Critical Encounters

A VOLUME IN A SERIES FROM
The Center for the Critical Analysis of Contemporary Culture

▼

Critical Encounters

Reference and Responsibility in Deconstructive Writing

▼

Edited by
CATHY CARUTH and DEBORAH ESCH

Rutgers University Press
New Brunswick, New Jersey

Library of Congress Cataloging-in-Publication Data

Critical encounters : reference and responsibility in deconstructive writing / edited by Cathy Caruth and Deborah Esch.
    p.   cm.
  "A volume in a series from the Center for the Critical Analysis of Contemporary Culture"—P. precedes CIP t.p.
    Includes bibliographical references (p.) and index.
    ISBN 0-8135-2085-1 (cloth) — ISBN 0-8135-2086-X (pbk.)
    1. Criticism. 2. Deconstruction. 3. Structuralism (Literary analysis) I. Caruth, Cathy, 1955– . II. Esch, Deborah, 1954– .
PN98.D43C75   1994
801'.95—dc20   93-39309
                                                                  CIP

British Cataloging-in-Publication information available

This collection copyright © 1995 by Rutgers, The State University
For copyrights to individual pieces please see first page of each essay.
All rights reserved
Manufactured in the United States of America

PN
98
.D43
C75
1995

▼ Contents ▼

Prefatory Note   vii

CATHY CARUTH   1
Introduction: The Insistence of Reference

Reference, Materiality, and History

ANDRZEJ WARMINSKI   11
Ending Up/Taking Back (with Two Postscripts on Paul de Man's Historical Materialism)

CYNTHIA CHASE   42
Literary Theory as the Criticism of Aesthetics: De Man, Blanchot, and Romantic "Allegories of Cognition"

CATHY CARUTH   92
The Claims of Reference

DEREK ATTRIDGE   106
Singularities, Responsibilities: Derrida, Deconstruction, and Literary Criticism

E.S. BURT   127
Hallucinatory History: Hugo's *Révolution*

KEVIN NEWMARK   155
Nietzsche, Deconstruction, and the Truth of History

DEBORAH ESCH   184
The Work to Come

Rethinking Responsibility: Politics and Ethics

JUDITH BUTLER   213
Contingent Foundations: Feminism and the Question of "Postmodernism"

DIANA FUSS   233
Inside/Out

HARRIET DAVIDSON   241
"I Say I Am There": Siting/Citing the Subject of Feminism and Deconstruction

THOMAS KEENAN   262
Deconstruction and the Impossibility of Justice

JILL ROBBINS   275
Visage, Figure: Speech and Murder in Levinas's *Totality and Infinity*

Notes on Contributors   299

Index   301

▼ PREFATORY NOTE ▼

THIS VOLUME EMERGED from a conference collaboratively organized and sponsored by the Center for the Critical Analysis of Contemporary Culture at Rutgers University and the Mellon-funded Theory of Literature and History Group at Princeton. That event took place in April 1989, under the title "Deconstruction Reviewed." It was conceived, in the organizers' formulation, as "an attempt to consider the achievements and the limitations of deconstruction seen as an important movement and to examine its future possibilities." The present collection gathers a number of essays based on papers presented at the conference, as well as several others subsequently solicited as assessments of the possible pasts and futures of what has come to be called deconstruction.

The editors would like to thank Tom Keenan, George Levine, Earl Miner, and the staff of the CCACC for the time and energy they devoted to making the conference such a success. In addition, we are grateful to Leslie Mitchner of Rutgers University Press, who has been the most cooperative and patient of editors.

Critical Encounters

▼ CATHY CARUTH ▼

Introduction
The Insistence of Reference

ONE OF THE CENTRAL CONCERNS in literary criticism and theory is the relation between literature and reality, or language and experience. In recent years, the questions raised by poststructuralist criticism, and particularly deconstruction, concerning the establishment of reference have seemed to many readers to involve a dangerous denial of any link between texts and reality: the possibility that reference is indirect seems to mean that we have no reliable access to experience or to history and hence no basis for political action or ethical decision. The essays in this volume put in question the presuppositions underlying this critique of deconstruction: the assumption that experience is constituted in large part by self-awareness and thus by meaningful perception, that history is available primarily as the completed knowledge of a past, that political and ethical decisions can and do arise only from a position of understanding and self-understanding. What would it mean, on the contrary, to conceive of an experience that is constituted by the very way it escapes or resists comprehension? How might one have access to a history that is constituted by its continually delayed entrance into experience? In what ways could we define a politics or ethics that derives from a position in which full understanding is not possible? Taking as their starting point the attempt to rethink fundamental questions of reality and of reference, the essays in this volume ultimately ask how we might learn to recognize and to respond to the realities of a history, a politics, and an ethics not based on straightforward understanding. At the heart of this volume, beyond any local argument about literary theory, is thus the urgent task of discovering the ways in which texts render legible those realities that may not be available to preconceived notions of language and the world.

Reference, Materiality, and History

When we look at recent trends in history, psychiatry, and literary theory, it would seem that whenever the power of language to name or give access to reality is asserted or affirmed, there is always an emphatic response that either denies this power or places it in question. When texts that pose problems for interpretation (such as, most recently, survivor narratives, stories of rape or childhood abuse) emerge on the scene—texts that claim referential truth but may rely on metaphorical language or other indirect means of expression—then we find that the urgent claim of these texts to convey otherwise unacknowledged realities often meets with an opposing argument that their language distorts experience or reality and hence leaves it ultimately inaccessible.[1] These conflicts, which occasionally gain popular attention in the historical and psychiatric fields, have long been at the heart of literary studies, where the status of the literary text—which is always by definition possibly a fiction—is in question. Attempts to assess the truth value of such texts frequently oscillate between theories that claim that literary texts refer directly to a world outside the text, and theories that emphasize that because all texts can always be fictional, they therefore do not reliably refer to any reality, which consequently remains inaccessible or even in question.[2] In increasing numbers of books and articles, deconstruction has been wrongly identified with the second side of this debate (the claim that reference is a fiction), and has accordingly been dismissed as denying memory, history, and all notions of truth.[3] What is crucially important, on the contrary, about the intervention of deconstruction in literary theory—and by extension, within larger debates about history and memory—is precisely that it searches for a way to think of language, and specifically reference, in terms that do not fall prey to the dynamic in which every textual affirmation meets with a seemingly inevitable denial. How can we think of a referential—or historical, or material—dimension of texts that is not simply opposed to their potentially fictional powers? How might the very fictional power of texts be, not a hindrance to, but a means of gaining access to their referential force?

In response to these questions, the writers in this volume show that the effect of deconstructive writing is not to eliminate the referential power of texts, but rather to offer a rethinking of the terms in which we have conceived it. More specifically, in their own writings on literary texts as well as through careful analyses of the work of Paul de Man and Jacques Derrida, the essays here assembled argue that deconstruction does not deny reference, but denies that reference can be modeled on the laws of perception or of understanding. Such models, which suggest that reference is "seen" or grasped as outside the text, ultimately place limits on reference that, as Andrzej Warminski and Cynthia Chase show, in fact constrict it rather than open it to the new: for anything that is not accessible as a semantic content that can be "seen" or understood cannot be recognized as real. What cannot be simply perceived or grasped, that is, becomes from this point of view a mere fiction. Such theories, rather than assuring us access to reference, thus eliminate the possibility of recognizing it where it does not occur in preconceived conceptual terms: for example, in the gaps and breaks in survivor narratives, in literary texts, in redefinitions of identity, or even, as I argue in my essay for this volume, in the notion of a world of gravitation or falling. In the perspective of this volume, it may indeed be in those moments that are least assimilable to understanding that a referential dimension can be said to emerge. The analyses by which deconstruction comes to distinguish reference from perceptual or cognitive models thus do not eliminate reference, but rather examine how to recognize it where it does not occur *as knowledge*. It is indeed in this surprising realignment of reference with what is *not fully masterable by cognition* that the impact of deconstructive writing can be said precisely to take place.

This rethinking of our notions of reference does not, as the writers in this collection show, close down our access to reality, but rather opens up an inquiry in which our experience can be rethought and recognized anew. Each essay in this volume, taking up this critical task, thus combines a suspension of assumptions about reference with the commitment to a specific referential field:

> To reanchor a poem too quickly in a context by a referential determination is to foreclose on the very place where poems could be speaking to the question of their historicity. (Burt)
>
> As a question, any given system of values . . . has to be critically examined and interrogated before we can reasonably expect to cast our relation to it in terms of . . . friend or foe. For values . . . are never simply given. (Newmark)
>
> That a claim [for the possibility of justice] has been made goes, as they say, without saying, but the status of this claim must remain an open question, if we are to give justice its due. (Keenan)
>
> What would it mean . . . to confront the very opening of the question of ethics—the grounds of its possibility and impossibility—prior to the production and elaboration of all moral values or precepts? (Robbins)

By placing into question the way we understand the referential meaning of their central terms, these essays open an exploration and an analysis that discover the force and referential impact of history, value, justice, and ethics. "Paradoxically," Andrzej Warminski writes, "it is he (or she) who does not assume or start out with a presumed referential reality on the one side (outside) and language on the other (the inside) that ends up with a referential model, a movement that takes us 'out' (or 'in'?), *back,* to the other."

This movement can first be seen in its focus on the problems of history and singularity. Beginning his essay with an analysis of traditional models of history, in which history is understood as what is referred to outside the text or through its perceptual manifestation, Warminski shows how such models tend to reverse into their opposite and end up eliding the history they attempt to reveal: the certainty that a text points "outside" ultimately reverses, dialectically, into the certainty of a text pointing to itself. Cynthia Chase likewise analyzes the ways in which the doctrine of language's stable referentiality always remains symmetrical to the certainty that merely reverses it, and misguidedly asserts language's complete nonreferentiality and/or self-referentiality. This problem—which is also, as Derek Attridge argues, the problem of grasping the singularity of reference—is most clearly addressed, in the essays by Deborah Esch and Kevin Newmark, in regard to the question of how to preserve the uniqueness of the historical event, how to theorize its referential aspect as a "happening." Traditional models do not capture either the specificity of history or the way it may occur as a continuing event, which must be continually reconfronted:

> The space available for movement between any given text's formal coherence and referential force, or between its truth and history, always outstrips the possibility of a definitive calculation, and . . . always remains to be determined anew. (Newmark)
>
> The thinking of how the then and there . . . may implicate us, here and now, poses the challenge of thinking history, not as a symmetrical, totalizing narrative of origins and ends, but in the precise terms of the material specificity of the event. (Esch)

By examining the resistance of texts to the models of inside and outside, before and after, these essays show that it is not in the certain and calculable knowledge of their meaning, but precisely in the interruption of such cognitive frameworks, that texts may give access to the thinking and rethinking of historical particularity.

We might say, then, that it is the insistence of these essays on aspects of texts that resist or disrupt patterns of totalizable meaning—aspects of texts that put in question the assumptions that we make about them—that constitutes the attempt of the present volume to open and recognize the unerasable referential singularity of the works it studies. Far from generalizing a form of negative knowledge about the absence of meaning or reference in texts, these essays rather name precisely what makes such negative certainty impossible. In thus breaking the tie between *reading* and *certainty* they permit reference to arise where understanding may not.

Rethinking Responsibility

This analysis of reference, as the essays in the second part of the volume show, is intricately tied up with questions of politics and ethics, or the relation between knowing and responsibly doing. Drawing on the insights of the foregoing theorists of reference, these authors suggest that the demand for responsible action arises most urgently in the impossibility of a pregiven self-understanding or knowledge. Thomas Keenan thus argues that a thinking of political action and responsibility based only on the notion of possibility—of the possibility of choice and agency as determined action and decision—ultimately limits legitimate political action to the ideal of what is or can be known, and hence eliminates precisely its most radical potential. How can we conceive of a mode of action and decision that could legitimately arise from a position in which self-understanding is not necessarily complete or possible? In Judith Butler's terms, the demand for a self-knowing subject actually eliminates the reality of the differing ways in which agency emerges:

> We may be tempted to think that to assume the subject in advance is necessary in order to safeguard the *agency* of the subject . . . but . . . agency can be *presumed* only at the cost of refusing to inquire into its construction. . . . In a sense, the epistemological model that offers us a pregiven subject or agent is one that refuses to acknowledge that *agency is always and only a political prerogative*. . . . We need instead to ask, what possibilities of mobilization are produced on the basis of existing configurations of discourse and power? . . . for that subject is never fully constituted.

For Diana Fuss, it is indeed only a politics that begins with the impossibility of defining a simple identity, with the impossibility, that is, of locating oneself either inside or outside of a social system, that can take into account the reality of a problematically gendered and sexed world. Both she and Thomas Keenan suggest that it is from this lack of the certainty of knowing, rather than from knowledge, that the thinking of action actually begins:

> Questions of epistemology ("how do we know?") enjoy a privileged status in theorizations of gay and lesbian identity . . . The

> very insistence of the epistemological frame of reference in theories of homosexuality may suggest that we cannot know—surely or definitively. . . . This is why . . . we need to shift . . . toward the performative mode. (Fuss)
>
> Perhaps right in general, the claim to rights, is another name for the complex strategic situation in which political demands are made because epistemologically justified grounds are not available, not in the nature or the essence of humanity, not in the experience of a subject or a group, not even in this very reality of the body, not anywhere. (Keenan)

Both Fuss and Keenan suggest that the political becomes most urgent not when it is possible to know simply and in advance what is right—that is, who one is, what society is, and what one deserves, or who indeed has a legitimate right—but when it is nonetheless necessary socially and politically to act: to claim rights, or to decide whose rights have priority. A thinking of politics can thus only address its reality when it begins not with the smooth transition from knowing to doing, but with an attempt to understand the notion of responsibility as emerging precisely in the ineradicable conflict between them.

The critical argument in these essays thus attempts to discover the paradoxical traps and limitations of a politics that does not recognize the opacities and complexities of self-understanding, identity, and decision. The thinking of politics, that is, like the thinking of reference, seems to require a way of recognizing and taking into account the force of what is not known, of allowing for, and negotiating, the powerful effects of the ill-understood and the not yet known in human experience.

An Act of Listening

The rethinking of responsibility also opens, necessarily, onto an ethical dimension that is closely tied to the problematic of reading and understanding. As Jill Robbins's essay implicitly suggests, the problem of reading is not only a struggle with meaning, but the encounter with an *imperative to listen*, the demand for an *act of listening* that is nonetheless *not simply an act of comprehending*. It is this demand, Robbins tells us, that Emmanuel Levinas describes as the encounter with the "face of the other," the incursion of the otherness of the other upon our self-reflexive acts of understanding. Thus the encounter with the face of the other in Levinas, Robbins argues, "interrupts the play of the Same"—the adequating relation of understanding, theorizing, and recognizing that eliminates the other's singularity—and thereby opens a dimension of "response" that originates precisely in

Introduction: The Insistence of Reference ▼ 7

this interruption of understanding. We might say that the problem of the "response"—in its ethical as well as epistemological dimensions—lies at the heart of the readings undertaken here.

The demand for the response is indeed also, as Robbins notes, a demand for an act, a doing, a speaking that is specifically not only a discourse "about" the other (or we might add, the "text") but also an "address": the other is not spoken about, says Robbins, but addressed. We might think of deconstructive writing, indeed, as struggling with the difficulty of listening to a certain address and of writing in a mode that is not a statement but itself a paradoxical address, governed by the ethical question of how to speak without reducing the text to a form of comprehension. Such an act could perhaps be described as what Harriet Davidson calls a "witnessing without experience," a registration of what impacts upon us even beyond our capacity to integrate it as experience or knowledge. Levinas, as Robbins tells us, describes the paradoxes of such a witnessing as what he calls an "ingratitude," in response to the gift of otherness, that is paradoxically necessary in order to respect, to guard the singularity of this other (not to assimilate otherness to the understanding implied by the notion of a grateful exchange): "A work conceived in its ultimate nature requires a radical generosity of the same who in the work goes unto the other. It then requires an *ingratitude* of the other. Gratitude would in fact be the *return* of the movement to its origin."[4] I would propose that we understand the attentive yet resistant readings and arguments in this volume as the display of such a respectful ingratitude, an ingratitude that in Maurice Blanchot's words "turns away" in order that it might listen better.[5] As the essays in this volume show, such an ingratitude is also the exercise of a complex and attentive act of engagement with the texts of our experience, an attempt to convey, and to respond to, what may not be heard in a reading founded on the comfortable anticipations of understanding.

Notes

1. For example, increasing interest in child abuse, and the insistence by experts trained in the treatment of trauma on listening to child witnesses for the truth of their testimony, has led most recently to a spate of articles in the media about the possibility of false testimony (as well as false memory), and increased work in forensic psychiatry on the significance of suggestion in the questioning process as well as on the problem of so-called false recovered memories.

2. One prominent example of the argument emphasizing the fictionality of texts would be the narratological extension of structuralism, or some literary

extensions of semiotics. The argument that a text is ultimately "self-referential," which appears in some of these readings, can be understood in many cases as a claim for the text's fictionality in relation to any truth outside the text.

3. A recent article (which attests to the ongoing, heated response to deconstruction) takes this misunderstanding to the limit when it compares deconstruction to revisionism (see "When History Is a Casualty," by Michiko Kakutani, in the *New York Times,* April 30, 1993).

4. Levinas, "The Trace of the Other," cited in Jill Robbins, "On Call from the Other," in *Ethics and the Literary Instance: Reading Levinas* (forthcoming).

5. This is, I believe, one way to read Blanchot's analysis of Hölderlin's notion of "le retournement catégorique," the double turning away of gods and men that guards or preserves a space of difference. See "L'Itinéraire de Hölderlin" in Maurice Blanchot's *L'Espace littéraire* (Paris: Gallimard, 1955).

Reference, Materiality, and History

▼ ANDRZEJ WARMINSKI ▼

Ending Up/Taking Back
(with Two Postscripts on Paul de Man's Historical Materialism)

J. DERRIDA: I have the feeling—again speaking hastily in straightforward terms of immediate feelings—I have the feeling that what I am doing is more referential than most discourses that I call into question. The impossibility of *reducing* reference, that is what I am trying to say—and of reducing the other. What I'm doing is thinking about difference along with thinking about the other. And the other is the hard core of reference. It's exactly what we can't reinsert into interiority, into the homogeneity of some protected place. So thinking about difference is thinking about "ference." And the irreducibility of 'ference' is the other. It's what is other, which is different.
J. CREECH: The irreducibility of what, did you call it?
J. DERRIDA: "Ference." Re*ference*. Of "that which carries."
J. CREECH: Ah, I see.
J. DERRIDA: Yes, a *referent* is what "carries back to." Referent, means "referring to the other." And I think that the ultimate referent is the other. And the other is precisely what can never allow itself to be closed again within any closure whatsoever. So that's what I'm trying to say. It is just as paradoxical for me to see this thought translated as a thought without reference, as it is to see textual thought translated as thought about language. Language games. It's just as topsy-turvy in the one case as in the other.
—*from "Deconstruction in America: An Interview with Jacques Derrida," James Creech, Peggy Kamuf,* and *Jane Todd*[1]

PAUL DE MAN'S WORK—his writing, his teaching—had and continues to have a way of getting under people's skin.[2] (Indeed, as de Man himself said at one lecture occasion, this is the moment when things become interesting: "when one gets under people's skin, when some resistance

Copyright © 1994 by Andrzej Warminski.

develops.") Among the many statements and pronouncements that have succeeded in provoking this kind of response, perhaps one of the most notorious, one that seems to have rankled longer and more intensely, is the well-known sentence toward the end of "Semiology and Rhetoric": "This will in fact be the task of literary criticism in the coming years" (p. 138).³ In the immediate context of the essay, "this" refers to the "kind of analysis" that de Man has just performed on a passage in Proust. The analysis demonstrates that this passage—whose seductive power seems to rest on an entire tropological system of metaphorical exchanges and substitutions and which itself, on the thematic level, values the "necessary link" of a figuration based on the constitution of entities and their intrinsic properties *over* a figuration that works by the contingent juxtaposition of merely contiguous elements—that this passage in attempting to complete and close off its system of metaphor nevertheless has recourse to an idiomatic expression, a cliché, an automatic juxtaposition of words whose epistemological authority is at the very least questionable since it is as mechanical as the workings of grammar. "This," then, is a demonstration of what de Man here calls "the grammatization of rhetoric," a certain demystification of the authority of metaphor—whose claim to authority is by no means negligible, for if inquired into rigorously enough, it would coincide with the authority of what can be called "metaphysics." ("It turns out," writes de Man, "that in these innocent-looking didactic exercises we are in fact playing for sizable stakes" [p. 136].) Hence it is not surprising that de Man does not hesitate to call "this" kind of analysis "deconstructive reading." "This" kind of reading, then—reading as such—is declared to be the task of literary criticism in the coming years.

But what has rankled the critics, gotten under their skins, has been not so much the meaning deposited in the term "reading" or "deconstructive reading"—or the apparently quick move from the microscopic analysis of a passage in Proust to "metaphysics"—but rather the claim that this kind of reading *will* be, "will in fact be," as the essay puts it, the task of literary criticism, our task, in the coming years. What overweening self-confidence about the future! What authoritarian bullying about the facts! This may have been the task of de Man when he was alive and it may remain the task of his disciples, but who is he to talk about the task of "literary criticism" itself? That "reading," even "deconstructive reading," has had its (brief) moment in the (metaphysical?) sun no one will deny. But that "it will in fact be the task of literary criticism in the coming years" is belied by the facts themselves, for those coming years have come and gone, and today it is only the unreconstructed fanatics, the faithful disciples or hopeless clones, who continue to chatter about "reading" (and about "rigor" and "stakes" and "epistemological authority"). In short, so runs the line, de Man may have been a smart fellow who may have been right about many things—including reading—but a prophet he was not. History, history itself, has caught up to him and overtaken him—and not least of all as the return of a certain repressed past in the form of the *Wartime Journalism*. Hence the irony—at de Man's expense—that has attended each republication and reprinting of "Semiology and Rhetoric" (originally published in *Diacritics* in 1973) and its apparently hapless prophesying first in *Allegories of Reading* in 1979 and since then in countless anthologies over the coming (and going) years. (One would indeed be tempted to apply the opening sentences of de Man's essay *to* the essay itself: "To judge from various recent publications, the spirit of the times is not blowing in the direction of formalist and intrinsic criticism. We may no longer be hearing very much about relevance, but we do continue to hear a great deal about reference, about the nonverbal 'outside' to which language refers, by which it is conditioned, and upon which it acts" [p. 121].)

If "history" (like "God") does not seem to have been on de Man's side—those "coming years" have been more cruel than kind—then perhaps we would be able to discover a more authentic, a more historically (never mind politically) "correct" account of the task of literary criticism in our time by moving to a critic who has apparently had the spirit of the times blowing in his direction: Fredric Jameson, whose motto ("Always historicize") and whose critical practice would seem to render him immune to misguided prophesies about the coming years and the hypostatization or reification or fetishization of a historically determined technique like that of de Man's "reading" or "deconstructive reading." Jameson's essay "Symbolic Inference; or, Kenneth Burke and Ideological Analysis" (originally published in *Critical Inquiry* in 1978 and now reprinted in his *The Ideologies of Theory* [1988]) states in no uncertain terms what he takes to be the task of literary criticism in our time. I quote from the last page of the essay, where Jameson recapitulates its beginnings and summarizes its conclusions: "At the beginning of the present essay, I proposed a checklist of the great contemporary critics, the great readers of an age that has discovered the symbolic; what I then neglected to add was that the art and practice of virtuoso reading does not seem to me to be the noblest function, the most urgent mission, of the literary and cultural critic in our time. In a society like ours, not stricken with aphasia so much as with amnesia, there is a higher priority than reading and that is history itself" (p. 152).[4] The contrast to de Man's ending in "Semiology and Rhetoric"—even though Jameson symptomatically (in 1978) does not list de Man among the virtuoso readers of our time[5]—could not be clearer: our time, our society, does not need readers, *especially* not those readers who have made fashionable what Jameson elsewhere in the essay calls "the primacy of language," "the more mindless forms of the fetishism of language," and "the ideologies of the intrinsic and of the antireferential text." Indeed, Jameson is so set on the priority of what he calls "history" over what he calls "reading" that he prefers critics who are positively *bad* readers—as though their lack of reading talent were a badge of honor or evidence that they had been man enough to withstand the seductive wiles and snares of the literary text. The paragraph continues:

> There is a higher priority than reading and that is history itself: so the very greatest critics of our time—Lukács, for example, and to a lesser degree, Leavis—are those who have construed their role as the teaching of history, as the telling of the tale of the tribe, the most important story any of us will ever have to listen to, the narrative of that implacable yet also emancipatory logic whereby the human community has evolved into its present form and developed the sign systems by which we live and explain our lives to ourselves. So urgently do we need these history lessons, indeed, that they outweigh the palpable fact that neither critic just mentioned is a good, let alone a virtuoso, reader, that each could justly be reproached for his tin ear and his puritanical impatience with the various *jouissances* of the literary text. (p. 152)

In short, hearing a joyless story—or rather a joy*ful* story joylessly told—is what is most important, most urgent, for us, and those who tell it to us are the most noble (if a bit dour) storytellers.[6] Again, the contrast to de Man's ending could not be more stark—*reading* versus *precisely not* reading—and a remark toward the beginning of "Semiology and Rhetoric" that one could take as a response to the tendency represented by Jameson's statements ("It is a fact that this sort of thing happens again and again in literary studies" [p. 122]) seems to ring hollow indeed when confronted with the authority of "history" itself.

On the one hand, this difference and this contrast between de Man (and reading) and Jameson (and history) is not at all surprising. Indeed, what could be more self-evident than this opposition between the "deconstructionist" who fetishizes language, the antireferential text, and its reading, and the "Marxist" who is *against* all that but *for* the mediation of text and context and the work of what he calls "transcoding" between superstructures and base. But things are a bit more complicated once we get past the labels and the name-calling and begin to inquire into what de Man means by language, text, and reading, and what Jameson means by history. For, on the other hand, despite the apparent divergence in their apparent evaluations of "reading," de Man's and Jameson's essays agree on one fundamental point: both have the same main target insofar as both are written against, both are a critique of, any simple division between sign and meaning, text and the referential reality putatively "outside" it, language and reality, and so on, hence both are a critique of the false division between "intrinsic" (or formalist) and "extrinsic" criticism. Jameson is particularly eloquent in negotiating the treacherous straits between the Scylla and Charybdis of literary criticism:

> Now to insist on either of these two dimensions of symbolic action without the other—to overemphasize the way in which the text organizes its subtext (in order, presumably, to reach the conclusion that the "referent" does not exist) or on the other hand to stress the instrumental nature of the symbolic act to the point where reality, understood no longer as a subtext but rather as some mere inert given, is once again delivered over into the hands of that untrustworthy auxiliary, Common Sense—to stress either of these functions of symbolic action at the expense of the other is surely to produce sheer ideology, whether it be, in the first alternative, the ideology of structuralism or, in the second, that of vulgar materialism. (p. 142)

If for Jameson the possibility of avoiding (or at least not producing) these two ideologies depends on the work of reconstructing the subtext and mediating it with the text—or as he puts it, "an imperative to reinvent a relationship between the linguistic or aesthetic or conceptual fact in question and its social ground" (p. 140)—a work that, in the end, cannot take place without the labor of the negative conceived of as a determinate negation, then for de Man the critique of the false division between intrinsic and extrinsic criticism takes place as a more difficult, more *retorse,* movement of thought that is anything but a mediation of the terms. Instead, de Man's text operates a wholesale rethinking and rewriting of both the terms—sign/meaning, text/referent, language/reality, "linguistic fact"/"social ground"—and their economy. (In fact, one could more easily speak of a "disjunction" rather than a mediation—as long, of course, as one reads the word disjunction the way de Man does.) It is in this movement of thought, of text, I would say, that we can begin to determine the real divergence between de Man and Jameson, reading and history. Neither Jameson's good intentions (to mediate text and context) nor his good conscience is in question here. But since the same cannot be said as easily for de Man, I am going to focus on de Man's critique of the intrinsic/extrinsic, inside/outside, opposition in "Semiology and Rhetoric."

"Semiology and Rhetoric" is not the most obvious place to look for a de Man *not* in the thrall of what Jameson calls the ideology "of the intrinsic and of the antireferential text" or "the fetishism of language." If one is looking for de Man's "materialism" or for his vision of "the materiality of actual history,"[7] the late work on the critique of aesthetic ideology would seem a more logical place to go—especially if one subscribes to the historicizing (in de Manian terms: pseudohistorical) account of de Man's progress as a story that goes *from* phenomenologico-Heideggerian beginnings *through* a "linguistic" or a "rhetorical" turn *to* the critique of ideology. ("If only he had lived . . . ," we would have gotten those fabled projected essays on Kierkegaard, on Marx, on Kenneth Burke. I don't subscribe to this history—that is, neither this "history" of the development of de Man's work nor the conception of history behind it.)[8] For, indeed, is not "Semiology and Rhetoric" the very place where one can locate that linguistic turn, the turn to a rhetorical model of language and the text? Well, yes and no—it all depends on how one understands language in this text. Let me remind you of the argument. The essay begins by identifying its main target: that is, the naive opposition of form and meaning based on a metaphorical inside/outside model—as though the text were a box to be opened. The extrinsic critic takes the *form* (the external cover or container) as the decorative, superfluous external outside and the *meaning* (the content or the text's reference to a psychological or a social or a historical reality, say) as the essential inside. Whereas the intrinsic or the formalist critic takes the *meaning* (the nonverbal outside to which the text presumably refers) as the external, and the *form* (that which is to be understood or made visible by the interpreter) as the internal, the inside, of the text.

The symmetrical chiasmic reversal is clear: what is called inside in one type of criticism is called outside in the other, what is called outside in the one is inside in the other. As de Man writes:

> When form is considered to be the external trappings of literary meaning or content, it seems superficial and expendable. The development of intrinsic, formalist criticism in the twentieth century has changed this model: form is now a solipsistic category of self-reflection, and the referential meaning is said to be extrinsic. The polarities of inside and outside have been reversed, but they are still the same polarities that are at play: internal meaning has become outside reference, and the outer form has become the intrinsic structure. (pp. 122–23)

Behind this metaphorical inside/outside model of the text (and of literature and of language) is the dream of a reconciliation between content and form, meaning and form—the dream of getting around the danger of having meaning blot out form or of allowing the opacity of the form to make meaning inaccessible. De Man summarizes:

> Thus, with the structure of the code so opaque, but with the meaning so anxious to blot out the obstacle of form, it is no

wonder that the reconciliation of form and meaning seems so attractive. The attraction of reconciliation is the elective breeding-ground of false models and metaphors; it accounts for the metaphorical model of literature as a kind of box that separates an inside from an outside, with the reader or critic as the person who opens the lid in order to release into the open what was secreted but inaccessible inside. It matters little whether we call the inside of the box the content or the form and the outside the meaning or the appearance. The recurrent debate opposing intrinsic to extrinsic criticism stands under the aegis of an inside/outside metaphor that has never been seriously questioned. (p. 123)

There are many implications to be drawn from this compact rhetorical reading of the history of literary criticism—not the least of which is the implication that in the passage from extrinsic to intrinsic criticism and vice versa, *nothing happens:* that, in short, such passages are not historical in any meaningful sense of history but rather are the simple working out of a pattern built into an inside/outside metaphor and the ideology that supports it, namely the ideology of the aesthetic.9 (As de Man writes, again: "It is a fact that this sort of thing happens again and again in literary studies" [p. 122].) These implications aside, what I would mark here is that the essay itself stands under the aegis of this opening critique of the inside/outside metaphorical model of the text (and of language) and the "easy play of [symmetrical] chiasmic reversals" (p. 123) that it leads to. If we remember this beginning, then we will be less likely to mistake the analyses that follow in the essay as ending up in any notion of the text or of language as simply "intrinsic" or "antireferential."

The analyses themselves are well-known—indeed notorious in the case of the Archie Bunker example—and there is no need to paraphrase them in detail for my purposes here. Instead, I will simply re-mark the pattern of their itinerary. In brief: What de Man proposes to do is to speculate on a different set of terms—"perhaps less simple in their differential relationship than the strictly polar, binary opposition between inside and outside" (p. 123)—which, in this case, are "grammar" and "rhetoric." He derives these terms—which, he reminds us, are as old as the hills (presumably because they come from the general linguistic model of the trivium: grammar, logic, rhetoric)—pragmatically from developments in current critical methodology. By these developments he means semiology, "the science or study of words as signifiers" which bases itself on the linguistic model of structural linguistics. One of the striking characteristics of literary semiology, says de Man, is its use of grammatical structures conjointly with rhetorical structures, in fact, its attempt to reduce rhetorical structures *to* grammatical structures, to reduce figure to grammar—as though they were continuous or homogeneous. The examples of rhetorical questions—Archie Bunker and the last line of Yeats's "Among School Children"—would put the possibility of this reduction into question. The examples would show that the clear syntactical pattern of the question becomes undecidable because we cannot decide the question's rhetorical mode by purely grammatical means, that is, by taking language as a grammatical code to be decoded. De Man summarizes: "The grammatical model of the question becomes rhetorical not when we have, on the one hand, a literal meaning and, on the other hand, a figural meaning, but when it is impossible to decide by grammatical or other linguistic devices which of the two meanings (that can be entirely contradictory) prevails" (p. 129). The point is clear: it's not just that there are two *meanings* (one literal and one figurative) that may contradict one another, but rather that the level of meaning, rhetoric, always comes to interfere with the grammar of the sentence. It is an example of what de Man in this essay calls "the rhetorization of grammar." The reading of the Proust passage that follows is, of course, an example of the reverse—there it is in fact a rhetorical, that is, metaphorical, model of the text that gets interfered with by the merely metonymical juxtaposition or contiguity of a grammatical structure. This is in turn an example of what de Man calls "the grammatization of rhetoric." So: the chiasmic reversal could not be clearer—we go from the rhetorization of grammar to the grammatization of rhetoric. Although there at first seems to be a difference where we end up in the case of the one and of the other—with the rhetorization of grammar we wind up suspended in our ignorance or undecidability, with the grammatization of rhetoric we get a negative assurance, a knowledge productive of more deconstructive activity—because of the apparent reversibility of each, both ultimately lead to "the same state of suspended ignorance" (p. 140). What is this, then, if not an example of our being stuck within language, circulating idly (or busily) from grammar to rhetoric and back? Is not this indeed the fetishism of language and the antireferential text? Not quite. Not quite not only because de Man explicitly stated at the beginning of the essay that the speculation on the terms grammar and rhetoric should not be confused with the inside/outside polarity and the easy play of chiasmic reversals. (In other words, grammar and rhetoric may be just other words for "form" and "meaning," but their relationship is not that of inside and outside—or outside and inside.) To take de Man's conclusion as one that deposits us, leaves us, *within* language would be a mistake, since whatever language is by this point it is not an inside (or an outside). Perhaps we could get at what else it may be by remembering the third articulating term crucial to understanding both the rhetorization of grammar and the grammatization of rhetoric: namely, *logic,* the third component of the trivium along with grammar and rhetoric. Logic enters upon the scene of both the grammatical and the rhetorical (or metphorical) models of language and the text. The project and the dream of the grammatical model is to reduce all utterances, all language, to a code which, *as a code* (that is, whose meanings need only to be decoded), is universalizable into a logic, "the possibility of the universal truth of meanings" (as de Man helpfully defines it for us in his discussion of Peirce [p. 128]). But because the rhetorical function of language always interferes with this project, de Man can say that rhetoric "radically suspends logic and opens up vertiginous possibilities of referential aberration." For indeed if the meaning of no utterance can ever be decided by purely grammatical means because its meaning always depends on some decision about its rhetorical mode, then the possibility of universalizing the truth of meanings and thereby making an unbroken passage to logic and from there to the arithmetical sciences of the quadrivium (and hence to the knowledge of the "outside," nonverbal, phenomenal world) is radically suspended.[10] What the rhetorization of grammar does, then, is to defeat the attempt to close off language, systematize it, and then to make an unbroken passage to a "referential" reality that would also be closed upon itself and closed off from language, in other words extralinguistic, nonverbal.

In the case of the reverse, the grammatization of rhetoric, logic enters in a different way, but with similar results. That is, the project and the dream of a "rhetorical" model of language is to conceive of language as a tropological system, a system of metaphor, of substitutions and exchanges based on a knowledge of entities and their (exchangeable) properties: in short, based on an ontology, an onto-logic, a logic of beings, of metaphysical meanings, one could say. What comes to defeat this project and this dream is the grammatical function of language, all its purely formal, mechanical structures that are necessary to constitute meaning but that are themselves not meaningful. In other words, the project of this "rhetorical" model of language is also to close it off, as a closed tropological system this time, and thereby to make an unbroken passage—"unbroken" because the passage can now take place as a controllable, reliable, metaphorical transfer—to a world of beings that is outside but that is as closed off, analogously, as the world of meanings in metaphor.[11] Now, since both of these models fail in their respective projects, *in* the demonstration of this failure (the rhetorization of grammar, the grammatization of rhetoric), to be brought back from one to the other—from grammar to rhetoric and from rhetoric to grammar—does *not* mean to be brought back to the same thing. Indeed, if anything, it means to be brought back to the other—that is, the other *of* language, that which always makes language different from itself, makes it defer itself, makes it carry *it* and *us* back . . . to the other.[12]

This carrying back could "properly" be called the *referential*—*re-fer,* to carry back—function of language, and to the extent that de Man's readings take us back to an other, or an otherness, of language, his "model" of language (and the text) is a truly *referential* model. And it is referential *not* because it takes us back to some "referential" reality "outside" language—for that would in fact only be the attempt to restitute the inside/outside model of language in relation to reality—but rather because it refuses *any* totalization of either what is called language or what is called reality. Paradoxically—but consistently and predictably—enough, it is he (or she) who does *not* assume or start out with a presumed referential reality on one side (outside) and language on the other (the inside) that ends up with a referential model, a movement that takes us "out" (or "in"?), *back,* to the other.[13] I use these idiomatic expressions—"end up in," "taking back"—advisedly, for they are the very expressions that riddle de Man's essay, whether in the form of these words or similar ones. For instance, at the "end": "We *end up,* therefore . . . ," or elsewhere, "We seem to *end up in* a mood of negative assurance . . ." or "The former *ends up in* indetermination . . ." among others. This "ending up" chain is doubled, shadowed, by another one, the chain of taking back: "We are back at our unanswered question" or "We return to the inside/outside model" or "The deconstruction of metaphor . . . takes us back to the impersonal precision of grammar" or "Our recurrent question" or "The recurrent debate" and so on. If the former, the "ending up" chain, would want to end up in a "theory" or a "model" of language—whether "grammatical" or "rhetorical"—the latter, the chain of "taking back," pulls back, away from any such ending and takes back to the impossibility of any "theory" or "model" of language and text. So where *do* we end up with "Semiology and Rhetoric"? It turns out that we end up precisely *with* semiology *and* rhetoric. That is, we don't end up anywhere—only in reference, in taking back, in being taken back, to the other. It's the sort of thing that happens again and again, but this time as a real, material happening, that is as a *text*—semiology *and* rhetoric as text—and hence as historical, history. And *as* history, it will in fact be the task of literary criticism in the coming years. No wonder it keeps getting under the skin.[14]

Postscript 1: History, Materiality, Reading

> In a genuine semiology as well as in other linguistically oriented theories, the referential function of language is not being denied—far from it; what is in question is its authority as a model for natural or phenomenal cognition. Literature is fiction not because it somehow refuses to acknowledge "reality," but because it is not *a priori* certain that language functions according to principles which are those, or

which are *like* those, of the phenomenal world. It is therefore not *a priori* certain that literature is a reliable source of information about anything but its own language.

It would be unfortunate, for example, to confuse the materiality of the signifier with the materiality of what it signifies. This may seem obvious on the level of light and sound, but it is less so with regard to the more general phenomenality of space, time or especially of the self; no one in his right mind will try to grow grapes by the luminosity of the word "day," but it is very difficult not to conceive the pattern of one's past and future existence as in accordance with temporal and spatial schemes that belong to fictional narratives and not to the world. This does not mean that fictional narratives are not part of the world and of reality; their impact upon the world may well be all too strong for comfort. What we call ideology is precisely the confusion of linguistic with natural reality, of reference with phenomenalism. It follows that, more than any other mode of inquiry, including economics, the linguistics of literariness is a powerful and indispensable tool in the unmasking of ideological aberrations, as well as a determining factor in accounting for their occurrence. Those who reproach literary theory for being oblivious to social and historical (that is to say ideological) reality are merely stating their fear at having their own ideological mystifications exposed by the tool they are trying to discredit. They are, in short, very poor readers of Marx's *German Ideology.*
—Paul de Man, *"The Resistance to Theory"*

In using terms like "material" and "history" we have all too abruptly made a passage to the terminology of de Man's last work on the critique of "aesthetic ideology." To make it less abrupt, it may be good to double back and explain how we got there—how de Man gets there—from what we have called the "referential" function of language. A good place to look for what de Man himself means by "referential" is "Roland Barthes and the Limits of Structuralism," an essay written around the same time as "Semiology and Rhetoric" (i.e., about 1972) and whose reading of Barthes no doubt formed the occasion for the writing of "Semiology and Rhetoric."[15] The essay is especially valuable not only because it is utterly straightforward in its assertion of what can be called the "irreducibility" of reference and of the referential function of language but also because it explicitly links this irreducibility to the question of ideology-critique.

De Man's reading of Barthes consists of an exposition and a critique. Since both exposition and critique are particularly clear, we can go a long way by simply paraphrasing it. The exposition begins by tracing the "euphoric, slightly manic tone" of Barthes' writing: "It is the tone of a man liberated from a constraining past, who has 'the earth . . . all before [him],' and who looks about 'with a heart / Joyous, not scared of its own liberty.' The exact nature of this liberation can best be stated in linguistic terms, in a formula partly borrowed from Barthes himself: it is the liberation of the signifier from the constraints of referential meaning" (pp. 166–167).[16] Barthes, in short, is a leading representative and advocate of the science of semiology—"the study of signs independently of their meaning" (p. 168). How is it, de Man asks, that the ideas about language leading to the science of semiology acquired such a polemical vigor in the hands of Barthes? After all, these ideas had been around for quite a while in various philosophies of language and in the formalist schools of literary criticism. (Indeed, as "Semiology and Rhetoric" puts it, semiology turned out to be the way that the nimble French literary mind finally made a contact with the question of *form,* something that American and other literary critics had faced without the help of linguistics—although this does not mean, adds de Man, that we can do without "a preventative semiological hygiene altogether" [p. 124].) What Barthes has done, however, is to use his gifted semiological eye "to scrutinize not only literature, but social and cultural facts as well, treating them in the same manner as a formalistically oriented literary critic would treat a literary text" (p. 168), his early *Mythologies* being the best example of "this kind of semio-critical sociology" (p. 169). And even though Barthes had probably not read the undisputed masters of the genre when he wrote *Mythologies*—Walter Benjamin and Theodor Adorno—the common ancestry is nevertheless apparent from his references, in the concluding essay on history and myth, to Marx's (and Engels's) *German Ideology,* "the model text for all ideological demystifications" (p. 169). How and why the science of semiology grants its practitioners considerable power to demystify ideologies is easy enough to understand. Fictions—what Barthes calls "myths"—are more persuasive than facts.

> Their order, their symmetry is possible because they are accountable only to themselves, yet these are precisely the qualities wishfully associated with the world of nature and necessity. As a result, the most superfluous of gestures are most likely to become the hardest to do without. Their very artificiality endows them with a maximum of natural appeal. Fictions or myths are addictive because they substitute for natural needs by seeming to be more natural than the nature they displace. The particular shade of bad conscience associated with fiction stems from the complicity involved in the partial awareness of this ambivalence coupled with an even stronger desire to avoid the revelation, public or private, of this knowledge. It follows that fictions are the most marketable commodity manufactured by man, an adman's dream of perfect

coincidence between description and promotion. Disinterested in themselves, they are the defenseless prey of any interest that wishes to use them. When they are thus being enlisted in the service of collective patterns of interest, including interests of the highest moral or metaphysical order—fictions become ideologies. One can see why any ideology would always have a vested interest in theories of language advocating the natural correspondence between sign and meaning, since they depend on the illusion of this correspondence for their effectiveness. On the other hand, theories of language that put into question the subservience, resemblance, or potential identity between sign and meaning are always subversive, even if they remain strictly confined to linguistic phenomena. (pp. 169–170)

The passage states concisely the reasons for semiology's demystifying power and its political implications—especially in the gifted hands of Barthes as he moves from the relatively innocent mystifications of catch-as-catch-can wrestling to consumer goods to reach finally the domain of the printed word and image in movies or in *Paris-Match*.

But this very demystifying power of semiology is both a source of strength and a danger. The danger comes from the seemingly perfect convergence between Barthes's social criticism and the means used to accomplish its highly desirable aims, for this convergence and its power engenders its own mystification, says de Man, this time on the level of method rather than of substance. In brief, the very power of the method creates an overconfidence in the possibility of grounding literary study on foundations strong enough to be called scientific. By asserting, as Roman Jakobson does, that in literature, the language is autotelic, that is, focused on the message for its own sake rather than on its content, one gets rid of all the mess and muddle of signification and thereby opens up a heretofore undiscovered world of scientific discourse. "With the inevitable result," continues de Man, "that the privileged adequation of sign to meaning that governs the world of fiction is taken as the ideal model towards which all semantic systems are assumed to tend. This model then begins to function as a regulatory norm by means of which all deviations and transformations of a given system are being evaluated. Literature becomes a degree zero of semantic aberration. We know that it owes this privileged position to the bracketing of its referential function, dismissed as contingency or ideology, and not taken seriously as a semantic interference within the semiological structure" (p. 172). The question remains, however, "whether the semantic, reference-oriented function of literature can be considered as contingent or whether it is a constitutive element of all literary language" (p. 173). The autotelic, nonreferential aspect of literature stressed by Jakobson cannot be seriously contested, but then why is it "always and systematically overlooked? (p. 173). "All theoretical findings about literature confirm that it can never be reduced to a specific meaning or set of meanings, yet it is always reductively interpreted as if it were a statement or message" (p. 173). Although Barthes grants the existence of this pattern of error, he denies that it is the object of literary science to account for it. It would rather be the task of historians— "thus implying that the reasons for the recurrent aberration are not linguistic but ideological" (p. 173). In other words, the bracketing of the referential function that grants the semiologist so much power of formal analysis and demystification also exercises a seduction (a properly *literary* seduction) on the interpreter that leads him to make claims for the scientificity of literary study. A methodological move that is perfectly legitimate as such— for a certain formalism is a necessary preliminary for any discourse about literature that would want to be more than gossip about texts—issues in unwarranted claims for the method and a mistaking of its object.

This is where we finally approach the main point of de Man's critique:

> That literature can be ideologically manipulated is obvious but does not suffice to prove that this distortion is not a particular aspect of a larger pattern of error. Sooner or later any literary study must face the problem of the truth of its own interpretations, no longer with the naive conviction of a priority of content over form, but as a consequence of the much more unsettling experience of being unable to cleanse its own discourse of aberrantly referential implications. The traditional concept of reading used by Barthes and based on the model of an encoding/decoding process is inoperative if the master code remains out of reach of the operator, who then becomes unable to understand his own discourse. A science unable to read itself can no longer be called a science. The possibility of a scientific semiology is challenged by a problem that can no longer be accounted for in purely semiological terms. (p. 174)

The passage is particularly instructive for us in several respects. First of all, although its critique of semiology is very much the same as that contained in "Semiology and Rhetoric," it is inflected differently: namely, on the problem of reference, of language's, *any* language's or *any* discourse's, irreducible *referential* function. Here it does not seem to be a question of semiology's attempt to grammatize rhetoric—and its inability to do so— but rather the impossibility that *any* language, *any* discourse, can gain a scientific vantage-point on another language. Why can't it? Because no matter how much it would want to bracket the referential function of its "object"-discourse, it can never "cleanse" its own discourse of "aberrantly referential implications." Although it may be easy enough to understand this in general terms—for instance, that de Man means that one language can never gain "scientific" distance or objectivity upon another one because, *as* language, it is included in its object and therefore can never define, de-limit, the borders and boundaries of its object and hence cannot perform the first step necessary for any science to constitute itself as such, *as a science*—there is a more precise way to read this passage in de Man's own terms once we note the verbal echo between the phrase "aberrantly referential implications" here and the sentence in "Semiology and Rhetoric" toward the end of the first demonstration of the way rhetoric interferes with grammatical models of language and the text: "Rhetoric radically suspends logic and opens up vertiginous possibilities of referential aberration" (p. 129). "Aberrantly referential," "referential abberation"—familiar, recurrent formulations in de Man's work: it's what his writing always again ends up taking us back to. And it takes us back not to some vague sense of aberration, but rather to what the word says quite clearly and distinctly: aberrant, ab-erration, it takes back to the error, the necessary error and *errance*, of reference, of taking back. *Accounting* for this necessary error is what de Man takes to be the task of literary study—and "accounting" for it does not at all mean making it the object of science, of epistemologically reliable knowledge—a task that Roland Barthes forgets when he would want to forget the referential function of language, *all* language, including the most "literary" or "fictional" or "mythic."

But the verbal echo also helps us because it identifies what makes it impossible for the literary critical discourse to cleanse itself of aberrantly referential implications: namely, *rhetoric*. It's rhetoric that does this—that "suspends logic and opens up vertiginous possibilities of referential aberration"—and if these aberrantly referential, or referentially aberrant, possibilities can be identified with *ideology,* with *the* ideology that is always already "built into" language (including literary language), then it is rhetoric that prevents the literary critic, semiologist, or other formalist, from cleansing his or her own discourse enough to be able to read it. How so? Presumably because the literary critic's own discourse is always subject to the same question of its rhetorical mode—a question that, like all questions, is undecidable as to whether it really asks or not because its rhetorical function may always interfere with its grammatical status—and hence can never *know* what it is talking about. In other words, because it is impossible to cleanse critical discourse of the question of rhetoric (or of the rhetorical question), it is impossible to demystify or unmask its ideologies once and for all. It's here that we are brought back to "Semiology and Rhetoric" and the critical ideology that forms its main target: that is, the division between an intrinsic (or formalist) and an extrinsic criticism "that stands under the aegis of an inside/outside metaphor that has never been seriously questioned." A criticism that stands under the aegis of the inside/outside metaphorical model of the text (and of language) is in the thrall of ideology, and all that it can do—whether it calls itself intrinsic and formalist or extrinsic and referential—is to reproduce more ideology. And ideology can be read here in de Man's own sense as formulated in "The Resistance to Theory": "What we call ideology is precisely the confusion of linguistic with natural reality, of reference with phenomenalism." In the case of the inside/outside metaphor as a textual model, the confusion consists in thinking of the text, a linguistic artifact, in terms consistent with a phenomenology of the self and its experience of the "natural," phenomenal world: here, as though the text were a box with an inside and an outside. To think language and text in this way is to take it as a mere content and an object of consciousness: in short, to take as language what is only its represented, alienated, ideological, ghostly self and not that which is its material reality. This is why the transition from an intrinsic to an extrinsic criticism (or vice versa) does not happen and hence is not historical, is not history. Since all that an extrinsic criticism does is to substitute a new content of consciousness for an old one, it is just as *non*referential as the intrinsic, formalist criticism, just as stuck in the predictable working out of an inside/outside metaphor and its ideologies. Only a criticism that is material, that butts up against the materiality of the text and of language, can be historical. Taken as an object or content of consciousness, language is not being thought in its materiality but only, as it were, according to its superstructures—and those, as ideology, have no history. But, according to de Man, language *as* language—in its materiality—can never be the object of consciousness (or of knowledge or of science). This is quite explicit in the short but packed reading of Hegel in "Hypogram and Inscription": "Consciousness . . . is not 'false and misleading' because of language; consciousness *is* language, and nothing else, because it is false and misleading."[17] One could summarize de Man here by rewriting the famous line of *The German Ideology,* "Life is not determined by consciousness but consciousness by life": "Language is not determined by consciousness, but rather consciousness is *over*determined by language." For just as "life" in Marx's sentence is not to be understood as mere natural, appetitive existence but rather as produced by labor and hence as *historical,* so language is not to be read as an object or content of consciousness but as the material, historical *life* of consciousness. Language is the material life of consciousness.

Using such Marxian terms to begin to explain history and materiality in de Man may sound all too much like "historical materialism" to some, but unless we are very poor readers of the *German Ideology* we should also remember that Marx can sound a great deal like de Man. In going through the premises of human existence and history—which is a history of the material production of life—Marx, after four steps, finally gets to consciousness:

> Only now, after having considered four moments, four aspects of primary historical relations, do we find that man also possesses "consciousness." But even from the outset this is not "pure" consciousness. The "mind" is from the outset afflicted with the curse of being "burdened" with matter, which here makes its appearance in the form of agitated layers of air, sounds, in short, of language. Language is as old as consciousness, language *is* practical, real consciousness that exists also for other men as well, and only therefore does it also exist for me."[18]

So: if de Man is Marxian, then Marx is certainly de Manian, but it is not just any Marx but the Marx of the *German Ideology* (a book he seems to have read better than some so-called Marxists), de Man's consistent reference whenever the question of ideology and reference comes up. What's the upshot? The upshot is that language, for de Man, is not an object of consciousness and therefore can never be the object of a science. This is because consciousness *is* language—meaning that it is "false and misleading," that is, ideology, aberrantly referential or referentially aberrant. The task of a truly historical, materialist criticism is not just to demystify the ideological aberrations—for that would mean to end up in a negative knowledge that, in the end, knows very little because it cannot know itself, cannot cleanse its own discourse of ideology—the task is to account for the recurrence of the mystification, aberration, or ideology. Such accounting would be historical, material, because it comes up against the materiality of language and the text, of language *as* text: its irreducibly referential function. What to call such accounting? De Man calls it *reading*. Language is a text in need of being read. But reading it does not mean emptying it out and filling it up with content. Those who do this—whether they fill up the content with form *or* with content, intrinsic *or* extrinsic, sign *or* meaning—and think that they are making a theoretical, never mind practical or political, difference, are only reproducing (and teaching) not history but ideology. And a specific ideology at that, one that has a name: German Ideology. They are indeed very poor *readers* of Marx's *German Ideology*.

Postscript 2: Language, Consciousness, Allegory

Rosso: Perhaps, now, you could tell us something about the book you are writing and about the "mysterious" chapters on Kierkegaard and

Marx you mentioned in the lectures, and the frequent recurrence of the terms "ideology" and "politics" we have noticed recently. . . .

de Man: I don't think I ever was away from these problems, they were always uppermost in my mind. I have always maintained that one could approach the problems of ideology and by extension the problems of politics only on the basis of critical-linguistic analysis, which had to be done in its own terms, in the medium of language, and I felt I could approach those problems only after having achieved a certain control over those questions. It seems pretentious to say so, but it is not the case. I have the feeling I have achieved some control over technical problems of language, specifically problems of rhetoric, of the relation between tropes and performatives, of saturation of tropology as a field that in certain forms of language goes beyond that field. . . . I feel now some control of a vocabulary and of a conceptual apparatus that can handle that. It was in working on Rousseau that I felt I was able to progress from purely linguistic analysis to questions which are really already of a political and ideological nature. So that now I feel to do it a little more openly, though in a very different way than what generally passes as "critique of ideology." It is taking me back to Adorno and to attempts that have been made in that direction in Germany, to certain aspects of Heidegger, and I just feel that one has to face therefore the difficulty of certain explicitly political texts. It is also taking me back constantly to problems having to do with theology and with religious discourse, and that's why the juxtaposition of Marx and Kierkegaard as the two main readers of Hegel appears to me as the crux, as the problem one has, in a way, to solve. I have not solved it and the fact that I keep announcing that I am going to do something about it is only to force myself to do so, because if I keep saying I'm going to do this and I don't do it, I end up looking very foolish. So I have to force myself a little to do this, both in the case of Kierkegaard and in the case of Marx. It's taking me first of all in a preparatory move, by forcing me to go back to Hegel and Kant, and I just hope that I won't remain stuck in that. So I felt ready to say something about the problem of ideology, not out of a polemical urge. What has been said about it, what now is around in the books of Jameson or of other people, is not what spurred me to do this. As I said, it has always been a major concern and I now feel this problem of language somewhat more under control. What will come out of it, I just do not know because I do not work that way. What will come out, will come from the texts of Marx and Kierkegaard as I think they will have to read. And they have to be read from the perspective of critical-linguistic analysis to which those texts have not been submitted. There has been very little on Kierkegaard along those lines and there has been even less on Marx, except, of course, for elements in Althusser that, I think, go in that

direction. But I look forward to seeing what I will produce and know as little about it as anybody else.
—*from Stefano Rosso, "An Interview with Paul de Man," in Paul de Man,* The Resistance to Theory

If the move to "history" and "materiality" at the end of the essay was a bit fast and required some explanation, the remarks on language and consciousness in the first postscript—and my assimilation of de Man to Marx (and vice versa)—may seem a still faster move requiring still more explanation. Explaining this move comes down to reading the apparently quick juxtaposition of two statements: (1) language is not (and cannot be) the object or content of consciousness (or of knowledge or of science); and (2) this is because consciousness *is* language (which, my remarks claim, is consciousness *in its materiality*). This move requires some explanation not least of all because what it takes to be the reason for the impossibility of making language the object of consciousness (knowing, science) could more easily be taken as the very reason why language would be the best, because most reliably knowable, object of consciousness. That is, if *consciousness* is language, then the truth and essence of language should be just as determinable as that of consciousness. For in attempting to make language an object of knowing, consciousness (which *is* language) is trying to make itself its own object. What it wants to know is *knowing,* and what better way to do so than to know an object that is also a subject: in short, to know an object that is its own object, an object that is in fact itself. As we know from the first two sections of the *Phenomenology of Spirit,* the essence and truth of consciousness, what consciousness has to be in order to be truly consciousness—that is, what knowing (as knowing *something*) has to be in order to be truly itself— is *self*-consciousness, self-knowing. In other words and in short, rather than presenting any problem for the dialectic of consciousness, language's being made the object of consciousness would in fact seem to provide consciousness with the object of knowing par excellence, the privileged object that it needs in order to become what it is in truth: itself, consciousness.

Understood in this way, saying that consciousness is language, as Marx and de Man do, can make no difference because it is something that could as well be said by Hegel—indeed, *is* said by Hegel. In order to have it make a difference, the statement "consciousness is language" needs to be said with a certain shift in emphasis from the word *consciousness* to the word *language.* In other words, to say that consciousness is *language*—with the stress on language—means at least to suggest that language should not be thought according to the determinations (and self-negations) of consciousness but rather that consciousness should be thought according to the determinations peculiar to language. And if these determinations of language were *not* subsumable under those of consciousness—that is, if they did not negate consciousness determinately—then consciousness's trying to make language its object would not at all be a dialectical movement in which consciousness could recognize and verify itself in its own negation. It would mean that language was constituted in such a way as to make it resist ever becoming just an object of consciousness, and its refusal to become an object of consciousness could mean that consciousness—which, again, according to Marx and de Man *is* language—could never *know* or *be* itself in truth, that is, self-consciousness. In other words, consciousness would turn out to be just a secondary, unreal, ghostly, ideological, alienated projection of something materially different from a mere *object* or *content* of consciousness: namely, language. But here is the crux of the problem and precisely what needs more explanation: summarily put, how to think language differently—differently enough so that it cannot be taken as a mere object and content of consciousness that would end up being consciousness's own negation, that is, self-consciousness? Abstractly, the answer is easy enough. Language has to be shown to be constituted by *over*determined contradictions, say, which cannot ever be totalized (through *any* process of self-mediation by negation) into one, simple negation—a negation that would be determined enough to allow one to define its limits and borders, that is, to determine it enough so as to be able to say that it is the negation *of* something and therefore has a positive content—precisely the content *of* that of which it is the negation.[19] And, still speaking abstractly, one of those who thinks language materially enough, in its overdetermined contradictions, is certainly de Man when he demonstrates that any attempt to construct a *model* of language—whether grammatical or metaphorical, say—to make language an object of knowing, consciousness, science (to be read in German: *Wissen, Bewusstsein, Wissenschaft*) by defining and delimiting its borders fails and *has* to fail because, for example, the grammatical model always gets interfered with by the rhetorical function, and the metaphorical model always gets interfered with by the grammatical function. Insofar as language is constituted by the unstable and asymmetrical "relation" of grammar and rhetoric, it is unable to come into being as an object of knowing, consciousness, science. The mutual interference of grammar and rhetoric would be *one* way—and not the only way—to see how language is overdetermined, how it is made up of contradictions that make language overdetermine *itself*, that prevent it from ever *being* a self—an object whose borders could be drawn and that could be identified *as* an (self-same, self-identical) object.

If one wants, one can take what is happening here schematically as the inversion and reinscription of the (hierarchical) relation of consciousness and language. That is, it's not enough to say that language should be first, that the primacy of consciousness (in the definition of man, say) has to be shown to be secondary and derived. For as long as the inversion is a *mere* inversion, then nothing has been done to change the ordering, hierarchical structure itself. To say that consciousness is determined by language is still to treat it as the determinate negation *of* consciousness, still to think language on the model of consciousness. In other words, in addition to the reversal or inversion of the hierarchy, language has to be re-defined, better, reinscribed, in such a way as to transform the structure of the relation between language and consciousness. For unless consciousness itself is tampered with—and in its materiality—all we do is to perform a mental critique, we only substitute one content or object of consciousness for another and therefore do nothing to challenge the (Hegelian or Young Hegelian) primacy of consciousness. And, as we know, to do this is precisely what German Ideology *is,* precisely the main target of Marx's critique: thinking that one can change the world *in thought,* by *thinking* it differently, substituting a new content of thought for an old one—man for God, for instance, or, say, an empiricist determination of man for an idealist one. No, what is necessary is—I might as well say it—a deconstruction of consciousness: an inversion and reinscription that changes not only the terms but also the ordering structure of relations like consciousness and language or consciousness and life.[20]

In order for Marx's statement "Life is not determined by consciousness but rather consciousness is determined by life" to make a difference (again, a difference from Hegel), "life" has to be thought differently: no longer as the determinate negation *of* consciousnesss but rather as made up of *overdetermined* contradictions that cannot ever be reduced to (sublated, *aufgehoben*) a simple, determinate negation—of consciousness by life, for instance. Indeed, as we know from Hegel's introduction to the chapter on self-consciousness in the *Phenomenology*, the way that self-consciousness verifies itself and becomes what it is, itself, self-consciousness, is by making *life* essential for self-consciousness, not just negating it immediately (as in desire, *Begierde*) but making it *essential* (true) for self-consciousness. Until we can say the difference between what Hegel means by *life* and what Marx means by *life,* we might as well let *Hegel* say Marx's statement "Life is not determined by consciousness but rather consciousness is determined by life." In short, Marx is already saying (and has to be saying in order to be Marx): "Life is not determined by consciousness but rather consciousness is *over*determined by life."[21]

I find several of the *Theses on Feuerbach* to be helpful on this aspect of Marxian deconstructive technique. For instance, Thesis 4:

> Feuerbach starts out from the fact of religious self-estrangement, of the duplication of the world into a religious world and a

> secular one. His work consists in resolving the religious world into its secular basis. But that the secular basis lifts off from itself and establishes itself as an independent realm is the clouds can only be explained by the inner strife and intrinsic contradictoriness of this secular basis. The latter must, therefore, itself be both understood in its contradiction and revolutionised in practice. Thus, for instance, once the earthly family is discovered to be the secret of the holy family, the former must then itself be destroyed in theory and in practice.[22]

The inversion of the religious world and the secular world, and the substitution of one for the other in the hierarchy, is correct enough but it remains a purely mental critique—one that leaves the structure of consciousness untouched—because it cannot explain why it is that the secular basis would alienate itself and invent a religious realm in the clouds in the first place. It does it, of course, on account of the material contradictions that already make up the secular basis—for instance, the division of labor between manual and priestly (mental) work which makes it advantageous for the priests to invent a religious realm in the clouds, grant it autonomy and primacy and assert that it is all that counts in the end—and these material contradictions are *overdetermined* in that they make of the secular basis an "entity" that is not just, and *cannot be* just, the determined negation of the religious realm in the clouds.

As with *life* or the *secular basis,* so with language. As is at least suggested by Marx's passage on consciousness and language that I quoted at the end of Postscript 1—consciousness first comes on the scene "burdened" with matter, a materiality that turns out to be *language*—language is on the side of matter, on the side of real life, it is the very materiality of consciousness and thought. But in order to change anything, it is not enough to assert the primacy of language over consciousness—that would be a Feuerbachian, German-ideological move—but rather one has to try to explain how it is that the overdetermined contradictions that constitute (and de-constitute) language were gathered together (totalized by mediation) to form one, simple negation that could then alienate itself in the form of that ghost: consciousness. In whose interest was it to alienate language from itself, set it up as that which is to be understood on the model of consciousness, knowing, as an object and content and simple negation *of* consciousness itself—as though language were an independent entity (like the religious realm in Thesis 4)?

In whose interest was it? Marx provides at least the beginnings of an answer in another passage of the *German Ideology:*

> One of the most difficult tasks confronting philosophers is to descend from the world of thought to the actual world. *Language*

is the immediate actuality of thought. Just as philosophers have given thought an independent existence, so they were bound to make language into an independent realm. This is the secret of philosophical language, in which thoughts in the form of words have their own content. The problem of descending from the world of thoughts to the actual world is turned into the problem of descending from language to life.[23]

Without going into the difficulties of this passage, it is easy to see that what "the philosophers"—that is, the ideology of philosophy as such—do is to perform a certain sleight of hand. Crudely put, they move *language*—the *actuality* (*Wirklichkeit*) of thought, its very material basis, on the side of real life—over to the side of *thought*. And they do this by alienating language from itself, making language into an independent realm (so that thoughts in the form of words may have their own content). To short-circuit a whole reading, one could say that philosophy alienates language from itself by occulting, covering up, its material, overdetermined contradictions and turning it into one, simple determined negation *of* consciousness, of thought—that, *as* the determined negation of consciousness and thought has *them* for a *content* and belongs to them as their own negation. Thus the problem of descending from the world of thoughts is turned into the problem of descending from language to life—when language was already life, already living![24]

So much for language and consciousness. But I think one more step and one more precaution is necessary. From what I have just said—and indeed from certain formulations of Marx—one could get the wrong impression that what one is doing here is indeed coming up with something like a *science*. As though once we "know" that consciousness is language and language is made up of overdetermined contradictions and therefore consciousness cannot ever be itself in truth, we can step out of or beyond ideology, if not into the truth, then at least further away from error. This is where de Man's help is indispensable, for the conception of ideology that we end up with here is—what can one say?—more negative, still more negatively other-than-dialectical.[25] For, in de Man, the materiality of language, materiality as such, is not ever something that we can know, and hence is never something that could be the object of consciousness or of science. This is the point of my attempt to read "Semiology and Rhetoric" and the Roland Barthes essay together. A "deconstructive," demystifying discourse, which is always the demystification of *metaphor, rhetorical delusion,* that is, referential aberration, that is, *ideology,* the ideology inevitably produced by language itself, no matter how demystificatory that language would want to be, is certainly possible and necessary, but it always remains impossible for that discourse to become scientific ("science" to be read in

German: *Wissenschaft*), to know what it knows with any epistemological reliability and consistency, because it itself is language, linguistic, and therefore can itself never rid itself of *referential aberration, ideology, rhetorical delusion*. (Perhaps I should note that it's the lining up of these last three—referential aberration, ideology, and rhetoric—in de Man's work that I see as the "contribution" of my remarks here.)

The demystifying, deconstructive discourse in fact always produces a "secondary figural superposition" (as de Man puts it on the crucial p. 205 of *Allegories of Reading*) that is a second story, a second narrative that narrates the impossibility of *reading* the "first" narrative, the story of the deconstruction of a figure or a system of figures, usually metaphor. This "second" narrative is what de Man calls allegory—the allegory of the impossibility of reading. Whatever *this* narrative knows, its knowledge is not that of a heightened, progressive self-consciousness. And whatever this allegory of unreadability does, it is not to get us further from error and closer to the truth. (This is, symptomatically, where the recent, very rich and generous essay by Jameson on de Man goes wrong: he takes allegory as an increase in self-consciousness. This in turn allows him to see not only metaphysical residues in de Man but also to take de Man to be privileging a certain aesthetic function of literary language—when the aesthetic is precisely the target of de Man's critique!)[26]

But then where does it get us or leave us—where do we end up with de Man? Not with truth, not with just error, but not just with negative knowledge of error either. A last quotation (from the Roland Barthes essay) helps: "The mind cannot remain at rest in a mere repertorization of its own recurrent aberrations; it is bound to systematize its own negative self-insight into categories that have at least the *appearance* of *passion* and *difference*" (p. 175, my emphasis). This systematization is of course the turning of negative self-insight into ideology, the phenomenalization (or phenomenology), re-metaphorization, re-ideologization of the deconstructive narrative and the allegory of unreadability. The mind is *bound* to do this—not on account of any subjective choice—it is *bound* to do it. It's a linguistic necessity, the ideology built "into" language, which is what makes it impossible to talk about an inside and an outside of language, which makes language always produce an "outside" or "other" that is not its own—an other speaking, a speaking of the other, *allos* + *agorein*, *allegory*—it's what is bound to happen. And that's history.[27]

Notes

1. The interview took place in the spring of 1984 and is published in *Critical Exchange* 17 (Winter 1985), pp. 1–33.

2. This essay was originally written for a conference on Paul de Man held at the University of Zürich in 1989. Its ending was deemed to require more explanation by some of the participants at this conference—in particular Cynthia Chase—and so the first explanatory postscript (on history, materiality, and reading) was written for delivery at Purdue University (and subsequently at UCLA, the Benjamin Cardozo School of Law, and Berkeley). Cynthia Chase quite justly felt that this postscript required still more explanation, and so the second explanatory postscript (on language, consciousness, and allegory) was hastily "written" in shorthand for delivery at the Society for the Humanities at Cornell University in February 1991. My thanks to those who prodded me to do more explaining—and thanks especially to those who let the essay and its explanations get under their skin.

3. All page references to "Semiology and Rhetoric" are to the original version of the essay reprinted in *Textual Strategies: Perspectives in Post-Structuralist Criticism,* ed. Josué Harari (Ithaca: Cornell University Press, 1979).

4. All page references to this essay are from Fredric Jameson, *The Ideologies of Theory,* vol. 1 (Minneapolis: University of Minnesota Press, 1988).

5. According to Jameson: "Besides Burke himself the list would probably include Empson and Frye, Roland Barthes, Walter Benjamin, Viktor Shklovsky" (p. 138).

6. Proleptic remark: that this narrative would be that of an emancipatory *logic* is not without interest for our reading of grammar and rhetoric (and along with them logic) that follows. One could say that all the difference between Jameson and de Man can already be read in Jameson's writing "logic" here.

7. This phrase is from de Man's "Anthropomorphism and Trope in the Lyric," in *The Rhetoric of Romanticism* (New York: Columbia University Press, 1984), p. 262.

8. Why not? Because, directly put, such historicizations of de Man's itinerary are pseudohistorical. To apply one of de Man's remarks about literary-historical periodization: the interpretation of de Man's work as a succession of periods manages to come up with, at best, "rather crude metaphors for figural patterns rather than historical events or acts" (ibid., p. 254). In fact, rather crude metaphors for the readings of the texts that have (or, as is more often the case, have *not*) taken place. One could use de Man's own early essay on Yeats ("Image and Emblem in Yeats," written in the late 1950s for his dissertation, and now reprinted in *The Rhetoric of Romanticism*) to explain how and why such periodization, rather than being historical in any meaningful sense of history, is rather allegorical, the working out and narration of a figural pattern of linguistic relations and functions rather than historical events or acts. In brief: Yeats, according to de Man's apparently still quite straightforward literary-historical interpretation, starts out writing a poetry of the "image" (i.e., symbolic imagery still consistent with the natural, phenomenal world and our experience of it), then moves to a poetry of the "emblem" (allegorical signs that have an arbitrary, i.e., conventional, link to what they signify, and whose meaning can be decoded by reference to a codebook of

emblems), and ends up in a poetry of the "image-emblem" (in which the figuration has a double function: on the one hand, it seduces with its natural imagery and all it can represent; on the other hand, what it actually means, emblematically, allegorically speaking, is the ontological nonexistence of the natural, phenomenal world). In short, the poetry (as image) represents one thing but (as emblem) means another, and what it means is the destruction of what it represents—as neat a "definition" of allegory as one could ask for, whether in de Man's or Benjamin's texts (compare de Man's favorite phrase from Benjamin's *Ursprung des deutschen Trauerspiels* [Frankfurt am Main: Suhrkamp, 1963], p.265, about allegorical signification: "Und zwar *bedeutet* es genau das Nichtsein dessen, was es *vorstellt*," "It *means* precisely the nonbeing of what it *represents*" [my emphasis]).

But one does not have to be a particularly astute "rhetorical reader" to ask the obvious question that arises: namely, if an emblematic, allegorical, function is always a possibility in any figurative language whatsoever, then what allowed us to periodize Yeats's work into "poetry of the image," "poetry of the emblem," "poetry of the image-emblem" in the first place? Perhaps the so-called "poetry of the image" is also full of emblematic, allegorical, meanings that we misread or cannot read only because we do not have access to the "codebook" that would allow us to interpret these emblems, and instead *mis*read the poetic language by taking it literally, as it were, only on the level of its mimetic, representational function. And the same thing could be asked in reverse about the so-called "poetry of the emblem": does its emblematic signifying function completely exhaust its capacity for meaning, or may it not also always carry along with it a symbolic, mimetic, representational function that, whatever the codebook may tell us, always brings us back to the natural, phenomenal world and our experience of it? But then if these questions are at all pertinent—and they most certainly are once something like a poetry of the "image-emblem" is said to be possible—in other words, if it is possible that Yeats's poetry from beginning to end was always already a poetry of the "image-emblem," then the apparently literary-historical periodization of his work into the succession of "poetry of the image"–"poetry of the emblem"–"poetry of the image-emblem" turns out to be not a history (of historical events or acts, of what actually happened) but rather an allegory of properties and functions proper to language "itself": in this case, the irreducible and mutually undoing "relation" of, call it, symbolic representation and allegorical signification. Meaning, then, that Yeats's poetry was always a poetry of the "image-emblem"/"image-emblem"/"image-emblem", and it is only the (inevitable) exigency of telling the story of our reading as a coherent narrative with a beginning, middle, and an end that makes us invent the devices of *first* a "poetry of the image" and *then* a "poetry of the emblem," and so on. In short, rather than a history of Yeats's work, such a story is in fact an allegory of a reading of Yeats's text—a reading that, in order not to start stuttering repetitively right at the outset (emblem/emblem/emblem, allegory/allegory/allegory), must unfold by mistaking itself for a history with its periods, beginnings, and ends.

The same thing holds true for de Man: we can tell the story of his itinerary as a history of successsive "periods" and development only at the cost of *not reading* his texts—for instance, the early Yeats essay which, in de Man's own words, was "a rhetorical analysis of figural language *avant la lettre*" ("Preface," *The Rhetoric of Romanticism*, p. viii)—whereas a reading of his texts not only gives the lie to the "recuperative and nihilistic allegories of historicism" ("Shelley Disfigured," in *The Rhetoric of Romanticism*, p. 122) but also stands a chance of getting closer to that which would be actually, materially, historical in de Man, what happened and continues to happen under the proper name "Paul de Man." This is not to deny the necessity, inevitability, and even usefulness of such (pseudohistorical) historicizations—indeed, as is clear from the above, de Man's readings always and again start out from the quite traditional questions of literary history—but only to underline the fact that the discipline of "history" can do its work only by suspending what in shorthand can be called "the rhetorical dimension of language" and hence by *not reading* the texts. Needless to say, those studies of de Man with the most global synthesizing ambitions to account for his "career"—no matter how friendly to de Man and well-intentioned (and, indeed, useful and even "correct" on a certain level) they may be—are most subject to such nonreading and have quite willfuly to suppress what the texts actually say in order to make them fit into their "history." See, for example, Christopher Norris's *Paul de Man* (New York and London: Routledge, 1988). Therapeutic in this regard are not only Jacques Derrida's *Mémoires, for Paul de Man* (New York: Columbia University Press, 1986) but also Werner Hamacher's "LECTIO: de Man's Imperative," in *Reading de Man Reading*, ed. Lindsay Waters and Wlad Godzich (Minneapolis: University of Minnesota Press, 1989) and Kevin Newmark's "Paul de Man's History" in the same volume and, in revised form, in his *Beyond Symbolism* (Ithaca: Cornell University Press, 1991).

9. This is already readable in "Semiology and Rhetoric." For instance, on pp. 121–122: "Behind the assurance that valid interpretation is possible, behind the recent interest in writing and reading as potentially effective public speech acts, stands a highly respectable moral imperative that strives to reconcile the internal, formal, private structures of literary language with their external, referential, and public effects." That this "moral imperative" to reconcile sensory form with spiritual meaning is in the thrall of "aesthetic ideology" becomes even clearer when on the following page de Man speaks of it as "so attractive" and "the attraction of reconciliation" of form and meaning. Beauty, "the sensory appearance of the Idea"—literary language (mis)taken as *art*—will respond to this "moral imperative" and give us a good "moral conscience." It would be instructive to compare de Man's remarks on this "moral imperative" here to Jameson on the "imperative to reinvent a relationship between the linguistic or aesthetic or conceptual fact in question and its social ground" (p. 140) quoted above.

10. Cf. de Man's remarks on the trivium/quadrivium relation in "The Resistance to Theory," in *The Resistance to Theory* (Minneapolis: University of Minnesota Press, 1986), p. 13:

The most familiar and general of all linguistic models, the classical *trivium*, which considers the sciences of language as consisting of grammar, rhetoric, and logic (or dialectics), is in fact a set of unresolved tensions powerful enough to have generated an infinitely prolonged discourse of endless frustration of which contemporary literary theory, even at its most self-assured, is one more chapter. The difficulties extend to the internal articulations between the constituent parts as well as the articulation of the field of language with the knowledge of the world in general, the link between the *trivium* and the *quadrivium*, which covers the non-verbal sciences of number (arithmetic), of space (geometry), of motion (astronomy), and of time (music). In the history of philosophy, this link is traditionally, as well as substantially, accomplished by way of logic, the area where the rigor of the linguistic discourse about itself matches up with the rigor of the mathematical discourse about the world. Seventeenth-century epistemology, for instance, at the moment when the relationship between philosophy and mathematics is particularly close, holds up the language of what it calls geometry (*mos geometricus*), and which in fact includes the homogeneous concatenation between space, time and number, as the sole model of coherence and economy.

That de Man conceives his reflection on the critique of aesthetic ideology very much in terms of these seventeenth-century questions (in particular the articulation of number and space or extension) is clear from his "Pascal's Allegory of Persuasion" and "Phenomenality and Materiality in Kant," in *Aesthetics, Rhetoric, Ideology*, ed. Andrzej Warminski (Minneapolis: University of Minnesota Press, 1995). See my introduction to that volume.

11. It would be instructive here to read closely de Man's critical reading (in *Allegories of Reading* and elsewhere) of Genette's interpretation of Proust. On the one hand, Genette does something like a "deconstructive reading" in demonstrating that the metaphorical structures of Proust's text are grounded in metonymical structures; on the other hand, it is not difficult to see that these metonymical structures are, for Genette, themselves grounded in still more powerful, all-embracing metaphors like that of the self and its experience of the phenomenal world. Hence Genette winds up restoring the "necessary link" between the phenomenal world and linguistic structures—the link that, in de Man's terms, is the very definition of ideology: "What we call ideology is precisely the confusion of linguistic with natural reality, of reference with phenomenalism" ("Resistance to Theory," p. 11). It should perhaps be noted that de Man's remarks on ideology nearly always take place in close proximity to a discussion of semiology, the demystifying power of its "non-phenomenal linguistics," and its self-ideologization when it confuses the *materiality* of the signifier with *phenomenal* (perceptible, sensory) forms that can become the object of consciousness. See the introduction to my forthcoming book of essays in allegorical reading. (My thanks to Cathy Caruth for discussion of the "*unbroken* passage" here.)

12. Our references here to "the other" should not be taken in any "idle or mystical sense," but only as "the other," truly, really, actually, other, and not

the same. The fact that we—the text—have been led to this formulation on the back of a metonymical juxtaposition of words in a mechanical idiomatic expression ("to be brought back from one to the other" above)—the grammar of the language, as it were—is no doubt no accident.

13. It would be instructive to compare this to de Man's reading of Kant and Schiller, in which the "formalist," "theoretician," "philosopher" Kant, because he thinks through "form," "the theoretical," "the philosophical," butts up against something material; whereas the one who would empiricize Kant on the sublime, Schiller, winds up in a frightening, utter idealism. All too predictable and all too evident on the current scene of what passes for "theory." "We are all Schillerians, no one is Kantian any more," as de Man quipped on a lecture occasion. See "Kant and Schiller" in *Aesthetics, Rhetoric, Ideology*. Cf. also my "Terrible Reading (Preceded by 'Epigraphs')" in *Responses: On Paul de Man's Wartime Journalism*, ed. Werner Hamacher, Neil Hertz, and Thomas Keenan (Lincoln: University of Nebraska Press, 1988).

14. A reading of de Man's Archie Bunker example (p. 128) would very quickly uncover a good example of our ending up/taking back "structure." Since the exchange between Archie and Edith Bunker is an *example,* its rhetorical mode needs to be decided, but it turns out that (as always) the example is more than just an illustration of the argument's logic. In this case, it is, on the one hand, quite clearly a "good" example of the "rhetorization of grammar"—de Man's argument's illustration of how it is that rhetoric interferes with grammar—and hence an example consistent with the logic of the essay at this point. Nevertheless, we also have to read the *rhetoric* of this example, and, once we do so, we find that it is also a "good" illustration of the reverse, "the grammatization of rhetoric." For in this example, Edith Bunker is clearly a *figure*—and a figure for *grammar* at that (something always forgotten by those who would "critique" de Man's example from a pseudo-feminist point of view), indeed the grammatical reader who reads Archie's "What's the difference?" strictly according to its grammar, and thereby punctures the balloon of Archie's rhetorical pathos (or rather "provokes only ire," as de Man puts it, i.e., has Archie substitute one self-inflated metaphorical transport for another). And that Edith Bunker is a "reader of *sublime* simplicity" (my emphasis) who "patiently" explains the difference (between tying bowling shoes over and under) to Archie is not without interest for the reader of the later de Man, since it is in the theories of the *sublime* (in Kant and Hegel, for example) that something like a radically "linguistic moment" takes place to puncture the rhetorical ("poetic") pathos of the sublime with a resolutely *prosaic* instance that disarticulates the projects of aesthetics. In short, it is Edith Bunker here in her sublime simplicity who is already a figure for the "deconstructive," indeed *allegorical,* reader.

15. Unpublished until 1990, the essay appeared in *Yale French Studies* 77 and is now included in Paul de Man, *Romanticism and Contemporary Criticism,* ed. E. S. Burt, Kevin Newmark, and Andrzej Warminski (Baltimore: The Johns Hopkins University Press, 1993). It was originally commissioned by *The New York Review of Books* and then rejected by it. Correspondence

indicates that the editors found the essay's terminology too technical for a general audience.

16. All page references to "Roland Barthes and the Limits of Structuralism" are to de Man's *Romanticism and Contemporary Criticism*.

17. See Paul de Man, "Hypogram and Inscription," in *Resistance to Theory*, p. 41.

18. Karl Marx and Frederick Engels, *Collected Works* (New York: International Publishers, 1976), 5:43–44.

19. For a shorthand definition of "determined negation" (*bestimmte Negation*), see the introduction to Hegel's *Phänomenologie des Geistes* (Berlin: Felix Meiner, 1952), pp. 68–69; or, in English, in *Phenomenology of Spirit*, trans. A. V. Miller (Oxford: Oxford University Press, 1977), p. 51.

20. For consciousness is "the most theoretically sensitive point in the entire system of bourgeois ideology," as Louis Althusser puts it in "On Marx and Freud" (*Rethinking Marxism* 4 [Spring 1991]: 25). Althusser is particularly rigorous and eloquent on this question:

> In the category of the self-conscious subject, bourgeois ideology *represents* to individuals what they *must be* in order for them to accept their own submission to bourgeois ideology; it represents them as endowed with the *unity* and *consciousness* (which is this unity itself) that they must have in order to *unify* their different practices and actions under the unity of the dominant ideology. . . . *Consciousness* is *necessary* for the individual who is endowed with it to realize within "himself" the unity required by bourgeois ideology, so that every subject will conform to its own ideological and political requirement, that of unity, in brief, so that *the conflictual violence of the class struggle will be lived by its agents as a superior and "spiritual" form of unity.* I emphasize this unity, otherwise known as the identity of consciousness, and the function of unity because it was this unity that Marx's critique called most forcefully into question when Marx dismantled the illusory unity of bourgeois ideology and the fantasy of unity that it produced in consciousness as the effect it needed in order to function. (pp. 24–25)

21. Cf. my "Hegel/Marx: Consciousness and Life," forthcoming in *Hegel after Derrida*, ed. Stuart Barnett (Stanford: Stanford University Press, 1995), for a detailed discussion of the Hegel/Marx "relation." Needless to say, a reading of Althusser is indispensable for any such discussion.

22. Marx and Engels, *Collected Works*, 5:4.

23. Karl Marx and Frederick Engels, "The German Ideology," in *Collected Works*, 5:446.

24. Cf. Marx on "the language of real life" at the beginning of *The German Ideology*.

25. As de Man says toward the beginning of "Anthropomorphism and Trope in the Lyric" (*The Rhetoric of Romanticism*, p. 242): "Whatever truth may be fighting, it is not error but stupidity, the belief that one is right when one is in fact in the wrong." In any truly critical philosophy, says de Man, "truth is always at the very least dialectical, the negative knowledge of error."

26. See Fredric Jameson, "Deconstruction as Nominalism," in *Postmodernism* (Durham: Duke University Press, 1991):

> In the case of de Man's work, however, I feel that it is fatally menaced at every point by a resurgence of some notion of self-consciousness that its language vigilantly attempts to ward off. Surely the deconstructive narrative always risks slipping back into that simpler story in which the initial figure, having brought illusion into being, then somehow achieves some more heightened awareness of its own activity; while the allegory of reading, or of unreadability, comes before us in his work with a heightened charge of renewed consciousness of its own processes, consciousness ever more intensely becoming conscious of itself, "to the second (or third) degree," in a never-ending progression. (p. 245)

Jameson misreads the crucial passage on allegory (p. 205 of *Allegories of Reading*) here in part because he does not read the meaning and function of *number* and *enumeration* in de Man: that is, allegories "to the second (or third) degree" are by no means to be understood as a heightening or progression of consciousness. It would take some time to demonstrate this, but a passage from de Man's "Aesthetic Formalization: Kleist's *Über das Marionettentheater*" (in *Rhetoric of Romanticism*, p. 266) that summarizes the reading of Baudelaire's "Correspondances" can provide a hint here: "The tension, in this poem, occurs indeed between number as trope (the infinitesimal as the underlying principle of totalization) and number as tautology (the stutter of an endless, but not infinitesimal, enumeration that never goes anywhere)." In other words, allegories (of reading or unreadability) "to the second (or third) degree" are anything but "a never-ending progression." If anything, they always again "start out from scratch"—from the irreducible, incommensurable, and unmediatable (dis-)articulation of number as trope and number as mere enumeration (or, as p. 205 puts it, the deconstructive narrative "of a figure [or a system of figures]" and the allegory of [the impossibility of] reading). On de Man's always again starting out from scratch, see Samuel Weber's "Disfiguring the Monument" in *Responses*. On de Man's crucial page 205, see J. Hillis Miller's helpful " 'Reading' Part of a Paragraph in *Allegories of Reading*" (in *Reading de Man Reading*).

27. For texts on allegory and history in de Man "worth reading," see, in addition to Derrida's *Mémoires*, the essays by Werner Hamacher and Kevin Newmark mentioned in note 8 above.

▼ CYNTHIA CHASE ▼

Literary Theory as the Criticism of Aesthetics
De Man, Blanchot, and Romantic "Allegories of Cognition"

> . . . he conjures you to weep for him no longer.
> —William Wordsworth, *Essay upon Epitaphs*

"LITERARY THEORY"—THE NAME AND THE THING—has a quite peculiar historical specificity, intimated by the name's ambiguous grammatical structure. It shares the ambiguity of the phrase "the criticism of aesthetics," which evokes the criticism carried out by aesthetics, as well as criticism that takes aesthetics as its object. Paul de Man's criticism has aesthetics as its target, but it does so by remaining, as I shall try to describe, an *aesthetic* criticism, and one that explicitly invokes "the critical thrust of aesthetic judgment."[1] Literary theory as de Man conceived of it is not the set of theories about literature—its social function, its historical character, its formal resources, its structures. Rather, it takes as its subject the literariness of literature and investigates the problems that arise from this potentiality of language. Literature provokes theory (and not only interpretation or evaluation) because it invites "reading": in the absence of obvious pertinence as a message, it requires attention to its medium as potentially distinguishable from its meaning. To cite the terms that de Man derives from Walter Benjamin, literary texts raise the possibility of a conflict or even an incompatibility "between proposition (*Satz*) and denomination (*Wort*)" or between the literal and the figurative meaning of a text or, within the symbolic dimension itself, between what is being symbolized

---

This essay takes up arguments developed in a different way in Cynthia Chase, "Translating Romanticism: Literary Theory as the Criticism of Aesthetics in the World of Paul de Man," *Textual Practice* 4 (1990): 349–375. I am grateful to the editors of *Textual Practice* and Routledge for permission to reuse some of this material.

and the symbolizing function"—"in the most general terms, . . . between what language means (*das Gemeinte*) and the manner in which it produces meaning (*die Art des Meinens*)."[2] Ineluctably literary as well as inescapably theoretical, literary theory carries a peculiarly double critical force. De Man's criticism is acutely alert to the mutual interference rather than mutual reinforcement of different sorts of "meaning"—the felt meaningfulness or gratuitousness of form, the referential, metadescriptive and ideological meanings of a text. To what extent does the understanding of a work of language consist in the understanding of form? Literature, as language that is "art," becomes the site of this question.

Literary theory thus involves "examining if and how the *poetics* of literary *form* can be made compatible with the *hermeneutics* of *reading*" (*RT*, 31): if and how the description of a self-disclosing form can accord with the interpretation of a referential as well as self-reflexive system.[3] Insofar as description and interpretation are in accord, literature fulfills an aesthetic function, and, by implication, can be ascribed "a reliable, or even exemplary, cognitive and, by extension, ethical function"—the grounds on which literature is traditionally professed and taught. "The link between literature (as art), epistemology, and ethics is the burden of aesthetic theory at least since Kant," de Man writes. "Burden" here has the sense of "onerous task" and even of "reiterated refrain" as well as "main assertion." For the link that aesthetic theory assumes or asserts, *literary* theory confronts as an "unavoidable question"—"whether aesthetic values can be compatible with the linguistic structures that make up the entities from which these values are derived" (*RT*, 25).

I want to elucidate these claims (including my claim that they are de Man's) by examining an essay originally entitled "Hypogram and Inscription: Michael Riffaterre's Poetics of Reading."[4] It is a text in which the criticism of aesthetics reveals its scope as well as its predicament.

But first I want to invoke some passages indicating how de Man's essays locate "theory" in "history," and thereby do the inverse as well.

It can be illuminating if also misleading to evoke a particular locus of the interplay between literature and aesthetics, to lend a historical dimension to this argument about theory. To conceive theory as the critical encounter of aesthetics and literature is on the one hand to locate it historically, to see its enabling conditions in "the rise of aesthetics as an independent discipline in the later half of the eighteenth century," as de Man notes (*RT*, 25). But it is on the other hand to undercut conceptions of history dependent upon the possibility that literature and literary theory put into doubt (including period concepts, such as "Romanticism"): the possibility of access to reliable knowledge via the aesthetic totalization claimed by means of texts' narrative or spatial figures. In questioning whether aesthetic values are compatible with the linguistic structures of literary works, literary theory takes up "a recurrent philosophical quandary," writes de Man in "The Return to Philology": "Such questions never ceased to haunt the consciousness of writers and philosophers. They come to the fore in the ambivalent rejection of rhetoric at the very moment that it was being used and refined as never before, or in the assimilation of the considerable aesthetic charge emanating from rhetorical tropes to the aesthetic neutrality of a grammar" (*RT*, 25). The rise of aesthetics happens concurrently with the fall of rhetoric: it is the institutionalized discipline of "Rhetoric" that is displaced by aesthetics, and it is the power of "rhetoric" that is castigated in the literature and the politics which in this respect it may be right to call "romantic." Crucial in the rhetoric of Romanticism (including, by a seemingly unbreakable law, the rhetoric *about* "Romantic literature") is the "ambivalent rejection of rhetoric"; de Man's phrase evokes such texts as Wordsworth's *Lyrical Ballads* and Preface (1800) and *Essays upon Epitaphs*, Rousseau's "Lettre à d'Alembert sur les spectacles" and *Du contrat social*. The literature and philosophy of the Romantic period are one of the main referents of de Man's allusion to times when an "unavoidable question . . . come[s] to the fore." Kant's *Critique of Judgment*, de Man observes, assigns aesthetics its ultimate significance: guaranteeing the continuity of perception with rational judgment. Questioning how and whether literature can fulfill that function is the defining feature of "Romantic" literature (de Man's comments suggest); hence, for de Man, Romanticism's importance and ambiguity, as suggested in this striking characterization of Nietzsche's "Über Wahrheit und Luge im Aussermoralischen Sinn": "Like the Third Critique, this late Kantian text demonstrates, albeit in the mode of parody, the continuity of aesthetic with rational judgment that is the main tenet and the major crux of all critical philosophies and 'Romantic' literatures."[5] Here the significance and difficulty of Romantic literature and critical philosophy are ambivalently affirmed, with de Man describing as their "crux" what he has also termed their "tenet"—the meaningfulness for "Reason" of disinterested aesthetic judgments, the accessibility of meaning via phenomenal intuition.

To have as a "tenet" what is also set out as a "crux" seems an untenable or contradictory critical position. It is the position, by de Man's account, of "all critical philosophies and 'Romantic' literatures." And, in a telling alignment, it is also the position (by de Man's account) of structuralist poetics and semiotic approaches to literature, insofar as they let "come to the fore" questions about the compatibility of aesthetic values and linguistic structures. They do so, de Man suggests, in the poetician's very attempt to reduce the ambiguous rhetorical force or "aesthetic charge" of a text's tropes to the predictability and "aesthetic neutrality" of a grammatical system. In other words it is the "ambivalent rejection" or the unsuccessful reduction of rhetoric and rhetorical force that brings out the questions addressed in literary theory; and that conjunction constitutes a similarity, continuity, or repetition between Romanticism and modern formalist criticism or poetics. If " 'Romantic' literatures" take up the problem assigned to aesthetics in the Third Critique—"the continuity of aesthetic with rational judgment"—modern literary criticism and interpretation at their most effective remain "Romantic" in this respect, inasmuch as they focus deliberately on the perceptions of the reader as the basis of the text's "reception."

The essays in *The Resistance to Theory* demonstrate this in some detail, analyzing with particular care the exemplary critical labors of Michael Riffaterre (*Semiotics of Poetry, Text Production*) and of Hans Robert Jauss (*Literaturgeschichte als Provokation, Aesthetic Experience and Literary Hermeneutics*). De Man argues that central among their critical premises is the axiom that "it is not sufficient for a poetic significance to be latent or erased, but that it must be manifest, actualized in a way that allows the analyst to point to a specific, determined textual feature." The basic premise of a "poetics of reading" is "that the articulation of the sign with its signification occurs by means of a structure that is *itself phenomenally realized*" (*RT,* 33–34). This premise underlies "close reading," the affirmed commitment to deriving interpretations from the text "itself." An equal dependence on post-Kantian and Hegelian aesthetics is reflected in Marxist and historicist approaches to the extent that they presume the phenomenality (and the availability to positive knowledge) of the social and historical causes and effects held to be the work's signification. In essays brought (or to be brought) together in *The Resistance to Theory* and *Aesthetic Ideology,* De Man's readings disentangle texts of Kant and Hegel from the post-Kantian aesthetics they ostensibly authorize, such as the view that the possibility of "the sensory appearance [or manifestation] of the idea" (to cite Hegel's *Aesthetics*) is made manifest in the apprehension of the "beautiful," of coherent formal wholes—including and especially the *self*-referential (not referential *and* figurative or fictional) structure that defines (for Riffaterre and for others less deliberately explicit than he) a work of literature. These guiding principles of modern poetics and aesthetics assimilate the process of signification to perception or phenomenal intuition, as well as to understanding or knowledge. Aesthetics thereby fulfills its deepest vocation: to confirm the phenomenality of language. Language, through its appearance as literature or poetry, is understood as art: as human making, and ultimately, as symbolic—intentionality and its mediations superseding the arbitrary relation between meaning and form.

Before examining de Man's analysis of how these conclusions come under pressure in the elaboration of a poetics of reading, I want to extrapolate from his argument an account of why or how *in " 'Romantic' literatures"* the "continuity of aesthetic with rational judgment" emerges not merely as a tenet but also as an uncertainty and "crux." In this regard Maurice Blanchot's writing on "literature" and "Romanticism" is an inviting resource, since it conceptualizes these terms in relation to, as it were, certifiably "historical" events, the French Revolution and the Terror. That they are represented as events with a fabulous character makes Blanchot's account akin to the gesture whereby de Man places ironic quotation marks around the aesthetic and period term "Romantic." Blanchot draws all these terms into interpretations which, in their insistent focus on the "act" of writing, have complex affinities with de Man's work. Analytical reading of Blanchot texts that deliberately propound a Romantic connection between literature and theory can improve the chances of a good-enough reading of a perhaps more obvious resource, de Man's essays and lectures from the sixties. In those texts (de Man's) the significance of Romantic literature is equally charged and the understanding of history even more enigmatic; they require a separate reading from the later essays I interpret here.[6]

Both Blanchot's and de Man's writings complicate and disqualify the idea of an "expressive" function displacing a "mimetic" function of literature in the Romantic period. The Romantic crisis of "literature"—the "Romantic" element of literature—takes place not in a changed alignment of priorities between an outside and an inside (a metaphorical model that maintains the phenomenal and cognitive identity of language), but rather in this model's disruption by the coming to the fore of language's performative force. What language *does*—not simply in specific performatives or speech acts, but in its figural and constative functions, in naming and thereby negating and yet apparently gaining a phenomenal world—emerges as literature's subject and aim. "The power, for the work, to be" becomes, in and through literature, a stake and a question. Thus a passage in "L'Absence de livre" proposes that "one of the tasks of romanticism was precisely to introduce a totally new mode of fulfillment and even a veritable conversion of writing: the power, for the work, to be and no longer to represent, to be everything [*tout*], . . . yet in a form that, being all forms (that is to say being, at its limit, no form), does not realize the whole [*le tout*], but signifies it in suspending it, indeed in shattering it."[7] This comment appears in the last section of *L'Entretien infini,* in pages entitled "The Athenaeum," an explicit allusion to Friedrich Schlegel's periodical published from 1798–1800 in Jena. Bringing to life the word's own allusions (to a temple, to reason, to rhetoric, to the *polis*), Blanchot's text also recycles "the Athenaeum" as the name for a peculiar aspect of the history of thought:

a name for thought that "has a history," so to speak—namely the moment of excess or aberration in which "literature announces that it is taking power" (Ath, 167). It is quite compatible with the argument of Blanchot's earlier essay that the title of the later one is a word defined also simply as "a literary magazine." The argument that literature or writing can only contradictorily be conceived in terms of "action"—as "inaction," *or* as authentic act—is evoked in the ambiguous resonances of a title that alludes to literature's periodical publication, in, say, London, as well as Jena: contexts more and less recalcitrant to "undocumented" argument that the self-publishing of literature implies and emulates "the right to death" (unpromising condition for a "public sphere"). The implication of such a title is that the very precincts of fundamental consensus (the "Athenaeum" of "Athens"), the very grounds of "the social contract" in common "sense" and "taste" (Addison's, Adam's, Keats's)—notwithstanding the equanimity of the style in which they are sometimes announced—may be, like the Jena *Athenaeum* in its very marginality, places where in the guise of literature "Reason" "encounters its most dangerous meaning—which is to interrogate itself in a declarative mode" (Ath, 167).

De man, like Blanchot, envisions literature as the tangling of "knowledge" and "power," as unpredictable kinds of complicity and conflict between two inescapable functions of language. De Man locates in literature or in the text as rhetoric—and, repeatedly (in readings of Rousseau, Wordsworth, Hegel, Shelley, Hugo) in the writing of Romanticism—a "force" or "power" of figuration or positing that disrupts the process of understanding. Reading the texts of "Romantic literatures and critical philosophies" uncovers "force" of an order that conflicts both with their status as aesthetics and with the status of the aesthetic as a value. It ruins the relation of linguistic structure to aesthetic values and the "continuity of aesthetic with rational judgment" that are the "burden," "tenet," and "crux" precisely of Romantic literature.

Blanchot's account of why such darkness makes abode in Romantic literature stems from an argument about the "work" of writing and its turning on the writer's encounter with "those decisive moments in history when everything seems put in question, when . . . everything sinks effortlessly, without work, into nothingness."[8] Romantic literature recognizes itself in the French Revolution, Blanchot observes—which means that Romantic writing conveys its affinity with "events that are declarations," and that "the French Revolution" is the name for the occurrence of events of this kind. Events such as "the Terror" with a capital *T*[9]—"the scaffold, the enemies of the people presented to the people, beheadings performed simply for show, . . . constitute not historical facts, but a new language" (Ath, 167), with all a language's force, to "foster alike by beauty and by fear."[10]

This observation of Blanchot's *also* means that themes and rhetorical modes of a text that identify it with "events" that are "language"—events with untrammelled power to mean—mark the impressive power of the "actual" (as we say) French Revolution; yet that impact is inseparable from the events' allegorization and monumentalization. An inescapability of ideology that begins in the time of the French Revolution, perhaps ("perhaps" here indicating the impossibility of knowing whether the previous phrase should be read in quotes), appears in the impossibility of isolating from an ideological effect (of "the Revolution"?) the insight that the French Revolution inaugurates and manifests the power of ideology.

Blanchot's essays abide with these difficulties. They leave unsettled whether the historical referent or the historical monument has priority. Their subject could be stated as literature's inescapable affinity for ideology, except that this summation would tell much less than the Janus-faced interpretation Blanchot's texts set up. The interpretation can point in two directions, toward Romantic poetry and toward literary theory; toward, say, the question of Wordsworth's "jacobinism," which needs to be addressed from within the framework Blanchot evokes, that of the poetic text's identification with and self-interpretive distancing from the Revolution; and toward, say, the question of de Man's theory of Romanticism, which can be advanced within the framework of Blanchot's discussion of the "act" or the "work" of writing. For the latter question comes (as I will argue) to asking in what respect de Man's finding, in Romantic writing, *language as sheer (non-)event*—called in one context "the forgetting, by inscription, of terror"—checks the power of "events that are language."[11]

Blanchot undertakes in "La Littérature et le droit à la mort" to reread "work," as it figures in Hegel's *Phenomenology*, as the work of *writing*.[12] De Man's reading of the *Phenomenology*'s first chapter, in his review esssay on Riffaterre's poetics, is in one sense a critical rewriting of "La Littérature et le droit à la mort," Blanchot's rewriting of Hegel on "Absolute Freedom and Terror":

> The man [l'écrivain] knows he has not stepped out of history, but history is now the void, the void in the process of realization; it is *absolute* freedom which has become an event. Such periods are given the name Revolution. At this moment, freedom aspires to be realized in the *immediate* form of *everything* is possible, everything can be done. A fabulous moment—and no one who has experienced it can ever completely recover from it, since he has experienced history as his own history and his own freedom as universal freedom. These moments are, in fact, fabulous moments: in them, fable speaks; in them, the speech of fable be-

comes action. That the writer should be tempted by them is
completely appropriate. Revolutionary action is in every respect
analogous to action as embodied in literature: the passage from
nothing to everything, the affirmation of the absolute as event
and of every event as absolute. Revolutionary action explodes
with the same force and the same facility as the writer who has
only to set down a few words side by side in order to change the
world. Revolutionary action also has the same . . . certainty that
everything it does has absolute value, that it is not just any action
performed to bring about some desirable and respectable goal,
but that it is itself the ultimate goal, the Last Act. This last act is
freedom, and the only choice left is between freedom and nothing. This is why, at that point, the only tolerable slogan is: *freedom or death*. Thus the Reign of Terror comes into being. . . .
When the blade falls on Saint-Just and Robespierre, in a sense it
executes no one. Robespierre's virtue, Saint-Just's restlessness,
are simply their existences already suppressed, the anticipated
presence of their deaths, the decision to allow freedom to assert
itself completely in them and through its universality negate the
particular reality of their lives. (Lit, 38–39)

Blanchot redoes and outdoes Hegel in interpreting the Terror as the fulfillment of the demand of a writer, of one in whom resides "that negation that is not satisfied with the unreality in which it exists, because it wishes to realize itself and can only do so by negating something real" (Lit, 38). In "The Athenaeum"—which can refer back to and reinterpret this *récit*—this account of the Terror is succeeded by an observation about the "curious exchange" that takes place, with romanticism, "between the two movements, the 'political' and the 'literary' " (Ath, 167) and by reflection upon an unresolvable confusion of language and event. The work of the poet, Blanchot's texts suggest, unravels the aesthetic work. An attitude still often associated with the notion of Romanticism, the notion of poetry's value as "expression," is undercut by the question, read by Blanchot and de Man in Romanticism, of how and what poesis ("making") produces ("itself"), or, as de Man writes, "the enigma of the relationship between the aesthetic and the poetic" (*RT*, 70).

Thus "The Athenaeum":

The poet becomes the future of man at the moment when, being nothing but one who knows himself to be a poet, he designates (in this knowledge for which he is intimately responsible) the place where poetry will no longer be content to produce beautiful, well-defined works, but will produce itself in a movement without termination or determination. In other words, literature encounters its most dangerous meaning—which is to interrogate itself in a declarative mode: at times triumphantly in the discovery that everything thereby belongs to it, at others in the distress at discovering that it lacks everything, for it only affirms itself by default. There is no need to insist on what is well known: it was the French Revolution that gave the German romantics this new form constituted by the declarative imperative, the *éclat* of the manifesto. . . . It is not from the revolutionary orators that the romantics will seek lessons in style, but from the Revolution in person, from this language made History, signified by events that are declarations. (Ath, 167)

The "considerable aesthetic charge" of this passage has to be taken account of in interpreting it. Yet its rhetorical resourcefulness makes very difficult the task of determining the meaning of the relation between the text's statement and its performance. The passage both refers to and evokes—if not enacts—the literary text's capability of grammatically formulating as statements, as assertions, claims that are rather questions or attempts at persuasion. ("To interrogate," moreover, is a term that threateningly blurs the distinction between the attempt to know and the use of force. And it is not really reassuring that it is "literature" that interrogates "literature," or "itself.") Declarative self-interrogations, like so-called rhetorical questions, exemplify the fact that the text's rhetorical mode or force is not within the control of its lexical and grammatical form. The doubleness and ambiguity of the "declarative imperative" is like that of the rhetorical question as it is analyzed by de Man in a famous and funny passage of "Semiology and Rhetoric." Derrida is adduced as Archie (De-)Bunker asking "What is the Difference?" along with the Yeats of "Among School Children" asking "How *can* we know the dancer from the dance?" Whereupon de Man concludes, "Confronted with the question of the difference between grammar and rhetoric, grammar allows us to ask the question, but the sentence by means of which we ask it may deny the very possibility of asking. For what is the use of asking, I ask, when we cannot even authoritatively decide whether a question asks or doesn't ask?"[13] De Man's analysis shows up the hegemonizing power of literary rhetoric as exemplified in the rhetorical question that forecloses questions about what it technically (grammatically) asks—*and* demonstrates the subversive or unreliable effect of rhetoric's deployment in a literary text. Blanchot's analysis manifests or mimes "the *éclat* of the manifesto," even in the very process of forging a historian's *récit*.

De Man's "Promises" (1979) and Derrida's "Declarations of Independence" (1986) have since analyzed the rhetorical mode termed here the "declarative imperative" as it functions in Rousseau's *Du contrat social* and in "the" Declaration of Independence.[14] Such a "Declaration" turns to its own purposes the grammatical indistinguishability of constative and performative utterance; its "felicity" depends on there being no law whereby a text's grammar controls or generates its rhetoric (nor the reverse). The positing power of literary *fiction* would be realized in the Revolutionary rhetoric that would *bring about* the existence of a state or a nation by stating that it exists already or forthwith. An "ideological"—and a fictive—moment. Yet it is the case that the conditions of modern politics—democracy, the nation, the constitutional state—depend on the possibility of literature: of the institution of literature, and of the act of writing.

How, however, are specific instances of written language linked with a "language" "made History"—with "events that are declarations"? The connections between written texts and "events" or practices—precedentless rituals, or reiterated traumas or epiphanies—are not straightforward. They form unreliable tropes, they are unpredictably symbol, synecdoche, metonymy, metaphor. As de Man writes, Rousseau's text "promises" and goes on promising, notwithstanding its deconstructive theorizing of the legitimate or lawful State. Blanchot's text conveys the enigma and the prestige of "style"—a "form" constituted by an "*éclat*." Thus "there is no need to insist on what is well known"—"well known," at least, since the publication of "La Littérature et le droit à la mort." In various ways, Blanchot's pages give short shrift to the presumption that it would be decisive to find "actualized in a particular feature" of a Romantic text its looking to "the Revolution" for "lessons in style." Not decisive not because such *trouvailles* are simply dispensable, but because they are conditioned by the unreadable figure of personification or prosopopoeia, the model of the "model." That figure of a "face" that "speaks" subtends the figure of "the Revolution in person" demonstrating "style," and the figure of "literature" (or the German Romantics) seeking out uncalled-for initiations and meeting with dangerous close calls. To *promise* and to *experiment:* such is the practice of that unnatural role model "the Revolution," "literature," or "text," a difficult-to-circumscribe Don Juan (*AR,* 268).

In setting up such loose connections between texts and events, Blanchot's essays manifest the negative power of rhetoric: literature's power to make linguistic structures' meaning undecidable, hence only "decidable." The sentence stating one of the essays' main contentions, that literature has a point of convergence with Revolution and the Terror, is the sort of language usually called "highly rhetorical"—rife with metaphor, prosopopoeia, the future anterior, personifications that may or may not be in "free indirect discourse" (a variety of prosopopoeia), and the figure of a scene of instruction. Let us cite that again: "There is no need to insist on what is well known: it was the French Revolution that gave the German romantics this new form constituted by the declarative imperative, the *éclat* of the manifesto. . . . It is not from the revolutionary orators that the romantics will seek lessons in style, but from the Revolution in person, from this language made History, signified by events that are declarations (Ath, 167)." What does this rhetoric mean for the text's implied judgment of the stance it describes, and of the language in which it is named or conceptualized, such as the notion of "language made History"? One can only doubtfully "decide"—on the watery ground of the text's emphasis on the fact that a text's grammar or structure does not control its meaning or force—that writers' emulating the style of a "language" consisting in "events" with the violence of "declarations" is being represented as a false step. Working against that inference, though, is the passage's implication that the illusion of power vested in the notion of "language made History" is an illusion with real power; its vindication of "the journal" (*The Athenaeum*) against the suspicion that it "dream[s] of rejecting freedom's conquests," harbors a counterrevolutionary or a totalitarian politics; its unironical formulation of what the journal wants or dreams of, namely, "endowing the revolutionary act with all its decisive force in establishing it as near as possible to its origin: where it is knowledge, creative word and, in this knowledge and this word, the principle of absolute freedom" (Ath, 167). Yet there is no escaping the implication of this text that there is no language, "History," within which the rhetorical force or the occurrence of an event or a text predictably instantiates a given grammar. Nor the implication that this nonexistence is not only due to the volatile character of the declarative and the question.

To what is literature entitled, according to Blanchot's refiguring of Hegel's account? What it attains is an insistent, highly demanding question: "Then where is literature's power? . . . Then where is literature's force?" (Lit, 58–59). (" 'Thea! Thea! Thea! Where is Saturn?' ")[15] About to resume a thesis, that "literature is language turning into ambiguity," Blanchot's essay calls up its title and refers to "literature's *right* to affix a negative or positive sign indiscriminately to each of its moments and each of its results" (Lit, 58). "Right," here, suggests the idea of a historical link between this conception of "literature" and the concept of a "right." With disconcerting implications for both. What if the notion of a "right," also that of a "man" or of a "citizen," were bound up with that Ovidian metamorphosis "language turning into ambiguity"? A transmutation hard to grasp, a most elusive difficulty, for, as Blanchot writes, "It is not just that each moment of language can become ambiguous and say something different from what it is saying, but that the general meaning of language is unclear: we don't know if it is expressing or representing, it if is a thing or means that thing; if it is there to be forgotten or if it only makes us forget so that we will see it; if it is transparent because what it says has so little meaning or clear because of the exactness with which it says it . . ." (Lit, 59). (I have quoted this seemingly interminable sentence only to the point at which any sense of a binary opposition of alternatives breaks down.) "This" ambiguity, de Man will argue, signifies the merely positional status of "grounds"—of reasons for appearance; it signifies the figural (or catachrestic) status of "voice" and "face." The general meaning of language is ambiguous insofar as its "speaking" is a fiction: insofar as "intentionality" is a figure. As literature reveals: in the very gesture of *manifesting* its emulation of "the speaking face of earth and heaven" or "language made History"; in the very act of propounding its faith in a "language" providing determinate relations between law and example; *and* in the envisaging of the possibility of "absolute freedom," the possibility of *exercising* the "right to affix a negative or positive sign to each of [a text's or event's] moments and each of its results." "Language" is a catachresis—like the "right" to "death."

These essays of Blanchot's help lend a content to de Man's allusion to the "ambivalent rejection of rhetoric at the very moment that it was being used and refined as never before" (RT, 25). Linking the literary imagination with the power of fable contained in the French Revolution, as is also done in *The Prelude* (not to mention, for the moment, *The Republic,* nor the mythification of Rousseau), leaves a writer with lots to reject and lots to regret. (It leaves "literature" a lot, too. "The post-Romantic predicament" (AR, 322) comes out at times in abjection and in reconstructed trauma.) The very "freedom" of the work of writing—from the constraints of forms known not to add up to meaning, as well as from the specific restraint of social reference—holds open the question of how, or whether, its formal and referential aspects converge. With work, one could socialize this argument, one could reform it along the following lines:

The very freedom of utterance—both of literature no longer produced for patrons, and of political discourse no longer descriptive or administrative but constitutive and legislative—means also its detachment from the constraints of representation and its discrepancy from the phenomenality of the social world. Why does the condemnation of "mere rhetoric," "false rhetoric," become a central gesture? That gesture repeats and reacts to the unleashing of the performative power of language through the political power of print.[16]

De Man: What comes to the fore is an unavoidable question, the question whether aesthetic values can be compatible with the linguistic values that make up the entities from which they derive.

Blanchot: This question haunts and galvanizes those romantics and revolutionaries who proceed to the denunciation of literary and political discourse as rhetoric. One can describe that antirhetorical gesture in historical terms. But it is not determined by history; it is the perennial incitement of Letters, as has been demonstrated in Jean Paulhan's *Les Fleurs de Tarbes, ou la Terreur dans les lettres*. It is part of that book's meaning, but not a condition of its origination, that it was written in Paris in 1941.

(End of the prosopopoeia.)

The rise of aesthetics can be seen as making it possible to meet a threat: the danger of the gap opened between meaning and language, between the phenomenal world and the materiality of language. One seems to see the urgency of the hegemonizing task of "taste," "reading," or the making of a reading public. That aesthetics comes to replace the institutionalized discipline of rhetoric, in the late eighteenth and early nineteenth century, is a scenario that makes sense. For in an epoch marked by "events which are declarations"—or by a journalism that tries systematically to provide them—conceding authority to a traditional "rhetoric," whether codified rules of style or that "large portion of phrases and figures of speech which from father to son have long been regarded as the common inheritance of Poets," is at once too threatening, too close to the bone (Paris) and too tame—too boring.[17] The only traditional rhetoric one can be interested in is commemorations of the dead. Whence *Essays upon Epitaphs;* and (in Prefaces to *Lyrical Ballads* 1800 and 1802) a radical reappropriation of aesthetic categories—turning on "Taste" as a taste for rhetoric without meaning, and convoking in accord with "the native and naked dignity of man, the grand elementary principle of pleasure, by which he knows, and feels, and lives, and moves," all elements resistant to "pre-established codes of decision."[18] The writer must take *such* codes as "enemies," and not alone "large codes of fraud and woe." Liberal remonstrance against abrupt unenlightened decision, like the plain style epitaph, "seems to me upon the whole greatly preferable," Wordsworth would intimate, to lines that carry on as if dead can speak: epitaphs that "personate the deceased"; apostrophes that throw their voice to a blank (such as "Thou hast a voice, great Mountain! to repeal / Large codes of fraud and woe").[19] The limited circumstances and the defensiveness—but *also* the insidiousness, the promise—of this particular Romantic aesthetic comes through in Wordsworth's surprising word for the antagonists of these "enemies" the "codes": "pleasures" (not justice, not judgment; not the people). Aesthetic criticism of this scope retains the sharpness of a "crux" and requires of its contesters irony, but not dismissal. The rhetorical power of a liberal aesthetic repeatedly eludes being grasped as what it shows, the power of its announced adversary, "rhetoric."

These critical texts arising with the "rise of aesthetics" manifest literature's "strange right," to change meanings, to invert values: "to affix a negative or positive sign indiscriminately to each of its moments and each of its results" (Lit, 59). The pitiful or pitiless unraveling of a poetics of remembrance that occurs in Wordsworth's *Essays upon Epitaphs*—which offer, against their declared aesthetic intent, repeated evidence that the relationship between word and thing, between features of style and features of grief, is not phenomenal but conventional—manifests the antagonism I have been asserting, that of aesthetic and poetic or literary functions. "Literature," Romantic writing—including romantic aesthetics—"involves the voiding, rather than the affirmation, of aesthetic categories" (RT, 10). Of the antirhetorical gesture of Romanticism it can be said, as Blanchot says of the "struggle" with "ambiguity," that it is "like the struggle against evil Kafka talks about, which ends in evil, 'like the struggle with women, which ends in bed' " (Lit, 59).

Given all that is at stake along with the vocation of aesthetics, as this essay began by trying to recall—even if one overlooks questions relating to the value (of all kinds) of vocations generally known as "rewarding" (like teaching literature)—"it should come as no surprise" that few institutions wittingly buy into ensuring "literariness." Vainly does de Man's essay on literary theory describe literature's work, "voiding," as an appreciable public service—advertising "literature as the place where this negative knowledge about the reliability of linguistic utterances is made available" (RT, 10). No doubt: an indispensable address. Passed along, this address reveals something else. "Literature" indicates all the ways a shelter can become a threat (to borrow Neil Hertz's remarking of an odd figure in de Man's text "Wordsworth and the Victorians"). Thus "the rise of aesthetics" is not the response to a threat. The aesthetic is a shelter that *is* a "threat," making audible the Siren promise of knowledge as action. Neil Hertz reads this figure in a way that calls attention to how it marks the occurrence of reverses not necessarily recouped by any dialectic, which alienate the experience of Consciousness as well as the priority of Life.[20]

Say that one says, for instance, rightly, that in the same period as the rise of aesthetics, the subject and aim of literature become what it *does,* or *that* it can be. That act and that operation of literature oscillate between being a praxis that is the very mainspring of aesthetic criticism and its decisive interruption. It is its mainspring insofar as language, as literature, concentrates on its formal, not merely its referential, properties, and the formalization thereby achieved appears as an action or entity that the text or the reader can also *know*. The formalization achieved in the literary work seems to make it available as both a model and object for knowledge. The substantiality precisely of a language shaped by the play of form rather than the arbitrary constraints of reference, freed for the totalizing self-generated interplay of figure, promises as it were even despite itself the substantiality of a world, the availability, in language, of a phenomenal reality. Literature—certainly Romantic literature—houses this belief. Poetics—even Riffaterre's—reverts to it, in the form of "the postulate of self-referentiality which defines and delimits for him the specificity of literature" (*RT,* 31). Back comes the ghost host, the still-game guardian, antagonist of the Don: the phantom of "the category of the aesthetic as guardian of the rational cognition it appears to subvert." Its inviting reconciliation has to be exposed; it is the phantom of the opera: "the *aesthetic* ideology." This job falls to rhetorical reading, that is, to a reading able to spell out again, rather than come to terms rhetorically with, "the claims of reference."

The work is carried out in the essay by Cathy Caruth in this volume, and of course elsewhere (it is hard to finish off). It entails rethinking the related roles of trope and grammar. Caruth writes about de Man's interpreting the graceful puppet dance evoked in Kleist's "Über das Marionetten-Theater" as a particular model of a written text, the model that conceives the text as a sequence of tropes—tropes seen as spatial (ultimately, mathematical) figures, whose aesthetic charm and power lies in their link to an author or intentional agency, as this link appears in "the transformations undergone by the linear motion of the puppeteer" into the beautiful display of curves and arabesques. De Man writes,

> This text is the transformational system, the anamorphosis of the line as it twists and turns into the tropes of ellipses, parabola, and hyperbole. . . . The indeterminations of imitation and of hermeneutics have at last been formalized into a mathematics that no longer depends on role models or on semantic intentions. . . . Balanced motion compellingly leads to the privileged metaphor of a center of gravity. . . . On the other hand, it is said of the same puppets, almost in the same breath, that they are *antigrav* [antigravitational], that they can rise and leap, like Nijinsky, as if no such thing as gravity existed for them. . . . By falling (in all senses of the term, including the theological Fall) gracefully, one prepares the ascent, the turn from parabola to hyperbole, which is also a rebirth. (RR, 285–286)

With a blandly approbatory assent one is tempted to connect with her personal knowledge of dancing on ice, Caruth's essay carries on de Man's deadpan exegesis (holding off tactfully, though, from more of its murderous *style indirect libre*):

> The exhilarating, graceful freedom of this movement lies in its elimination of any referential weight of a personal authorial self; the puppeteer is lost entirely in the movements of the puppets. The graceful image of the human body arises precisely, here, in the *loss* of any referential particularity. What makes this possible is indicated by de Man when he calls this a "transformational system" as well as a system of "tropes" or figures. For, as a transformational system, it is a grammar, a grammar conceived as a coded set of differences not based on any extralinguistic reality; what is at work here is the power of a grammar that incorporates referential differences into nonreferential, intralinguistic ones. Yet at the same time this loss of referential particularity appears, surprisingly, in the very *figure* of a human being. The paradox of this writing system is that it produces the human figure of the author in the very elimination of authorial referentiality. Precisely when the text appears most human, it is most mechanical.[21]

This passage pinpoints the frightening metamorphosis of meaning into force, tropes into grammar, grammar into figure, and event into "language" (or language into "events"), that aligns "aesthetic education" with the "aesthetic state" ("not just a state of mind or soul") (*RR*, 264). The power of the "literature" or the "writing system" generated by the textual model these essays so gravely pan is that of ideology—pleonastically speaking, of "aesthetic ideology" ("an *empty* void"—W. Allen): the power of the aesthetic (an idea of freedom inseparable from the idea of the beautiful) to conceal its force as law. De Man's strategy, as Caruth shows, is to bring out what he elsewhere calls "the shift to a performative model of language": to put a name—"transformational system," "force," "power," "charm"—to the incoherence of the process whereby referential differences become intralinguistic ones, and to the disguising of that process by and as a formal structure of law available to perception and for inspection.

This convocation of texts is enough and more than enough to evoke the double problem at which this essay aimed. It is the problem of how Romantic literatures inaugurate literary theory, and of how that name or phrase relates to a problem that is also a historical and historic one—the relation between literary theory and literature, and the relation between Romanticism and what comes after it (over the ice; and to the brink of the futile recourse by which the writer tries sometimes to shake off identification with a secret—heading for a harbor hoping to "pass immediately into Holland").[22] For it is not so clear, given the analysis I have just outlined, how literature could be exceeded or grasped by its theory, or how the Romantic era could come to a close. The problem of differentiating literature, as "available" knowledge of the specificity of literary as distinct from aesthetic or mimetic principles, from literary theory, can be seen as converging with the problem of defining a relation to Romanticism, as to the historical "event." How to find or make the difference between "our" situations as readers of Romantic writing from those of the Romantic literary and philosophical texts "themselves": that elusive separation may illustrate—better than it explicates—the tension between literary and aesthetic functions. I want to return to de Man's enigmatic insistence on the fact of our distance or difference from "Romanticism," keeping these problems in mind.

We have experienced this event, de Man asserts, "in its passing away." The 1966 essay "Wordsworth and Hölderlin" describes in these terms a point of access to "approaching by way of the comparative path that truth of romanticism that is beginning to be indicated by some specialized works of criticism" (*RR*, 49).

> In the case of romanticism . . . [t]he proximity of the event on the historical plane is such that we are not yet able to view it in the form of a clarified and purified memory. . . . We carry it within ourselves as the experience of an *act* in which, up to a certain point, we ourselves have participated. . . . To interpret romanticism means quite literally to interpret the past as such, *our* past precisely to the extent that we are beings who want to be defined and, as such, interpreted in relation to a totality of experiences that slip into the past. The content of this experience is perhaps less important than the fact that we have experienced it *in its passing away,* and that it thereby has contributed in an unmediated way (that is, in the form of an act) to the constitution of our own consciousness of temporality. Now it is precisely this experience of the temporal relation between the act and its interpretation that is one of the main themes of romantic poetry. (*RR,* 50)

It is unmediately, in the form of an act, that something experienced in its passing away contributes—has contributed to—framing "our" consciousness of temporality. (Syntax can do only so much. Nearly every one of these words would need to be printed in quotes and woven into and out of its historical contexts, those of an existentialist vocabulary de Man won't long maintain, but never erases.) We carry it within us uninterpreted, like a stone supper or an unforgettable and unperformable refrain, a deaf man's notes. Wind of an unaccommodatable lyre. It permits no adjustment—in the sense that this text accommodating a voice, this figure of "the experience of an *act,*" wheels round upon itself and "treads in its own steps" (like the image in "A Defense of Poetry" of the lyre that is not like a lyre but like a musician adjusting his voice to a lyre that is or is not like a lyre), bending its path back away from "the truth" in a way that precludes rather than allows repose.[23] Nobody is exempted from anything by the qualifying remark that allows one to read it as saying that precisely the wish to be interpreted in relation to a totality defines or constitutes "the past as such"—calling it "*our* past to the extent that we are beings who want to be interpreted in relation to a totality of experiences that slip into the past." It is *our* past—is an act in which we have participated—precisely to the extent that we are beings who want to be defined, and, as such, interpreted.

That is, precisely to the extent that we want to stand in an interpretive relation to the event of Romanticism, we don't, we are involved in it as in an act in which we have taken part or parts. Our part was to lose it: to lose a loved figure, that of the theme—"one of the main themes of romantic poetry"—of the "experience of the temporal relation between the act and its interpretation." The difficulty of interpreting Romanticism is the difficulty of turning this traumatic loss of the figure of "experience," or of the experience of interpretation (or the "experiencing" of a temporal relation), into an object or a subject of interpretation. The dialectical resourcefulness of the terms "act" and "interpretation" in this particular passage of de Man's essay discourages attempts to meet the difficulty they describe by redefining it as a "problem," whether an addiction or a technological challenge. Realizing that the problem with interpreting Romanticism is that you turn Romantic, trying to make over into an experienced loss what is rather an array of differences and discontinuities, may feel good (or bad) but doesn't give more than flash-in-the-pan alternatives to interpretive readings of texts; reselecting the texts to be read is a way back but not a way out.

Staying with de Man's text requires a sort of running in place. Thus for instance it might well be that the above reading is erroneous, since the final sentence ought rather to be read, "it is precisely *this* experience" (namely that of the loss—the passing away—of experience), "*this* experience of the temporal relation between the act and its interpretation," namely, "unmediated" relation to that relation; trauma, the "slip into" the past—"that is one of the main themes of romantic poetry." Yet the occurrence if not the content of "themes," in Romantic poetry, allows for a distinction between the readers of Romanticism or trauma and the writers. Romantic writing has taken as a theme the relationship between act and interpretation, the relation that is also "our" relation to this act of thematization. We are positioned as the interpreters of the act that is or was Romanticism, the act of being beings who want to be interpreted ("in relation to a totality" could go without saying; "of events that slip into the past" stamps this remark as European, un-American). At the same time we are positioned as those who have experienced only in an unmediated fashion, as an act, that is, not via an interpretation, the passing away of the act constituted by a *thematizing* of the relation between interpretation and act. This represents a difficult "position" to get down or take up, for it lies in what was supposed to be the object of interpretation carrying (or not carrying) it out, while the would-be interpreters are cut off from that activity by the "act" of losing it. "Our temporal consciousness" is neither a consciousness nor ours, one infers, but is the fading, the ever-increasing precariousness, of the representation or the *thematization* of temporal discontinuity, of the disjunctions of language or consciousness. The "temporal," the non-"relation between the act and its interpretation" is forgotten or becomes invisible. Given the fix of this glazing eye, the only sobering possibility is that of once again taking it as a theme.

De Man's essays in various ways emphasize the possibility of having to examine the idea that an empty link (as of sign with meaning) could be "pointed out" or marked. One finds the gist of this "suggestion" or argument in a passage in "The Resistance to Theory" taking note of a telling insight or doubleness of contemporary theory (Barthes's, Jakobson's, Genette's; the same could be said of Riffaterre's): these contemporary theoretical texts are and are named "semiology," but intermittently misname or misrepresent the functions of the "poetic" sign as an *aesthetic* function, that of making available perceptually the links between a language's signs and its meanings. "It is inevitable that semiology or similarly oriented methods be considered formalistic, in the sense of being aesthetically rather than semantically valorized," but that is nevertheless a mistake—the misdescription of systematic attention to *signs* as attention to *forms,* whereas the apprehension of "forms" and the attention to "signs" are mutually antagonistic (*RT,* 10). "Semiological" approaches, as readings or studies of trope or "rhetoric," manage to make this observation. For instance,

> the convergence of sound and meaning celebrated by Barthes in Proust . . . is also considered here [i.e. in Barthes] to be a mere *effect* which language can perfectly well achieve, but which bears no substantial relationship, by analogy or by ontologically grounded imitation, to anything beyond that particular effect. It is a *rhetorical* rather than an *aesthetic* function of language, a . . . trope that oper-

ates on the level of the signifier and contains no responsible pronouncement on the nature of the world—despite its powerful potential to create the opposite illusion. The phenomenality of the signifier, as sound, is unquestionably involved in the correspondence between the name and the thing named, but the link, the relationship between word and thing, is not phenomenal but conventional. (*RT,* 10)

Semiological analysis, to the extent that it gets involved with the reading or theory of rhetoric, has the not inconsiderable demystificatory potential of indicating why a state or a society, inasmuch as it is constituted by signs and language, could not and should not be organized or conceptualized as an aesthetic whole—a dance, a self-solidary array of meanings all present in potentia without conflict in the same time frame. "The prisonhouse of language" is no descending house or shade at all, but the being sentenced to uncertainty whether and which, among a variety of possible syntaxes, the operations of meaning are being levied for—whether and among whom words, "clocks," and fixes on the world are being shared. "This gives the language considerable freedom from referential restraint, but makes it epistemologically highly suspect and vulnerable," de Man comments (*RT,* 10).

That it is possible to write all in one breath of the anxieties of "the language" and of the state, the writer and the citizen, appears at times as a solution to the problem it imperfectly describes, but just as likely, repeats or redisguises it.[24] Redisguises it by reaestheticizing it: by making the indeterminable borderline between the "social" and the "linguistic" seem to take shape as a principle of analogy, one offering real knowledge, between the social and the text. So states and societies are structured like a language—that is, by languages (by overlapping idioms in the literal and figurative sense, by rival or mutually oblivious "natural" languages, and by all sorts of writing and written texts); what follows? The slides and the differences still have to be placed, located—with all the "undecidability" and interminableness that that labor implies. It "would be" and it is an error and a misfortune to believe, for instance, that one *knows* something (useful; about the world; "about" and "of" the law or the text) by "knowing"—even if by heart as well as by rote—that the "text" is like a legal text, and that the law (or "legal text") is *like* (not *is,* though it also "is") a text. The discussion of the " 'definition' of text" along these lines, in de Man's reading of the *Social Contract,* "Promises"—and the unfolding of that definition or figure, in Derrida's "Force of Law," in juxtaposition with a reading of Walter Benjamin's "For a Critique of Violence"—in being much more complex and rigorous than this rote rendering of one of their main themes, do have the value of providing a reader with exercise in a practice that may have appreciable exchange value as well as aesthetic charm; they do-not-and-should-not, though, offer access to the possession or exercise of knowledge or power in any but this very limited sense.[25] Stated in this way, this point may seem as obvious and stupefying as claiming to observe, "in earnest," that "un chat est un chat et Rolet un fripon."[26]

Blanchot's essay explains and alludes in passing to the "hypocritical violence" that is the sole content of the claim, by a writer, to "believe that he is on the way to health and sincerity" in "mak[ing] it his ideal to call a cat a cat" (Lit, 30–31). Plenty of such writers will claim, of course, the precedent and the exemption of the "physician to all men," treading on the heels of Freud in "Fragment of an Analysis," in which, however, Mnemosyne's charge that "The poet and the dreamer are distinct, / Diverse, sheer opposites, antipodes" has been modulated into its seeming opposite. Editors hesitated, one was told, (fascinated), whether or not to allow into the canonical *The Fall of Hyperion* what, in not every manuscript, comes next: It is the poet shouting "Spite of myself and with a Pythia's spleen," to "faded, far flown Apollo":

> Where is [i.e., give me, give it to them] thy *misty pestilence* to creep
> Into the dwellings, through the door crannies,
> Of all mock lyrists, large self worshipers,
> And careless Hectorers in proud bad verse.
> Though I breathe death with them it will be life
> To see them sprawl before me into graves

(This is, mind you, Keats!)[27]

Only an ever-rarer discipline in keeping eyes on "the ball" could steel one to resist the pleasure of unveiling the discreet footnote on this page in "Literature and the Right to Death." Behold the remarkable poetic and exegetic resourcefulness of the path of the translator, which drops from Blanchot's passage above to the following facts: "Blanchot is referring to a remark made by Nicolas Boileau (1637–1711) in his first Satire: 'J'appelle un chat un chat et Rolet un fripon' ('I call a cat a cat and Rolet a rascal'). Rolet was a notorious figure of the time. — *Tr*" (Lit, 31n). This signature hums to the very note of the cracked bell of the text on facts on figures; its angelically ambiguous modesty and penetration ("angelic penetration" is "The Antenaeum" 's praise for a Novalis text of 1798, "Monologue") makes such a text seem able and willing to *earn* the "right" to the same sometime residence as, for de Man, *Glas*. The right to "significance"; since we're staying with de Man (or Blanchot), "poetic significance": as "Hypogram and Inscription" notes of *Glas,* the text's "patent overdetermination . . . is of poetic significance only if, like Saussure's hypogram [a reference] to the preferred word fixed upon by the Saussure of *Les Mots sous les mots* for the uncertifiable anagrams he has traced in Latin and Vedic poetry], it cannot be determined whether it is random or determined" (*RT*, 43).

The insight propounded above as an ideological insight about ideology (putting every word of this phrase under the stress of ironic emphasis without the shelter of erasure) becomes, in effect, significant or interesting only as it is hauled back to the argument about and of a particular given written text. So—bearing in mind the impossibility of recalling now even one or two of the multitude of genuinely philosophical texts on the notorious figure of "the time"—I will stake these claims in a reading of de Man's reading of Hegel (the first chapter of the *Phenomenology*), together with Victor Hugo's lyric on the "*carillon Flamand.*" The anti-"Victorian," subversive and troubling nature of such an incongruous and worn-out pair, such a combining of the rhetorics of poetry and of philosophy—in an elusive alignment in which de Man would scent the lingering force of Wordsworth—will have to be drawn out elsewhere.[28]

▼ ▲ ▼

The most rapid access to a reading of de Man on "inscription" might be via the half-reading, half-paraphrase (or perhaps only what one "now" "experiences" as such) of passages from Nietzsche's so-called *The Will to Power* in the last chapter of the first half of *Allegories of Reading,* "Rhetoric of Persuasion (Nietzsche)." His reading of Nietzsche is for the reader of de Man a critical "critical" statement of the point that will bear upon literature and rhetoric, writing and politics. Key pages in this (the third) Nietzsche chapter set out the problem and the "relation" of trope and performance, rhetoric and grammar. Since these have been reframed with the utmost competence by William Ray and others, I'll cut to my take on their interest for the present argument: the take they imply on the "shift to a performative model."[29] It's just "this." The unavoidable necessity of shifting in this way with the hardships of "consciousness" has painfully uncertain results. It's the same beam in the eye over again—that is, that *noting* the deflection or wounding of the even most competently troping text's vision by "its" (—a—) "rhetorical force" can displace, but not spare, its violence. Having or wishing to note it does not imply, nor allow, a *knowledge* or a *model* of how "the true" (is what) happens. An "example": once again, of the powerlessness of a given text either to produce, or *not* produce, the effect of symbol, with "all" its susceptibilities to forced repatriation. Thus: not withstanding the executive as well as administrative capabilities implied by the ability to forge into a title, say, the disempowering quandary at work in the naive query, "Is there a 'text' in this class?" the example falters before its *general* implications. A reconceptualization of rhetoric or of the text (social or otherwise) as "force" or "performance" fails to work. The text, the model, is too curious, too "queer." What do I know from Nietzsche?—This:

> ("*first* we imagine an act that does not exist . . . and *second* we imagine a subject-substratum for this act . . ."). The aberrant authority of the subject is taken for granted; the new attack is upon the more fundamental notion ["*Mehr Licht!*"] of "act." Hence also the *apparent* [my emphasis—C. C.] contradiction between this text and the one on the phenomenalism of consciousness alluded to earlier. . . . The first passage (section 516) on identity showed that constative language is in fact performative, but the second passage (section 477) asserts that the possibility for language to perform is just as fictional as the possibility for language to assert. (*AR*, 128–129)

This conclusion *is played out* in de Man's readings in "Hypogram and Inscription," and there is where one might grasp the thread again of our investigation and quandary—the necessity of a relation and/or the lack of any relation between "the linguistic" and "the aesthetic." Who or what sends the letters, the letter bombs?

What is going on as de Man's text arrives at the following answer: "an obtuse bore: forget it! Which turns out to be precisely what Hegel sees as the function of writing"—The context, quickly please.—Yes. I quote, again, at length.

> Language appears explicitly for the first time in Hegel's chapter in the figure of a *speaking consciousness:* "The assertion (that the reality or being of external things possesses absolute truth for consciousness) does not know what it *states* (*spricht*), does not know that it says (*sagt*) the opposite of what it wants to say (*sagen will*). Every consciousness *states* (*spricht*) the opposite (of such a truth)" [*Phänomenologie des Geistes*, sect. 20, p. 87. Translation and italics are de Man's]. The figure of a speaking consciousness is made plausible by the deictic function that it names. As for written or inscribed language, it appears in Hegel's text only in the most literal of ways: by means of the parabasis which suddenly confronts us with the actual piece of paper on which Hegel, at that very moment, has been writing about the impossibility of saying the only thing one wants to say, namely the certainty of sense perception. Particularity (the here and now) was lost long ago,

even before speech: writing down this knowledge in no way loses (nor, of course, recovers) a here and now that, as Hegel puts it, was never accessible (*erreichbar*) to consciousness or to speech. It does something very different: unlike the here and now of speech, the here and now of inscription is neither false nor misleading: because he wrote it down, the existence of a here and now of Hegel's text is undeniable as well as totally blank. It reduces, for example, the entire text of the *Phenomenology* to the endlessly repeated stutter: *this* piece of paper, *this* piece of paper, and so on. We can easily learn to care for the other examples Hegel mentions: a house, a tree, night, day—but who cares for his darned piece of paper, the last thing in the world we want to hear about and, precisely because it is no longer an example but a fact, the only thing we actually get. As we would say, in colloquial exasperation with an obtuse bore: forget it! Which turns out to be precisely what Hegel sees as the function of writing: writing is what prevents speech from taking place, from *zum Worte zu kommen,* from ever reaching the *word* of Saussure's hypogram, and thus to devour itself as the animal is said to devour sensory things [sect. 20, p. 87], in the knowledge that it is false and misleading. Writing is what makes one forget speech: "Natural consciousness therefore proceeds by itself to this outcome, which is its truth [the knowledge that the Now or the Here is really a universal—C. C.] and experiences this progression within itself; but it also always *forgets* it over and over again and recommences this movement from the start" [sect. 20, pp. 86–87, de Man's italics]. As the only particular event that can be pointed out, writing, unlike speech and cognition, is what takes us back to this ever-recurring natural consciousness [or the drive to translate as to re-find what was there in the original, to state the certainty of sense perception—my translation, C. C.]. Hegel, who is often said to have "forgotten" about writing, is unsurpassed in his ability to remember that one should never forget to forget. To write down *this* piece of paper (contrary to saying it) is no longer deictic, no longer a gesture of pointing rightly or wrongly, no longer an example or a *Beispiel,* but the definitive erasure of a forgetting that leaves no trace. It is, in other words, the determined elimination of determination. As such, it goes entirely against the grain of Riffaterre's rational determination of unreason. (*RT,* 42–43)

This elastic encirclement of murmuring stones, word-things from "the tradition,"[30] burns for a reading, even as it draws a curtain upon language. It is equipped for in the passages that precede and follow my long quotation. Along with some enigmas, these offer plenty of reassuringly technical or "traditional" discursive moves. The anomaly of explicating together a poem and a philosophical text is balanced, for instance, by the enumerable themes that draw them together. Both texts bring out the supposed Romantic commitment to *time* as the preeminent condition of human experience, and both turn upon the appearance and the status of *perception*. And yet—any reflection, a fortiori any reflection on Romanticism and the criticism of aesthetics—necessarily distinguishes, in principle as well as in practice, even if its privileged object is to *identify*, two orders, the phenomenal aspect of language (sound) and its semantic and referential functions. Their identification with one another is delusive, de Man argues. "Voice" is a figure; in fact, the sound and the meaning of a linguistic utterance do not coincide. A lyrical-or-not "voice" is—not the generating principle, but the *figure* for figure that is the meaning that lies—"behind, not beyond," as Blanchot says—"words." Just as much as lyric, philosophical texts are dominated (domineered over) by the notion of a speaking consciousness. That notion, or that of "voice," is a figure for "the deictic or demonstrative function of language," a function that itself involves a conflict between the function of language as representation and its function as postulation.

These things have become "well known." But see what it takes, to repeat them without stumbling. Thus for instance one rereads, "The figure of a speaking consciousness is made plausible by the deictic function that it names" (*RT,* 42); and also, there is a crucial "logical difficulty inherent in the deictic or demonstrative function of language" that the figure of a speaking consciousness conceals ("Sign and Symbol in Hegel's *Aesthetics,*" 768). It is the double function of the deictic function, in other words, to make plausible *and* to exist as, or constitute, a fundamental implausibility, a "logical difficulty"—inasmuch as its impossible "function" is to *constitute*, to "represent," not *Wahrscheinlichkeiten* but *Wahrhaftigkeiten* (improbable as they may be).[31] The conflict is present (or waiting) in the "fundamental" linguistic "gesture"—predication. In the passages I am still en route to reading closely, de Man analyzes the account of the conditions of predication he finds in chapter 1 of the *Phenomenology,* together with the precisely comparable "allegory of cognition" he finds in a lyric of Victor Hugo entitled "Ecrit sur la vitre d'une fenêtre flamande."

Here comes something good, at last. But it's not what you think. "Hypogram and Inscription," as I could show you, "says the same thing" as the following key passage in *The Resistance to Theory.* (A cut to another phantom synthesis, here. It would bring together the work of the freshman writing seminar and the work of Paul de Man. No doubt over *The Resistance to Theory.* "Not only in this class, this text should be carried at all times.")

"In a genuine semiology as well as in other linguistically oriented theories, the referential function of language is not being denied—far from it; what is in question is its *authority* as a *model* for natural or phenomenal cognition" (*RT*, 11). What then, if there must always be a "model," of sorts.

The best would be a notation; the deploying, the recalling, of a notation. A notation of indeterminably significative status. Which means, maybe meant, maybe not. Anyway, there (again). Inscription, there, yet at any moment dissolvable into the background pattern of mere referents (things) or mere syntax-in-the-service-of a meant representation, *"inscription"* would be (this is why de Man found it so necessary to write on Riffaterre, so hard to find the place where they *do not agree*) what lasts, what makes for writing. In calling it, against Riffaterre, not a "hypogram" but an "inscription," de Man insists on the fact that the code word or words out of which the text unfolds is *not* a cliché or a "semantic given": *is* not, even if it is, for—so radically inserted, framed, dispersed—its meaning and its meaningfulness are not given; indeterminable, they are only *to be* determined, *to be* decided, by the reader who writes. The code-word, the kernel, is *not* the "given," but the gift and *Gift*.

To take as a model, then, a notation. Such is the inspiration that de Man finds blindly in practice in Riffaterre's theory and reading, under the cover of a claim to be blasé, to know, to know the "everybody" who knows, the "clichés" or semantic givens generative of French poetry. Thus de Man surmises that Riffaterre

> is probably the happiest when he can detect and identify the Virgilian hypograms that structure the system of French poetry from Hugo to surrealism; the fact that the citations from Virgil are most often grammatical examples culled from textbooks used in French *lycées* should be particularly satisfying, since it underscores that the virtue of the hypogram is certainly not its semantic "depth" but rather its grammatical resourcefulness. In Riffaterre's very convincing view of canonical literary history, Virgil has, for Baudelaire or for Hugo, a function close to that of Diabelli's little waltz theme for Beethoven. (*RT*, 38)

To take as one's Virgil a certain Diabelli's "little waltz theme": this has been the gift of two otherwise very different critics, Andrzej Warminski and Neil Hertz. The former, as Rodolphe Gasché shows in his introduction to Warminski's *Readings in Interpretation* contains an *entretien* with de Man and Derrida as well as Nietzsche, Hölderin, Hegel, and Heidegger in the reading he delivers of the "asymmetrical chiasmus" that is the "theme" or "notation" he discovers in literary and philosophical texts.[32] The interchange around chiasmus is joined as well in the discussion of *Essays upon*

Epitaphs' citation of Milton's "On Shakespeare" in De Man's "Autobiography as Defacement" and de Man's "Kant and Schiller" (in *The Aesthetic Ideology*). The latter notation—Hertz's "*T* on its side"—has offered a couple of generations of students a key (replaced over and over) to the reading of Romantic and psychoanalytic texts.[33]

Hertz (*The End of the Line*) has his own ways of "reading" Being—including a recent essay analyzing the poetic and rhetorical gesture of evoking "this," as it takes place in certain texts of Dr. Johnson, Robert Penn Warren, Descartes, and a former Ithaca vet.[34] Hertz's essays should be read "against" and alongside each of a series of texts on the gesture of pointing—especially the series on pointing and on the example that begins with Hegel's "Now is the Night," and includes, in addition to texts of Hölderin, Mallarmé, and Wordsworth, texts of Blanchot ("Je dis, Une femme," and Ponge on "trees," in "Literature and the Right to Death"), Warminski ("*I* say, 'That cat,' " massacred every time it tries to get out of or into the bag; "Reading for Example: . . . ," "Dreadful Reading," and "Terrible Reading"); and de Man, especially the closing lines of "The Return to Philology" (again the cat) and "Reading and History" (the "sign"; the sphinx).[35] De Man in "Hypogram and Inscription" reads a literary and a philosophical text as alike pointing to pointing—as revealing what pointing entails.

The texts' pointing to pointing should not be confused with the conception of literature as self-referential or non-referential. Sometimes erroneously taken to define Romanticism, sometimes equated with deconstruction, that conception belongs rather to a structuralist understanding of literary language. In this view—the riff de man would pan, not sell—literature stands to ordinary language as language stands to things: as their "determinate negation." This is the relation in which, in Chapter 1 of *The Phenomenology of Mind,* "perception," *Wahrnehmung,* "taking truly," stands to "sensory evidence" or "sense-certainty." De Man argues the inadequacy of such a conception of literary language and of language in general by re-reading a poem of Victor Hugo singled out by Riffaterre as a "descriptive" lyric—and to that extent a kind of pointing or perception—and the opening section of *The Phenomenology*'s first chapter, "Sense-Certainty: Or the 'This' and 'Meaning.' " These texts disclose, he argues, not the determinate negation of entities or of pieces of ordinary language (the clichés, topoi, commonplaces, Riffaterre identifies as the objects of literary discourse), but rather the indeterminable negativity of materiality and figure: the existence of language as mere inscription and the gratuitous *positing* of "hypograms," of determined or determining semantic kernels, in the process of "reading." The seal is there; someone needs to hear the seal bark.

The discrepancy between these two understandings of the self-reflexive character of literary language is the very distinction that Blanchot names as Romantic writing's precarious discovery:

> that to write is to forge a work of speech, yet that this work [*oeuvre*] is idleness [*desoeuvrement*]; that to speak poetically is to make possible an intransitive work whose task is not to say things (to disappear in what it signifies), but to say (itself) in letting (itself) be said, *without however making itself the new object of this objectless language (if poetry is simply speech* [la parole] *that claims to express the essence of speech and of poetry, one returns, scarcely more subtly, to the use of transitive language*—a major difficulty, through which one comes to circumscribe, within literary language, the strange lacuna that is its own difference and, as it were, its night. (Ath, 169–170)

De Man's readings attempt to locate in the texts of Hegel and Hugo the factors whereby they depart irreversibly from the transitive use of language—even though they enable that departure or difference to be "circumscribed" in a way that will justify their being called, as de Man calls Hugo's poem, an "allegory of cognition."

This is the allegory:

Ecrit sur la vitre d'une fenêtre flamande

> J'aime le carillon de tes cités antiques,
> O vieux pays, gardien de tes moeurs domestiques,
> Noble Flandre, où le Nord se réchauffe engourdi
> Au soleil de Castille et s'accouple au Midi!
> Le carillon, c'est l'heure inattendue et folle,
> Que l'oeil croit voir, vêtue en danseuse espagnole,
> Apparaître soudain par le trou vif et clair
> Que ferait en s'ouvrant une porte de l'air.
> Elle vient, secouant sur les toits léthargiques
> Son tablier d'argent plein de notes magiques,
> Reveillant sans pitié les dormeurs ennuyeux,
> Sautant à petits pas comme un oiseau joyeux,
> Vibrant, ainsi qu'un dard qui tremble dans la cible;
> Par un frêle escalier de cristal invisible,
> Effarée et dansante, elle descend des cieux;
> Et l'esprit, ce veilleur fait d'oreilles et d'yeux,
> Tandis qu'elle va, vient, monte et descend encore,
> Entend de marche en marche errer son pied sonore![36]

That Flemish chimes provide a privileged experience of time: perhaps the contents of the poem's statement, as well as its opening address ("*I love* the chimes of *your* ancient cities"), impels de Man to query Riffaterre's classification of this text as "description." De Man stresses the description's dependence on a performative—a "declaration of love"—and a personification. De Man's reading will analyze how the figure of *time* is constituted: how it clings to the figures of "voice" and of "face."

The cliché "carillon flamand" (the piece of language, and not thing, that is the poem's object, in Riffaterre's account) is a sign of time, having the phenomenal presence of sound, which is personified and given a face in Hugo's text as a costumed female figure descending a crystal staircase. De Man's analysis focuses on how the phenomenality *of time and of language* depends upon the linking, *in a figure,* of the phenomenal aspect of language, sound, to the semantic function of "the mind" or consciousnesss. He stresses that the poem's feat lies in giving a phenomenal shape to an imaginary entity, time or "the hour." "If there is to be consciousness (or experience, mind, subject, or face)," de Man writes, "it has to be susceptible of phenomenalization. But since the phenomenality of experience cannot be established a priori, it can only occur by a process of signification" (*RT,* 48). In Hugo's poem praising the *carillon* that chimes from the bell towers of Flemish towns, the ringing of the bells, the *carillon,* de Man writes, "is the material sign of an event (the passage of time) of which the phenomenality lacks certainty." Its evocation is important because "The phenomenal and sensory properties of the signifier have to serve as guarantors for the certain existence of the signified" (*RT,* 48). This takes place via a specific figuration: chiasmus set up by prosopopoeia. The opening of the poem is, "J'aime le carillon de tes cités antiques, / O vieux pays gardien de tes moeurs domestiques, / Noble Flandre" ("I love the chime of your ancient towns, / o old land, keeper of your domestic customs / noble Flanders"). The underlying figure or "matrix" of the poem, de Man establishes, is the prosopopoeia, the face-giving figure, "*I love time.*" That figure "accomplishes the trick [of] arbitrarily linking the mind to the semiotic relationship that connects the bells to the temporal motion they signify." The phenomenality of the mind or cognition or the semantic function can seem to be ensured by the phenomenality of the signifier because the mind and time are linked in a chiasmus by the prosopopoeia "*I love time.*" "The senses become the signs of the mind as the sound of the bells is the sign of time, because time and mind are linked, in the figure, as in the embrace of a couple" (*RT,* 48–49). The chime is apprehensible as a sign of time, which in turn makes consciousness apprehensible, because signifier and signified have been united in a *form* by the giving of face to the chime, by means of the figure linking time and its sign to the mind and its senses. Thus the phenomenalization of consciousness occurs, the apprehension of the *indicating* of something occurs, through an act of reading, the *giving* of figure, the prosopopoeia that gives a face to the sound of the bells.

I will come back to the fact that it is a *feminine* figure and *Flemish* towns that are personified and apostrophized in Hugo's prosopopoeia, and also to the comparable though dissimilar figures in Hegel's text. But the significance of de Man's reading lies first of all in results that can be stated abstractly. The generative principle of the poetic description, according to Riffaterre, was a "semantic given"—the cliché or topos "Flemish carillon." To the contrary, de Man stresses: the generative principle of the description or deixis—and by the same token, the generative principle of perception or consciousness—is a fiction, a figure, the "face"-allowing figure "I love time," which frames and generates the description. The I that loves time sees it as "l'heure," the hour, which "arrives" as if she were suddenly opening a door and descending a stair ("it is the hour, unexpected and mad," seen to "appear suddenly through the keen, bright hole / that a door of air would make, in opening. . . . By a fragile stairway of invisible crystal / she descends"). "I love time" is the prosopopoeia that "*posits* voice or face by means of language" (*RR,* 80). Thus we are dealing with an asymmetrical configuration as well as with the symmetrical chiasmus, "the senses are to the mind as the chime is to time."37

mind	senses
time	chime

The prosopopoeia sets up that signifying structure; the face-giving figure "I love . . ." gives the face of a meaningful sign to the material signifier and the signified:

	chime
	(signifier)
"I love time"	
("matrix," figure)	
	time
	(signified)

This structure is—that is, needs or ought to be read, correctly, as—asymmetrical rather than specular or one of equivalence. It is the radically asymmetrical relationship between the semantic or cognitive and the figural or *positional* dimensions of language. The crucial inadequacy of the symmetrical structure—or *ratio*—to conceive how phenomenalization takes place is that it fails to register the *force* of this operation "of a grammar," that of *conferring* semantic status on indeterminably meaningful marks. The symmetrical chiasmus represents this operation as the correspondence between two already constituted significative structures (such as "the mind" and "nature" or "subject" and "object").[38]

In effect the symmetrical chiasmus misconstrues *syntax*—the linguistic devices of meaning, "die *Art* des Meinens"—as inherently meaningful, the symmetrical correspondent of semantics; as though syntax were the mirror of logic, or of the real, and thus always already semantic and cognitive. By the same token the symmetrical ratios misconstrue *semantics*, or questions of meaning, which always involve questions of rhetoric, as a lexical order, as a matter of a lexicon: the totality of "semantic givens," in Riffaterre's expression, or essentially a "grammar" or a "code." Effacing the *disparity* between the cognitive and the positional dimensions of language, between "what language means" and "the manner in which it produces meaning" (*RT*, 62), the linked ratios efface, clear, void, the nontransparency of language. Such is the operation—performed within and *on* literature—of aesthetics.

What aesthetics has to foreclose, or disguise, is the *figural* condition of its own operation: the face-giving figure that underlies perception. Such foreclosure, such nonrecognition of the "face" that gives or promises the possibility of meaningful faces and surfaces, is the cost and the ruin of aesthetics' rationalist vocation—its vocation of ensuring a consistent, determinable ratio between transcendental philosophy and phenomenology. De Man's argument (in "Hypogram and Inscription" and in another essay largely concerning prosopopoeia, "Autobiography as De-Facement") is that a certain manifestation of the role of figures—of the *figure* of figure—puts a strain on this system in such as way as to reveal that it never worked. That is, the temporal existence of an "I," or the "experience" of *perceiving* time, is as much the product of a fiction as the experience of "seeing" the Hour when one hears the sound of (Flemish, for instance) bells. Aesthetics tries to preserve perception distinct from hallucination. It fails as a result of the authentic critical power lying in literature, in the possibility of marking the irreducible difference *and* collusion between the constative character and the force, the positional character, of language.

Allegories of Reading uses the word *performative* in order to indicate that language or "rhetoric" is irreducible to trope, metaphor, measured swerve from a "proper" sense—in order to recall rhetoric's having always meant "persuasion" or "force" of language, as well as trope. With this usage, de Man's writings on "rhetoric" tap into not only the ancient reservoir of guilt and uncertainty about "fiction," "poetry," and "rhetoric," but also the reservoirs of trust and amusement accumulated by J. L. Austin in *How to Do Things with Words*. Speaking in such a manner of the "performative" perhaps needs to be grasped as an example of the operation that de Man, writing about Benjamin, holds up as *monstrum* and example: "translation." In the context of *this* essay's undertakings, all we can say is that, encountering de Man's not immediately obvious definition of "translation"—that it "relates to what in the original belongs to language and not to meaning" (*RT,* 84)—one knows something of what is meant: that in the reading operation de Man calls "translation," the irreducibility to cognition of the syntactical and figural aspects of language is admitted and verified, and, even in being registered, repeated.

Just as de Man objected to Riffaterre that the matrix of the Hugo lyric was not "le carillon flamand" but more precisely "*j'aime* le carillon," not a "semantic given" but a figure, so he objects that the crux of the Hegel text is "the *figural enigma* . . . of a conscious cognition being in some manner akin to the certainty of a sense perception": "a classical philosopheme," as de Man writes, "not a kernel of determined meaning" (*RT,* 47). In addition to the figure, the other element in Hegel's and Hugo's texts not fully assimilable to semantic structures or phenomenal or symbolic aspects is inscription. Hugo's lyric about the carillon is entitled "*Ecrit* sur la vitre d'une fenêtre flamande"—"*Written* on the pane of a Flemish window." De Man "notes" a drastic asymmetry between the written word "written" and every other element of the text: "Every detail as well as every proposition in the text is fantastic," he writes, "except for the assertion, in the title, that it is *écrit,* written" (*RT,* 51). Consciousness, in Hegel's text, is similarly "false and misleading" or fantastic, de Man argues:

> At that moment in the *Phenomenology* Hegel is . . . speaking . . . of consciousness in general as *certainty* in relation to the phenomenal categories of time, space, and selfhood. The point is that this certainty vanishes as soon as any phenomenal determination, temporal or other, is involved, as it always has to be. Consciousness ("here" and "now") is not "false and misleading" because of language [as Riffaterre had paraphrased Hegel's argument]; consciousness *is* language, and nothing else, because it is false and misleading. (*RT,* 41–42)

De Man's reading of Hugo's "allegory of cognition," as he calls it, guides, or retraces, his reading of Hegel's chapter on "Sense-Certainty." To put it another way, the reading of Hugo translates into the reading of Hegel. This is the case not because each text "means the same thing." It is because both texts "mean" the validity of the experience of time, and in each case, the reading, as a reading, has to say what the text *says* as against what it *means,* and as against staying with its own (the reading's) "meanings." Each of the readings is itself a translation—in the first place, the literal translation of a single word: the German word *geschrieben* and the

French word *écrit*. These translate, of course, into the written word "written"—and it like them proves *un*translatable in the sense that it is simply an inscription: that is, one could say that it does not necessarily say or mean anything that the perceptible marks do not already manifest merely by being inscribed, "written," on a surface. Such a reasoning by the present (i.e. the past) reader (C. C.) is no more—or no more (non-)decisive—than a literal and literalistic "reading." But let us let it hold us for a while.

According to "this" "sense" (that of a "literal" reading), the word "written," written, does not really function as a sign. To "see" this, though—to see "written" as an inscription and not a name or a sign—takes some effort, some work; translating work, once again. Here de Man's labor of translation consists in peeling off or screening out the usual meanings we grant to the word "written" as we read it on the page and leaving visible just the opaque bit of writing, of writtenness.[39] De Man's translation makes us relate to that in the original word that relates to language and not to meaning. The result is a bit of language that lacks the phenomenal properties supposed to belong to a mother tongue or language of a fatherland. Within and outside three languages, the written-down word "written" persists as what it is, that is, neither a signification, nor a verbal sign or sound (*geschrieben*, *écrit,* and *written* are not the same sounds or letters). In such a way, in its material inscription, language remains to be read. It is the inscription that brings on *die Aufgabe des Übersetzers*.

No doubt it is necessary to *re-quote* the long passage from "Hypogram and Inscription." Please see again the long quotation a few pages earlier.

The "elimination of determination" is the elimination of the possibility of determining once and for all whether a pattern is or is not significative, is or is not determined by a semiotic process rather than mere probability, which emerged in Saussure's study of anagrams.

To make his argument—that, rather than being non-*referential,* literature, and language, is in some crucial respect non-*semantic,* inasmuch as it is inscription, or *indeterminably* significative marks—de Man recalls Saussure's abortive project on anagrams, anagrammatic patterns in Latin and Vedic poetry. Saussure eventually abandoned the project as he discovered that no evidence could be adduced, either historical or mathematical, that could determine whether the patterns he had identified were deliberate or random, were encoded or merely the effect of probability or chance. This undid the premise with which Saussure began, that the formal aspect coincided with a semantic one, that the anagrammatic patterns concealed significant proper names, and it altered the sense of his term "hypogram" for what he had been perceiving: "hypograms," from *hypographein,* "to underline by means of make-up the features of a face" (*RT,* 37).⁴⁰ Saussure discovered the impossibility of perceiving the semiotic process without *conferring* on some patterns of recurrence and not on others the status of meaningful articulations: only by means of makeup is a "face" there. De Man's essay describes the *giving* of face—*prosopopoein,* the figure (or catachresis) *prosopopoeia*—as the "move" that enables the predicative and deictic function of language to take place.

De Man thus views Saussure as making an important theoretical inference precisely insofar as his work approaches Hegel's texts on the sign and the symbol, which imply that the sign is only preserved, only apprehended or manifested, in the formal alignment of signifier and signified, form and meaning, which makes it in some sense a symbol, and which takes place through a gesture of predication that is essentially figural, a giving (not merely underlining) of face. "The relationship between sign and symbol however is one of mutual obliteration," writes de Man in "Sign and Symbol in Hegel's Aesthetics." For for the sign to operate as a symbol, in signifying, is for the functioning of language as signification to cancel what allowed it to come into being in the first place, the arbitrary power of position of the sign.⁴¹ The "symbolic manifestation" of the sign—its phenomenal status—implies also its obliteration: that is the confounding lesson of Saussure's encounter with the disappearance of the significative status of the sign in the very attempt to determine its formal and phenomenal limits. The irreducibly unrecognizable dimension of the signifying process, which de Man reading Hegel and Nietzsche had called the sign's arbitrary power of position, is newly theorized in "Hypogram and Inscription" as the *materiality* of those marks that may or may not be signs—that *can* be signs precisely because they *may or may not be* significative.

The nonsemantic, material dimension of the sign radically affects the conditions and status of deixis (indicating, pointing) and of perception. Those conditions are the topic not just of Hegel's but of Hugo's text, as Riffaterre acknowledges in selecting it as his example of "descriptive" poetry (hence the best place to prove his claim that all poetry is not referential but self-referential).

Such is the impact of Hegel's text, according to "Hypogram and Inscription," specifically because that text includes, not only an account of the negative correlation between what consciousness "wants to say" and what it "says," but the occurrence of inscription. In this essay de Man argues from Hugo's descriptive poem and from chapter 1 of the *Phenomenology* that the conditions of cognition are prosopopoeia and inscription. His argumentt does not simply *interpret this to be the meaning* of Hegel's or Hugo's text. His reading *follows the occurrence* of prosopopoeia and inscription: it summons up a moment in Hegel's text that corresponds both to the word "Ecrit" in the title of Hugo's poem and to the prosopopoeia that frames the description of the sound of the bells (or of the sign that points). This moment in Hegel's text is the passage that alludes to "this piece of paper I am writing on, or rather have written on," in the next-to-last paragraph of the first chapter. This written-down "this piece of paper on which I am writing" differs altogether from "this" or "here" or "now" as they are spoken—including the spoken reference to "this piece of paper" that the paragraph goes on to discuss, presenting it as one more example of pointing and of the logical contradiction inherent in the deictic function: natural consciousness's meaning to say the particular but stating the general. Like the written word "written" in Hugo's title, the written-down "this" differs from the demonstratives described and carried out in these texts. It is not pointing, but inscription. It is of the order of the anagrammatic patterns observed by Saussure: the distribution of letters was undeniably there, but its meaningfulness or nonmeaningfulness was indeterminable; it is "undeniable," as de Man writes, but "blank." This is the really disruptive indetermination, de Man argues—not the ultimately stabilizing indetermination between reference and the absence or negation of reference—that Hegel's chapter brings out.

And yet, as an exceptionally acute reader of de Man and of Hegel commented, on this paragraph of "Hypogram and Inscription," "he doesn't just assert inscription but must find it as it 'appears' in the text, when it says 'I am written.'[42] Cathy Caruth was referring to de Man's remark that by way of a "parabasis," inscription "appears" in Hegel's text: "As for written or inscribed language, it appears in Hegel's text only in the most literal of ways: by means of the parabasis which suddenly confronts us with the actual piece of paper on which Hegel, at that very moment and in this very place, has been writing about the impossibility of ever saying the only thing one wants to say" (*RT,* 42). The "parabasis," namely, in which Hegel suddenly writes of "this piece of paper I am writing on, or rather have written on." The written-down word "written" is inscription; the allusion, the pointing to it, is a parabasis, a gesture of address that suddenly confronts the audience of a representation with the framework of its performance. (De Man takes the term "parabasis" from the *Athenaeum* editor's definition of irony as "eine permanente Parekbase.")[43] This parabasis suddenly gives a face to the agent that has been producing the text. The passage is a prosopopoeia of inscription, and it culminates by reproducing the gesture of "*pointing out* this bit of paper," at the close of the final paragraph. The gesture asserting that what one means is precisely this thing here, for instance this bit of paper, repeats and renews the illusion of sense-certainty that the chapter has revealed to be false. The possibility of pointing to "this bit of paper," then—the prosopopoeia of inscription—enables the process of consciousness as Hegel described it earlier in the chapter, in a sentence de Man quotes: "Natural consciousness . . . proceeds by itself to this outcome, which is its truth [i.e., the knowledge that the "now" or "here" is really a universal] . . . ; but it also always *forgets* it . . . and recommences this movement from the start." A complex and ambiguous effect takes place, then, with prosopopoeia: both the "appearing" of inscription, of the materiality unassimilable to meaning, and the *adducing* of that materiality as the certainty of sensory evidence. This latter gesture is itself ambiguous, as the forgetting, on the one hand, of the disparity between "what one says" and "what one wants to say," between "what language means" and "the manner in which it produces meaning," but on the other hand, the forgetting also of the *negative certainty* of the *universality* of the "this" exemplified in "this bit of paper," a certainty which simply reverses sense-certainty, just as the doctrine of the *non*-referentiality of literary language merely reverses and remains symmetrical with the doctrine of language's stable referentiality.

De Man's reading of Hegel reads and reproduces this proposopoeia of inscription in his own essay: "We can easily enough learn to care for the other examples Hegel mentions: a house, a tree, night, day—but who cares for his darned piece of paper, the last thing in the world we want to hear about and precisely because it is no longer an *example* but a fact, the only thing we actually get. As we would say, in colloquial exasperation with an obtuse bore: forget it!" (*RT,* 42). Hegel's text as "an obtuse bore," the reader-function as a bored listener rebuffing him: such is the unromantic scene in which de Man casts the activity of historical self-consciousness. The act of forgetting—remembering to forget—"the fullness of thought" or the attempt to coincide with, return to, the original. What takes place in de Man's Hegelian—or Benjaminian—figure is not a union but an *interruption.* But also, as it were by the same token, a *repetition,* for to "forget it!" is precisely what Hegel sees as the function of writing." "Writing is what makes one forget speech," de Man writes further, in a dense and untranslatable passage. "Writing is what prevents speech from taking place, from *zum Worte zu kommen,* . . . and thus to devour itself as the animal is said to devour sensory things, in the knowledge that it is false and misleading." For for "what is meant" to "get into words" (if I may quote Hegel now from the Miller translation), would be for language to be supererogatory, for "what is meant," "what one means to say," means in this context simply the certainty of sensory evidence. Inasmuch as language subverts that implied assertion, it is necessarily "false and misleading," in de Man's words; in the words of Hegel he is translating here, language "has the divine nature of directly reversing the meaning of what is said, of making it into something else, and thus not letting what is meant *get into words* at all."[44] What does not finally "get into words" once and for all, thanks to language or to writing, is not only sense-certainty, however, but also its symmetrical opposite, or the negative knowledge that language is *non*-referential. For the referential, and the semantic, function of language remain, with the *inscription* that "appears" as a text, the indeterminably meaningful linguistic signs that require, like Hegel's "bit of paper," to be read.

The possibility of writing and of history—like the possibility of writing history—thus is conditioned by, in de Man's reading of Hegel, a "forgetting" that occurs through writing. There are no doubt *two* forgettings involved in the scene or operation de Man describes. One is the reversion of consciousness to the certainty of perception and the conviction it can *say* what it *means*. Consciousness always forgets the negative insight it had achieved, says Hegel, and "recommences that movement from the start." That forgetting of what is achieved or past, in a recommencing that marks the passage of time, can be equated with the carillon, the chiming of the bells that Hugo's poem reveals as a process of phenomenalization, and that de Man sees the poem's fundamental trope figuring as the embrace of a couple. It comes about due to what seems another, different forgetting at issue in Hegel's text, the forgetting done not by the reader or consciousness, but by "Hegel" or the writing of writing. This moment corresponds not only to the inscription of the word "écrit" in the title of Hugo's poem, but to the asymmetrical configuration that makes legible the incommensurability between that nonsemantic element and the trope that links the mind and time. De Man alludes to it in these terms: "Hegel, who is often said to have 'forgotten' about writing, is unsurpassed in his ability to remember that one should never forget to forget."

This may be the place to consider the references to place or nation that mark, fleetingly, de Man's Benjamin talk, and more prominently, of course, Hugo's poem on Flemish chimes, which I should point out however was cited first by Riffaterre, and only in that context by de Man as an exemplary "allegory of cognition." The Hugo lyric apostrophizes "Noble Flanders, where the North warms itself, benumbed, / In the sun of Castille, and couples with the Midi!" Flanders is identified as the site of the coming together of polarites evoked in geographical and national terms.[45] The attenuated, picturesque opposition evoked in Hugo's lyric belongs to a highly charged history of European or Western self-definition in opposition to and identification with the Orient or Greece, a history which to many in 1942, as also to a few in 1795 (the year of publication of Schiller's "Über naive und sentimentalische Dichtung"), seemed a question of the history of Germany.

De Man's commentary on the Hugo poem more or less ignores the national or geographical topoi and focuses on the erotic imagery that fills in the decisive structural framework for the description: the address to Flanders that frames the praise for the feminine figure of the carillon. De Man notes, "The poem is a declaration of love addressed to something or someone, staged as an address of one subject to another in a *je-tu* situation which can hardly be called descriptive. . . . these 'descriptions' can only occur because a consciousness or a mind (*l'esprit*) is figurally said to relate to another abstraction (time) as male relates to female in a copulating couple (line 5)" (*RT,* 47). No doubt it is the case that in the chiasmus which de Man successfully establishes to be the main tropological scheme in the poem, the mind and time are "coupled," and exchange properties, and this coupling can be assimilated to the one named in the text, in lines 3–4, which address Flanders as the place where "le Nord . . . *s'accouple* au Midi." De Man's reading displaces the figure of coupling from the geographical or *national* entities onto the phenomenological ones, "mind" and "time."[46]

▼ ▲ ▼

De Man's literary theory is perhaps necessarily "aesthetic criticism" (as well as the criticism *of* aesthetics) in the sense that it retains the features, even if half effaced, of the *topoi* of European poetry and politics. And it would not be in those terms—aesthetics, its criticism, objective or subjective genitive—that one could make the critical distinction between two sorts of forgetting that are named by and take place in de Man's writing and other critical writing as well. One has to go back to the technical terms of the rhetorical reading. There one can "distinguish"—telegraphically, hieroglyphically—between the inscription and the parabasis: between the material, the nonphenomenal, inscription, and the deictic magic of "pointing it out." Inscription is "forgetting" in the sense that uncertainly significant marks (like the written-down word "written") interrupt the process of understanding or cognition. *Pointing* to an inscription, as an instance of a thing that coincides with itself, is a "forgetting" of the elusiveness of that materiality, the figural force involved in perception. But it is not as though (or maybe it *is, as though*) "remembering" that elusiveness (that force) were an available alternative, except—again—for the monster "itself": the sign, sketch, hieroglyph, diagram, model, *T* on its side, that "indicates" a discrepancy between the performative and the cognitive, the material and the phenomenal, grammar and trope, figure and syntax, an obtuse bore, and an angel.

Yet the necessity of the *appearing* in Hegel's and in Hugo's text of the inscription—or rather: the apparently irresistible "necessity" of *claiming*, as even de Man, and in *this* argument (with actualists) does, that just "here," it was necessary that inscription appear (in an actual textual feature such as the word *écrit* or the word *written*—poses once again the difficulty of making that distinction. De Man, just as he criticized Riffaterre for doing, seems to depend on an "actualization" of a significance in the texts. Yet the point is that inscription is not a signification, and that by themselves those inscriptions tell us nothing. Tell us nothing until they appear in a scenario set up in the text by means of a prosopopoeia. The prosopopoeia and parabasis in de Man's text, as in Hegel's, produce distinguishable but inseparable (as one fall is "inseparable" from another) figures of forgetting: on the one hand, "Natural Consciousness," or the bored reader saying "Forget it!" to Hegel's insistence on "this piece of paper"; on the other hand, "We" or Hegel forgetting the universality of the particular as he writes down "this piece of paper"; Hegel's writing down of writing, eliminating the structural determination of the sign.

Who is "Hegel"? Who, the hands?

A collage:

Shelley Disfigured

> . . . while digging in the grounds for the new foundations, the broken fragments of a marble statue were unearthed. They were submitted to various antiquaries, who said that, so far as the damaged pieces would allow them to form an opinion, the statue seemed to be that of a Roman satyr; or, if, not, an allegorical figure of Death. Only one or two old inhabitants guessed whose statue those fragments had composed.
> —*Thomas Hardy*, "Barbara of the House of Grebe" (*RR*, 93)

And from the last two paragraphs of "The Image of Rousseau in the Poetry of Hölderlin":

> Why, then, does Hölderlin identify the moment of retreat in Rousseau with the act of forgetting (l. 160 and n. 50)? What is it one "forgets" when consciousness bends back on itself in this way? It is not being, for it was never known in the first place; it is not the source, for it is proper to the demi-god never to leave sight of it. Rather we have to forget the fullness of our thought itself when it has been put back on the path of truth—especially in its almost uncanny understanding of the past and its concrete anticipation of the future. . . .
>
> Nothing summarizes better what Rousseau signifies for Hölderlin than the conclusion that imposes itself as a result of this

preparatory examination: the "one" ("*einer*") designated in these lines can be none other than Rousseau. There was a man who, in reaffirming the ontological priority of consciousness over the sensuous object, put the thought and the density of the West back on its authentic path; the same man had the wisdom and the patience to remain faithful to the limits that this knowledge, in accordance with its own laws, imposes upon the human spirit. He was thus able to safeguard the future of mankind. His name: Rousseau. His act: to re-collect oneself. (*RR*, 44–45)

These texts tell, in many ways, this. That it is alluring but incorrect to imagine that one could legislate, *or* receive, principles allowing one to distinguish, *in principle*, between "we" and "him," between "forget it" and "remember to forget"; between ideology, and the critical force of language or "theory." The two *occur together,* according to de Man's figure of a scene of reading (and according to the abstract statement of "Phenomenality and Materiality in Kant," with regard to the mutual intrication of ideology or metaphysics and transcendental or critical philosophy).[47]

That the first figure ("we," the unforgivably bored with reading) represents ideology, and the second figure ("Hegel," the "unsurpassed in his ability to remember that one must never forget to forget" about them), represents the critical power of language or theory—and never the twain shall meet—would be a conclusion one might draw strength for from a favorite passage of "The Resistance to Theory," for it is perfectly possible to say (or mean to say) something along these lines:[48]

So de Man maintains (namely, that the first figure represents ideology, the second the indeterminable negativity of the Letter) in "The Resistance to Theory," in a passage that alludes to Marx's *German Ideology* and "very bad readers of it" (an allusion which should be proof enough, of course, that, *here,* no ideology is going or is to be going on):

> It would be unfortunate, for example, to confuse the materiality of the signifier with the materiality of what it signifies. This may seem obvious enough on on the level of light and sound but it is less so with regard to the more general phenomenality of space, time, or especially the self; no one in his right mind will try to grow grapes by the luminosity of the word "day," but it is very difficult not to conceive the pattern of one's past and future existence as in accordance with the temporal and spatial schemes that belong to fictional narratives and not to the world. (*RT,* 11)

Sheer "reading" and "interpretation," "interpretation" and "ideology," can by certain guidelines again and again be differentiated, but will not have been able to be held apart. Such is the sense of this culmination of a *tranche d'analyse* in "Phenomenality and Materiality in Kant"—

> Ideologies, to the extent that they necessarily contain empirical moments and are directed toward what lies outside the realm of pure concepts, are on the side of metaphysics rather than critical philosophy. The conditions and modalities of their occurrence are determined by critical analyses to which they have no access. The object of these analyses, on the other hand, can only be ideologies. Ideological and critical thought are interdependent and any attempt to separate them collapses ideology into mere error and critical thought into idealism. The possibility of maintaining the causal link between them is the controlling principle of rigorous philosophical discourse: philosophies that succumb to ideology lose their epistemological sense, whereas philosophies that try to by-pass or repress ideology lose all critical thrust and risk being repossessed by what they foreclose.[49]

Distinguishing between the two figures—ideology and the critical force of language—constitutes the ethics of reading. Nevertheless, the distinctness of those figures is a representational effect of the prosopopoeia and an effect it also dissolves. According to a prescription from Wordsworth: "The character of a deceased friend or beloved kinsman is not seen, no—nor ought to be seen, otherwise than as a tree through a tender haze or a luminous mist, that spiritualises and beautifies it; that takes away, indeed, but only to the end that the parts which are not abstracted may appear more dignified and lovely; may impress and affect the more."[50] The faces we are and see are, writes Wordsworth, "the joint offspring of the worth of the dead and the affections of the living." That is, almost impossible bastards, violently allegorical signs. The *ethics* of reading will ever and again consist in saying, "There's nothing wrong with X"—X here being a soldier, sailor, tinker, tailor, cripple, beggarman, or thief (recalling figures Wordsworth cared for)—"he's just confused." The drastically disorienting effect of prosopopoeia, in the readings of de Man, is to deprive us of a phenomenal or fixed distinction between ideology and the material conditions of cognition. The distinction between them is attenuated into the distinction between two recurrences of a linguistic function, *reference:* on the one hand, the inscription's appearance in the text in a parabasis that refers to a fact (the undeniable but blank fact of the existence of writing); on the other hand, and *with* it, the reversion to the notion of sensory evidence, "the forgetting that is experienced by consciousness as an attempt to refer."

The distinction can be drawn in a *notation* I evoked earlier: the asymmetrical configuration that differs from chiasmus, that notes the disparity between the *figural condition* of meaning and the semantic structure of the sign. Such a notation—like a capital *T* lying on its side, is the way Neil Hertz, who long ago first thought of it, described it, is something different from a concept and an image. It can tell you nothing you did not already know. It is not a symbol, but an inscription. It does not ensure, rather it *interrupts* cognition, the discursive understanding of the distinction that it cites. It is of the same order as the first, and not the second, kind of forgetting we have distinguished: the materiality of the indeterminably significative marks that are the condition of the possibility of language, and the condition of that second forgetting which can come to be motivated, meaningful, a defense, a trope. Some of any woman's tropes are of that kind, no doubt, up to and conceivably including the figure of "forgetting," to the extent that it is a trope, though one with unusual powers of translatability. Much of literary theory has the peculiar precision and instability of a notation, of uncompleted discursive form, since literary theory, unlike political or aesthetic discourse, does not attempt to saturate the context of its assertions. (—You're doing it again: those "declarative imperatives.") For the impossibility of ever doing so is something that—as literary—theory "knows" from the start. This does not mean that theorists need not take decisions, on the contrary. The irreducible priority of "forgetting" in the first sense—the nonsemantic, nonphenomenal dimension of language and history—implies that forgetting in the second sense may always take place, and implies the permanent uncertainty of distinguishing between them.

"Hypogram and Inscription," for instance, falls into the error that it names, or *manifests* the impossibility it asserts—that of *determining* the significative or nonsignificative status of marks, of letters, for example Saussure's Latin and Vedic anagrams—in drawing, at the close of the long passage I quoted earlier, a hard and fast distinction between inscription and pointing, and between inscription and example. This is also, interestingly, occurring in an allusion that seeks to separate his argument in this essay from a previous essay by Andrzej Warminski, a reading of Hegel's "Sense-Certainty" chapter or rather of the Introduction to the *Phenomenology* in terms of the bizarre aporia of the "example."[51] (Praising Lindsay Waters for publishing Warminski's book, de Man observed—and one knew this was the highest praise, or *jouissance*—"It will sell three copies—and they will be returned.") For the point is that not just "the word 'written,' *written,*" constitutes an indeterminably significative sign (or nonsignificative, random, mark: mere syntax—not meaning, but "the prop on which meaning leans and with which it is immediately confused").[52] So does the least *remaining*—the least *literary*—form or mark, the mark, or form, for whom literariness or figurality constitutes even the remotest possibility. It *could be* framed. It *might be* an example. And, then, of what.[53]

The same gratuitous stamping in of an impression—the same intensifying tone of a lurid figure—takes place in Warminski's "Facing Language," his reading of the drowned man episode in *The Prelude*.[54] The remarkable pedagogical breakthrough made in that reading derives almost equally from the analytical resourcefulness of the diagram Warminski draws and discusses and from the literalistic insistence that it is *because that schoolteacher left behind his clothes* before disappearing into the lake that we have the sort of sinister predicament evoked by Wordsworth near the close of *Essays upon Epitaphs:* language cut off from meaning, the garment of a garment, or, in Warminski's equally resonant words, "a dead spirit" or "a living dead," "zombies," who "will get you," just *because* you only "killed" them by "finding them already dead." For the point of the diagram and of the reading, finally—"Facing Language" does in fact get this into its text—is that *from the very moment* you have *figura*—the body/spirit, letter/spirit analogy or correspondence—the changes rung by that chiasmus give you a spirit which is letter of a letter, or a "ghost." Such was also the uncanny ferocious inference de Man read out of Wordsworth's ringing lines on "language as counter-spirit" (near the end, again, of *Essays upon Epitaphs*). Here is Wordsworth according to de Man.

> Language, as trope, is always privative. Wordsworth says of evil language, which is in fact all language including his own language of restoration, that it works "unremittingly and *noiselessly*" (p. 154). To the extent that, in writing, we are dependent on this language we all are, like the Dalesman in the Excursion, deaf and mute—not silent, which implies the possible manifestation of sound at our own will, but silent as a picture, that is to say eternally deprived of voice and condemned to muteness. No wonder that the Dalesman takes so readily to books and finds such solace in them, since for him the outside world has in fact always been a book, a succession of voiceless tropes. [Watch out for those books—those "ready comrades, whom he could not tire"!] As soon as we understand the rhetorical function of prosopopoeia as positing voice or face by means of language, we also understand that what we are deprived of is not life but the shape and the sense of a world accessible only in the privative way of understanding. (*RR*, 81)

This comes near an issue raised at the beginning of this essay, that of the difference between literary theory and literature, and between contemporary writing and Romanticism. The distinction is difficult insofar as literature, like theory, is "the voiding of aesthetic categories," and Romanticism the self-discovery of literature. And that lack of distinction is painful, not only because nonidentity is painful, but because literature and Romanticism now carry a history, like politics and philosophy, that includes inconceivable suffering and disaster. It's with this in the background that I read de Man's formulation of the difference I need to describe between literary theory and Romanticism, between *translation* and poetry:

> Of the differences between the situation of the translator and that of the poet, the first that comes to mind is that the poet has some relationship to meaning, to a statement that is not purely within the realm of language. That is the naiveté of the poet, that he has to say something, that he has to convey a meaning which does not necessarily relate to language. The relationship of the translator to the original is the relationship between language and language, wherein the problem of meaning or the desire to say something, the need to make a statement, is entirely absent. (*RT*, 81–82)

The predicament of the translator is to say the same things that the original text says, rather than meaning them; to write down what the previous text says or states, not what one wants to say. This could describe de Man's own situation with regard to Hugo's poem celebrating the coupling of the mind and time in terms of an imaginary geography of Europe. That "*allegory* of cognition," as de Man pointedly calls it, is what his translation finds the poem to say. One would have to decide what one wants that to "say."

Notes

1. Paul de Man, "Hegel on the Sublime," in *Displacement: Derrida and After*, ed. Mark Krupnick (Bloomington: Indiana University Press, 1983), 153. De Man writes, "Poets, philosophers, and their readers lose their political impact only if they become, in turn, usurpers of mastery. One way of doing this is by avoiding, for whatever reason, the critical thrust of aesthetic judgment."

2. Paul de Man, *The Resistance to Theory* (Minneapolis: University of Minnesota Press, 1986), 62; hereafter cited as *RT*.

3. On the tension between hermeneutics and poetics, see *RT*, 55–56.

4. First published under this title in *Diacritics* 11, no. 4 (1981): 17–35, it is reprinted without the subtitle in *RT*, 27–53, from which it is cited here.

5. Paul de Man, *The Rhetoric of Romanticism* (New York: Columbia University Press, 1984), 239; hereafter cited as *RR*. See also Cathy Caruth, *Empirical Truths and Critical Fictions* (Baltimore: Johns Hopkins University Press, 1990); Cynthia Chase, *Decomposing Figures: Rhetorical Readings in the Romantic*

Tradition (Baltimore: Johns Hopkins University Press, 1986); Jacques Derrida *La Vérité en peinture* (Paris: Flammarion, 1978), and Philippe Lacoue-Labarthe and Jean-Luc Nancy, *The Literary Absolute,* trans. P. Barnard and C. Lester (Albany: State University of New York Press, 1988).

6. Such a reading would of course be required in a full-scale inquiry into de Man's interpretation of "Romantic literatures" and could do a good deal as well for the understanding of "the aesthetic ideology" (the name and the thing). See Christopher Norris, *Paul de Man: Deconstruction and the Critique of Aesthetic Ideology* (New York: Routledge, 1988); Terry Eagleton, *The Aesthetic Ideology* (Oxford: Blackwell, 1990); and Paul de Man, *Aesthetic Ideology,* ed. Andrzej Warminski (Minneapolis: University of Minnesota Press, forthcoming).

7. Maurice Blanchot, *L'Entretien infini* (Paris: Gallimard, 1969), 518; "The Athenaeum," trans. Deborah Esch and Ian Balfour, *Studies in Romanticism* 22 (1978): 167. Further references will be to this translation, cited as Ath.

8. Maurice Blanchot, "La Littérature et le droit à la mort," in *La Part du feu* (Paris: Gallimard, 1949), 309; "Literature and the Right to Death," in *The Gaze of Orpheus,* trans. Lydia Davis (New York: Station Hill Press, 1981), 38; henceforth cited, in this translation, as Lit.

9. "The Terror, [which] asserted itself in capitalized form" (Ath, 167).

10. Wordsworth, *The Prelude* 1805 (New York: Norton, 1979), 1.306.

11. See de Man's reading of Baudelaire's "Spleen" (ii), "Reading and History," in *RT* 70.

12. See Andrzej Warminski, "Dreadful Reading: Blanchot on Hegel," *Yale French Studies* 69 (1985): 267–275.

13. Paul de Man, *Allegories of Reading: Figural Language in Rousseau, Nietzsche, Rilke, and Proust* (New Haven: Yale University Press, 1979), 10; hereafter cited as *AR*.

14. See Paul de Man, "Promises," in *AR*, 246–277; Jacques Derrida "Declarations of Independence," *New Political Science* 15 (1986): 7–16; and Neil Saccamano, "Rhetoric, Consensus, and the Law in Rousseau's *Contrat social,*" *MLN* 107 (1992): 730–751, and *Rhetoric, Politics, and Rousseau's "Contrat Social,"* forthcoming.

15. John Keats, *Hyperion: A Fragment,* 1.134, in *The Poems of John Keats,* ed. Jack Stillinger (Cambridge: Harvard University Press, 1978), 333.

16. For further discussion, see Cynthia Chase, "Translating Romanticism: Literary Theory as the Criticism of Aesthetics in the Work of Paul de Man," *Textual Practice* 4 (1990): 349–375. Neil Saccamano, *Publication and Poetics in the Eighteenth Century* (Ithaca: Cornell University Press, 1995) argues along these lines, in scrupulous detail responsible to the texts' complications.

17. "Preface to *Lyrical Ballads* (1800)," *The Prose Works of William Wordsworth,* ed. W. Owen and J. Smyser (Oxford: Oxford University Press, 1974) 1:600–601.

18. Wordsworth, "Preface" (1800), 1:140.

19. Wordsworth, *Essays upon Epitaphs,* in *Prose Works* 2:60–61; Percy Bysshe Shelley, "Mont Blanc," lines 80–81, in *Shelley's Poetry and Prose,* ed.

Donald Reiman and Sharon Powers (New York: Norton, 1977), 91. Wordsworth's ambivalent practice and denigration of prosopopoeia is one of the cruxes of de Man's reading of *Essays upon Epitaphs:* see "Autobiography as Defacement," *RR,* especially 74–81.

20. Neil Hertz, "Lurid Figures," in *Reading de Man Reading,* ed. Wlad Godzich and Lindsay Waters (Minneapolis: University of Minnesota Press, 1988) 87–88. Cf. de Man: "As we know from Kant, and as is certainly not openly contested by Hegel, this interiorization of intuition as meaning is entirely compatible with the phenomenalization of aesthetic experience. In his insistence on actualization, Riffaterre makes the perennial and necessary gesture which founds the category of the aesthetic as a confirmation of the phenomenality of language. Whenever this phenomenality is being contested— and it always is—aesthetics, in one of its numberless guises, comes to the rescue" *(RT,* 34).

21. Cathy Caruth, "The Claims of Reference," *Yale Journal of Criticism* 4 (1990): 188–189; reprinted in this volume.

22. I allude to Dr. Frankenstein at the North Pole and to his forerunner Caleb Williams, pursued to Harwich by the noxious Gines. William Godwin, *The Adventures of Caleb Williams; or, Things as They Are* (London, 1794), vol. 3, chap. 15.

23. Wordsworth, *The Prelude* (1805) 10.71; *Shelley's Poetry and Prose,* ed. D. Reiman and S. Powers (New York: Norton, 1977), 480. A reading of these lines, upon which I am drawing here, is found in Carol Jacobs, *Uncontainable Romanticism* (Baltimore: Johns Hopkins Press, 1989), 17–18. On repose, in relation to the bending back of the power of thought, cf. the image of Macbeth in the *Prelude* passage cited above and de Man's "The Image of Rousseau in the Poetry in Hölderlin" *(RR,* 44–45).

24. This means, among other things, that there is an inherent tension between the telegraphy that would be required to complete this paper in the time allowed, namely having recourse, like one of the Guys, to conveying the combat by dashing off images ("it is a stretch, but a perfect stretch"), and the maintaining of the "disjunctions" that are its purpose and theme. See de Man, "Literary History and Literary Modernity," in *Blindness and Insight,* 2d ed. (Minneapolis: University of Minnesota Press, 1983), 158, where de Man is reading, in Baudelaire's "Le Peintre de la vie moderne," the description of M. G.'s capability of "synthesizing" a record of a moment of history or fashion by means of a rapid pencil sketch. "That Baudelaire has to refer to this synthesis as a 'fantôme' is another instance of the rigor that forces him to double any assertion by a qualifying use of languauge that puts it at once into question."

25. *AR,* 246–277, and Jacques Derrida, "Force de Loi: Le 'Fondament Mystique de l'Autorité,' " *Cardozo Law Review* 11 (1990): 919–1045.

26. The rhetorical violence in pronouncements upon what does or does not constitute useful knowledge should be recognized as a version of the also-classic affliction of denouncing art, rhetoric, or literature. For the latter at least

holds out the hope that it could be brushed off again to reveal a *philosophical* (although recurrent) quandary and an unavoidable, ethical, "crux"—"the unromantic essence of romanticism," as "The Athenaeum" calls it: the impossibility of ruling—that is, in any way that could claim to set a legitimate precedent—on how linguistic structures stand in relation to aesthetic categories and values. On literature, on "the question it contains," Blanchot's closing chapter of *La Part du feu* has this, first off, to say: it "has properly speaking nothing to do with [literature's] value or its rights. The reason the meaning of this question is so difficult to discover is that the question tends to turn into a prosecution of art and art's capacities and goals" (Lit, 22). The complex and painful wrenchings that have followed upon the death and the *chosification* of Paul de Man and of writing relating to him are only the to-this-writer apparently most "available" of referents, which does not mean that they are any the less a case of "literature." If "romantic literatures and critical philosophies" deserve some privileging, it is just to the extent that they risk investing in a similar singularity. The Wordsworth of *The Prelude* is one of the few who are able to get into the record a "trouble" that comes into their mind "from unknown causes"—not excluding too-long-to-read-through plans of Political Justice, murmurings of thwarted laws or of removed parents, of alien peoples, and unlucky manifestos.

27. John Keats, *The Fall of Hyperion: A Dream*, 1.199–210.

28. See de Man, "Wordsworth and the Victorians" (*RR*, 84), Hertz, "Lurid Figures," 85, and Chase, "Translating Romanticism."

29. William Ray, *Literary Meaning: From Phenomenology to Deconstruction* (Oxford: Blackwell, 1984), 199–205. Or again, "better," a long shot, in a different vein, Werner Hamacher, "Lectio: De Man's Imperative," in Godzich and Waters, *Reading de Man Reading*, 171–201.

30.   This solitary Tree!—a living thing
      Produced too slowly ever to decay;
      Of form and aspect too magnificent
      To be destroyed. But worthier still of note
      Are those fraternal Four of Borrowdale,
      Joined in one solemn and capacious grove;
      Huge trunks!—and each particular trunk a *growth* . . .

—so, Wordsworth, *Poetical Works*, ed. E. de Salincourt (Oxford: Oxford University Press, 1952) 2, 210. Just here, along the wayside, comes a message regarding tradition. It's the closing footnote of de Man's Introduction for the first full-length republication in English of writings by H. R. Jauss, introduced in 1969 in *New Literary History* as the author of an essay titled in translation "Literary History as a Challenge to Literary Theory" (1980). It concerns finding that Baudelaire and Hegel "hit on the same emblematic sequence" (pyramids, sphinxes, statues) in saying that the symbol is not a sign: "That the coincidence may be due to common occult sources in Hegel and Baudelaire obscures rather than explains the passage. It distracts the reader from wondering why the use of this particular emblematic code can be 'right' in a lyric poem as well as in a philosophical treatise" (*RT,* 72). A throwaway line that preserves the dreamy and jacobin accents of the earliest Romanticism.

31. See Heinrich von Kleist, "Improbable Veracities" ("Unwahrscheinliche Wahrhaftigkeiten") *Sämtliche Werke,* ed. Helmut Sembdner (Munich: Hanser, 1964) 2:278–282; the chapter regarding it in Carol Jacobs, *Uncontainable Romanticism* (Baltimore: The Johns Hopkins University Press, 1989); and Cynthia Chase, *Decomposing Figures,* 220 nn 1, 5.

32. On the way what was the "theme" becomes the allegorical "figure," or "notation," in the course of a reading, e.g., de Man's of the Winander Boy passage in Book V of *The Prelude,* see de Man, "Time and History in Wordsworth," the editor's footnotes by Warminski, and C. Chase, Introduction, *Romanticism* (London: Longman, 1993), 18–19.

33. Hertz, *The End of the Line: Essays on Psychoanalysis and the Sublime* (New York: Columbia University Press, 1985). Most ready to hand as reference, my own attempt along these lines, "Primary Narcissism and The Giving of Figure," *Abjection, Melancholia and Love: The Work of Julia Kristeva,* ed. John Fletcher and Andrew Benjamin (London: Routledge, 1990), 124–136.

34. Neil Hertz, "Dr. Johnson's Forgetfulness, Descartes' Piece of Wax," *Eighteenth Century Life* 16 (1992): 167–181.

35. The sources are: Andrzej Warminski, *Readings in Interpretation: Hölderlin, Hegel, Heidegger* (Minneapolis, University of Minnesota Press, 1982) chap. 4; *Yale French Studies* 69; and *Responses: On Paul de Man's Wartime Journalism,* ed. Werner Hamacher, Neil Hertz, and Thomas Keenan (Lincoln: University of Nebraska Press, 1989).

36. Victor Hugo, "Ecrit sur la vitre d'une fenêtre flamande," Poem 18 of *Les Rayons et les ombres, Oeuvres poétiques,* ed. Pierre Albouy (Paris: Gallimard, 1964) I, 1062–1063: I love the carillon of your ancient towns, / O old land, keeper of your domestic customs, / Noble Flanders, where the benumbed North warms itself / in the sun of Castille and couples with the South! / The carillon is the unexpected and mad hour / that the eye thinks it sees, dressed as a Spanish dancer, / appear suddenly through the keen, bright hole / that a door of air would make, opening. / She comes, shaking over the lethargic rooftops / her silver apron full of magical notes, / quivering like a spear vibrating in the target. / By a fragile stairway of invisible crystal, / alarmed and dancingly, she descends from the heavens; / And the mind, that watchman made of ears and eyes, / as she goes and comes and climbs up and down again, / hears her sonorous foot wandering from step to step!

37. G. F. W. Hegel, *Phenomenology of Spirit,* trans. A. V. Miller (New York: Oxford University Press, 1977), 60–61.

Andrzej Warminski defines symmetrical and asymmetrical chiasmus and the crucial difference between them. See *Readingss in Interpretation,* xxxix–li; and "Facing Language: Wordsworth's First Poetic Spirits," *Diacritics* 17:4 (1987), 18–31.

38. In so doing, the symmetrical chiasmus in Hugo's text performs the same rhetorical operation as the founding "social contract," which has to

posit, as one of the "respondent parties" to the contract, a respondent party which it is the very purpose of the "contract" to "constitute" or produce. Such is the rhetorical operation of Rousseau's *contrat social* (the name (the book) and the thing). See the important analysis of that text by Louis Althusser, "Rousseau: The Social Contract," in *Montesquieu, Rousseau, Marx* (London: New Left Books, 1972), and Saccamano, "Rhetoric, Consensus, and the Law."

39. For the figures of peeling and screening here as well as the "observation" to me that "Hypogram and Inscription" 's statement of this point about the "written" required, of me, some "translating," I am grateful to Neil Hertz.

40. See also Sylvère Lotringer, "The Game of the Name," *Diacritics* 3, no. 2 (1973): 8–16; and Jean Starobinski, *Les Mots sous les mots; Les anagrammes de Ferdinand de Saussure* (Paris: Gallimard, 1971).

41. De Man, "Sign and Symbol," 770.

42. Cathy Caruth, in a letter to the author dated Jan. 31, 1986.

43. Cited in de Man, *Blindness and Insight*, 218; Schlegel, "Fragment 668," in vol. 18 of *Philosophische Lehrjahre (1796–1806)*, ed. Ernst Behler (Paderborn: Ferdinand Schöningh, 1962), 85.

44. Hegel, *Phenomenology*, 66.

45. Some of de Man's earliest published writing, in 1941 and 1942 in Brussels in the collaborating newspapers *Het Vlaamsche Land* and *Le Soir* "volé," sought to define a Flemish and a European identity in not unsimilar terms, as the coming together of "northern" and "southern" or of "German" and "French" characteristics.

46. This is interpretively legitimate and precise. For "us" it could distractedly suggest a repression of a loaded historical scenario, one which had had a peculiar resonance for de Man. The image of a coupling or an erotic encounter can be glimpsed or projected, perhaps, in this passage from de Man's review of *Journal de France,* by Alfred Fabre-Luce, in *Le Soir* on 21 July 1942: "Quelle utile sujet de méditation, quel fertile terrain d'observation que les convulsions de la France vaincue! L'histoire offre peu de thèmes d'étude aussi attachants que celui qui se déroule sous nos yeux à notre frontière méridionale: le choc de deux civilisations complémentaires mais souvent hostiles, la naissance d'un esprit nouveau sur les ruines des erreurs passées, l'angoissant problème de savoir si un des piliers de la culture occidentale parviendra à s'adapter aux exigences d'une autre ère"; "Chronique littéraire. L'histoire vivante. *Journal de la France* (Tome ii) par Alfred Fabre-Luce," in *Wartime Journalism, 1939–1943,* 253. The notion that de Man "repressed" this memory and that that repression is evidenced in the misattribution of line 5 to lines 3–4—my notion in an earlier version of the present essay—is an especially banal and delusive variety of the belief in the actualization of texts' (supposedly essentially "referential" or autobiographical) meaning (in a specific textual feature). See, on such interpretations, Caruth, "The Claims of Reference," especially pp. 199–202. The allusions to the "embrace of a couple" between "the mind" and "time" bear, rather, one ought to notice, upon what might be a permanent undercurrent of

de Man's writings—*l'entretien infini*—with Heidegger and Friedrich Schlegel (i.e. with *Sein und Zeit* and *Lucinde,* favorite books).

47. De Man, "Phenomenality and Materiality in Kant," in *Hermeneutics: Questions and Prospects,* ed. Gary Shapiro and Alan Sica (Amherst: University of Massachusetts Press, 1984), 121–144.

48. See also the previous version of the present essay (Chase, "Translating Romanticism").

49. De Man, "Phenomenality," 122–123.

50. Wordsworth, *Essays upon Epitaphs,* in *Prose Works,* 2:58.

51. Warminski, *Readings in Interpretation,* chap. 1.

52. Caruth, *Empirical Truths and Critical Fictions,* 55.

53. On this problem and how it upset the original receivers of, e.g., Coleridge's poetry, vid. Karen Swann, "Lovely Ladies and Literary Gentlemen," *ELH* 52 (1985): 397–418.

54. Andrzej Warminski, "Facing Language: Wordsworth's First Poetic Spirits," in *Romantic Revolutions: Criticism and Theory,* ed. K. Johnston (Bloomington: Indiana University Press, 1990).

▼ CATHY CARUTH ▼

The Claims of Reference

IN THE WAKE OF STRUCTURALIST and poststructuralist developments in literary theory, a good deal of concern has arisen that these linguistically oriented theories of reading deny the possibility that language can give us access to history. The constant focus by poststructuralists on the linguistic devices by which meaning is produced, and by "deconstruction" on the difficulties these devices create for our understanding of a text, seems to amount to a claim that language cannot refer adequately to the world and indeed may not truly refer to anything at all, leaving literature and language, and even consciousness in general, cut off from historical reality.[1] Responding to this concern, Paul de Man states, in his 1982 essay "The Resistance to Theory," that linguistically oriented theories do not necessarily deny reference, but rather deny the possibility of modeling the principles of reference on those of natural law, or we might say, of making reference like perception.[2] De Man's attempt to distinguish reference from natural law, which is tied to his understanding of the relation between constative and performative language, far from denying access to history, is a way, I will argue, of precisely keeping history from being swallowed up by the power of abstraction. This emphasis is to be read not only in de Man's statements about language, however, but most concretely in a story he repeatedly tells: the story, specifically, of a fall, not just a figurative fall but also the story of a very literal falling. It is de Man's unexpected association of theory with falling that, I will suggest, constitutes the original insight of his theory, a theory which does not eliminate reference but precisely registers, in language, the impact of an event.

The essay "The Resistance to Theory" is a good framework for this inquiry because it is specifically about reference, and it is also about fall-

From *The Yale Journal of Criticism* 4/1 (Fall 1990).

ing. It begins by addressing the resistances, or objections, to theory made in the name of referential reality, or of an external world. It responds both by arguing conceptually for a resistance that stems from "within" theory, and by associating this referential "resistance" with the additional connotation of something concrete, something like the resistance one feels upon impact, the impact, for example, one feels falling down. Those who resist theory in the name of perceptual reality, de Man seems to be arguing, are in fact resisting the force, or impact, of a fall.

In order to understand de Man's argument we can turn to a narrative that is not explicitly articulated but can be read, I would suggest, in de Man's essay, the story of how the problem of reference became, in the history of thought, inextricably bound up with the fact of literal falling. This story emerges when de Man compares contemporary problems of reference to problems arising in the traditional philosophical project of linking the sciences of language (logic, rhetoric, and grammar) with the sciences of the world in general (arithmetic, geometry, astronomy, and music). The example de Man offers of such a project is seventeenth-century epistemology, which attempted to link language with mathematics through a logic comparable to analytical geometry, a geometry which articulated number with the phenomenal, spatial figures of curves and lines. The use of analytical geometry as a model for language exemplifies, de Man implies, the attempt to assimilate language to phenomenal reality.[3] But the example of seventeenth-century geometry as an ideal model of language bears special weight because the phenomenal world which this geometry seemed to describe so successfully was a world thought to be governed entirely by motion, a world whose phenomenal coherence *as motion* would come to an end toward the close of the seventeenth century. De Man appears to allude to this end when he follows the example of the philosophical ideal with the example of a literary text which this philosophy cannot account for, the title of Keats's poem "The Fall of Hyperion." For the world of simple motion was ended, once and for all, with the discovery, by Newton, of gravitational force, or the revolutionary notion, introduced in Newton's *Principia,* that objects fall toward each other. Newton suggested that the motions of massive bodies separated in space can be explained by an attractive force pulling them toward each other. It could be said indeed, that with this assertion, the world of motion became, quite literally, a world of falling. I would suggest here that the history of philosophy after Newton could be thought of as a series of confrontations with the question of how to talk about falling. And similarly, the problem of reference, in so far as de Man implicitly associates it, in my interpretation, with this development in the history of philosophy, is: *how to refer to falling.*

If we step back for a moment, we can see how the problem of gravitation or universal falling could indeed by considered a problem of reference. Newton, in the story of his discovery of gravitation, sees an apple fall, and understands in a flash that the objects of the universe are all falling toward each other by the same force that pulls this apple, invisibly, toward the ground. In so far as this notion was made by Newton into a law, or was represented by a *mathematical formula,* it allowed mathematical science to explain aspects of the world it had not been able to explain previously. But insofar as gravitation was also a concept—represented by the *word* "gravity"—it remained philosophically incomprehensible, and seemed an "occult quality" or magical invisible entity that made no rational sense. That is, as a mathematical formula it could be applied perfectly to the world, but as a thing *referred* to by philosophical discourse, it seemed a pure fiction.[4] Thus, with the introduction of gravitation, the only thing that was adequate to the world was, paradoxically, that which didn't refer (mathematics); and what did refer, language, could no longer describe the world. In a world of falling, reference could not adequately describe the world.

I would argue that de Man's allusion to this moment in the history of philosophy suggests that it is a paradigm for a problem that is central to contemporary theory: the recognition that direct or phenomenal reference to the world means, paradoxically, the production of a fiction; or otherwise put, that reference is radically different from physical law. Many of de Man's works indeed connect problems of theory with literary and philsophical scenes of falling,[5] but two in particular, his essay on Kant's *Critique of Judgment,* and his essay on a story by Kleist, which also involves an implicit reading of Kant, can be seen as illuminating his arguments about theory, because Kant might be said to represent, in the history of philosophy, the attempt to deal rigorously with the referential problem by founding his theory on the very knowledge of its independence from empirical referents.[6] In the following pages I will sketch briefly how de Man's readings of Kant and Kleist trace, first of all, the philosophical attempt to distinguish language from empirical law by making theory into a self-reflexive system. I will then show how de Man's reading also uncovers a resistance to this project arising within the language of philosophy that emerges in its use of examples, a referential resistance de Man will associate with a performative dimension of discourse. Both the necessity of theory and the resistance to it will occur, in de Man's analysis, in the transformation of a specific example—the example of falling—and through the appearance of a specific figure—the figure of a body. It is in de Man's insistence on the centrality of the body, I would suggest, that we can best understand how his own theory both conceptualizes and enacts a mode of referential resistance.

De Man's introductory discussion of Kant focuses on the definition philosophy offers of itself, and the example by which it illustrates this definition. Kant defines philosophy by distinguishing what he calls metaphysics—basically an expansion of Newton's laws of motion—as an empirically determined set of laws, from the principles of pure or "transcendental" philosophy, which is entirely conceptual.[7] Thus empirical law tells us facts about the world, while transcendental philosophy tells us the conceptual conditions of possibility for thinking about the empirical world in the first place. The importance of this distinction, de Man tells us, is that it distinguishes between an empirical discourse that depends on given empirical facts, and a philosophical discourse that is purely conceptual and hence does not depend on empirical givens. In other words, one might elaborate, pure philosophy defines itself as that which does not depend for its meaning on the empirical world; it knows itself *as* that which does not directly know the empirical object.

Just as significant as this conceptual distinction, however, is also, in de Man's analysis, the way in which philosophy uses an example—the example of bodies in motion—to define its conceptual purity. Kant illustrates the distinction between metaphysics and transcendental philosophy with the example of how each relates the phenomenon of bodies in motion to causality. Thus for example, Kant says, a metaphysical law tells us that all changes in a moving body have an external cause (in Newtonian terms, all nonlinear motion is caused by external forces); the corresponding transcendental law tells us, rather, that all changes in bodies must have some cause. Remarking on this example, de Man notes its significance in relation to the definition of philosophy:

> The example of bodies in motion is . . . more than a mere example that could be replaced by any other; it is another version or definition of transcendental cognition. If critical philosophy and metaphysics are causally linked to each other, their relation is similar to the relation, made explicit in the example, between bodies and their transformations or motions. (PMK, 123)

If philosophy gives up direct reference to the body in its definition of itself, it nonetheless reintroduces it, figuratively, in the example, which becomes a kind of implicit or secondary definition alongside the conceptual one. The body becomes in this secondary definition a figure for the very knowledge philosophy has about its inability to refer to bodies. Indeed, later in the essay de Man points to the appearance of an explicit bodily figure in Kant's description of the unified system of transcendental philosophy and metaphysics:

> That this unity is conceived in organic terms is apparent from the recurring metaphor of the body, as a totality of various limbs and parts (*Glieder,* meaning member in all the senses of the word, as well as, in the compound *Gliedermann,* the puppet of Kleist's *Marionette Theater*). (PMK, 142)

When the body reenters philosophy as a figure for its own knowledge, it is not only a moving body but a moving organic body, and ultimately a moving *human* body: a body that is a series of articulated parts. The human body, as a figure for a self-knowing philosophy, is also the figure for the knowledge of a difference: the difference of pure philosophy from empirical discourse. The possibility of a self-knowing, self-referential system of discourse—the paradigm of theory as the knowledge of its independence from empirical referents—is contained in its self-representation as a human body. Philosophy, or theory, incorporates its loss of reference to the falling empirical body into the conceptual gain of the presumably upright body of the philosophical system.

The means by which philosophy would achieve this conceptual and linguistic freedom is suggested, in the lines quoted above, by de Man's surprising association of the limbs of the philosophical body—its *Glieder*—with the puppet—*Gliedermann*—of Kleist's story "On the Marionette Theater." In this story, the acclaimed principal dancer of a local opera admires the gracefulness of marionettes which he claims to be superior to that of human dancers, and suggests that, indeed, a dancer who wanted to perfect his art "could learn a thing or two from them." The perfection is purely mechanical: merely by manipulating, with his strings, the puppet's center of gravity, the puppeteer creates in the limbs of the puppets the perfect curving motions of a dance, without the clumsiness of the human dancer, because in the puppets, the limbs are "what they should be: dead, mere pendula, governed only by the law of gravity." While this unsettling vision of swinging mechanical limbs surpassing human grace seems an unlikely comparison to the serious rationality of Kant's philosophical project, de Man's linking of the two suggests an uncanny similarity. Indeed, in an essay he wrote directly on Kleist's "Marionette Theater," de Man suggests that the puppet-dance can be read as the representation of a certain aesthetic model of self-knowledge in the tradition developing out of Kant.[8] De Man thus suggests that behind philosophy's own figure of its conceptual project, which would incorporate force, as an unknowable event, into the articulated body of philosophical thought, lies the ideal of a mechanism that lifelessly transforms the laws of force and motion into superhuman grace. The philosophical body, in other words, should not simply move upright, but dance: and dancing, its movements are no longer strictly human, but are rather the movements of lifeless, mechanical limbs. To understand Kant, de Man implies, is to grasp how the body of the system is both a human body and at the same time the gracefully inhuman body of a marionette.

The superior gracefulness of the marionettes, de Man insists in the Kleist essay, lies specifically in the transformations that occur between the puppeteer and the puppet. The gracefulness of the puppet body is the result of the union between the mechanical puppet and the particular agency who directs it:

> The puppets have no motion by themselves but only in relation to the motions of the puppeteer. . . . All their aesthetic charm stems from the transformations undergone by the linear motion of the puppeteer as it becomes a dazzling display of curves and arabesques. . . . The aesthetic power is located neither in the puppet nor in the puppeteer but in the text that spins itself between them. (AFK, 285)

De Man suggests that the dance of the puppets represents a particular model of a written text, a text created by the relation between the puppeteer and the puppets. As de Man's essay continues, the relation between puppeteer and puppet, figured as the transformation of puppeteer-held strings into puppet motions, appears to represent the relation between the author and his writing. This, we may conjecture, is what de Man sees as a primary referential relation behind the text, and the beauty of the marionette-dance is that it permits the difficulties of such referentiality to be lost, entirely, in a formal, quantified system that is as predictable, and ultimately nonspecific—or nonreferential—as a mathematics:

> This text is the transformational system, the anamorphosis of the line as it twists and turns into the tropes of ellipses, parabola, and hyperbole. Tropes are quantified systems of motion. The indeterminations of imitation and of hermeneutics have at last been formalized into a mathematics that no longer depends on role models or on semantic intentions. . . . Balanced motion compellingly leads to the privileged metaphor of a center of gravity. . . . On the other hand, it is said of the same puppets, almost in the same breath, that they are *antigrav* [antigravitational], that they can rise and leap, like Nijinsky, as if no such thing as gravity existed for them. . . . By falling (in all senses of the term, including the theological Fall) gracefully, one prepares the ascent, the turn from parabola to hyperbole, which is also a rebirth. (AFK, 285–286)

The exhilarating, graceful freedom of this movement lies in its elimination of any referential weight of a personal authorial self; the puppeteer is lost entirely in the movements of the puppets. The graceful image of the human body arises precisely, here, in the *loss* of any referential particularity. What makes this possible is indicated by de Man when he calls this a "transformation system" as well as a system of "tropes" or figures. For, as a transformational system, it is a grammar, a grammar conceived as a coded set of differences not based on any extralinguistic reality; what is at work here is the power of a grammar that incorporates referential differences into nonreferential, intralinguistic ones. Yet at the same time this loss of referential particularity appears, surprisingly, in the very *figure* of a human being. The paradox of this writing system is that it produces the human figure of the author in the very elimination of authorial referentiality. Precisely when the text appears most human, it is most mechanical. And this autobiographical paradox is also the philosophical paradox, de Man implicitly suggests, underlying Kant's bodily figure of philosophy: when philosophy conceives itself as a human form, it is in fact dependent on the workings of a purely formal grammar.

The appeal and tempting power of this formalization is indicated, moreover, in what happens, specifically, to falling. For in this system, falling, as de Man remarks, is only a means of rising. And yet, if motion and force are easily assimilated by this system, de Man also notes a less easily assimilable element: "One must . . . have felt some resistance to the unproblematic reintegration of the puppet's limbs and articulations, suspended in dead passivity, into the continuity of the dance" (AFK, 288). The resistance one "must" have felt is not only a moral one but also the difficulty, arising within the formal system, of incorporating dead limbs into its phenomenal geometry, of turning death into life as falling was turned into rising.

Indeed, de Man points out that the dancer accompanies his example of marionettes with an example that is less easily formalized:

> The passage is all the harder to assimilate since it has been preceded by the briskly told story of an English technician able to build such perfect mechanical legs that a mutilated man will be able to dance with them in Schiller-like perfection. . . . The dancing invalid in Kleist's story is one more victim in a long series of mutilated bodies that attend on the progress of enlightened self-knowledge. (AFK, 288–289)

In the context of de Man's reading of the marionette-dance, this mutilated invalid can be nothing other than the reassertion of reference, which, from the perspective of the system, can appear only as a disruption and mutilation. Elsewhere in his essay, de Man makes it clear what figure, exactly, the dancing invalid comes to disrupt. It is the figure of the traditional autobiographical interpretation of Kleist:

> The received opinion is that, in this late work, Kleist achieves self-control and recovers a "naive form of heroism" by overcoming a series of crises, victories over "Todeserlebnisse" [death-experiences] that can only be compared to as many deaths and resurrections. This is, of course, a very reassuring way to read *Marionettentheater* as a spiritual autobiography and . . . it is not entirely compatible with the complications of the tone and the diction. (AFK, 283)

The marionette-dance, it turns out, describes the very reading by which critics have found the story to be Kleist's own spiritual autobiography. Believing they are finding, in "The Marionette Theater," the moving human figure of Kleist himself, resurrected in his writing from the deaths of his experience, these critics have unknowingly described only the purely mechanical movements of a system that easily exchanges rising for falling, life for death, because all are equally free of referential weight. The dancing invalid disturbs this graceful, yet mechanical, illusion of autobiography with the suggestion of another, less formally recognizable life story.

De Man himself offers an alternative autobiographical reading in his essay, one which is, in contrast to the traditional spiritual biographies, somewhat more difficult to integrate: "The only explicit referential mark in the text is the date of the action, given as the winter of 1801. Now 1801 is certainly an ominous moment in a brief life rich in ominous episodes." In de Man's reading the referential potential of the story thus seems to derive not from the figure of the dance, but rather from what he will later call an "innocuous-looking notation," the innocuous number marking a date. If this date is to refer us to the referential Kleist, however, what we find most immediately is a series of crisis-ridden relations between Kleist and others with whose name he had become associated:

> [1801] is the year when Kleist's self-doubts and hesitations about his vocation culminate in what biographers call his "Kant crisis." It is also the year during which Kleist's engagement to Wilhelmine von Zenge begins to falter and during which he is plagued by doubts similar to those which plagued Kierkegaard in his relationship to Regina and Kafka in his relationship to Felice. Between the two events, the Kant crisis and the forthcoming breach of promise with Wilhelmine (the final break occurred in the spring of 1802), there seems to be a connection which, if only

> he could understand it, would have relieved Kleist from his never resolved self-desperation. To uncover this link would be the ground of any autobiographical project. (AFK, 283–284)

As de Man reads Kleist's "life" from the notation 1801, he produces a series, not of movements, but of breaks, or rather of proper names which name particular discontinuities in the life: the crisis of reading Kant, the breach of promise with Wilhelmine, not to mention the introduction of several new proper names in the status of biographical analogues. The possibility of referential self-recognition becomes in de Man's story the possibility of providing a meaningful continuity between these breaks—a continuity presumably provided by the spiritual biographers when they speak of "death experiences" that will ultimately be redeemed through writing. The stakes of such autobiographical self-recognition are clear in de Man's reference to Kleist's self-desperation, which would eventually lead to a horrible suicide. But as de Man's story continues, Kleist's own attempts within his life to make meaningful links between events appear to be thwarted, precisely, in the bewildering displacements and substitutions that occur between the proper names attached to them, names which at times appear to take over the very reality of the unfortunate Kleist's life:

> The link [between the Kant-crisis and the break with Wilhelmine] actually and concretely existed in the reality of Kleist's history, but it took a somewhat circuitous route. For when Kleist next met his bride-to-be, in 1805 in Königsberg, she was no longer Fräulein Wilhelmine von Zenge but Frau Professor Wilhelmine von Krug. Dr. Wilhelm Traugott Krug was Kant's successor in the latter's chair in philosophy at the University of Königsberg. Kleist, who had wanted to be, in a sense, like Kant and who, one might conjecture, had to give up Wilhelmine in order to achieve this aim, found himself replaced, as husband, by Krug, who also, as teacher philosopher, replaced Kant. What could Kleist do but finish writing, in the same year 1805, a play to be called—what else could it have been—*Der zerbrochene Krug* [The broken jug]?
>
> All this, and much more, may have been retained, five more years later, in 1810, when he wrote *Über das Marionettentheater,* in the innocuous-looking notation winter of 1801. (AFK, 284)

If there is indeed a link between the crises in Kleist's life, it is not one that Kleist could easily have grasped: where he apparently attempted to exchange one event for another—to gain Kant in his loss of Wilhelmine—he instead loses Kant *and Wilhelmine* precisely because *Wilhelm* gains them both. The figure for any Kleistian autobiography, de Man suggests, would thus be less appropriately the graceful and figurative falling and rising of dancing puppets, than the smashed pieces of "the broken jug," a play which, incidentally, opens on the scene of a man who is injured from falling, not from falling figuratively, but from falling quite literally, and rather less exaltedly, out of bed. It would appear to be this unredeemable *literality* of the events of Kleist's life that emerges, then, in de Man's final insistence on the incomprehensible agency of the *letter* in Kleist's life:

> To decide whether Kleist knew his text to be autobiographical or pure fiction is like deciding whether or not Kleist's destiny, as a person and as a writer, was sealed by the fact that a certain doctor of philosophy happened to bear the ridiculous name of Krug. A story that has so many K's in it (Kant, Kleist, Krug, Kierkegaard, Kafka, K) is bound to be suspicious no matter how one interprets it. Not even Kleist could have dominated such randomly overdetermined confusion. (AFK, 284)

Read alongside the dancer's story of the marionettes, de Man's story of numbers and names, and their simultaneous connection and dispersal through names and letters, reveals a break, a mutilated limb, perhaps, in the continuity of the abstract, formal, philosophical dance of Kleist's traditional biographers. The proliferation of letters in *de Man's* story is less a denial of reference, indeed, than the active assertion of a literality, the disruption of any so-called autobiographical reading that would, in perceiving behind Kleist's writing the figurative face of his past, in fact reduce his referential specificity to a mere figure. It is paradoxically only through such a disruption, through such "randomly overdetermined confusion," or through the interruption of the marionettes by the falling of a broken body, de Man strikingly implies, that a shadowy autobiographical reality first begins to emerge.[9]

In the essay on Kant, similarly, de Man remarks on a break within the system, a system which also, as in the puppet theater, models itself as a formal articulation of phenomenal motions deflected by forces. The break occurs in Kant's text precisely in the attempt to integrate force into the system of motions. In his analysis of Kant, de Man identifies this break specifically as a disruption in the phenomenal self-representation of language, or in the appearance in language of a performative dimension:

> From the pseudo-cognition of tropes, language has to expand to the activity of performance. . . . The *Critique of Judgment* therefore has at its center, a deep, perhaps fatal, discontinuity. It depends on a linguistic structure (language as a performative as well

as a cognitive system) that is not itself accessible to the powers of transcendental philosophy. (PMK, 131–132)

Knowing itself as a grammar or a system of tropes, philosophy must, and yet cannot, fully integrate a dimension of language that not only shows, or represents, but acts. Designating this moment as "fatal," de Man associates it, as in the Kleist story, with death. It is paradoxically in this deathlike break, or resistance to phenomenal knowledge, that the system will encounter the resistance, de Man suggests, of reference.

Indeed, just at that point in the *Critique of Judgment* that the figure of force is being integrated into the body of philosophy, de Man locates an oddly unassimilable model of reflection: the model of a vision, not exactly a perception, which is not aimed at the unification of the whole, but is rather a vision of individual parts. This model is accompanied, again, by an example, the example of the human body, not however as a unified whole but as a system of nonpurposive parts, parts seen, as Kant says, "without regard for the purposes which all our limbs serve." As de Man remarks, this example reflects on the self-knowledge of the philosophical system; but in this case we no longer perceive a unity but read a kind of disarticulation:

> We must, in short, consider our limbs, hands, toes, breasts, or what Montaigne cheerfully called "Monsieur ma partie" [Mister Member] in themselves, severed from the organic unity of the body. . . . We must, in other words, disarticulate, mutilate the body in a way that is much closer to Kleist than to Winckelmann, though close enough to the violent end that happened to befall both of them. (PMK, 142)

In de Man's reading of this example the body does not represent philosophy figuratively as the *formalization of number,* but rather comes to have, in the list of individual body parts, the *force of enumeration.* This force disarticulates the system as it attempts to distinguish and unify empirical and conceptual discourse, that is, to know itself as independent of empirical referents. The disarticulation of the body is thus not something known or stated by philosophy, but something that occurs in its attempt to free itself from reference. While this can only appear, from the perspective of philosophy, as a mutilation, such mutilation also designates the reassertion of a referential moment, a referentiality that is not, however, to be understood within the phenomenal, formalizable opposition of empirical and conceptual knowledge. In terms of the example, we could say that while the force of enumeration mutilates the body as a whole, it at the same time establishes, in this disarticulation of limbs, or naming of parts, the very specificity of a human, as opposed to puppet, body. The reappearance, through de Man's reading, of a body, while mutilated, is thus the paradoxical evocation of a referential reality neither fictionalized by direct reference nor formalized into a theoretical abstraction.[10]

We can only recognize such a referential force, however, if we take into account what happens in de Man's own text when he introduces, as Kant before him, an example; that is when he compares the mutilation we "must" do in reading Kant to two very specific deaths, the "violent end" that "happened to befall" Kleist and Winckelmann. The names of Kleist and Winckelmann here—two prominent writers in the German aesthetic tradition—are not figures for their thoughts or writing, but are rather attached to the specificity of the two men's actual deaths: the death of Kleist, who, following a suicide pact contracted with Henriette Vogel, shot first her and then himself with a gun; the death of Winckelmann who, on the other hand, was murdered in Trieste, for a couple of gold coins, by an Italian named Arcangeli. The particularity of this double example is itself a referential moment in de Man's text, but it is not, however, a referentiality we can subsume or understand in either a purely conceptual, or in a purely phenomenal, way. Indeed, it is an example of the occurrence of a difference: the difference between living and dying—which resists being generalized into a conceptual or figural law. This is the difference that, we recall, appeared in, but remained unassimilable to, the formal system, a difference it could not know just as, we could add, the system was unable to know the event of falling. And this is also what de Man's text does not know when it refers to Kleist's and Winckelmann's deaths as something that "befalls" them; when it names, that is, a befalling. In de Man's text as in Kant's, the impact of reference is felt in falling: in the resistance of the *example of falling* to a phenomenal or perceptual analogy that would turn it into the mere figure of an abstract principle. In naming a befalling, de Man's text no longer simply knows what it says, but indeed does more than it knows, and it is in this that we can read the referential significance of his own theory.

This significance has the weight of a paradox: that reference emerges not in its accessibility to perception, but in the resistance of language to perceptual analogies; that the impact of reference is felt, not in the search for an external referent, but in the necessity, and failure, of theory. This theoretical knowledge, however, cannot be separated from the particular performance of de Man's own text, which always accompanies its theoretical lesson with a story. It is the originality and unique referential resonance of de Man's writing, I would suggest, to discover the resistance of theory in the story it tells of its own falling. What theory does, de Man tells us repeatedly, is fall; and in falling, it refers. To capture the reality of this falling is the crucial task de Man's theoretical work is engaged in, and it is the task that falls upon us as we read the very particular story of de Man's writing.

Notes

1. See for example S. P. Mohanty, "Radical Teaching, Radical Theory: The Ambiguous Politics of Meaning," in *Theory in the Classroom,* ed. C. Nelson (Urbana, 1986), and David Simpson, "Going On about the War without Mentioning the War: The Other Histories of the 'Paul de Man Affair,' " in *The Yale Journal of Criticism* 3, no. 1 (1989).

2. Paul de Man, "The Resistance to Theory," in *The Resistance to Theory* (Minneapolis: University of Minnesota Press, 1986). Quotations from this text refer to this edition.

3. De Man says simply "geometry" but is clearly referring to analytical geometry; compare his description of analytical geometry in his essay, "Aesthetic Formalization in Kleist," as "an attempt to articulate the phenomenal particularity of a spatial entity (line or curve) with the formalized computation of number"; *The Rhetoric of Romanticism* (New York: Columbia University Press, 1984), p. 266.

4. For a discussion of the distinction between the law of gravitation and the concept of gravitation see Gerd Buchdahl, "Gravity and Intelligibility: Newton to Kant," in *The Methodological Heritage of Newton,* ed. Robert E. Butts and John W. Davis (Toronto: University of Toronto Press, 1970).

5. See for example Paul de Man, "The Rhetoric of Temporality," reprinted in *Blindness and Insight: Essays in the Rhetoric of Contemporary Criticism,* 2d ed., rev. (Minneapolis: University of Minnesota Press, 1983), and "The Epistemology of Metaphor," in *On Metaphor,* ed. Sheldon Sacks (Chicago: University of Chicago Press, 1978).

6. Paul de Man, "Phenomenality and Materiality in Kant," in *Hermeneutics: Questions and Prospects,* ed. Gary Shapiro and Alan Sica (Amherst: University of Massachusetts Press, 1984), and "Aesthetic Formalization in Kleist," in *The Rhetoric of Romanticism*. Quotations from these texts (cited as "PMK" and "AFK") refer to these editions. The description of critical philosophy as a theory founded on the "independence [of knowledge] from its empirical referents" does not imply the irrelevance of the empirical for Kant but rather the fact that critical philosophy is able to articulate its own transcendental rules for the conditions of possibility of experience as in some sense prior to the knowledge of empirical law.

7. See Kant's *Metaphysical Foundations of Natural Science,* trans. James W. Ellington, in *Immanuel Kant: Philosophy of Material Nature* (Indianapolis: Hackett Publishing Co., 1986). The *Foundations* is an elaborate conceptual system which is meant to be a reformulation of Newtonian law in terms of its combined conceptual presuppositions and material givens which link it to transcendental philosophy as the latter's "example." Metaphysics is partially empirically determined, and is linked on its side to fully empirical laws.

8. Cynthia Chase offers a brilliant reading of de Man's essay in relation to aesthetic theory and politics in "Trappings of an Education," in *Responses to Paul de Man's Wartime Journalism,* ed. Werner Hamacher, Neil Hertz, and Thomas Keenan (Lincoln: University of Nebraska Press, 1989); see also the excellent analysis in Andrzej Warminski, "Terrible Reading," in the same volume.

9. We may understand this dynamic of autobiography also in terms of de Man's own writing/nonwriting on his past and the attempts to create autobiographical accounts of it.

10. On the figure of hanging and the appearance of other bodily figures in de Man, see the fascinating essay by Neil Hertz, "Lurid Figures," in *Reading de Man Reading,* ed. Lindsay Waters and Wlad Godzich (Minneapolis: University of Minnesota Press, 1989), and "More on Lurid Figures," *Diacritics* 20/3 (Fall 1990); on the function of reference as an "imperative" in de Man's writing, see Werner Hamacher, "LECTIO: De Man's Imperative," in *Reading de Man Reading.*

▼ DEREK ATTRIDGE ▼

Singularities, Responsibilities
Derrida, Deconstruction, and Literary Criticism

WE LITERARY CRITICS ARE DOUBTLESS always a little intimidated by philosophy: it refuses us the pleasures by which we set most store—the sensuous movements of language, the hilarious accidents of comedy, the surge and release of narrative, the intimacies of shared emotions, the particularities of concrete observation—and demands instead, with joyless exigency, the abstractions of pure thought, the progressions of cold logic. True, we read many philosophers with pleasure, but we do so with an edge of guilt, as we relish the modulations of their phrasing, trace their metaphorical patterns, respond to their irruptions of feeling, and take delight in the minute precision of their representations. At the backs of our minds is the discomfiting thought—implanted by three millennia of cultural history—that in the largest scale of things, the practice of literature can provide only an attractive garnish for the strong meat of philosophical enquiry.[1]

When a philosopher speaks up for literature, therefore, we are quick to take notice. The literary critic who defends the status of literature is inevitably suspected of special pleading, even if the defense is couched in impeccably philosophical terms; but when we find an accredited member of the institution of philosophy—someone who in his work traverses the entire tract of Western philosophical writing—arguing that literature might hold a key to the problems with which philosophy has never ceased to grapple, our reaction is understandably different. Perhaps we're not as peripheral as we feared; perhaps we weren't wrong to believe that Dante probes as deeply as Descartes, that Aristophanes' insights are as

Copyright © 1994 by Derek Attridge.

profound as Aristotle's. This, at least, is one possible reason why Jacques Derrida's words have found within the literary academy such fertile ground.²

In accordance with the same logic, of course, Derrida's words have found among philosophers, for the most part, only the stoniest of ground. I can't say if philosophers suffer from a mirroring sense of inadequacy to that of critics, a sense that their own poker-faced efforts are always vulnerable to the sprightly corrosions of the literary, but it's clear that appeals for philosophy to open itself to an other called "literature" fall mostly on deaf ears, as if the contemplation of such a prospect endangered not only the *traditions* of philosophy (philosophy is hardly loath to challenge its own traditions) but the very possibility of philosophical activity.³ This general picture is not significantly altered by the fact that philosophers who choose to regard philosophy as a kind of ongoing conversation rather than a quest for truth have found Derrida's literary bias appealing—a somewhat surprising fact, given Derrida's relentless engagement with traditional philosophical questions in what one must assume is the belief that they matter to the human community in fairly traditional ways.

Turning back to the reception of Derrida's work by literary critics, which is the main concern of this essay, we find some rather surprising configurations.⁴ Let us recall that Derrida has written widely on literary as well as philosophical texts (using these categories for the moment in an entirely conventional sense): not only on Plato, Aristotle, Leibniz, Kant, Hegel, Husserl, Heidegger, Austin, and many others who unquestionably nail their colors to the philosophical mast, but also on Shakespeare, Baudelaire, Mallarmé, Valéry, Joyce, Kafka, Artaud, Celan, and many others whose work clearly answers to some notion of the literary.⁵ Let us recall, too, that Derrida has on several occasions stressed the importance of literature to his work. For instance, in one of the interviews collected in *Positions* (an interview which took place no later than 1967), it was to certain literary texts that he gave the leading role in the contemporary activity of deconstruction: "If we had the time, we could . . . ask ourselves too, why the irreducibility of writing and, let us say, the subversion of logocentrism are announced better than elsewhere, today, in a certain sector and certain determined form of 'literary' practice" (11). In his thesis defense of 1980 he commented: "[M]y most constant interest, coming even before my philosophical interest I should say, if this is possible, has been directed toward literature, towards that writing which is called literary" ("The Time of a Thesis," 37). And most recently, in a 1989 interview published in *Acts of Literature* (" 'This Strange Institution' ") he elaborated at length on the centrality of literature to his intellectual development and philosophical concerns. "It's the most interesting thing in the world," he said of literature, adding only half-jokingly, "maybe more interesting than the world" (47).

In the light of Derrida's constant emphasis on literary writing, the first surprise we encounter when we consider his influence on literary studies in the English-speaking academy is the place of his own work on literature. Jonathan Culler provides an economical formulation of the situation: "Derrida's own discussions of literary works draw attention to important problems, but they are not *deconstructions* as we have been using the term, and a deconstructive literary criticism will be primarily influenced by his readings of philosophical works" (*On Deconstruction* 213). This is not, of course, a simple objective statement: not only is it uttered in defense of the selectivity of Culler's own representation of Derrida, but given Culler's influence *as* a representative of Derrida in the Anglophone world, it has helped to fulfill the very prediction it claims to make. Nevertheless, it does serve to mark a peculiar feature of the reception of Derrida's work: Derrida the reader of *philosophical* texts has been much more important for literary critics than Derrida the reader of *literary* texts.

Another conventional subdivision of Derrida's writing—equally problematic, and problematized by Derrida, but widely assumed nevertheless—is into a more "philosophical" portion and a more "literary" portion; the criterion this time being not the text under consideration but the mode of Derrida's own writing. One might expect that the influence upon literary criticism would be exercised largely by the "literary" texts—those that exploit language in a way traditionally regarded as the preserve of literature, and as inimical to philosophy's task of passing through the veil of language to truth itself. But, if we leave aside the stylistic mannerisms that have infected a great deal of critical writing, it is Derrida's "philosophical" writing that has had the most significant impact on literary criticism. A few critics have been encouraged by Derrida's "literary" example—in *Glas,* for instance—to write texts that play ingenious games with the signifier, but they appear to have relatively little interest in one of Derrida's major concerns, which is also one of my concerns here: the place of philosophy in relation to literature, and of literature in relation to philosophy. Such critics have been influential in one respect, however: the view of "deconstructive criticism" from the outside, from those who haven't read much Derrida or his more philosophically inclined mediators, is heavily colored by a notion of something called "freeplay," as if this meant some kind of escape from all the demands of careful thought that Derrida in fact exemplifies and insists upon.

This double discomfort with the more "literary" Derrida leads to another surprising phenomenon: we find literary critics (or at least academics speaking from the institutional site of the literature department) not only encouraging us to concentrate on the "philosophical" Derrida, in both senses, but stressing the importance of Derrida *for philosophy*, rather than for literary criticism. Thus Rodolphe Gasché tells us in *The Tain of the Mirror*, having admitted at the outset that he has "given greater prominence to the more philosophically discursive texts" (4), that "Derrida's marked interest in literature . . . has in his thinking never led to anything remotely resembling literary criticism or to a valorization of what literary critics agree to call literature" (255). And Christopher Norris, in one of his introductory books which are read widely in literature departments (though probably less widely in departments of philosophy) focuses his attention on what he calls the "more substantial and significant portion of [Derrida's] work" (*Derrida* 20)—that is, the texts which do not employ a "literary" style (which he believes, rather quaintly, was adopted to gratify the peculiar taste of American readers)—and goes on to assert that he is "more interested in the philosophical consequences of deconstruction than in its current high prestige among literary critics" (22).[6] Both writers are reacting against much of what has been done in the name of deconstruction: Gasché accuses so-called "deconstructive literary critics" of having "chosen simply to ignore the profoundly philosophical thrust of Derrida's thought" (3), while Norris assails "those zealots of a limitless textual 'freeplay' who reject the very notions of rigorous thinking or conceptual critique" (27). While I'm not sure that it's appropriate to describe the nonphilosophical cast of much of what passes for deconstructive criticism as the result of a simple choice, as Gasché does, and while I find Norris's phrase "conceptual critique" doubly unsuitable for Derrida's engagements with texts, this reaction is understandable and largely justified. But it doesn't seem to follow with any philosophical rigor that Derrida's *own* use of a more literary style, and his writing on literary texts, need to be set aside, nor that Derrida's work is of only limited interest to literary critics. It *does* follow, however, that the significance of his work for literary criticism has yet to be fully explored.[7]

▼ ▲ ▼

Now that a good twenty years have passed since the impact of Derrida's work was first strongly registered in the literature departments of the English-speaking world, the time is perhaps ripe to embark on such an exploration, taking into account the whole range of Derrida's work, including his less obviously philosophical texts and his writings on literature. We now know—or have no excuse for not knowing—that deconstruction is not a technique or method, and hence that there is no question of "applying" it. We know that it is not a moment of carnival or liberation, but a moment of the deepest concern with limits. We know that it is not a hymn to indeterminacy,[8] or a life-imprisonment within language, or a denial of history: reference, mimesis, context, historicity, are among the most repeatedly emphasized and carefully scrutinized topics in Derrida's writing. And we know—though this myth perhaps dies hardest of all—that the ethical and the political are not avoided by deconstruction, but implicated at every step. None of what we have learned has been easy, and this above all has conditioned the reception of Derrida's work within the domain of literary criticism; the temptation to substitute a simple formula for laborious intellectual activity is understandably powerful and ever-present.

Derrida isn't, it turns out, saying that we literary critics are doing better than the philosophers; on the contrary, we are probably more damagingly caught up in the centuries-old philosophical presuppositions and practices he has questioned than are most philosophers. Our literary pleasures don't hold any simple lesson for philosophy, and what we like to term "reading philosophy as literature" doesn't begin to engage with the issues that deconstruction—like the philosophical tradition it participates in while contesting—repeatedly broaches. The heady enthusiasm of the early days of Derrida's reception has now been qualified by the careful work of a number of able commentators, and Derrida himself has published a series of texts that have extended and complicated our understanding of "deconstruction," as well as reiterating some of the overlooked dimensions of his early work.[9]

How, then, do Derrida's dealings with works of literature differ from those we might consider characteristic of literary criticism? We can start with some comments in one of the *Positions* interviews, where Derrida claims that criticism is dominated by such typically philosophical categories as "the values of meaning or of content, of form or signifier, of metaphor/metonymy, of truth, of representation" (69), and some of its "reductions and misconstruings" of literature are listed as "thematism, sociologism, historicism, psychologism," as well as a "symmetrical reaction" to this closure on the signified, an isolation of the literary in formal terms (70). (It is no doubt this allegiance of literary criticism to philosophy which explains the relative weakness of the impact of Derrida's "literary" essays upon it.) One prevalent reductive approach to literature, which Derrida terms "mimetologism" and links to the tradition of philosophical discourse on truth, he discusses and exemplifies at length in "The Double Session." In other words, we spend a great deal of our energy as critics (professional or casual) responding to literature as something else: as social history, as personal confession, as formal object, as ideological weapon, as moral lesson, as cultural instruction, as linguistic exercise, and so on. The texts of literary criticism down the ages would no doubt offer the same opportunities for deconstruction as philosophy: one could demonstrate their reliance on logocentric, phonocentric, phallocentric assumptions— their domination by the signified as meaning or by the signifier as form, or some organic or dialectical relation between them, for instance—and at the same time the exclusions on which those assumptions depend, as well as the structural necessity for that exclusion.

Deconstructive criticism, by contrast, would be an attempt to do justice to what is "literary" about a literary text (though not just as a formal category), and in so doing to put into play, and reinforce, its potential for unsettling philosophical categories—and with them, of course, a whole series of political and ethical positions. Much that has passed for deconstructive criticism in the past twenty years operates just as much on the basis of philosophical assumptions as do the more traditional modes it attempts to displace, whether it evinces its deconstructive allegiance by verbal frolics and open-ended interpretations or by the strenuous teasing-out of metaphysical oppositions. To treat the literary text as an indeterminate self-referential game is to reinforce the philosophy/literature, or serious/nonserious, opposition by which philosophy constitutes itself (the notion of literature as ungoverned rhetoricity being a philosophical notion par excellence); and to treat the literary text as a structure of thematic oppositions is to turn it into a philosophical argument. But what sense can we give to the apparently tautological notion of doing justice to literature "as literature," in the light of Derrida's own readings of literary texts? And what has literary criticism to gain from the difficult task of familiarizing itself with Derrida's dealings with literature—if those strange texts could ever be said to become familiar? All I can do in this limited space is offer a few preliminary pointers to a future practice.[10]

First, a caution about the term "literature." Derrida uses the word in three distinct but related ways: sometimes to refer to a specific Western historical institution whose beginnings lie in the eighteenth century, in which case he contrasts it with "poetry" (as an earlier term for a different institution); sometimes it means the body of texts from Homer to the present that have come to be called "literature," or the concept that governs this textual classification; and sometimes the term is reappropriated (like the terms "writing" or "trace") to signal a movement or a moment that exceeds (while at the same time it makes possible) what we call "philosophy," which Derrida identifies with "logocentrism" and the "metaphysics of presence."[11] The shiftiness of the term "literature" is frequently evident in Derrida's writing; thus in the statement to his thesis jury one should note the cautious qualification of the word: "towards literature, towards that writing which is called literary." And in *Positions,* having referred to a recent " 'literary' practice," he adds "But you can very well understand why I would write this word ['literary'] between quotation marks, and what equivocality must be brought into play. This new practice supposes a break with what has tied the history of the literary arts to the history of metaphysics" (11).

This linking of the history of literature—in the first two senses—with the history of metaphysics is a constant and crucial emphasis in all Derrida's dealings with the question of the literary text. Here is a relatively early statement, from *Of Grammatology:* "With the exception of a point of advance or a point of resistance which has only been very lately recognized as such, literary writing has, almost always and almost everywhere, in accordance with diverse fashions and across diverse ages, lent itself to that *transcendent* reading, that search for the signified which we here put in question" (160, translation modified). "Literature" does not, therefore, name a privileged body of texts in which the hold of metaphysics on Western thought is loosened; on the contrary, literature has generally been read (and not *mis*read) in terms of the presuppositions of logocentrism, phallocentrism, presence, and transcendence that Derrida has traced as a ubiquitous impulse in the philosophical tradition. (Bad news for those critics who thought that deconstruction spelled the revenge of literature on philosophy.)

Derrida insists that there is no "essence" of literature, however; nothing that could protect a privileged corpus from the inroads of its changing discursive contexts. Here is a relevant passage from "The Double Session":

> This text [Mallarmé's "Mimique"] could be read as a sort of handbook of literature. . . . If this handbook of literature meant to *say* [*voulait-dire*] something, which we now have some reason to doubt, it would proclaim first of all that there is no—or hardly any, ever so little—literature; that in any event there is no essence of literature, no truth of literature, no literary-being or being-literary of literature. (223)

Depicted in this way, literature doesn't appear a very potent ally for the practice of deconstruction, and the emphasis placed by Culler, Gasché, and Norris on Derrida's work on, and within, the *philosophical* tradition might seem to be vindicated. Yet we need to place against this apparent disqualification Derrida's repeated insistence on the importance of literature, especially of the "point of advance or point of resistance" mentioned in passing in the passage from *Grammatology*. In *Positions* he comments more fully on this claim:

It is incontestable that certain texts classed as "literary" [again in quotation marks] have seemed to me to operate breaches or infractions at the most advanced points. Artaud, Bataille, Mallarmé, Sollers. Why? At least for the reason that induces us to suspect the denomination "literature," and that which subjects the concept to belles-lettres, to the arts, to poetry, to rhetoric, and to philosophy. These texts implement, in their very movement, the demonstration and practical deconstruction of the *representation* that was made of literature. (69, translation modified)

And the passage from "The Double Session" that I quoted earlier, although it asserts that there is hardly any literature, ever so little literature, asserts that it is a *literary* text—Mallarmé's "Mimique"—that would tell us this, if texts could tell us things.

Some texts, then, largely texts of modernity, do *not* lend themselves to the transcendent reading that has dominated the history of literature, thwarting the urge to move through the writing to a self-sufficient, preexisting theme, intention, historical or psychological cause, referent, model, or moral, and thwarting too the formalizing drive which would divorce the text from questions of reference, ethics, and history.[12] Instead these texts pose these very questions, and in a way that does not permit of philosophical answers, because they shake the ground upon which philosophical thought rests: they question the very question, "What is?" In doing so, Derrida argues, they expose the inescapable "ground" of philosophy—which is not a ground at all, but a primordial movement or structure of differing/differentiating/deferring/being-deferred (all these, together with a challenge to phonocentrism, are implied in Derrida's invented word *différance*) that both makes philosophy possible and renders its task of totalization and mastery unachievable. This exposure does not present itself as a substantive feature of the literary text, however. It is not a particular *place* in the text, since there is no law that forces every text to show its literary hand at some specific point; dreams may have navels, if Freud is right on this issue, but texts are not organic unities, and can be endlessly cut and regrafted without excising what I'm calling the literary moment—indeed, as Derrida has shown, the capacity to be so cut and regrafted is constitutive of all textuality. And its evanescent quality is suggested by the unstated statement of "Mimique" ("there is no—or hardly any, ever so little—literature"): not that the quantity of literature among the texts of the Western library is small, but that the literary event, the one that shakes the "is" before you are able to ask "What is?," can hardly be said to "take place" at all, is exiguous, minimal, gone before you know it is there.

Our term "literature," in so far as it names not an institution, a body of writing, or a concept, but a structural logic that breaks through the limits of institutions and textual categories, remains appropriate, in the same way that Derrida is willing to retain a number of the terms of metaphysical discourse which mark moments of uncertainty or excess, however suppressed, within that discourse. It is not incorrect, therefore, to say that Derrida's readings of philosophical texts are particularly concerned with their "literary" dimension; but only if we have understood that "literature" here is not a matter of sensuous movements or narrative satisfactions, nor of the inevitable recourse to metaphor,[13] nor even of "textuality" (in Barthes's sense) or the much talked-about "materiality of the signifier." Questioned in a 1981 interview whether literary and poetic language can be the "non-place which would be the 'other' of philosophy" he is trying to discover, Derrida replies, "I think so, but when I speak of literature it is not with a capital L; it is rather an allusion to certain movements which have worked around the limits of our logical concepts, certain texts which make the limits of our language tremble, exposing them as divisible and questionable. This is what the works of Blanchot, Bataille or Beckett are particularly sensitive to" ("Deconstruction and the Other" 112).

However, we should not think in terms of an *opposition* between literature and philosophy; this is already itself a philosophical structure, needing to be undone. No text, for Derrida, is completely dominated by metaphysics, just as no text can completely escape metaphysics.[14] From this perspective, "literature" is not confined to the institution or corpus of literature; it is a moment or a structural possibility in every text, whatever its public genre. Those texts which qualify neither as literature nor as philosophy—Derrida has written on letters, autobiographies, notebooks, dialogues, and other uncertain or mixed modes—offer peculiar opportunities of their own to exploit the "literary." Of course many of Derrida's own texts are equally uncategorizable, and take advantage of devices associated with literature without marking themselves as belonging to a recognizable genre.[15] To the extent that they do this, they avoid reinstating the categories of metaphysics, but by the same token they call for a "reading" which is not governed by those categories—the kind of reading of which Derrida's texts on literature offer a number of instances.

▼ ▲ ▼

Does this leave us with, on the one hand, a mass of texts called "literature" which merely reproduce logocentrism, and thereby sustain the ethical and political structures which depend on and follow from logocentrism, and, on the other hand, as "a point of resistance which has only very lately been recognized as such," a few "radical" texts, largely of the twentieth century, which subvert it and challenge its ethicopolitical corollaries? Since Derrida has used philosophical texts from all periods to demonstrate the unsettling of logocentrism at the very moment it is being reinforced, while devoting relatively little attention to literary texts from earlier periods, are we to assume that literature has been, for most of its history, even more complicit with metaphysics than philosophy?[16] In beginning to answer this question, we might pay particular attention to the careful phrase by means of which literature's solidarity with metaphysics is described in the passage I quoted earlier from the *Grammatology:* "literary writing has . . . *lent itself* to this transcendent reading" (*s'est prêtée d'elle-même à*). This phrase signals the *possibility* of other kinds of reading, or other ways of dealing with a text, which go against the metaphysical grain to find, or rather to produce in collaboration with one aspect of the writing, a movement that would unsettle philosophy's assumptions—and therefore those of the bulk of literature (and, or course, literary criticism) as well. In "The Double Session," in the course of a discussion of imitation, Derrida comments that it is "the precedence of the imitated . . . that governs the philosophical or critical interpretation of 'literature' [again in quotation marks], if not the operation of literary writing" (192). In that "if not" we have the same hesitation about the degree of literature's domination by philosophy and metaphysics, in contrast to the indubitably logocentric tradition of literary criticism. Let us note, too, the phrase in the passage from *Positions* already cited: "These texts implement, in their very movement, the demonstration and practical deconstruction of the *representation* that was made of literature" (la manifestation et la déconstruction pratique de la *représentation* qu'on se faisait de la littérature"—not very clearly translated in the published English version). What these modern texts deconstruct is not literature *as such*—there is no literary essence, no being-literary of literature, "Mimique" has (almost) told us—but what has been made of literature: a "representation" of literature (as representation, among other things). The passage continues: ". . . it being well understood that long before these 'modern' texts a certain 'literary' practice was able to operate against this model, against this representation. But it is on the basis of these last texts, on the basis of the general configuration to be remarked in them, that one can best reread, without retrospective teleology, the law of the previous fissures" (69).

Derrida's interest in a particular set of modern texts springs, then, from his sense that here, more saliently than elsewhere in literature, is perceptible the rupturing of the classical scheme of presence and transcendence. However, these texts draw this quality not just from their modernity, but also from their being literary: no nonliterary text, according to Derrida, stages this rupturing as forcibly. And he leaves open the possibility of examining that "certain 'literary' practice" of earlier periods, though warning us against the danger of "retrospective teleology": we should not read earlier texts as if they were imperfect realizations of what has finally been achieved in modernity. Their specificity is to be respected, and the "literariness" whereby logocentrism is put in question takes a unique form in each text. If we read a text along with a contemporary (or more recent) commentary that works in the reductive, "philosophical" way typical of the tradition of literary criticism, we might find that the literary text being read had "lent itself" to such a reading, but we might also be able to show that it exceeds or undermines such a reading by its own "literariness," its own staging and unsettling such issues as interpretation and form/content relations. The objective in every case would be to examine how *this* reading of *this* text at *this* time engages with or evades these issues, and thence to understand more fully the differences between readings, styles of reading, historical periods, cultural sites, and so on.

When Derrida writes on *Romeo and Juliet* (in "Aphorism Countertime"), for instance, he focuses on, and weaves together, two motifs, "aphorism" and "contretemps," by means of which he engages with some of the best-known features of the play: the plot of unlucky accidents, the absoluteness of the declarations of love, the question of the "name" in the balcony scene, and so on. But what he writes is also a text of thirty-nine aphorisms, or aphoristic paragraphs, conveying in their own dissociated definitions the unmastering rhythm of the contretemps, the truncating stroke of the aphorism. As in Derrida's treatments of modernist literature, there is an *alliance* here between his text and the text he writes on: an alliance which, like Romeo's and Juliet's, is subject to chance and contretemps, but which clearly involves an answering, a commitment, an acknowledgment of a certain responsibility. Most of Derrida's writing on philosophical texts is more guarded, less open to the chance of contretemps, and therefore more summarizable, more teachable, more transferable. But what the writing on literary texts offers the reader—in concert with the texts themselves—is something like the *experience* of the testing of the limit, the shaking of the frame (though we have to divest the notion of "experience" of any simple, originary, "natural" force). It is not an experience that can be conveyed by description or summary; there is no substitute for reading the text itself.

We can trace this double movement—all literature offering the possibility of readings which shake the metaphysical grounds of philosophy and criticism, yet some texts offering particular opportunities for such readings—in the 1981 interview from which I've already quoted. First, the more general statement:

> In literature, . . . philosophical language is still present in some sense; but it produces and presents itself as alienated from itself, at a remove, at a distance. This distance provides the necessary free space from which to interrogate philosophy anew; and it was my preoccupation with literary texts which enabled me to discern the problematic of *writing* as one of the key factors in the deconstruction of metaphysics. (109)

Then, in the next reply, a narrowing of focus as Derrida explains his difference from Heidegger partly in terms of the writers who interest him (he names Mallarmé and Blanchot) and those who interest Heidegger (Hölderlin and Rilke)—a distinction, in other words, between a literature that foregrounds the relays and mediations of all knowing, all thought, and one that strives (or at least appears to strive) for some kind of unmediated access to Being.[17]

Thus the peculiar ontological status of literature—without essence, without boundaries—does not entail leveling and homogenization: "If one can re-read everything as literature, some textual events lend themselves [that phrase again] to this better than others, their potentialities are richer and denser" (" 'This Strange Institution' " 46). But the word "potentialities" signals that the process of *reading* is crucial, and Derrida emphasizes that our readings, too, always take place in specific contexts:

> Even given that some texts appear to have a greater potential for formalization, . . . works whose performativity, in some sense, appears the greatest possible in the smallest possible space, this can give rise only to evaluations inscribed in a context, to positioned readings which are themselves formalizing and performative. Potentiality is not hidden in the text like an intrinsic property. (46–47)

Derrida's focus on modernist texts does not constitute a claim for some absolute superiority, but a recognition that, as a particular reader in a particular time and place, he can most productively respond to literature as manifested in these texts.

▼ ▲ ▼

The way remains open, then, for the reading of *any* literary text—just as of any philosophical or critical text—in an attempt to track down, or at least make evident the tracks of, the "literary" moment or movement. These encounters with texts would not be "readings" in any conventional sense of the term, of course; they would not attempt an interpretation, or an evaluation, or a cultural placing of the text, nor would they make any claim to dominate other, past or future, encounters with the text. We might get a better sense of the status of these encounters if we hold on to Derrida's word *events,* events of responding as responsibly as possible to the event of the text, answerable to the uniqueness of the text and thus producing their own uniqueness. (Derrida uses the term "signature" and "counter-signature" in " 'This Strange Institution' " and elsewhere in relation to literary response: the text is that unique but iterable structure that requires an equally unique but iterable response to validate it, to allow it to speak its "own" name.) The responsibility involved in such an event of response is a responsibility to the other, a notion which plays an important part in Derrida's thought (derived partly from Levinas's extended interrogation of the term), and at the same time a responsibility to the future, since it involves the struggle to create openings within which the other can appear beyond the scope of any of our programs and predictions, can come to transform what we know or think we know.[18] But responsibility for Derrida is not something we simply take: we find ourselves summoned, confronted by an undecidability which is also always an opportunity and a demand, a chance and a risk.

It is important to stress this concern with the uniqueness and singularity of the text, its difference from all other texts, its historical particularity and irreducibility, since this aspect of deconstruction is often overlooked; for Derrida, the question of the relation between the singular and the general, the unique and the universal, is one of the questions that literature persistently stages in its full undecidability.[19] But at the same time, such responses to literary texts would be very different from the responses of the critical tradition to literary objects seen as unique forms: they would make evident the fact that, far from being punctual and self-enclosed, both events, the text and the reading, have a structure that renders them repeatable, readable, misreadable, divisible, graftable within an infinite variety of contexts, open to an unpredictable future. Their uniqueness is not opposed to their iterability and citability, it is constituted by it. The event of the "primary" text is brought about by the event of the text that answers to and affirms it, thus complicating the opposition of a pure primariness and a pure secondariness on which traditional criticism depends. The encounters I am describing would not be attempts to "prove" some general philosophical truth, or to illustrate some general movement of deconstruction; rather, they would be engagements with the specificities of texts in order to dramatize, to make happen, each in its own unique way, the staging, the self-dividing, of presence, of meaning, of reference. They would, of course, be themselves "literary" texts.

This sense of what a deconstructive criticism might be has a clear ethico-political dimension. It's not a question of the moral power of great literature as traditionally taught in humanistic criticism, nor of the detection of morally and politically suspect ideological positions concealed in literary texts that is typical of some more recent approaches, but of the supremely difficult ethical act of responding to the singularity and otherness of the unique instance—whether person, act, or text—while bringing to bear on it, without merely *applying* them, all the general laws and norms which constitute both it and the judging discourse. Philosophy—and both literary criticism and ethics count here as domains of philosophy—can offer little help; its founding principles and its continuing institutions are undermined by any such act. This is not to decry critical analysis which operates by means of the application of rules, under the aegis of philosophy; most of what we do as critics is just such an activity, and the skills involved in this activity form the basis of all reading. But just as no *literary* text is ever entirely the programmable reaction to events or experiences, but reinvents the very conditions which enable it to come into being, surpassing the logic of computers or psycho- or sociological rules, so no *critical* text that does justice to what is literary in literature, and to the specific literary text it's answering to and affirming, can be solely a skillful application of existing rules. Its singularity affirms, countersigns, makes possible, the singularity of the other, of the text, but also necessarily betrays it, does violence to it (otherwise it could not be a singular, but merely an algorithmic reaction); and we touch here on the difficult, and essential, question of the violence at the heart of any ethical relation.[20]

An obvious question is whether Derrida's published writings on literary texts could provide a model for such activity of literary response and responsibility. Since one of the metaphysical relations that they would work to undermine is that between a model and an imitation, it's hard to give a positive answer. To do so would be to imply that from Derrida's diverse texts some useful paradigm could be produced, and then reproduced; whereas any such paradigm would leave out precisely what constitutes the efficacy of Derrida's engagements: their unique responsiveness to the uniqueness of the text. One might just as well try to produce a paradigm of the literary text by abstracting from, say, *La Folie du jour,* "Mimique," and *Vor dem Gesetz*. But Derrida's texts, too, call for a response, not only as one reads them, but in going on to read other texts as well; and this response may produce further texts that also possess a singular respect for singularity, an iterable recognition of iterability, and a deconstructive concern for deconstruction. No one is ever going to be able to say with finality: "these critical texts are deconstructive and these are not," because there is no place outside the chain of signatures and counter-signatures, responses and responses to responses, from which such a statement could be made. It's tempting to replace the word "literature" in some of Derrida's formulations by the term "deconstruction": there is no essence of deconstruction, no truth of deconstruction, no being-deconstructive of deconstruction, by which a deconstructive text could be infallibly recognized. All one can do is testify to the deconstructive effect, which is to say the "literary" effect, of a certain text (literary or critical), in a certain reading, and to attempt to fulfill one's obligation, as a responsible reader who is also a writer, to do justice to that quality, trusting to future readers to confirm, and reenact, one's testimony.

Let me return, then, to the question I posed earlier: what has literary criticism to gain from becoming more fully acquainted with Derrida's texts on literature? The existence of these texts, it should be clear, does not imply an injunction to put a halt to all the many things that make up the diverse activity of literary studies in order to do something else (though it's hard to imagine any intellectual activity that would not be touched in *some* way by as fundamental a rethinking of the grounds of thought—and action—as Derrida's). Even limiting the question to the tradition of critical interpretation and evaluation, it would hardly be responsible to ignore the importance of work that has been done, and will continue to be done, by way of literary commentary and explication, the kind of work that Derrida calls, in *Of Grammatology,* an "indispensable guardrail" (158). (The last thing Derrida does with the philosophical tradition, after all, is to *dismiss* it.) But anyone who finds that Derrida's claims for the deconstructive potential of literature carry some weight (and this implies also some acceptance of his more general arguments concerning the role of metaphysical thinking in our history and contemporary culture), and who experiences in reading his texts on literary texts a series of events which seem to manifest, however fleetingly, that potential, may feel impelled to work toward strategies of literary engagement which produce events of a similar sort (though always, of course, singular events—with a singularity that is crucial to their effect).[21] The result may be less recognizable as literary criticism than most of the "deconstructive criticism" written in the wake of Derrida's texts on philosophy (and here we see the force of Gasché's insistence, cited earlier, that Derrida's writing on literature is far removed from literary criticism), but, in combining a concern for that which marks literature as a site of resistance to metaphysics and transcendence (an ethico-political as well as an intellectual resistance) with a response to the iterable singularity of the literary text, it would be a way of allowing the text to speak that does not immediately subject it to history, sociology, dogmatics, aesthetics, or some other philosophically determined discipline.

It's not just philosophy which, since Plato, has marginalized literature; our political and social histories show that no matter how radical or progressive a literary text is in terms of *content,* its being placed in the category of "literature"—as traditionally understood—functions to take away its potential force as praxis. Derrida refers in " 'This Strange Institution' " to the space of literature in our culture as the space where, in principle, *anything and everything may be said,* the space of *"tout dire"* (36–39); a cultural positioning which gives literature enormous power by means of the same act which takes all power away. A deconstructive literary criticism will not be the one that apes Derrida's writing on literature; it will be, in fact, one that does *not* ape Derrida, or anyone else (and so I should talk of deconstructive literary criticism*s*, with of course both the words "literary" and "criticisms" doing duty for as yet unnamed activities). It will be a series of events allowing literature, that "so little" literature, to be heard in a way that, for once, actually matters.

Notes

1. The fact that the philosophers are now in the process of being banished from certain cultures—as is brutally evident in the United Kingdom today—is perhaps in part a delayed revenge for what Plato did to the poets. Not that anyone would suspect the British government of acting in the name of literature as they shut down philosophy departments, but there is a certain degree of continuity between a political attitude which can claim "There is no such thing as society" (one of Margaret Thatcher's more memorable utterances) and what have traditionally been thought of as the (un- or antiphilosophical) pleasures of literature. See Eagleton's discussion of the way in which in Britain "the aesthetic becomes a weapon in the hands of political reaction" (60).

2. Even the texts of a number of quite unphilosophical literary critics have been invested with a philosophical aura by the invocation of Derrida's name. Perhaps all major critical movements during this century have claimed some authority from an allegiance that can be called, in the broadest sense, philosophical, whether openly as in the scientific pretensions of I. A. Richards's "practical criticism," the appeals to Marxism in leftist criticism, and the use of linguistics in structuralism, semiotics, and stylistics, or covertly, as in the Wittgensteinian cast of F. R. Leavis's criticism and the quasi-technical approach of New Criticism.

3. A recent instance of the philosophical establishment's perception of Derrida as the most potent of all imaginable threats was the opposition by a number of senior philosophers at Cambridge University to the proposal to award him an honorary degree. Their names appeared below a statement which included such comments as this: "By denying the distinctions between fact and fiction, observation and imagination, evidence and prejudice, [Derrida's 'doctrines'] make complete nonsense of science, technology and medicine.... These doctrines threaten the very basis of all subjects" (flysheet circulated by the Council of Cambridge University, 1992). Readers of such comments might well wonder whether the blatant failure to read the texts at issue does not constitute a somewhat graver threat to "all subjects."

4. What follows is, inevitably, a highly simplified sketch of the impact of Derrida's work on North American literary studies; in particular, it omits the crucial mediating role played by a number of critics based in the United States. It might be said that the shape taken by "deconstructive literary criticism" in the Unites States was determined more by Paul de Man than by Derrida—though Derrida was the seminal influence on the phase of de Man's work that had this effect. A more detailed sketch is offered by Leitch in *American Literary Criticism,* chap. 10; by his silence with regard to Derrida's writings on literature and the issues they raise, Leitch confirms my sense of the slightness of their impact on the United States.

5. For a selection of Derrida's writings on literary texts, and an annotated bibliography of works by Derrida of special relevance to literature, see his *Acts of Literature.*

6. Norris somewhat surprisingly claims that Derrida's more overtly "literary" kind of writing represents the dominant way in which his work has been used in literary criticism: "Hence their [deconstructive critics'] strongly marked preference for those texts where the deconstructive groundwork (so to speak) is very largely taken as read, and where Derrida most thoroughly exploits the resultant opportunities for experiments in style" (*Derrida* 21). Perhaps this is a necessary falsification in order for Norris to be able to dismiss the field of literary studies and concentrate on Derrida's importance for philosophy.

7. Even Culler, who offers a manual of critical maneuvers derivable from Derrida's work, stresses that "the implications of deconstruction for the study of literature are far from clear" (*On Deconstruction* 180).

8. The sticking-power of the term "indeterminacy" is evident in the recent republication of Derrida's *Limited Inc,* with an "Afterword" in which he makes abundantly clear his distance from it; all in vain, for the back-cover blurb exults in "Derrida's most controversial idea, that linguistic meaning is fundamentally indeterminate."

9. Among the most important of Derrida's recent works that are engaged in elaborating, extending, and/or reiterating the operation of deconstruction are "Afterword," "Donner la mort," "Force of Law," *Mémoires, Parages,* "The Politics of Friendship," "Ulysses Gramophone," and many of the essays collected in *Du droit à la philosophie* and *Psyché.* Since it is sometimes

asserted that Derrida's early writing is more "philosophical" in its style and his later writing more "literary" or "eccentric" (for example, by Rorty [123]), it might be worth pointing out that these works, while extremely varied, include many that belong to the former end of the spectrum. For a scrupulous "nonliterary" account of Derrida's thought, see Bennington, "Derridabase."

10. I have considered these issues from a different perspective and at somewhat greater length in "Derrida and the Questioning of Literature," the introduction to *Acts of Literature*.

11. This is not the place to rehearse Derrida's arguments about the history of philosophy since Plato as a history of "the metaphysics of presence," of "logocentrism," of the privileging of the signified, of the reliance on origins, teleology, and transcendence, and so on; in using such terms, I'm obliged to take those extended and complex discussions as read.

12. Of course, they *are* subjected to transcendent readings, often applied with impressive skill and conspicuous success—one only has to glance at the critical history of writers like Joyce, Stein, Woolf, or Beckett. If these works of literature performed the task of deconstruction on their own, Derrida's strenuous texts would be unnecessary.

13. The notion that deconstruction involves the demonstration that philosophical texts are, in spite of themselves, metaphorical or rhetorical, is a widespread one, but not one that could be derived from Derrida's writing; indeed, the essay most explicitly concerned with metaphor and philosophy, "White Mythology," works hard to make such a simplification impossible. The idea persists in introductions to Derrida, however; thus Norris can represent Derrida as "arguing that philosophy—like literature—is a product of *rhetorical* figures and devices" ("Deconstruction" 7). (The book in which Norris exemplifies his version of deconstructive readings of philosophical texts—*The Deconstructive Turn*—is largely based on this premise, and makes no mention of "White Mythology," though Derrida's essay was published twelve, and translated into English nine, years earlier.)

14. Discussing "transcendent" and "nontranscendent" readings in " 'This Strange Institution' " (that is, readings which do or do not close upon the meaning or referent), Derrida insists both that "one can do a nontranscendent reading of any text whatever" (44) and "a literature which forbade . . . transcendence would annul itself" (45).

15. In "Deconstruction and the Other" he says of *Glas,* "I try to compose a *writing* which would traverse, as rigorously as possible, both the philosophical and literary elements without being definable as either" (122). And in " 'This Strange Institution' " he states: "Still now, and more desperately more than ever, I dream of a writing that would be neither philosophy nor literature, nor even contaminated by one or the other, while still keeping—I have no desire to abandon this—the memory of literature and philosophy" (73).

16. The point of Derrida's focus on twentieth-century literature should not be exaggerated, however; the authors he has written on include Shakespeare (in "Aphorism Countertime"), Marvell and Milton (in *Mémoires*

d'aveugle), Baudelaire (in *Donner le temps*), Flaubert (in "An Idea of Flaubert"), and Mallarmé (in "The Double Session" and "Mallarmé").

17. De Man, by contrast, prefers to see Romantic literature as equally alert to the relays and mediations of thought, and Heidegger's reading of Hölderlin as one example of a repeated misreading of Romanticism; see, especially, "Heidegger's Exegeses of Hölderlin."

18. I present a longer discussion of this set of issues, which I can only briefly allude to here, in "Modernist Form."

19. See, in particular, "Before the Law," "Donner la mort" (especially pp. 56–79, on responsibility and ethics), and the discussion of singularity in " 'This Strange Institution' " (58–70).

20. The issues addressed in this paragraph are central to Derrida's "Force of Law," though they are not discussed there with any reference to literature. See also the accompanying essays in the special issue of *The Cardozo Law Review, Deconstruction and the Possibility of Justice,* in which this essay first appeared (some of which are reprinted in Cornell, Rosenfeld, and Carlson), and those in the section entitled *On the Necessity of Violence for Any Possibility of Justice* in a later issue.

21. Or, indeed, to seek out texts of the past that function, or can be shown to function, in a similar way. "Deconstructive" responses to literature, in the sense in which I am using the term, did not come into existence with Derrida's writings. A fruitful place to look would be literary works themselves.

Works Cited

Attridge, Derek. "Derrida and the Questioning of Literature." Introduction to Derrida, *Acts of Literature*. 1–29.

———. "Modernist Form and the Demands of Politics: Otherness in Coetzee's *Age of Iron*." *Aesthetics and Ideology*. Ed. George Levine. Rutgers UP, 1994.

Bennington, Geoffrey. "Derridabase." *Jacques Derrida*. By Geoffrey Bennington and Jacques Derrida. Paris: Seuil, 1991. 6–292.

Cornell, Drucilla, Michel Rosenfeld, and David Gray Carlson, eds. *Deconstruction and the Possibility of Justice*. New York: Routledge, 1992.

Culler, Jonathan. *On Deconstruction: Theory and Criticism after Structuralism*. Ithaca: Cornell UP, 1982.

Deconstruction and the Possibility of Justice. Spec. issue of *Cardozo Law Review* 11.5–6 (1990): 919–1726.

De Man, Paul. "Heidegger's Exegeses of Hölderlin." *Blindness and Insight: Essays in the Rhetoric of Contemporary Criticism*. 2nd ed. Minneapolis: U of Minnesota P, 1983. 246–266.

Derrida, Jacques. *Acts of Literature*. Ed. Derek Attridge. New York: Routledge, 1992.

———. "Afterword: Toward an Ethic of Discussion." Derrida, *Limited Inc.* 111–60.
———. "Aphorism Countertime." Derrida, *Acts of Literature.* 414–433.
———. "Before the Law." Derrida, *Acts of Literature.* 181–220.
———. "Deconstruction and the Other." *Dialogues with Contemporary Continental Thinkers.* Ed. Richard Kearney. Manchester: Manchester UP, 1984. 105–126.
———. "Donner la mort." *L'Ethique du don: Jacques Derrida et la pensée du don.* Ed. Jean-Michel Rabaté and Michael Wetzel. Paris: Métailié-Transition, 1992. 11–108.
———. *Donner le temps: 1. La fausse monnaie.* Paris: Galilée, 1991.
———. "The Double Session." *Dissemination.* Trans. Barbara Johnson. Chicago: U of Chicago P, 1981. 173–285.
———. *Du droit à la philosophie.* Paris: Galilée, 1990.
———. "Force of Law: The 'Mystical Foundation of Authority.' " Cornell, Rosenfeld, and Carlson, *Deconstruction and the Possibility of Justice.* 3–67.
———. *Glas.* Trans. John P. Leavy, Jr., and Richard Rand. Lincoln: U of Nebraska P, 1986.
———. "An Idea of Flaubert: 'Plato's Letter.' " *MLN* 99 (1984): 748–768.
———. *Limited Inc.* Ed. Gerald Graff. Evanston: Northwestern UP, 1988.
———. "Mallarmé." Derrida, *Acts of Literature.* 110–126.
———. *Mémoires d'aveugle: L'autoportrait et autres ruines.* Paris: Réunion des musées nationaux, 1990.
———. *Mémoires: For Paul de Man.* Trans. Cecile Lindsay, Jonathan Culler, and Eduardo Cadava. New York: Columbia UP, 1986.
———. *Of Grammatology.* Trans. Gayatri Chakravorty Spivak. Baltimore: Johns Hopkins UP, 1976.
———. *Parages.* Paris: Galilée, 1986.
———. "The Politics of Friendship." *The Journal of Philosophy* 85 (1988): 632–644.
———. *Positions.* Trans. Alan Bass. Chicago: U of Chicago P, 1981.
———. *Psyché: Inventions de l'autre.* Paris: Galilée, 1987.
———. " 'This Strange Institution Called Literature': An Interview with Jacques Derrida." Derrida, *Acts of Literature.* 33–75.
———. "The Time of Thesis: Punctuations." *Philosophy in France Today.* Ed. Alan Montefiore. Cambridge: Cambridge UP, 1982. 34–50.
———. "Ulysses Gramophone: Hear Say Yes in Joyce." Derrida, *Acts of Literature.* 253–309.
———. "White Mythology." *Margins—of Philosophy.* Trans. Alan Bass. Chicago: U of Chicago P, 1982.
Eagleton, Terry. *The Ideology of the Aesthetic.* Oxford: Blackwell, 1990.
Gasché, Rodolphe. *The Tain of the Mirror: Derrida and the Philosophy of Reflection.* Cambridge, Mass.: Harvard UP, 1986.

Leitch, Vincent B. *American Literary Criticism from the 30s to the 80s.* New York: U of Columbia P, 1988.

Norris, Christopher. "Deconstruction, Post-Modernism and the Visual Arts." *What is Deconstruction?* By Christopher Norris and Andrew Benjamin. London: Academy Editions, 1988.

———. *The Deconstructive Turn: Essays in the Rhetoric of Philosophy.* London: Methuen, 1983.

———. *Derrida.* Cambridge, Mass.: Harvard UP, 1987.

On the Necessity of Violence for Any Possibility of Justice. Spec. issue of *Cardozo Law Review.* 13.4 (1991): 1081–1349.

Rorty, Richard. *Contingency, Irony, and Solidarity.* Cambridge: Cambridge UP, 1989.

▼ E. S. BURT ▼

Hallucinatory History
Hugo's *Révolution*

READERS OF POETRY AND ITS CRITICISM have long been accustomed to mixed reviews of its alleged autonomy. The lyric is generally the target here, although other poetic forms are also open to the charge of retreat from the public arena of history and politics. The loss of reference to empirical experience, deplored by some, has been felt by others to be a sacrifice made for gain: what poetry loses in concrete historical veracity, in attachment to a context, it makes up for by its achievement of the self-sufficiency and meaningful ideality of a fiction. What poems sacrifice in the way of a capacity to portray events or historical personages, they regain by depicting the human in all its generality.

Structuralist and post-structuralist critiques of the subject have modified the assessment somewhat. A theory of texts as self-reflexive structures has dispelled the illusion that poems represent a generalized, fictional self. One tends in recent times to praise poetry for its undoing of ideal fictions, rather than for its production of them.

It is no doubt natural that, in the wake of the undoing of the self as the meaning of the lyric, critics should cast around for something to put in its place and should ask whether they had not been too hasty in accepting the poem's autonomy. Even a poem understood to forego the representation of empirical experience can be considered in terms of a referent—for instance, as portraying a subject's wishful production of a self.[1] Poems do more than signify, they also refer. Words are not only interpretable figures, they are also signs that point. Some critics have therefore felt

From *MLN* 105.5 (1990): 965–991. Copyright © 1990 by The Johns Hopkins University Press.

justified in asking whether, having passed through the bath of the theory of language as the locus of the poem's meaning, we cannot now place poems in a larger historical picture. In short, they have sought for poetry a place in the new historicism.

The return to questioning poetry as to its possible referent in experience has of course not meant the return to a literal referent provided by the author's biography or by a single historical event. Instead, the self-reflexive language of poetry having been identified as the source of meaning and its undoing in the poem, it becomes possible to suggest that the referent of modern poems could be precisely the historical event of a change in the way that poets think about language and poetry, the event of the establishment of a new and more modern understanding of literature and literariness. A Foucauldian epistemic shift moves a poet away from the naive wish to polish language so it can prove the perfect mirror of the self, toward a more sophisticated understanding, where language, recognized to be the stuff of poetry, stands revealed as always dulplicitous, a structure always capable of saying more and less than the ideality of the self.

An historical thesis of this sort shows up in an admirable essay by Joel Fineman entitled "Shakespeare's "Perjur'd Eye."[2] Fineman finds in the space of the slim volume of Shakespeare's *Sonnets* two conflicting poetic practices that suggest to him just such an epistemic shift. Fineman explains:

> . . . Shakespeare's sonnet sequence marks a decisive moment in the history of lyric, for when the dark lady sonnets forswear the ideally visionary poetics of the young man sonnets, when poetic language comes in this way to be characterized as something verbal, not visual, we see what happens to poetry when it gives over a perennial poetics of *ut pictura poesis* for . . . a poetics of *ut poesis poesis,* a transition that writes itself out in Shakespeare's sonnets as an unhappy progress from a poetry based on visual likeness . . . to a poetry based on verbal difference. . . . ("Eye" 71)

For Fineman, the visionary, idealizing poetics of the young men sonnets implies a metaphorical system based on vision in which sensuous form and idea have an adequate relation to one another, and poetic language is Cratylic, its signifiers and signifieds brought by the poet's craft into harmonious relation. In the dark lady sonnets, on the other hand, language is not the transparent language of pure visibility, but a verbal, performative language, full of artifices and duplicity, and one that, capable as it is of showing the idealism of the homogeneous vision-centered sonnets to be predicated on an illusion, has a life and force to be reckoned with. Language does not mirror without distorting; the ideal image is, upon closer examination, itself a distortion, since metaphor makes things look alike that are in fact very different. Shakespeare's sonnets thus serve Fineman as the index of a decisive move from a poetry that wants to reflect only the self and its self-sameness, to a poetry far shrewder about language as difference. That poetry, he claims, is the product of a subjectivity that has undergone alteration in its understanding of language and has recognized itself to be belated and historical. It takes only a little forcing to make the sonnet sequences—whose organizing principle is not necessarily that of a progressive narrative—into a *Bildungsroman* ordered around a moment of conversion that entails an increased awareness in poetic consciousness.

Thus, the highly formalized construct that is the poem finds itself cleared of any charge of ahistoricity. Shakespeare's sonnets refer to the event of a change in consciousness within Shakespeare's history as a poet, an event that marks the appearance of a new subjectivity ("Eye" 71–72) and that corresponds to a shift from the Elizabethan lyric, with its tired Petrarchan themes, to a more modern and sophisticated literature of belatedness. Fineman is then able, in a polemical move, to suggest that recent language-centered theories are an epiphenomenon, a coming-into-theoretical consciousness of the crucial insight that Shakespeare had already figured in the dark lady sequence ("Eye" 78–79) as long ago as the Renaissance.

But to make the lady and her sexual difference stand for the difference of language is a decisive, stabilizing move on Fineman's part. On the one hand, it establishes the possibility of each poem or poem sequence operating autonomously as a system of meaning in which things as unlike as women and words can substitute for one another by way of a shared property, here, their difference. The dark lady is a figure within the sonnets for the language of the sonnets. On the other hand, it also establishes the possibility of reference for each poem or poem sequence, since a language known to be false can be a reliable vehicle for communication, at least about its own gainsaying ("Eye" 77). The figure of the lady consoles us for the revelation that language is a lie by telling us that we can trust it at one point, at the point that it identifies itself as lie: we can know, in a word, when we are dealing with liars and literary language, and when not. What Fineman calls a second degree of Cratylism makes the signifiers of lying language correspond to their signified, the lie of language.[3] Any language that tells us that it lies reveals the truth about language, and is literary. Any language that does not tell us its lie, lies with respect to itself, but we can then know it is not poetry, and so does not mean to deceive us by what it says. Fineman's interpretation of the figure of the dark lady thus allows a distinction between a poetic space where an interrogation into the verbal nature of literary language goes on, and the public, historical space where language aims to represent the world as in a painting.[4]

But one can wonder whether poems (and poets) are as certain about the status of their language as Fineman wants them to be. The indeterminacy of texts touches on the impossibility of deciding whether a given use of language is a referential use or a self-referring one. One would expect poems to address this undecidability and the pressures exerted toward deciding it in their self-referential discussion of their language. To reanchor a poem too quickly in a context by a referential determination is to foreclose on the very place where poems could be speaking to the question of their historicity.

The question to be pursued in what follows, then, is the question of what poems have to say about the pressures in language toward reference and signification, as also what they have to say about their historicity. My example will be a poem by Victor Hugo that ostensibly refers to the historical event of the French Revolution, an event credited by the idealist tradition of Kant and Hegel with having opened modern history as the actualization of the idea of history itself.

The poem, entitled *La Révolution,* dates from 1857 and was originally to have been included in a group called the *Petites épopées,* the little epics.[5] Reworked and expanded in 1870, shortly before Hugo's return to France, it was destined to figure in a collection called *Les Quatre vents de l'esprit,* as the single example of the epic spirit. The title—translatable as *The Revolution* or as *Revolution*—suggests that the poem will be about the famous Revolution of 1789, or else about revolution in general.[6] But to all appearances, the poem takes neither tack. Instead, it seems an hallucinatory history. It recounts the coming to life of the equestrian statues of three French kings, which it follows as they trot through Paris (in the first section, *Les Statues*); it apostrophizes the long-dead sculptor of the Pont-Neuf, and then sets down the thoughts of that downtrodden and speechifying bridge about the reigns of the kings (in the second section, *Les Cariatides*); it concludes with a brief dialogue concerning the meaning and authorship of the guillotine, a dialogue between the statues of the kings and the talking head of Louis XVI, which floats by (in the third section, *L'Arrivée*). An epilogue affirms that the outcome of all this delirium is progress toward peace, harmony and love. If the poem has a bearing on the real Revolution, or on the reality of revolution in general, it is as an hallucination relates to the real.[7]

A brief commentary on the term "hallucinatory" is in order. Hugo's hallucinations and his experiments with the occult in the *tables tournantes* during his exile are not at issue here. Riffaterre has already demonstrated that one does not have to have recourse to Hugo's biography or psychology to understand the hallucinatory effect of his poetry, which is produced by linguistic structures and figures. I will not be attempting the formal description of those structures either, Riffaterre having already done so in *Essais de stylistique structurale;* besides, the hallucinatory raises issues for the consciousness that are not accounted for by the formalism of that early essay.[8] Nor will I be seeking to establish a causal connection between the events of the French Revolution and a psychology, be it that of an individual Revolutionary, or of the Parisian masses.[9] The poem does not support a crude causality of this sort. Finally, however tempting it would be to explore *La Révolution* as a history written within a psychoanalytic framework, there are reasons for preferring to start with a less subjective landscape. One reason for resisting psychoanalytic terms is that it is entirely uncertain whether the poem presents itself as the description of an hallucinatory vision or is rather the fiction of an hallucination, made up to elucidate something else, say the effect of figuring poetic language in terms of a subject and its experience of language.

The etymology of the word "hallucinate" supports the contention that a relation between consciousness and signs is at stake. "Hallucinate" is derived from the Latin *alucinari,* a term meaning "to wander in mind, to dream," but also, "to talk idly, to prate, to discourse freely." The etymology suggests that Hugo's hallucinatory poems might best be considered in the line passing from Montaigne's logorrhaeic *Essais* through the Cartesian digressive *Discours* and *Méditations,* to the discursive vagaries of Rousseau's *Rêveries du promeneur solitaire.* The locus of exile from which the later Hugo speaks is analogous to the dislocation of the I of the *Rêveries,* whom a catastrophic loss of intersubjective and subject-object relations forces back upon itself and its own resources. The Rousseauian *I* has nothing left to affirm itself over and against the void except its experience of memory and memory-signs. A similar intense epistemological uncertainty and a resultant forcing back of the self onto its experience of signs are characteristic of the hallucinatory poems of the second half of *Les Comtemplations,* as well as of *La Révolution.*[10]

And it is indeed into a landscape from which human subjects and their objects of perception have disappeared that the poem introduces us, offering its horrific visions of mobile bronze, "visions où jamais un oeil humain ne plonge" (220) to "on ne sait quels spectateurs funèbres" (218). Against the landscape denuded of human subjects, in a night too dark to see anything but more darkness, move the statues with their human visages, endowed with sight, hearing, speech, and motion.

The walking statue is a redoubled prosopopeia. A statue is a work of art that gives a face to a dead or absent entity—the definition of prosopopeia—in a material very unlike that of the entity, be it granite or bronze in the case of sculpture, or, as Hugo says in the case of poetry, "le bronze dithyrambe et le marbre épopée" (230). To call such a work to life and motion is a prosopopeia to the second power, the prosopopeia of a prosopopeia. The poem is thus allegorizing its central figure, which is precisely the kind of figure by which Fineman decrees the lady's difference to stand for the language's difference. Like a metaphor for metaphor, the walking statue meditates on itself as statue, as prosopopeia. But unlike a metaphor for metaphor, which tends toward the stasis of a revelation, giving a face to the giving of face has to concern itself with an open and undeterminable series of effects. It asks about the responsibility of and for the human face incurred by the work of art when it endows an inhuman material with human characteristics, about what Hugo calls the "Responsabilité de la figure humaine / Prise dans le granit ou le bronze fatal" (220). Prosopopeia faces the possibility of ungovernable referential effects engendered by the making of fictions about man. This possibility is carried to an extreme in the poem when the poet credits an obscure artist under Henri IV, the putative sculptor of the mascarons of the Pont-Neuf, with having unwittingly roughed out a sketch of Robespierre in one of his farcical masks: "Mais à ton insu même . . . tu mettais la lueur / Des révolutions dans le regard les faunes . . . Et ta fatale main, o grand tailleur de pierre / Dans Trivelin sinistre ébauchait Robespierre" (230). The prosopopeia to the second power, then, raises the specter of ungovernable repetition. For even should the poem manage to bring a closure to the effects of a first giving of human face to an inhuman material, it would nonetheless incur a second set of debts and responsibilities by the second prosopopeia, the very one that lets it assume a discourse of responsibility for the effects of the first.

And it is in their effects that the statues reveal their nature as redoubled prosopopeias. In the following passage these effects are divisible into two rough categories: the statues bring the immutable and the dead to life; they chill or petrify the mutable:

> Visions où jamais un oeil humain ne plonge!
> Et comme par la rampe invisible d'un songe,
> La statue à pas lents du socle descendit.
>
> Alors l'âpre ruelle au nom fauve et maudit,
> L'échoppe, la maison, l'hôtel, le bouge obscène,
> Le mille toits mirant leurs angles dans la Seine,
> Les obscurs carrefours où, le jour, en tous sens,
> Court l'hésitation confuse des passants,
> Les enseignes pendant aux crocs de fer des portes,
> Les palais crénelés comme des villes fortes,

Le chaland aux anneaux des berges retenu,
S'étonnèrent devant ce cimier inconnu
Dont aucun ouragan n'eût remué la plume,
Entendirent le sol tinter comme une enclume
Et, tandis qu'au fronton des tours l'heure étouffait
Sa voix, n'osant sonner au cadran stupéfait,
Virent, dans l'épaisseur des ténèbres accrues,
Droit, paisible et glacé, s'avancer dans les rues,
Accompagné d'un bruit funèbre et souterrain,
L'homme de bronze assis sur le cheval d'airain.

L'eau triste frissonnait sous la rondeur de l'arche. (220)

[Visions where never a human eye plunges!
And as if by the invisible ramp of a dream,
With slow steps the statue from its pedestal descended.

Then the precipitous lane with its fierce and accursed name,
Streetstall, house, mansion, obscene hovel,
A thousand roofs mirroring their angles in the Seine,
Obscure crossroads where, by day, in every direction,
Runs the confused hesitation of the passersby,
Signs hanging from the iron hooks of doors,
Palaces crenellated like fortified towns,
Barge held at the rings of banks,
Were astounded by this unknown helmet crest
Whose feather no hurricane could move,
Heard the earth ring like an anvil,
And, while on the fronton of towers the hour stifled
Its voice, not daring to sound to the stupefied clock,
Saw, in the thickness of the gathered gloom,
Straight, peaceful and icy, advance in the streets
Accompanied by a funereal and subterranean noise
The man of bronze seated on the horse of brass.

The sad water shivered under the roundness of the arch.]

Note that, upon the dramatic passage of the statue of Henri IV, a structure, the city of Paris, takes on human features: it sees, hears, and is surprised. A little further on, a bone structure, a skeleton, turns in its grave and voices questions. Similarly, in the poem as a whole, each monument mobilized will ride up to the next and, by an apostrophe—"Viens voir si ton fils est à sa place encore"—will awaken it.[11] On the other side, however, the fugitive and figural is arrested in the passage. Time does not flee, but is, on the contrary, paralysed; the temperature of the Seine drops and it becomes chilly enough to shiver; further on, the dream loses its transforming and distinguishing capacities. A double movement is uncovered: the work of art endows with and deprives life, or what is the same thing here, feeling, movement, voice, distinctness.

What does this chilling and mobilizing mean with respect to a dynamic pressure toward reference and signification? Hugo is commenting upon the problem in this passage where, as exchanges take place between the spatial and temporal dimension of the text, the city, the text as structure or semiotic system, starts to take on intention and meaning, while time, the text as figural system, loses its mobility and gets fixed into a denominative system.

The arresting of time is indeed one of the most notable effects of the statue's passage. It would seem that a poem ostensibly about the historical event of the French Revolution, and one appearing, at that, as the example of the epic spirit, ought to be regulated by some overriding temporal scheme. Instead, among the various astonished spectators of the mobile statues an immobilized clock informs us of the suspension of objective time: "Et, tandis qu'au fronton des tours l'heure étouffait / Sa voix, n'osant sonner au cadran stupéfait. . . ."

The oddity of the figure lies partly in the fact that the hour is not perceivable by the means that human beings have found to make their rational constructs of time felt, i.e., by the clock. Time cannot make itself heard or seen; its bell is silenced, its hands stunned into immobility. With the loss of time as we perceive it by the clock are also lost the constructs that go with it. The linear progression made perceptible by the sounded hour as it disrupts a continuum of silence is not operative.[12] Nor is the cyclical model for which the turning hands of the clockface is the visual analogy. The familiar rational structures—both of which are associated with the modern meaning of revolution—are suspended along with the familiar sensible manifestations that are their correlative.[13]

Hugo is well aware that we do not experience time directly, but as a language, by way of signs. The rest of the poem bears out the contention that the arrested clock signals an end to objective time. The poem does not narrate the events of the the Revolution or suggest that the Revolution returns man to a more original state of virtue and freedom, as Hugo's novel *Quatrevingt-treize* will do. Only in the most oblique of ways—by an allegory developed in *Choses vues*[14] which says that a statue off its pedestal is like a dethroned king—can the moving statues be said to point to such empirical events of the Revolution as the destruction of the royal statues, the renaming of the Place Louis XV, or the beheading of Louis XVI. Hugo's stilled clock stops correlating the perception one has of the clock as signifier to an objective construct.

But, in another sense, the clock does not cease to keep time. It is still a sign and can refer to itself as an empty order or construction. The clock stilled is still a clock, just as a representation that represents nothing is nonetheless something, i.e., a representation or sign of nothing.

Is the objective time scheme then voided in order to open time and revolution to a subjective interpretation? The poem might be asserted to be self-referential in order to allow Hugo to focus on the Revolutionary crisis as a crisis of spirit in which the French nation found its identity, and watching Europe found confirmation that history was not a set of random events but reason actualizing itself.

By way of prosopopeia, the gift of voice, of feeling, and of the capacity for voluntary action associated with the inner time of the self is conferred upon the hour: ". . . l'heure étouffait / Sa voix, n'osant sonner au cadran stupéfait." But the gift of life is only equivocally a gift. The hour is endowed with human characteristics so that it may have more of which to be deprived. It gets the passion of fear to petrify passion's mobility, action to deprive itself of action. More tellingly, in a poem where the human is represented by the qualities specific to the poet, the hour is given voice only to mute it. Even its vestigial ears—for the root of *oser,* to dare, is *audere,* to hear—are taken away from it: *n'osant,* not daring / not hearing. The hour is made human so as to assert its striking resemblance—death-like stillness and stupefaction—to a suicide. The prosopopeia gives us to know the hour by an odd likeness to ourselves: it is like us when we have called into question our selfhood by an act of self-annihilation. The hour is the time ushered in when, in an act of Mallarmean self-doubt, the self ceases to exist as an operative category. Thus, the hour's stifled voice undoes the harmonious correlation between signifier and meaning. Time is not a signified expressed by ringing bells, as voiced language expresses human feeling; just as the stupefied clock interrupts passage by way of meaning from the sign to an outside referent, so the stifled voice, the suicidal hour interrupts the process of signification itself, the passage from the outside of perception to the inside of meaning.

Bergsonian duration, introspective time, is not operative in the poem either. It is a poem about statues and masks, things devoid of inner life. The most human figure is that of the dead sculptor, Germaine Pilon. But even this representative artist is no self-conscious genius; he is said to have been a prophet who was not in on his own secret, a soul who did not have the revelation of his whole thought, a dreamer who did not know what symbol he had thrown across the Seine in the Pont-Neuf. *La Révolution* does not promise the great interpretative wealth of an introspective poem, centered on a self's return to itself, or on a radical transformation it brings about in its mental or moral order. The stifled voice of the hour speaks rather of a discrepancy between consciousness' understanding of poems as expressive totalities and the actual structure of the poetic text, which is non-homogeneous, non-totalizing and cannot necessarily be reduced to meaning.

The point is made in part by the undoing of prosopopeia as seductive human figure. Prosopopeia transfers face and voice to a dead or absent entity; here, the transfer also works in the reverse direction: the humanized hour is made a dead or absent entity. The figure speaks against the construction of the language of time along the model of the self.

But the hour is an houri, *l'heure est un leurre,* a lure, a trap, a Nervalian will o' the wisp, a gleam (or *lueur*). It is seductive in the first place because, in undoing itself as human figure, it becomes convincingly more and more like a human figure, endowed as it seems with a purposiveness in its act of self-stifling. It turns itself into a not-self by a fearsome, murderous gesture, and in so doing, hides itself as not-self by the apparent intentionality of its turn. The prosopopeia undoes the first figure only by reconstituting it.

The seductiveness involved in the reconstituting of the figure is, however, a blind that conceals a less graceful and more threatening spectacle. For we should remember that the hour and the clock are not coming to life in this passage, but are tending toward progressive petrification. The distinctive feature of the passage on time is the seizing of the mobile, the figural, the human, in stone. The clock is stupefied, the hour is strangled; the fronton of towers turns to us a stony forehead (*fronton* derives from *front*, forehead). A rigor mortis seizes the temporal, after its reference to the objective word and its meaning for a self have both been evacuated in favor of a self-referential structure of uncertain or no meaning.

The syntagm *fronton des tours* accomplishes the rigidification by freezing in a single place the two functions evacuated. It is by way of the plural, *des tours,* which effaces the gendered article, that two different kinds of *tours,* both of which have been at work in the passage, are coupled: on the one hand, *tour* as tower, la Tour de la Bastille, la Tour de Nesle or La Tour de Babel; on the other hand, all the turns of *le tour,* from trope and turn of phrase, from sleight of hand or trick, from circuit or circular walk to rotation or revolution. As in Baudelaire's *Thyrsus,* where the hieratic emblem of a wand around which dances a snaky line of flowers allegorizes the indissociability of trope and sign, Hugo's twin *tours,* the referential and the tropological, are yoked together by a single—indeed a singular—*fronton.*

For a *fronton*—an architectural term designating a frontal or small pediment—like its near synonyms, pediment and façade, names by catachresis, that is, by abusive metaphor. A catachresis does not exchange terms between known entities but rather sets up an unequal exchange by means of which a known entity can give a term to an unknown entity so that the latter can get a name for one of its parts. The human body is often pillaged for these unequal exchanges, to name the teeth of a comb, the arm of a chair, the eye of a camera, or the face of a building. As catachresis *fronton* is both a name and a figure, as as such can successfully bridge the gap between signification and reference, trope and name, turn and tower.

However, the *fronton des tours* presses the passage—as passage allegorical of its language—away from the seductions of the self-undoing hour toward a rigid system of names, of conventional, referential language. As proper term for part of a tower it makes the figurality of the passage recede, giving to it the quality of a description of the literal scene of a tower on whose pediment is a stopped clock. One could, for example, read the passage as inspired by an event of the 1848 revolution described by Hugo in *Choses vues:* "Le cadran des Tuileries arrêté à 3 heures. (N'a pas été remonté depuis la révolution.) Marque l'heure de la chute de la monarchie."[15] As name, the catachresis presses the passage about the undecidability of language toward reference, and thence toward such referential towers as the *Bastille,* and such referential events as the French Revolution.

The figure is not far off, of course. We have been talking about language in this passage because time can come before us only by a process of signification, by the mediation of a language.[16] In a word, talking about time is to talk figuratively about a language, as to talk about the arresting of time arrested is to talk figuratively about bringing a stasis to a mobile, figural system. If the passage tends toward a sudden collapse into reference, that is precisely what it has been preparing all along in its discussion of rigidification. The figurative meaning of the catachresis is: meaning and reference are collapsed into reference when language stops meaning the self or referring to the world outside, and starts referring to itself as undecidably trope or sign. The stopped clock of *Choses vues* confirms the insight of *La Révolution* that there is a pressure in language toward the loss of a distinctness between names and tropes.

The loss of that distinction is here considered to be a precondition for the revolutionary turn. Of course Hugo is not claiming that the shots of the 1848 Revolution were fired by language. But he is suggesting that the collapse of the two disparate functions of language into a single referential function is necessary for revolution to be conceivable.[17] This is not a delirious notion on Hugo's part. We can certainly understand that, in order for the attack on the Bastille to touch off a revolution, the Bastille had not only to be the name of a literal tower and a symbol of the king's power, but also that, for the time it took to destroy it, it be treated as if those two functions were collapsed into its very stones. The Revolution is defined here as the collapse of the figure into a name.

This collapse has an equivalent on the other side of the equation, in a collapse taking place in the city. The city is a spatial structure standing for other structures, which is given the pathos of a human subject, and an object of knowledge—the moving city monument—that can well represent it. The poem sets up an opposition between space and time that suggests how we are to read this animation and attempt at self-understanding on the part of the city. While, *tandis que,* time is seized in stony structures and signification falls into reference, spatial constructs, the text as organized grammar, starts to move or get emotional, and language as a structured set of conventional signs takes on meaning for a subject. The dramatic change takes place around the monumental statue.

Now the statue is of the city, insofar as it is a structure, but insofar as it advances, it is not entirely like the city. It has some of the features of the time system, and can be said, if not absolutely to be replacing time broken down on the other side of the equation, at least to have appropriated some of its properties. Its advance, its passage, is the signified that clock and bells ordinarily mean: time does not advance or pass, but the statue advances and passes. Furthermore, the ringing that should be the perceptual sign of time passing shows up here as a funereal and subterranean noise, the ringing of the ground itself that accompanies the statue's advance. The hour stifles its voice, but the earth rings. The clock hands cease to turn, and the turn of *tour* tends to disappear, but, as I will show in a minute, the towering statue can be said to turn. When we look to one of the representative structures of a text—the organization of its signifiers—for understanding, we do so by importing the discredited interpretative framework from the other side. In the structure that is the work of art the inside/outside polarity that reigns when we think of a perception corresponding to an understanding is not the primary function. But when the work of art is taken to be representative, to be a figure, it is by way of the worn-out relation.

It is to the poem's signifiers, as to its very ground, that we need to look for the meaning. It is there that we hear time advancing, for example. For *heure* continues to sound its passing in odd ways and places: *épaisseur, rondeur, horreur, roideur, leur, grandeur, stupeur,* etc. Similarly, although time's turns are no longer visible on the dial, they can be sighted in a signifier, indeed in the signifier of vision itself, the peculiar *virent,* the past tense of the verb *voir,* to see, but which is also the present tense of *virer,* to veer, to round a corner. A strategic placement makes this *virent* turn to turn. It is distanced from its subject by the clause about time, and is thus

Hallucinatory History ▼ 139

close to the *tour* and the unturning hands; the object of vision, the man of bronze and the horse of brass, are quite capable of serving as the subject of *virent*, giving us a wheeling man and horse.[18]

The poem is commenting on itself as a structure that offers itself, by way of a new figuration, as a perception of sorts. Language is getting phenomenalized in the passage, its grammar and signs being treated as audible and visible. This phenomenalization is described as the descent of the dream into a mental maelstrom ("comme par la rampe invisible d'un songe / . . . dans l'égarement d'un orage mental . . . / Le rêve . . . / . . . s'épouvante . . . / Et frémit . . ." [220-221]) and what it raises is the issue of whether the text *advances* by way of such play with signifiers. For the system of signifiers, with accidents of grammar and the sonorous plays it brings into view, does not merely serve as the correlative of meaning, as the voice expressing a thought. It seems actually to advance meaning. Thus, the *épaisseur des ténèbres* seems more than just a nonsensical tolling of "heure," a resounding of its signifier after its meaning has been emptied out. It seems to ring the changes of a new hour, an hour substantializable, spatializable, an hour made thick (*épaisse-heure*), an hour outside the hour, *hors-heure*, a weighty hour, *une lourde heure*, an upright and kingly hour, *roi d'heure roide-heure*, a great hour, *une grande heure*, the impersonal hour itself, *l'heure elle-même, enfin!*

We are familiar with the engenderment of texts around their babbling, prating signifiers. This is one model for engendering texts at work in Rousseau's *Rêveries*. What is striking about the passage from *La Révolution*, however, is that, as it refers to its own phenomenalization of language, it moves away from the original comparison of the vision to dreaming and thus from the hope of achieving a Cratylic correspondence between signifier and signified. It suggest, as I will show in a minute, that the phenomenalization of language involves a kind of madness, for the dream collapses into hallucination. The prosopopeia endowing the city with intention reintroduces a dysfunctional model that first has us rubbing our eyes, wondering if we see or just think we see a turn in *virent*, and has us checking our ears, wondering if we hear the voice of the stifled *heure* or the sound of the wind, favored topos of Hugo, in *devant, s'avancer, s'avança,* etc. But the dream begins to turn toward hallucination as the poet starts to ask about the status of the event on which he is focussing and of the subject who sees it: ". . . qu'est-ce qui passait? . . . / Qui donc a vu lentement passer les statues?" (220). The point is less whether we see or don't see any of these phenomena, and whether they actually have a meaning or not, than the fact that one apparently prefers to make sense of nonsense rather than to have no meaning at all. The pressure toward meaning is great enough that when all sense has been evacuated and we are left with just a "nom fauve et maudit (220)," one prefers to hallucinate meaning and intention rather than that there be none.[19]

Laplanche and Pontalis, in an article on "Fantasy and the Origins of Sexuality," suggest that when signifiers get treated as objects of perception, we are in the domain of hallucination.[20] When an infant hallucinates a breast, it is not attempting to get milk, which it knows is not there. Its "vision" of the breast is not the means by which it tries to satisfy its physical hunger. For the child, in the dearth of milk and breast, thinks it sees "not the real object, but the lost object; not the milk, but the breast *as a signifier*" (15). The infant substitutes the signifier for the milk, a substitution that is possible because the signifier, like an object, has a phenomenal existence. Whatever satisfaction the child gets from the hallucination comes from the linguistic operation of substituting signifier for object, and then from sucking it for all it's worth, that is, for mental nourishment, for extra signifieds, to give nascent consciousness some sense of its own life and operation.

In "Hypogram and Inscription" de Man further elaborates the distinctive character of hallucination: "in hallucination, the difference between *I see* and *I think I see* has been one-sidedly resolved in the direction of apperception[.] Consciousness has become consciousness only of itself" ("Hypogram" 49). Toward the end, the passage from *La Révolution* talks about such a collapse in the dreamspace itself:

> . . . et le rêve lui-même,
> Qui distingue à minuit dans l'immensité blême
> Tout un monde terrible à travers l'oeil fermé,
> Le rêve, aux habitants de l'ombre accoutumé,
> S'épouvante de voir cette lugubre espèce
> De fantômes entrer dans sa nuée épaisse,
> Et frémit, car le pas de ces noirs arrivants,
> N'est ni le pas des morts ni le pas des vivants. (221)

> [. . . and the dream itself,
> Which at midnight distinguishes in the colorless immensity
> A whole terrible world through closed eye,
> The dream, to the inhabitants of the shadow accustomed,
> Is terrified at the sight of this lugubrious species
> Of phantoms entering in its thick cloud,
> And shudders, for the step of these black ones arriving
> Is neither the step of the dead nor the step of the living.]

The dream can see with a closed eye because it knows no difference between waking and sleeping. But it is accustomed to distinguishing between the dreamspace (*dans l'immensité blême*) and the dream world with which it furnishes that space (*tout un monde terrible*). When the lugubrious phantoms arrive, however, they render the space into which they enter (*dans une nuée épaisse,* into a thick cloud) indistinct from themselves as intruders (they enter *dans une nuée épaisse,* that is, *as* a thick cloud or swarm). The dream no longer knows how to distinguish its habitual space from the inhabitants that occupy that space. It cannot differentiate between what it "sees" with its closed eye, the cloud of phantoms, and itself as dreaming consciousness, the thick cloud of thought. Phantom thought grips itself in phantom perceptions.

The lines that explain the cause of the dream's terror yield an example of the way that reference and signification get conflated into a meaning undifferentiated from perception when language is phenomenalized. The explanation reads: "Car le pas de ces noirs arrivants / N'est ni le pas des morts ni le pas des vivants." It is hard to seize the distinctions the poet is trying to make, as the attempt to translate them shows. If we translate them with respect to the referential event of stepping as "For the step of these black arriving ones / Is neither the step of the dead nor the step of the living" we suggest that, for the poet, there are three distinct ways of walking, one for the living, one for the dead, and one for statues. The living do indeed have a step, but what madman has seen the dead or a town's monuments walking? The step of the dead is a no-step, a *pas de pas,* that is, a *pas* in its other sense, of negation. To translate *pas* as step is to lose the distinction between the dead and living, as well as what separates both dead and living from the statue.

Could we then translate them, by way of the *pas de pas,* as the difference between three kinds of negativities: "For the negativity of these black arriving ones / Is neither the negativity of the dead nor the negativity of the living"? But can the living be said to have a negativity? There are no negatives in nature; the living have to take a positive step, to posit a death to get an idea of negativity, which thus involves a move to the level of signification. And what about the black arriving ones? They are said to be arriving. Even if their arrival does not involve a referential step, it is at any rate not the no-step of the dead. The lines are trying to distinguish the referential event (the *pas* of the living), and the event for signification (the *pas de pas* of the dead), which exist in a specular opposition, from a third *pas,* the *pas* of the statues.

One could propose a third translation that would try to take this distinctness into account: "For the *pas* of these black arriving ones / Is neither the negativity of the dead nor the step of the living." What distinguishes the *pas* of the statues is that it has neither the meaning of negation nor does it point to a referential event, a step: it is a signifier, a sounded *pas,* distinct by virtue of its indifference to the difference between steps and negations. It functions as an empty piece of language, irrespective of all questions of reference and significance.

But the third translation is problematic in a different way. When we translate the lines in this way, we lose their triple *pas,* reducing it to a single *pas.* We localize in one place the rule of "es-*pa*-cement" giving rhythm to the poem throughout. Furthermore, the translation makes the problem into that of distinguishing between three separate species of signifieds (step, negation, the signifier itself), when in fact, the difference that language makes appears phenomenally here—to ear and eye—as a slide from one *pas* to another to another. In rhythm, an aspect of poetic language everywhere available, signifier and signified are not yet distinct sign features for consciousness. It is a reduction to make a rhythm either a signified, an object of knowledge, or a mere set of signifiers sounded to the inner ear of readers. Rhythm is at once perception and meaning, insofar as it is organized perception. It is also a reduction to discover rhythm at a single point when the suggestion is that any understanding of the *pas,* as step or negation, necessarily rests on the insistent recalling of the signifier.

The hallucinatory passage of the statues signals the movement of the poem away from the specular oppositions of dead and living, reference and signification, to the level of a language treated as an object of the senses undifferentiated from its signified.

The effect Fineman notes in Shakespeare's dark lady sonnets, namely, the effect of a secondary Cratylism in which a language that does not say what it means ends by saying exactly what it means, i.e., "I lie," is under discussion in this kind of text. The *pas* of the statues declares itself to mean neither step nor negation but to be just a signifier, *pas.* In so doing it reintroduces the equivalency of sound and meaning previously undone when the hour was stifled, since the sound *pas* gives us access to the meaning of the poem as rhythm, as ordered signifiers. But Hugo does not find this secondary Cratylism to be just a problem of poetic language, nor does he see it as the proof of an advance in understanding, as does Fineman. He sees it as hallucinatory and he sees it as laying the groundwork for the real. Consciousness in its infancy, prior to any distinction between its inside as consciousness and the outside of perception, is only conscious of itself in apperception. As de Man graphically puts it: "In that sense [the sense of consciousness as conscious only of itself], any consciousness, including perception, is hallucinatory" (49). A consciousness that subsists by producing meaning out of empty signifiers, milkless breasts, is certainly not a "wiser" consciousness, either. The triple *pas* of the statue gives access to an organizaion at work in the poem and can be said to add the signified "language" to *pas*. But this is emphatically not a poem in which sound echoes or engenders meaning or theme (except in the mode of illusion). Rather sound gives us access to a consciousness that cannot advance past the stage of hallucinatory, apperceptive consciousness. Hallucinatory consciousness just glides from *pas* to *pas* to *pas,* in what can be called a *pas-sage,* a wise step, only to the extent that a canniness is evinced with respect to the poem's rhythmic, sonorous dimension. This consciousness lives in proximity to a kind of terror, the terror of the sign that seems to engender thoughts instead of representing them. But there is a certain consolation even in this obsessive consciousness. One may not move ahead by way of this kind of play, but at least there is an organization that provides evidence that there is a consciousness around. When the possibility arises that we may not escape out of language to an outside referent, at the very least, the poem suggests, we can get evidence of the reality of consciousness.

Are we then to consider that, for Hugo, the track through the poem is finally that of a consciousness that constitutes itself over and over as apperception each time it gets deconstituted as self and finds itself confronted with a meaningless set of names?

In such a view, the poem would get its title from its understanding of the Terror as the equivalent, for a collectivity, of the threat of a disintegration into sheer difference, a threat over and against which it would constitute itself as a one-sided consciousness of consciousness. The very term "Reign of Terror" is instructive here. Fear is alienated from subject and object in the term "Reign of Terror." We do not say the Terror of Robespierre, for example. We do not think of it as the fear he invokes in others, or as his own fear. It is a structural Terror, it is the law as producing not the unity of the collectivity living under it, but sheer, uncollectable difference. The Terror, as defined by the *Petit Robert,* is exactly the reign in which laws are measures of exception. The rule of difference, of exception, can indeed be said to be a rule of law of sorts: the rule of producing rules out of exceptions, of which the rule of *pas* would be one example. Against the threat of a chaos, utter loss, no order, to find an overall sense of patterning, even of the unlikely sort that rhythms the poem as the pursuit of *pas,* or that makes rules of exception into the rule, is consoling. Is Hugo then proposing, in lieu of a poem on the French Revolution, or on the meaning of revolution, to track the subterranean, hallucinatory history of revolution, defined as the rule by which signifiers operate to produce meaningful effects for consciousness, independent of any literal reference or signification? Unlike Kant or Hegel, for whom the French Revolution turns out to be proof that the idea of history actualizes itself in events, which are thus demonstrably not random, for Hugo, the

Revolution would provide evidence that consciousness can only grasp itself in the textualized event by superimposing upon it a phenomenal grid that is in point of fact lacking. The Revolution would be the turning point when, faced with the likelihood of an ungovernable chaos, consciousness would have preferred the mad assertion of mastery and of law to a recognition of the true state of affairs.[21]

But the hallucinatory is a permanent interpretative possibility, and indicates the underlying possibility of consciousness as nonhistorical, as a-progressive, as obsessive repetition.[22] In its first part, the poem does concern itself with the phenomenalization of the signifier, and with the Terror as the equivalent of such a concern, but that is not where its historicity is situated. One would also have to take into account the second and third parts of the poem, which follow to its conclusion the logic of the promenading statues, and more especially, the epilogue, originally a separate poem whose title indicated a diferent and opposed logic. The poem from which the epilogue was excerpted was to have been called "Le Verso de la page."[23] From its first words, "Soit. Mais . . . ," it sets itself up as a postscript opposing the main thesis. The epilogue tells us that the Revolution is a stage, the lair of a divine monster into which Progress strays, but from which it then departs: "Le Progrès n'a pas peur d'entrer, lui qui s'envole, / Chez ce monstre divin, la Révolution. / . . . Puis il sort de la haute et grondante tanière . . ." (246). The poem insists that it *traverses* hallucinatory consciousness and that its historicity is not to be reduced to that dark moment of madness when reference and meaning are collapsed into one another, be it by the abusive naming of catachresis, or by a one-sided, hallucinatory consciousness recognizing itself in a prosopopeia.

The passage we have been reading contains a clue as to where Hugo situates the historicity of poetry. There is a dominant element in the passage, an element characterized by a repose beyond the reach of all the vertiginous activity of the figural system, and that, as unknown, excites its transports. This element makes the immobile clock towers and the advancing statues appear as inadequate translations of a source for all rest and energy. The element is the feather that no hurricane can move, found on an unknown cimier: "Ce cimier inconnu / Dont aucun ouragan n'eût remué la plume."[24]

It is perched atop a *cimier,* a helmet crest, from the word for summit, *cime*. A feather on a helmet crest can be said to dominate even the high forehead of the towers. This feather is not a feather of the sort that birds shed and that could be tossed about by a light wind. By virtue of its immobility, it is not even a feather of the sort that one might find atop the forehead of a man of bronze. Bronze men are moved by the wind of inspiration in this poem, just as the hurricane that was the Revolution had no trouble melting down Henri IV's statue. "Rien, pas même l'airain, pour jamais ne s'arrête" (219), Hugo tells us in the passage just preceding this one. Nothing, no *thing,* even something made of bronze, can be arrested forever. Insofar as it can be made into a thing, even a creature of language, a work of art, can be moved. What is this feather atop this unknown helmet crest, that stands for the non-thing, for language as non-phenomenalizable, and that cannot be budged even by a hurricane?

Why is the *cimier* characterized as "unknown," anyway? A *cimier,* the *Petit Robert* tells us, is not only a term for a part of a helmet; it is also a heraldic term, indicating the uppermost part of an escutcheon. The whole of the passage can then be read as an escutcheon, of which this is just the uppermost part, the part that indicates that it is an escutcheon. Certainly, unknown escutcheons can come one's way. Indeed, the whole art of blazonry can be said to be pretty well unknown in our day. Of it, Hugo says: "Le blazon est une langue. . . . Ce sont les hiéroglyphes de la féodalité."[25] The language of blazonry is not an oral language to which the phenomenalized signifier could be the key. It is a written language which has as a precondition for its understanding an act that is not an act of perception but rather of reading, and that involves a preliminary organizing of its marks as a meaningful language system. The act of reading is active; it confers orderliness onto potentially random marks. One has, at the very least, to recognize that it is writing, to know anything about it. The *cimier* that reveals that we are reading an escutcheon, a written passage, part of the archive, suggests that the question of reading and writing is the unknown around which the rest is elaborated; the feather atop this escutcheon signals the writerly pen.

The quiet eye of the hurricane is writing, material inscription. Around it systems of exchange get set up and undone. In the face of its materiality, consciousness feels threatened enough to grasp at the straw of language as phenomenalizable. But also with respect to writing's materiality, the hallucinatory and repetitive history of the first part can be considered just a bad passage inscribed in a longer poem, or a bad reading of what shows up as inscription on the page's other side.

The unruffled emblem doesn't move partly because inscriptions don't move or get moved by hands, or even by whatever consciousness confers perceptibility and meaning on them. It also doesn't move because the wind that blows from it blows in one direction, forward, *devant.* It blows all its signs toward the future-oriented history of the epilogue. I'd like to conclude with an example from that epilogue which gives an idea of why, for Hugo, the historicity of poems resides in inscription, and is future-oriented. Two lines tell us:

> A qui te cherche, ô Vrai, jamais tu n'échappas.
> Une étape après l'autre. Après un pas, un pas.
>
> [From who seeks you, o Truth, you never escape.
> One stage after another. After a step, a step.]

The short sentences restate the old cliché about the seeking of truth as the only way to grab hold of it. The ideology it defines, Progress with a capital *p,* seems equally a cliché. But the last sentence, which repeats the problematic found in the earlier passage on the stepping statues, does so with a difference worth noting. Unlike the earlier lines about the statue's step, which ordered apparently alternative translations but in fact made sense only in the light of the system of meaning provided by the sounded signifier, this line defining Progress is very generous to the translator. One can translate it in many different ways, according to various systems of meaning: after a step, another step; after a negation, another negation; after a negation, a step; after a step, a negation. All these translations of the line are possible. All affirm, albeit in very different ways—from the pre-dialectical to the dialectical to the negatively dialectical—that progress toward truth is the law of history. The poem—and indeed, the Hugolian corpus—can be understood in the light of each of these differing ideologies of progress. To those interpretations can be added a commentary on the obsessive *pas* that gives rhythm to the poem: after a *pas,* another *pas.* The definition of progress in this translation would be repetition, consciousness of consciousness as obsessive, as advancing madness. In short, progress would be the repetitive move whereby consciousness persists in seeing itself in structures voided of meaning for it. To that reading can be added another reading, however. A difference could be made between the obsessive *pas* of rhythm from which one can escape by forgetting about it, and the *pas* which one has more trouble getting away from, namely, the *p-a-s* of the inscription: after the sound *pas,* still another kind of *p-a-s*. This new *pas* is a stilled *pas,* one that allows the poem to proffer to whoever seeks it, not only all the erroneous readings of which it is susceptible, but also the inescapable truth of its materiality as what makes it possible to denounce those errors. On the other side of the page of the hallucinatory history of Terror, or rather, on the same side of the page, as its support, we find Hugo writing through the madness of the Revolution as Terror toward an opening. His understanding of revolution in linguistic terms is a double understanding. If, on the one hand, its worst moments came about as it tried to refigure an insight into language's inhuman difference in human terms, on the other, its best involved the discovery anew of inscription as the source of historicity. With that it became possible to glimpse an opening, within the text of *La Révolution,* toward a definition of revolution as text, as "poème inouï (231)," the unheard, the unheard of, the magnificent poem, the yea-saying, or rather, yea-writing (*oui*), future-oriented poem which broadcasts the wherewithal to undo its ideologies themselves.

The materiality of writing is threatening to consciousness because it denies its power to progress to a certainty of anything beyond it—to an outside referent, to the inside of consciousness, or even, as in Fineman, to a progress in consciousness's understanding of how language functions. But it also provides a resistance to consciousness that gives it a handle on, an opening to, an outside of consciousness. Given the delusions of which consciousness showed itself capable at the end of the Enlightenment, we must consider that a good thing. There is, I would maintain, in a final polemical outburst, a *yes* worth thinking about in this darkest and most-nihilistic seeming of deconstructive texts, *La Révolution*.

Notes

1. An example, by now classic, of the way that language's undecidability can operate at a greater level of complexity than that of a mere opinion between fiction or history can be found in Rousseau's dialogued preface to *Julie*. Paul de Man, in *Allegories of Reading: Figural Language in Rousseau, Nietzsche, Rilke, and Proust* (New Haven: Yale University Press, 1979) discusses the insistent assertion by one of the two interlocuters, "R," who says he really does not know whether he is the author of a tableau, a fiction of man, or the editor of documents portraying particular men and women. De Man shows a re-emergence—at the very moment when the question seems resolved in favor of the self-signifying tableau—of a referential moment: ". . . the more the text denies the actual existence of a referent, real or ideal, and the more fantastically fictional it becomes, the more it becomes the representation of its own pathos. . . . In the terminology of the text, the "tableau" has become a "portrait" after all, not the portrait of universal man but of the deconstructive passion of a subject" (198–199).

2. Appearing in *Representations* 7 (Summer 1984) 59–86; rpt. in *Shakespeare's Perjured Eye: The Invention of Poetic Subjectivity in the Sonnets* (Berkeley: University of California Press, 1986). All references to the work will henceforth appear in the text.

3. Fineman explains the effect aimed at:
Language thus speaks *for* its own gainsaying. The result is a new kind of Cratylism, a second degree of Cratylism, that, like the Liar's Paradox Shakespeare often flirts with in his sonnets—"Those lines that I before have writ do lie" (115)), "When my love swears that she is made of truth" (138)—is proof of its own paradoxicality. In this gainsaying way—a speech acquired on condition that it speak against

itself—Shakespeare accomplishes a limit case of the correspondence of signifier to be signified." ("Eye" 77)

4. Until fairly recently, New Historicism neglected poetry and Fineman's work could seem idiosyncratic. In the past few years, however, as attention has been turned to English Romanticism and Wordsworth, tacks similar to Fineman's have been taken. Alan Liu, for example, in his *Wordsworth: The Sense of History* (Stanford: Stanford University Press, 1989), starts by suggesting the pastoral to be an antihistorical or prehistorical mode: "The purpose of the mirror of georgic nature is to hide history in order, finally, to reflect the self" (19). The thesis about poetry's ahistoricism is then refined by a turn: "the denials of history are also the deepest realizations of history" (32). This turn, Liu suggests, is the one by which the self-referential language of poetry ends by referring to the ideology of its age: "the very scheme of differences that allows certain ages to define a 'literary text' separate from historical event (for example, as a representation rather than action, aesthetic object rather than utilitarian artifact, medium of the cultured rather than of popular culture) is a reference to, or mimesis of, the scheme of differences that divides and organizes the historical context of that culture" (47). Liu's notion that each age has its ideology of literature follows Fineman's idea of a shift in Shakespearian subjectivity taking place around a more sophisticated understanding of language's deceitfulness. Both share the further assumption that a literary text and an historical event are two distinct objects for study and that texts in no way tend to interfere with that distinction. Whereas Liu merely asserts the distinction, however, Fineman finds a basis for it in the Liar's paradox.

5. *La Révolution,* in *Oeuvres complètes,* vol. 10, ed. Jean Massin (Paris: Club Français du Livre, 1969) 217–247. The passage with which I will be working can be found pp. 220–221. All page references will henceforth be found in the body of the text. See the "Présentation" by Jean Massin, pp. 199–216, for further details as to the poem's composition and publication.

Only published in 1881, the poem might very well serve as a reflection on the major revolutions of the nineteenth century (1830, 1848, 1870) in which Hugo was more or less closely implicated.

6. The definite article, *la,* is a first indicator of the poem's hesitation between signification and reference. The definite article may modify a noun that designates a unique and well-known thing. *The* revolution, for a Frenchman, is, of course, the French Revolution. *La* may, on the other hand, modify a generic noun about which something is predicated, in a usage roughly synonymous to the English suppression of the article, as in the phrase "*Revolution* consists in a radical break with past forms of government." In the first case, the article suggests a referential language use; in the second, it introduces a meaningful fiction.

7. The choice of Hugo to pursue the argument with Fineman is not purely arbitrary. We have the testimony of Hugo on Shakespeare's influence. He not only admired Shakespeare and referred to his works often, but indeed

he mentions him in this poem as one in a series of unconscious geniuses with whom the poetic voice is identified. Furthermore, the play that scholars generally agree to have been Shakespeare's last, *The Tempest,* shows at least one important parallel to this poem: the court is driven mad by a series of hallucinations, as the invisible is rendered visible by Ariel's agency. The dark lady's deceptions are a relatively mild form of a problem that surfaces in Hugo's poem as a paralyzing terror and in Shakespeare's play as insanity.

    8. Michael Riffaterre, "La Vision hallucinatoire chex Victor Hugo," in *Essais de stylistique structurale* (Paris: Flammarion, 1971) 222–241.

    9. The tendency to psychologize the revolution, to make of it a kind of Racinian tragedy in which is represented a conflict of forces within a single personality, is very strong. François Furet, in his *Interpreting the French Revolution,* trans. Elborg Forster (Cambridge: Cambridge University Press, 1981), warns against the 200-year-old tendency of historians to perpetuate the notion of the Revolution as a mythic tale of new beginnings and thus of the formation of a self. Historians tend, he claims, to identify with the actors, to commemorate the founders, to execrate the deviants, as if compelled to re-enact the dramatic conflict they are writing about. In that they do a disservice to an analytical understanding of the event (which is not a tale of self-constitution), as well as to Leftist political thought. The latter has become imprisoned, Furet suggests, by thinking in terms of a promise of unity that has failed, in lieu of thinking new political alternatives (11). His argument against reading the Revolution in psychological terms has not been much heeded.

    10. See, for example, "Pasteurs et troupeaux," a rewriting of one of the earliest poems figuring in *Les Contemplations,* "Le firmament est plein. . . ." Riffaterre explains that in Hugo's hallucinatory poems, "metaphor disappears from his style" (*Essais* 239), as the figure gets treated as a "literal reality" (*Essais* 239). The most frequently commented lines in "Pasteurs et troupeaux"—"Le pâtre promontoire au chapeau de nuées / S'accoude et rêve au bruit de tous les infinis" (The promontory shepherd with hat of clouds / Leans on his elbows and dreams to the sound of all infinities) contain such a figure treated literally.

    11. Riffaterre defines this giving of movement to the immutable as hallucinatory: "It is not that movement of life that a good writer knows how to give to his creations, and without which some of Hugo's myths would only be allegories, mere rebuses telling stories, but an abnormal movement, one that transforms the reality to which we are accustomed. It is not the movement of what we know to be living, but the movement of what ought to be immutable. That is what alarms the imagination, that is what suggests hallucination" (*Essais* 226).

    12. In *Choses vues,* Hugo remarks à propos of the death of the son of Louis-Philippe, then king of France, that the law of history has recently gone against the law of patrilinear descent. This leads him to speculate not only about the failure of human attempts to foresee and regulate the succession of rulers, but also, more generally, about the failure of the teleological model and

of linear progression to account for history's laws. The laws of history, he suggests, are not rational, human schemes, but are as necessary as the laws that regulate "les faits matériels." The passage is worth quoting at some length:

> . . . quand on médite l'histoire des cent cinquante dernières années, une remarque vient à l'esprit. Louis XIV a régné, son fils n'a pas régné; Louis XV a régné, son fils n'a pas régné; Louis XVI a régné, son fils n'a pas régné; Napoléon a régné, son fils n'a pas régné; Charles X a régné, son fils n'a pas régné; Louis-Philippe règne, son fils ne régnera pas. Fait extraordinaire! Six fois de suite la prévoyance humaine désigne dans tout un peuple une tête qui devrait régner, et c'est précisément celle-là qui ne règne pas. Six fois de suite la prévoyance humaine est en défaut. Le fait persiste avec une redoutable et mystérieuse obstination. Une révolution survient, un universel tremblement d'idées qui engloutit en quelques années un passé de dix siècles et toute la vie sociale d'une grande nation; cette commotion formidable renverse tout, excepté le fait que nous venons de signaler; elle le fait jaillir au contraire du milieu de tout ce qu'elle fait crouler; un grand empire s'établit, un Charlemagne apparaît, un monde nouveau surgit, le fait persiste; il semble être du monde nouveau comme it était du monde ancien. L'empire tombe, les vieilles races reviennent, le Charlemagne se dissout, l'exil prend le conquérant et rend les proscrits; les révolutions se reforment et éclatent, les dynasties changent trois fois, les événements passent sur les événements, let flots passent sur les flots,—toujours le fait surnage, tout entier, sans discontinuité, sans modification, snas rupture. Depuis que les monarchies existent, le droit dit: *Le fils aîné du roi règne toujours,* et voilà que, depuis cent quarante ans, le tait respond: *Le fils aîne du roi ne règne jamais.* Ne semble-t-il pas que c'est une loi qui se révèle, et qui se révèle, dans l'ordre inexplicable des faits humains, avec ce degré de persistance et de précision qui jusqu'à présent n'avait appartenu qu'aux faits matériels? N'est-il pas temps que la providence intervienne pour déranger elle-même cela, et ne serait-il pas effrayant que certaines lois de l'histoire se manifestassent aux hommes avec la même exactitude, la même rigidité, et pour ainsi dire la même dureté, que les grandes tois de la nature?—*Choses vues:* vol. 1, *1830–1846,* ed. Hubert Juin (Paris: Gallimard, 1972) 234–236.

[. . . in meditating on the history of the past 150 years, a remark comes to mind. Louis XIV reigned, his son did not reign; Louis XV reigned, his son did not reign; Louis XVI reigned, his son did not reign; Napoleon reigned, his son did not reign; Charles X reigned, his son did not reign; Louis-Philippe reigns, his son will not reign. Extraordinary fact! Six times in a row human foresight has designated out of a whole people the head that is to reign, and it is precisely that one that does not reign. Six times in a row human foresight is mistaken. The fact persists with a redoubtable and mysterious stubbornness. A revolution arrives, a universal shaking of ideas that in a few years swallows up a ten-century-long past and the whole social existence of a great nation; that formidable commotion overturns everything, except the fact just mentioned; on the contrary, it makes that fact spring up in the midst of everything it is making crumble; a great empire is established, a Charlemagne appears, a new world arises, the fact persists; it seems to be with the new world as it was with the old. The empire falls, the old races return, the Charlemagne disintegrates, exile takes the conqueror and returns the banished; revolutions form again and break out, dynasties are changed three times, events pass over events, flood over flood,—always the fact floats up, entire, without discontinuity, without modification, without break. So long as monarchies have existed, positive law states: *The king's eldest son always reigns,* and it happens thus, over a hundred and forty years the fact answers: *The king's eldest son never reigns.* Doesn't it seem as if a law were being revealed here, and as if it were being revealed, within the inexplicable order of human facts, with that degree of persistance and precision that until now had only belonged to material facts? Isn't it time for providence to intervene to disturb this itself, and wouldn't it be terrifying should certain laws of history manifest themselves to men with the same exactness, the same rigidity, and so to speak the same austerity, as the great laws of nature?]

13. The two time schemes suspended are both associated with the interpretation of the French Revolution. Hannah Arendt, in her discussion of "The Meaning of Revolution" (in *On Revolution* [Middlesex: Penguin, 1984], 21–58) suggests that the modern concept of revolution involves linear time: it is "inextricably bound up with the notion that the course of history suddenly begins anew, that an entirely new story, a story never known or told before is about to unfold . . ." (28). "It is obvious," she states, "that only under the conditions of a rectilinear time concept are such phenomena as novelty, uniqueness of events, and the like conceivable at all" (27).

Arendt also reminds us of the persistence of an earlier meaning, carried over from the time when revolution was an astronomical term "designating the regular, lawfully revolving motion of the stars, which . . . was certainly characterized neither by newness nor by violence. On the contrary, the word clearly indicates a recurring, cyclical movement" (42). When the term is carried over into the political domain, it gives a distinctly restorative flavor to revolution, as revolutionaries "pleaded in all sincerity that they wanted to revolve back to old times when things had been as they ought to be" (44).

We can correlate Arendt's problematic to the one raised by Hugo's stupefied clock because in both cases it is the correspondence of an ideal, rational model to a perceptual experience by way of a mediating sign—clock, or narrative construct—that is at stake.

14. In 1841, describing the Invalides where Napoleon's casket is provisionally lying upon its return to France, Hugo comes upon three statues off their pedestals and develops their allegory:

J'ai retrouvé là, dans l'ombre, trois autres statues de plomb, descendues de je ne sais où, que je me rappelle avoir vues, à cette même place, étant tout enfant, en 1815, lors des mutilations d'édifices, de dynasties et de nations qui se firent à cette époque. Ces trois statues, du plus mauvais style de l'Empire, froides comme ce qui est allégorique, mornes comme ce qui est médiocre, sont là debout le long du mur, dans l'herbe, parmi des tas de chapiteaux, avec je ne sais quel faux air de tragédies sifflées. L'une d'elles tient un lion attaché à une chaîne et représente la Force. Rien n'a l'air désorienté comme une statue posée à plat sur le sol, sans piédestal; on dirait un cheval sans cavalier ou un roi sans trône. Il n'y a que deux attitudes pour le soldat, la bataille ou la mort; il n'y en a que deux pour le roi, l'empire ou le tombeau; il n'y en a que deux pour la statue, être debout dans le ciel ou couchée sur la terre.

Une statue à pied étonne l'esprit et importune l'oeil. On oublie qu'elle est de plâtre ou de bronze et que le bronze ne marche pas plus que le plâtre, et l'on est tenté de dire à ce pauvre personnage à face humaine, si gauche et si malheureux dans sa posture d'apparat: "—Eh bien! va donc! va! marche! continue ton chemin! démène-toi! La terre est sous tes pieds. Qui te retient? qui t'empêche?" Du moins le piédestal explique l'immobilité. Pour les statues comme pour les hommes, un piédestal, c'est un petit espace étroit et honorable, avec quatre précipices autour."—*Choses vues:* vol. 1, *1830-1846,* 213-214.

[There, in the shadows, I came again upon three other lead statues, descended from I know not where, and that I remember having seen in this same place, when still a child, in 1815, during the mutilations of buildings, dynasties, and nations going on in that period. Those three statues, in the worst Empire style, cold like all that is allegorical, dreary like all that is mediocre, are there upright against the wall, in the grass, amongst a heap of capitals, with I know not what false look of hissed-at tragedies. One of them holds a lion attached to a chain, and represents Strength. Nothing looks so disoriented as a statue standing level with the ground, without a pedestal; one would think a horse without a rider or a king without a throne. There are only two attitudes for a soldier, in battle or in death; there are only two for a king, an empire or a tomb; there are only two for the statue, to be upright in heaven or bedded on the earth.

A statue on foot astonishes the mind and bothers the eye. One forgets that it is made of plaster or bronze and that bronze walks no more than plaster, and one is tempted to say to the poor personator with its human face, so awkward and unhappy in its attitude of display: "Well then! Go ahead! Go! Walk! Who is stopping you?" At least the pedestal explains its immobility. For statues, as for men, a pedestal is a small space, confined and honorable, hemmed in by four precipices.]

15. *Choses vues:* vol. 2, *1847-48,* ed. Hubert Juin (Paris: Gallimard, 1972) 311.

16. See Paul de Man's "Hypogram and Inscription," in *The Resistance to Theory* (Minneapolis: University of Minnesota Press, 1986) 27-53. (All page

references to the work will henceforth appear in the body of the text.) De Man explains that the relationship between carillon and time "is analogous to the relationship between signifier and signified that constitutes the sign. The ringing of the bells . . . is the material sign of an event (the passage of time) of which the phenomenality lacks certainty." (48). He further explains that "the phenomenality of experience cannot be established *a priori*, it can only occur by a process of signification" (48). I have drawn heavily on de Man's analysis of prosopopeia and hallucination in this essay.

17. See Alexis de Tocqueville, L'*Ancien régime et la révolution*, in *Oeuvres complètes*, vol. 2, ed. J.-P. Mayer (Paris: Gallimard, 1953) 56, 80. Tocqueville attributes a revolutionary force to the transfer of the exaggerated language by which Parlement traditionally remonstrated with the king onto a new stage, in front of an audience unfamiliar with usage. The violence with which the Parlement addressed the king was a conventionalized figure, whose decoding was not problematic for Parlement and king. To those unfamiliar with the convention, however, the clichéd form of address appeared a literal, referential use of language. Tocqueville is then describing as a precondition for revolutionary violence the conflation of language's two functions into its single referential function.

18. A play earlier in the passage prepares the play of *virent* by suggesting that the city's corners can be thought as eyes: *mirer*, in "Les mille toits mirant leurs angles dans la Seine," can mean either to reflect, to mirror, or to sight, to look at. The roofs reflect or look at their angles, that is, depending on the perspective, at their corners or their eyes. The placement of a signifier, the angles it makes with other strategically located signifiers are, so to speak, the "eyes" of the text.

19. The engendering of a text by way of a play with the signifier takes place at various moments in the poem. In the discussion of the reigns of Henri IV, Louis XIII, Louis XIV, and Louis XV, the most referential of signs, the proper name, is treated as if it were a signifier devoid of meaning or reference from which the other elements in the passage can be discovered. Of Henri, we are told "Il fit tout *en ri*ant / Il *ri*ait à la guerre, il *ri*ait *en pri*ant." His wind of inspiration is a "*bri*se", and what puts his reign into question, "non loin de ces jeux et de ces *ris*" are the "*bri*uits" and debris of skeletons, ". . . bri*sés* / Nus. . . ." (234). Similarly, Louis XIV shines, "*lui*t" at Versailles, but his crimes "*Lui* firent dans son *Lou*vre un colossal trophée / De ruine. . . ." (236). There are a multitude of such "streets" running through the poem.

However, Hugo lets us know that this textual model is a game with serious consequences. Henri IV, the ruler of an aesthetic kingdom of laughter, where the play of signifiers is the rule, is undone, broken, because he is blind to a dimension of language that makes it escape the phenomenalization on which such play is based.

20. "Fantasy and Origins of Sexuality," in *The International Journal of Psychoanalysis*, 49.1 (1968) 1–18. All references to this work will henceforth appear in the text.

21. Laplanche and Pontalis suggest that by means of the phenomenalization of the sign the subject gets a glimpse of its own original fantasy, and thus of its origin. Further, by way of the sense of hearing, the subject inserts itself into "the history or legend or parents, grandparents, and the ancestors: the family *sounds* or *sayings,* the spoken or secret discourse, going on prior to the subject's arrival, within which he must find his way. Insofar as it can serve retroactively to summon up the discourse, the noise—or any other discrete sensorial element that has meaning—can acquire this value" (11). For Laplanche and Pontalis, the noise of the signifier, which often appears in a fantasy and is in fact the starting point for its elaboration, is eminently historical. It gives the subject its origins as subject, and inserts it as well in a family history.

22. Hugo thought the revolutions of the nineteenth century, particularly the 1848 Revolution, largely in terms of a parody of repetition at work in the French Revolution. At most the hallucinatory can explain the parody of the Revolution by the nineteenth century, parody which, for Hugo, does not constitute a genuine hisorical move. He returns over and over again in his writings on the 1848 Revolution to lament its plagiaristic bent: "O parodistes de 93 . . . Quoi la Terreur parodie! Quoi la guillotine plagiaire! . . . 93 a eu ses hommes, il y a de cela cinquante-cinq ans, et maintenant il aurait ses singes." (*Choses vues:* vol. 2, *1847–48,* 315). What is parodic about 1848 is not the fact that it repeats 1793. Rather it is the fact that it provides the repetition available in the Terror and the guillotine in 1793 with a friendlier face: a prosopopeia conflates mechanical repetition and man, bringing repetition into view in the humanoid, monkey-like features of today's revolutionaries. Both man and knowledge of repetition stand the losers by the conflation.

23. The text can be found as it has been reconstructed by Pierre Albouy in Victor Hugo, *Oeuvres complètes,* vol. 10, ed. Jean Massin (Paris: Club Français du Livre, 1969) 261–287.

24. A reader of Baudelaire's *Tableaux parisiens* cannot help but notice the affinity between this passage and "A une passante" with its "jambe de statue," its hurricane's eye, etc.

25. Victor Hugo, *Notre-Dame de Paris,* in *Oeuvres complètes,* vol. 4, ed. Jean Massin (Paris: Club Français du Livre, 1967) 100.

▼ KEVIN NEWMARK ▼

Nietzsche, Deconstruction, and the Truth of History

THERE IS A LOT OF TALK these days about values. Especially in the context of higher education, there is a widespread belief that a moment of real crisis is upon us and that this crisis within the university goes hand and hand with or is even the necessary reflection of a wider crisis of values. Hence the shrillness of the debates now taking place, both inside and beyond the university walls, about the desirability of core curricula, the inviolability of a canonical approach to cultural artifacts, the centrality of the principles and history of Western civilization for today's undergraduate programs in the humanities.[1] In each case the question tends to be thematized as a contest or agon in which the defenders of longstanding cultural values and the familiar modes of evaluation that go along with them are pitted against a confusing array of attackers whose sole point of agreement seems to be the individual and collective wish to undermine all established values and institutions, including the values of meaning, knowledge, and understanding on which the university itself is founded and can be maintained. Of course, when the debate is set up in such a lopsided and theatrical fashion it becomes all too easy to denounce and deride the so-called "attackers" for any number of sound reasons, including their alleged confusionism, self-indulgency, immoralism, or, and especially, the logical self-contradiction at the heart of such a project. For what would be more self-contradictory than to try to establish the aim to undermine all values as a (supreme) value in its own right?

Before taking a stand on one side or the other in the current debates, it

From [New School of Social Research] *Graduate Faculty Philosophy Journal* 15.2 (1991): 161–189. Reprinted by permission of the Editors.

might be more valuable to step back, for just a moment, and to consider what happens when the entire issue is replaced within a slightly different context. For, in truth, there is little hope for a genuine discussion where the temptation is nearly always overwhelming to decide—quickly, effortlessly, perhaps even precipitously—in favor of those who quite simply "have" values over those who clearly do not, or at least who do not clearly exhibit and valorize them at the expense of all others. Friedrich Nietzsche, who in one guise or another is often identified as the most guilty culprit in this tug of war over values, is also the one who tirelessly reminds us that the question of values is first and foremost precisely that, a genuine *question*. And as a question, any given system of values—its origins and effects in particular—has to be critically examined and interrogated before we can reasonably expect to cast our relationship to it in terms of such dramatically opposed roles as friend or foe. For values, unlike flowers or trees, rocks or birds, are never simply given; they must be produced or at the very least revealed, and as such they are always open to the rigor of philosophical debate and critique. As Nietzsche says in the preface to his study on the genealogy of moral values: "One has taken the *value* of these 'values' as given, as factual, as beyond all question. . . . Let us pronounce this new requirement: we are in need of a critique of moral values, the value of these values must itself be *called into question* for once."[2] While it would be naive or foolish to question the legitimacy of a rock or a tree to exist, this same question becomes a philosophical necessity for all values, and in fact it would be difficult to conceive of the operation of the secular university apart from its mission to ensure that such questioning be initiated and maintained—even in the face of an opposite tendency toward complacency and inertia.

What Nietzsche calls for, then, is *not* the annihilation of all values—which would ultimately be just as arbitrary and senseless as their blind acceptance and propagation—but rather their transvaluation or revaluation. This, according to Nietzsche, is the necessary task of putting into question, of weighing and assaying, the composition and status of values as values, since otherwise there can be no valid check against their potential to dissipate into empty slogans or even coercive programs. This is not an easy task, though, especially given the internal resistances such questioning is bound to meet. "Eine Umwertung aller Werte," a transvaluation of all values, Nietzsche says metaphorically in his forward to the *Twilight of the Idols,* is "a question mark so black, so huge, that it casts shadows over whoever goes about setting it up."[3] True to this prediction, moreover, such a huge, black shadow has not failed to attach itself to Nietzsche's own mode of questioning, threatening in the process to blot it out or keep it safely hidden from view. Among all the philosophical inquiries of the West, Nietzsche's examination of the fundamental principles and values of Western metaphysics is perhaps alone in its capacity to generate misrepresentations, scoffing, debunking, and out-of-hand condemnations that bypass entirely the effort of serious analysis, or even direct acquaintance with the text. The Nietzschean categories of the healthy, the strong, the *Übermensch,* and the eternal return of the same, rather than becoming a true source of critical reflection, are still treated most often as straightforward values to be adopted or discarded without further ado. If only on account of this deficiency with respect to our understanding of Nietzsche's own texts, it would be difficult to conceive how any true study of Western civilization, or at least of its canonical texts of philosophy and literature, could simply dispense with the obligation, called for by Nietzsche from *within* its very own precincts, of posing once again the question of the value of all these common values.

Paradoxically enough, however, whoever dares, like Nietzsche himself, to put these values seriously into question for once runs the risk of being accused and convicted, often without a hearing, of cultural and intellectual, if not political and religious, heresy. Why this should be so is suggested in a very economical way by Paul de Man in an essay entitled "Nietzsche and the Rhetoric of Persuasion."[4] Nietzsche's questioning of the main concepts of Western metaphysics, de Man argues, is difficult to take seriously, is therefore difficult not to resist or ignore entirely, to the precise extent that it intervenes in and tampers with the most volatile of all relationships: the relationship and possible equilibrium between knowledge and power. Starting out from a rather academic interrogation of the value of values, Nietzsche's work ends up by questioning the legitimacy of the actual structures of power in whose shadow the philosopher of knowledge is always obliged to carry out such interrogations. It is at this point, where Nietzsche's philosophical critique of the values of knowledge and power threatens to call into question the conscious exercise of its own powers, de Man suggests, that it is liable to produce reactions of extreme defensiveness. Such reactions may in fact have less to do with these values considered in themselves than with an interested attempt on the part of their appointed representatives to protect themselves from all questioning, and at any cost.

Now what is particularly relevant in the present context—epistemological as well as institutional—is that de Man himself refers to Nietzsche's mode of interrogating the value of all values and to the ensuing complications introduced by this questioning into the relations between knowledge and power as a kind of *deconstruction.* Analyzing a posthumous fragment that has as its subject the principle of noncontradiction and identity, which he also calls "the most fundamental 'value' of all," de Man locates an initial polarity and valorization in Nietzsche between the active performance of a deed and the passive truth of a cognition. Since, de Man argues, an extended reading of Nietzsche's text eventually discloses the instability of even this fundamental polarity, we must be willing to consder Nietzsche's writing as the place where the "possibility of 'doing' is as manifestly being *deconstructed* as the identity principle, the ground of knowledge, is being *put in question*" (126, emphasis added). If we follow this brief hint by de Man that "deconstruction" can be another name for the Nietzschean operation of putting values into question—especially the distinction and valorization of "doing" and "knowing"—this is not just because it seems to offer a key for understanding this overused underexamined term. No, it is for the much more practical and verifiable reason that the texts of "deconstruction"—that is, those signed by Jacques Derrida, Paul de Man, and others as well—now function regularly and systematically as the target of the same kind of "black shadow" that has befallen the question marks inscribed in Nietzsche's own text. For there is no more common response to the questionings of deconstruction than the attempt to silence it by assigning it the value of an antivalue whose alleged "nihilism," "irrationalism," or "meaninglessness" would relieve us of any further obligation to take it seriously, except perhaps to defend ourselves against it categorically. But what would happen if, for once, we did not immediately allow the philosophical necessity of asking questions to be engulfed in the shadows of unquestioned assumptions and values, if we actually made an effort to bring the questions of Nietzsche and of deconstruction out into the light of a truly open debate?

▼ ▲ ▼

"Deconstruction," then, following up on de Man's reference to Nietzsche, is one name among others for a certain mode of questioning, and this mode of questioning puts to the test and rearticulates our most familiar values as well as the expectations that necessarily go along with them. Not just any old expectations, of course—and this, perhaps, is the first source of possible misunderstandings. Say, someone has been invited to contribute an essay on Nietzsche and does not write it, or writes only about the most topical of matters, or writes about Nietzsche in only the most occasional and superficial of ways; that may test a certain kind of expectation, but it would have little or nothing to do with deconstruction as it is being understood here. For that kind of surprise to one's expectations would simply be gratuitous or, if you will, perverse or even fraudulently dishonest. Rather than putting something to the test, this kind of surprise would in fact close down the possibility of truly testing anything whatsoever—except perhaps the patience of whoever would continue to read such an exercise in frustration. No, we are talking about a mode of questioning that tests our expectations and values by subjecting the knowledge from which they have been derived to critical analysis. For we only expect certain effects to follow from our systems of value and evaluation because we think we have, or can eventually have, sound knowledge about them. There can be no system of values, much less a transvaluation of values, that does not imply at the very least a necessary process of cognition, no matter how provisional or problematical.

The kind of questioning we are talking about therefore tests our expectations by carefully following or retracing all the steps of an actual process of knowing, understanding, and evaluating the values that have been established and continue to be operable in any given context. Very often it happens, with de Man or Derrida, that the context in which the questioning of these values takes place has already been determined as being "philosophical" or "literary," but this is not always the case. Nor is it always the case that our very expectations about what constitutes, or limits, the philosophical or literary context in contradistinction to others—like the psychological and the social, that is, political—would be left unchallenged by such questioning.

At any rate, here is the main stumbling block for anyone who would write on Nietzsche or the various deconstructions that can be related to his writings through analysis: because deconstruction names this mode of questioning, because it designates only this operation of actually putting to the test and rearticulating what we understand (or thought we understood) about a particular text and the values associated with and derived from it, it is very difficult, if not strictly impossible, to *describe* deconstruction itself as if it were simply this or that identity or essence—a body of beliefs or values, a method, a system, what have you, that we could then understand outside the specific activity of just such testing. The problem is, how give a description that could adequately comprehend what names only the necessary work of testing and renewing the limits of all understanding—how describe such work, that is, without at the same time irremediably betraying that work? And, contrary to another common misunderstanding, the difficulty of these questions is by no means an invitation to provide the name with any meaning (or non-meaning) that one chooses. As a question about and determined by the specific limits of knowledge, deconstruction resists simple affirmations in a way that is itself not simply describable, since such descriptions themselves always function according to unquestioned principles of understanding and knowledge. This problem, and the literal efficacy with which it is confronted, become in turn the measure of any text's relation to the questioning of cognitive expectations and values that is named by the term, deconstruction. No description, account, or critique that economizes on this stumbling block can be said to have any genuine contact with deconstruction or Nietzsche, or with a good many other texts for that matter, since it can always be shown to have replaced the actual operation of such questioning with an ideal value—no matter how negative such evaluations tend to be—that would itself have to be challenged by this very questioning.

Deconstruction, it could be argued, ceases to be deconstruction the moment it ceases "working" on a particular understanding and starts "describing"—or being described as—what its work has accomplished or understood, or, more often than not, what it has thus far failed to understand and accomplish. In other words, there is no sabbath, no day of rest, for this kind of questioning: "On the seventh day, God completed all the work he was doing and rested" (Genesis 2:1–2). That is an interesting textual example in its own right and, indeed, the beginning of a very Nietzschean question: What happens to the certitude we have of all our values and knowledge at the precise instant that God himself takes a rest? Can God still be said to be God when he is just resting on that seventh day? It is not absolutely certain, of course, that there is a transcendental principle, like God, at the origin of the world and all its activities, but it is guaranteed, and not only by the Bible, that if there was once a transcendental principle it did rest, and this one day of rest was substantial enough to prolong its effects right up to the present day. That is why, according to Nietzsche, certain kinds of questions cannot themselves be put to rest once and for all. Kierkegaard, who, at least in this respect, is rather close to Nietzsche, says pretty much the same thing when he insists that "in the world of spirit," by which he means only that world of (Hegelian) understanding and its limits we have been talking about, "in the world of spirit, only the one who *works* gets bread."[5] No bread, no deconstruction, then, no Nietzsche or Kierkegaard, without working for it, and that means getting involved with it, doing it, giving examples of its work rather than just rehashing mere descriptions of it from afar. Such descriptions always bypass the actual work by keeping it at a safe distance and by refusing to test the limits of its own presuppositions and understanding. Deconstruction, like Kierkegaard, who in this respect is also a lot like Marx, insists on the necessity of *labor,* of work. Whenever it stops working and starts to rest by simply describing what its work consists or results in, then it is no longer deconstruction, much less Kierkegaard, Nietzsche, or Marx. It is what Kierkegaard called speculation and what Marx called ideology; that is, it becomes the neccessary object of critical analysis as well as its constant temptation.

So mere description, no matter what the level of its analytic precision or pretensions, is not deconstruction. But, one might now be tempted to ask, where is the originality in that particular restriction? Is this peculiarity not a characteristic of any genuine activity—physical as well as intellectual? Is a description of baseball an actual game of baseball, for instance? Or is a description of a grape a true grape? Or a description of mathematical computation a genuine computation? And isn't it helpful or even necessary sometimes to describe what baseball is—especially if you're wondering whether you may one day want to play or not? The trouble is, however, that "deconstruction," as has just been noted, names a mode of testing whose very object of interrogation turns out to be, or at least to include, the cognitive mode of "description" itself—and this complication is no longer simply true of baseball or of any other empirical or intellectual activity as such, especially the mathematical and physical sciences. Deconstruction always asks what kind of knowledge mere description is capable of providing us with. "Description," as a certain mode of affirmation, as a certain assurance about "knowing" or understanding certain things once and for all, is itself always implicated—and implicated as a question or a problem and not as a certainty—whenever something like the questioning of "deconstruction" is at issue. Unlike the example of baseball or even mathematics, then, a description of "deconstruction" is not just *not* deconstruction, it is an ouright resistance to and a refusal of deconstruction, and from the very beginning. Which is not to say that such a resistance and refusal is itself once and for all avoidable—since what have I been doing here if not *describing* the predicament to which all descriptions of Nietzsche and other deconstructions necessarily fall prey? But then that does not mean that *all* we can do is resist and refuse the necessary questioning of our own assumptions and values, that *all* we can do is describe, either.

Any text that has a relation to deconstruction—and no text, no matter what its overt or implicit stance, is excluded in principle from having such a relation—will at some point have to confront the problem of cognitive description as well as the challenge of somehow going beyond it. What is of interest here, as always, is not which texts happen to display the rather contingent banner—or, rather, stigma—of "deconstruction," but rather, how specific texts actually manage to put our expectations and their related values to a genuine test. In the case of those texts now going by the name "deconstruction," of course, this means putting to the test whatever values and expectations have themselves come to be associated with this term in the various contexts in which it today continues to operate and produce effects. There can be no contact whatsoever with deconstruction, much less a refutation, neutralization, or deconstruction of deconstruction, without taking the trouble—which is also a risk—of giving an actual example of its activity as well. In order to assess the "value" of Nietzsche's transvaluation of all values or of other deconstructions, then, it would first be necessary to show it "at work" or "in action," and this is not exactly the same thing as simply understanding it, explaining it, or evaluating it. To put Nietzsche or related deconstructions in question is first of all to read the specificity of the question marks that are actually inscribed in their texts. This also means that this particular essay can put the relation between Nietzsche and other deconstructions to the test only on condition of the following requirements: to describe *and* to put to work deconstruction as this enigmatic relation between describing— which seems inevitable if you ever want to "know" anything—and an activity that would no longer simply be describing—which seems necessary if you ever want to "do" something. Deconstruction names an operation that—because it always takes place between those typically Nietzschean poles of "knowing" and "doing"—always has to do, fundamentally and inescapably, with the categories of "truth" and "history."

In definitional terms, such a description may already come as something of a surprise to whatever expectations we bring to the name of deconstruction: Deconstruction is the enigmatic relation between truth and history. Or rather, since it tests the limits of knowledge and power, we could say that this kind of questioning has as its object the truth of history, the truth that actually does happen in preference to the one that is merely believed or described or promised.[6] Deconstruction, it could be argued, it not just philosophy, or literature, or theology, political science, psychoanalysis, history, or any other cognitive field of inquiry, but rather the critical analysis of what truly happens in all of them. This, it must be pointed out immediately, is by no means to privilege "deconstruction" as a particular name, to say that it and it alone is truth and history and that all else somehow misses the point or is inferior to it. No, it is merely to give a name to this operation of putting to the test that is made philosophically necessary whenever values like "truth" and "history," or "knowledge" and "power" are at issue, as they always are. What would seriously miss the point, on the contrary, would be to believe that deconstruction somehow tries to privilege itself in naming the truth of history—for in that case it might just as well call itself pure ideology from the start. There can be many names for the truth of history, provided only, of course, that one knows how to put them to the test as well.

But what about language, after all? Isn't that important for deconstruction, too? Yes. Is language not so important, in fact, that deconstruction can safely be identified with the outrageous claim that absolutely everything, including the truth of history, can simply be reduced to what is often derisively referred to as a "free play of language?" Not so fast, and then not quite. If deconstruction pays a considerable amount of attention to language this is not because it subscribes to the mindless or self-interested view that the truth of history is a mere fiction or myth that can be produced and manipulated at will. It is because "language"—and this term, as we now know, can be understood in a very extensive way—because language, of all the "things" that exist in the world, is the one in which it is always possible to notice, in which it is very difficult to ignore or not to notice, the strange relationship and potential gap that always holds between describing and doing, between modes of knowledge and action, between truth and history. A text—Hegel's *Phenomenology* or Rousseau's *Autobiography,* Marx's *Capital* or Proust's *Recherche, The Declaration of Independence* or Baudelaire's poem "Correspondances"—is made up of a language of description that can be analyzed for its logical or formal consistency and a language of action that can have historical effects by leaving material traces on the world. The "play" of language referred to by Derrida and others is a play in this sense, and therefore it can in no way be identified with mere frivolity. It is rather a term for the extremely serious recognition that the space available for movement between any given text's formal coherence and referential force, or between its truth and history, always outstrips the possibility of definitive calculation, and that it therefore acquires a dimension of historical and cognitive openness that always remains to be determined anew. And it is this play of language, aptly characterized by Jacques Derrida as a play between force and signification, that makes it necessary to *read* texts in the fullest sense of the term. A text like David Lehman's *Signs of the Times: Deconstruction and the Fall of Paul de Man,* for example.

This book by David Lehman is not a book that could itself easily be called an example of "deconstruction" in any legitimate sense. And there is very little or nothing at all to be learned about deconstruction by reading it, though that is certainly not a reason for recommending that it not be read. On the contrary, only by reading it with care would it be possible to learn firsthand about Lehman's antiintellectual attitude and the actual historical effects he is aiming for on colleges and universities all over the United States. Reading Lehman's book is an important task today because (1) as a book that responds to and nourishes certain ideas that are very much "in the air" these days it is "historical" in the most topical of senses, (2) as a book that promises to inform readers about deconstruction it should contain a certain dimension of purely descriptive "truth" that can be measured in more or less precise ways, and (3) as a good example of just what deconstruction is not, that is, as a book that is calculated to be serious about truth and history in only the most shortsighted and self-serving, that is to say, most terroristic manner conceivable, *Signs of the*

Times is itself, and for the time being, a necessary object of critical analysis and interrogation.[7]

First, let us ask about the descriptive truth of the book. On page 21, after rehearsing a broad sampling of the ways the word "deconstruction" is now more or less casually used within the American vernacular, Lehman stops short to ask a necessary question: "What *is* deconstruction?" Naturally, this should be a key moment in any attempt to describe with precision an operation, like that of deconstruction, that is exceedingly complex both in its relation to existing modes of thought and analysis and to any claim of absolute originality. One of the obstacles to describing just what deconstruction is, then, consists in its own prudence with respect to employing the definitional logic of possible entities that is assumed or provided by other cognitive disciplines. One cannot therefore simply ask, "What *is* deconstruction?" without taking the time to reflect, even if it is just a little bit, on the formal and logical presuppositions implied by the very question, "What is?" Even, or especially, Socrates, whose wise ignorance in these matters stands at the foundation of western thought, understood this much in his own way by tirelessly employing the question "What is?" to interrogate exactly what he could know for sure about anything. Be that as it may, when David Lehman responds to the definitional question of deconstruction for the first time in this book, he does so not by quoting or commenting Jacques Derrida, who coined the term for reading texts, or Paul de Man, whose "fall" Lehman is supposed to be charting, but by quoting an opinion piece by one Michael O'Brien that was published some years back in the pages of the *Chronicle of Higher Education:* "For deconstructionists," Lehman repeats, "the world is made up of empty rooms, with impenetrable walls and no doors, in which individual minds are bent upon reading texts with a slight smile" (21–22). The only thing worthy of note here, I'm afraid, is the dangling preposition that makes it unclear whether it is the texts themselves, rather than the so-called "deconstructionists," that would be "smiling" in this definition.

At this point it should already be asked, with or without a slight smile of one's own: is that a description to be recirculated by a serious intellectual study as a possible description for a complex intellectual and institutional phenomenon? How could we even begin to measure the "truth" of such a descriptive definition? Do the other examples of Lehman's descriptions—of the work of Paul de Man, of Jacques Derrida, of Saussure, and others—do anything to offset in any substantial way the derisive frivolity of this first definition of deconstruction?

These are some of the questions that any thorough study of Lehman's book should examine and attempt to answer with care. The overall tendency of the book, in any case, is to describe its object of study—the alleged "doctrine" of deconstruction and the allegedly mindless "dogmatists" who adhere to it—in such a way as to motivate the following summation, which is both very angry and flamboyant: "The impulse of deconstruction is profoundly inimical to art (which it subordinates to theory), to biography and history (whose relevance it denies), to conventional methods of critical analysis (which it considers retrograde), and to any philosophy of action (since existential choices are always transmuted into irresolvable linguistic predicaments)" (132). If, as any scrupulous reading of the texts of Paul de Man, Jacques Derrida, and others would easily demonstrate, every one of these claims is either completely wrongheaded or at the very least reductively and tendentiously overstated, then it becomes necessary to wonder about the reasons for such misleading and hyperbolical descriptions of deconstruction and of those who sign its texts. This, of course, is where the question of history arises. For if the purely descriptive affirmations of Lehman can be shown to be grossly untrue by putting them side by side with the texts they are purportedly about, then there is every reason to consider these affirmations less for the logical truth of what they "say" than for the performative force of what they "do," or would have us "do" after reading them. That is, all of Lehman's descriptions of deconstruction, whatever their truth—or rather lack of truth—are calculated to produce a very specific effect, to make us act, to make us participate in history by acting upon it. What historical role would such a book have us play?

In what is undoubtedly one of the most important—and questionable—moments of his exposition, Lehman affirms, "Whatever else it is, deconstruction is a movement, a network of like-minded professors who fiercely promote one another's works and use their institutional power to further the cause. . . . Initiates are rewarded with teaching appointments. . . ." (70). The cause that deconstruction is said to further, which is always interpreted by Lehman as a "doctrine" or "cult" propagated by what is here called a network of like-minded individuals, thus ends up being linked to a "conspiratorial view of the world" that "is pernicious to the precise extent that it acquiesces in the curtailment of human freedom" (267, 268). "Deconstruction," Lehman assures us beyond the necessity of any further questioning, "is a program that promotes a reckless disregard for the truth," and one of the effects of such a "programmatic scepticism" would be to "paralyze the will to act upon our destiny" (267, 77, 110, 111). The appeal to the will to act—an appeal that comes in the face of and as a response to an external threat to paralyze the will and deprive us of our destiny—is unmistakable in this book. This appeal to the will to act of a given community, and in response to the threat posed to its inner coherence and destiny by an invading network of outsiders, by what in this case

Lehman himself calls deconstruction's "persistent assault on our fundamental cultural assumptions" (26), is not new. Its many versions have their own logical constraints and their own history—and in the spirit of a mode of questioning that, unlike Lehman's own, takes the intersection of logical and historical truth seriously, the true logic and history of this particular appeal to the will should be analyzed patiently and as fully as possible.

It leads, when all is said and done, directly to the conclusion of Lehman's book, a conclusion that consists in a remarkable sentence—and this word is to be understood in both its senses, in its descriptive and performative usages, in its grammatical and juridical connotations—a remarkable sentence, then, pronounced by Lehman on that "universe of fierce cabalistic disputation" in which the network of deconstructionists "shrouds itself in cabalistic mysteries and rituals" in order to keep us in "a state of permanent mystification" that, ultimately, "would paralyze the will to act upon our destiny" (27, 55, 111). The intellectual and historical ominousness of such a sentence should be carefully read and interpreted before we allow ourselves simply to carry out its program: "The signs are all around us.... It would be a mistake to think that we cannot by conscious action do anything about them" (268). David Lehman—who especially in this respect is wholly unlike Nietzsche, or Derrida, or de Man—will have said something else quite extraordinary in the penultimate sentence of his book, in the sentence that comes just before he urges us on to conscious action by doing something about those signs that are all around us. He tells us in this book on "deconstruction and the fall of Paul de Man," which is a book that is also called "the signs of the times," that these signs about which he would have us do something, and do something consciously active, by an act of the will, then, these signs of the times "can all be interpreted correctly": "Many of [these signs] are ambiguous, some are confusing, but they can all be interpreted, and intrepeted correctly" (268).

This is a truly amazing affirmation coming as it does just before the incitement to action, presumably to save our destiny from those who would paralyze our will for the sake of their own pernicious cabal. For if we put to use even the most elementary of those "conventional methods of critical analysis" to which Lehman claims "deconstruction is profoundly inimical"—which methods, I hasten to add, neither de Man nor Derrida has ever suggested it would be possible or even desirable simply to dispense with—we cannot help but read the subtitle of this book as an apposition of the main title. Deconstruction and the fall of Paul de Man *are* the signs of the times, then, and this means that the signs of the times referred to in the last sentence of the book, the signs that are all around us, soliciting our conscious action, can also be neatly summed up as whatever traces of "deconstruction" have somehow survived the "fall of Paul de Man." And if it is further true—despite any nuances, ambiguities, or even potential confusions and misunderstandings on our part—that all these signs can be interpreted correctly in preparation for doing something about them, then what choice of conscious action are we finally offered by David Lehman? Once we assume that Lehman himself may be correct in interpreting and characterizing precisely these signs of "deconstruction" as signifying a cabalistic network of like-minded individuals whose conspiratorial view of the world would ultimately paralyze the will to act upon our own destiny, what exactly are we supposed to *do* about them? Just what sort of book is it, anyhow, that proposes we not mistake our potential to do something active about those omnipresent "deconstructioninsts" and their enigmatic will to paralyze our will to act? This question, which one should not too quickly or lightly answer for David Lehman or for oneself, contains the following question as well: Do we act consciously about whatever is signified by the name "deconstruction" by reading, analyzing, annotating, and perhaps even contesting in as scrupulous a way as possible the texts associated with it, or by doing something else with its texts and the individuals who write, sign, or even disseminate them?

▼ ▲ ▼

It is time once again to turn to Nietzsche. In the book of fragments called *The Gay Science,* there is a fragment, number 361, that is written under the heading, "On the problem of the actor": "The problem of the actor has troubled me for the longest time. I felt unsure (and sometimes still do) whether it is not only from this angle that one can get at the dangerous concept of the 'artist.' . . ."[8] Now this "concept" of the actor, or artist, also engages philosophical categories of considerable importance, for the questions of truth and history cannot fail to surface whenever the essential character trait of the actor, "dissimulation" (*Verstellung*), is at issue in any serious way. This is because dissimulation, for Nietzsche, is defined by its problematic relation to the disclosure or unveiling of truth, and this process of truth's disclosure, or *aletheia,* at least as it has most often been interpreted and understood on the basis of the canonical texts of western philosophy, is governed both by a logic of adequation and by a temporality of historical development.[9]

But what is perhaps most noteworthy in this fragment on the problem of the actor is not this very respectable and important inquiry into the philosophical relation between truth as the historical process of *aletheia* and a counter power that deflects or dissimulates this truth in what

Nietzsche refers to here as the falsity of appearance. Rather, it is also what is at first sight the fragment's most crudely topical, questionable, and even offensive, feature: at the end of the fragment, after discussing several of the philosophical aspects of artistic "dissimulation," Nietzsche quite simply comes out and names "Jews" and "women" as two particularly remarkable contemporary examples of accomplished "actors." Because of the seriousness of the issues involved here, the concluding passage of the fragment deserves citation in full:

> As for the *Jews,* the people who possess the art of adaptability par excellence, this train of thought suggests immediately that one might see them virtually as a world-historical arrangement for the production of actors, a veritable breeding ground for actors. And it really is high time to ask: What good actor today is *not*—a Jew? The Jew as a born "man of letters," as the true master of the European press, also exercises his power by virtue of his histrionic gifts; for the man of letters is essentially an actor—he plays the "expert," the "specialist."—Finally, *women.* Reflect on the whole history of women: do they not *have* to be first and above all actresses? Listen to the physicians who have hypnotized women; finally, love them—let yourself be "hypnotized" by them! What is always the end result? That they "give themselves out" as something else even when they—give themselves up [*Dass sie "sich geben," selbst noch, wenn sie—sich geben*]. . . . *Woman is so artistic.* . . . *(317)*

The fact is, though—and beyond or independently of the unquestionably justified sense of distress and even outrage we feel in registering the impact of these lines—a closer look at the *formal* organization of the fragment reveals a problem of a slightly different, yet not totally unrelated, order. For the initial problem of the actor, the problematic deflection of truth in falsehood necessarily introduced into the discussion by the conceptual potential to "dissimulate," is itself somehow displaced or deflected midway through the philosophical analysis to become a none-too-rigorous social history of "adaptability." This new deflection—which literalizes the terms of a general philosophical dilemma by replacing them with highly charged anthropological examples of self-preservation in the face of threatening circumstances—can be quite precisely located. It occurs in Nietzsche's text at the point where the purely aesthetic and nonutilitarian capacity to dissimulate the category of truth is illustrated in his writing with a reference to the overdeveloped ability of actual "Jews" and "women" to adapt themselves to any situation whatsoever by dissimulating the truth of their own essence.

The "problem of the actor," then, which is in a certain sense the fragment's own title, can now be taken to refer not only to the theoretical problem of truth's dissimulation that Nietzsche is himself describing, but also to the additional problem this particular fragment occasions or produces in a very literal way for any reading and understanding of such a description. For how can we as readers explain the fact that an epistemological examination of the problem of the "actor" swerves, without any apparent reason of justification, away from its original philosophical object of inquiry and turns into a rather shabby historical description, or even indictment, of "Jews" and "women"? Moreover, it could not be argued that a system of simple parallels and equivalences is at work between the two parts of the fragment, since the logical problem of truth and falsehood that is exemplified conceptually by the art of "acting" is in no way adequate to explain the kinds of historical adaptability required of given individuals for their survival in society; much less could it, by itself, help us understand why these specific character traits—posing, deceiving, manipulating—are allotted here in an insulting and derogatory fashion to all Jews and women. Of course, we know today, as if by instinct, that we will not have read Nietzsche adequately until we can account for the enigmatic place occupied in his writings—their analytical descriptions as well as in their historical effects—by Jews and women. But this issue is brought home to us in a much more pragmatic mode by this particular fragment: we will not even be able to begin reading the text until we try to account for the way this tension is in fact played out in the perplexing relation articulated here between the beginning of the fragment, which is about the logical problem of the actor, and the end, which inexplicably deflects this problem by referring it to the historical existence of actual Jews and women.

At any rate, it is not entirely by accident that the question of Nietzsche's relation to deconstruction finds itself embroiled in this way with the question of Jews and women. One reason for this, though perhaps not the only or even the most essential one, is that the question of deconstruction, as long as it will be linked to the name of Paul de Man, will necessarily be marked in some way by his involvement as a cultural correspondent for almost two years with a Belgian newspaper, *Le Soir,* that continued to function under and lend aid to the—anti-Semitic, but also misogynistic—authority of the Nazi occupation forces.[10] It is true that this knowledge, which came to light only in 1987, can have the explosive effect of a bomb on the work of Paul de Man and deconstruction. That is, such knowledge can easily turn into the conscious action of reducing all the texts associated with these names to nothingness; either by closing them up for good, or, what would amount to almost the same thing, by turning them into invisible but unshakable stand-ins for this one, true, historical knowledge. For if we know all we need to know about the truth and history of Paul de Man and deconstruction by knowing about this particular link between them and both Nazism and the nihilistic ideology tributary to it, then what possible need have we to continue bothering ourselves about Paul de Man and other deconstructions by reading and discussing them? But can the kind of knowledge that would act, as in this case, consciously or not, like a bomb of pure destruction and annihilation still be said to be either true or historical in any genuine sense?

In this unlikeliest of places, where the truth of actual historical knowledge threatens to explode with the self-destructive violence of a bomb, the French poet and theoretician, Stéphane Mallarmé, has something valuable to teach us. In his famous lecture on recent aesthetic developments in France, *La musique et les lettres,* which he delivered at Oxford in 1894, Mallarmé suddenly interrupts his reflections on music and poetry to ask about the very different kinds of relations that are possible in the world between literature and politics.[11] At issue for Mallarmé are two symmetrically related phenomena occurring recently in the popular press, and together he sees them posing a potential threat to the integrity of both literature and politics. On the one hand, Mallarmé singles out for attention the publication and reception of Max Nordau's *Entartung* (651–652). This book—a vulgar diatribe denouncing *fin-de-siècle* art, especially in France, as the "graphomaniacal" symptom of a general pattern of social and cultural "degeneration"—is of concern to Mallarmé only because of the potential danger inherent in the considerable popularity it enjoyed for a time in both Germany and France.[12] Books like this are politically explosive, according to Mallarmé, not because of what they say, but because whatever they say, including in the case of *Entartung* the most far-fetched, libellous, and misinformed provocations, can always be passed off and begin to function aberrantly as the objective and irrefutable truth of scientific knowledge. The real problem with such "legends" and "melodramas," Mallarmé suggests, is not that they are fictions with no claim to scientific standards of truth, but rather that they do not know, or have allowed themselves to forget, that they are such fictions.

On the other hand, Mallarmé refers to the accusatory suspicion, current in Paris newspapers of the early nineties, that a direct link could be made between the radical aesthetic theories of certain avant-garde literary movements and the revolutionary acts of political violence committed by contemporary anarchists (652). Using the occasion of a literal bomb that was exploded in the Chambre des Députés on December 9, 1893, by an anarchist named August Vaillant, Mallarmé makes several key points about his own, subtly differentiated, thinking of the relation between writing, violence, history, and truth. First of all, Mallarmé says in no uncertain terms, the light that emanates from a literal bomb is by no means the same kind of light that emanates from the pages of a real book, and any insinuation to the contrary is an insult to both social community and literary activity. For the kind of light that illuminates a bomb of pure destruction, which also always has the disadvantage of injuring innocent bystanders, is all too brief to teach us anything, and therefore this kind of self-obliterating light can result only in a display of what Mallarmé calls "definitive incomprehension." In other words, we could never truly understand what we simply destroy and thereby definitively erase from history and the kind of critical light that alone can help to reflect and extend all its truths. In the second place, according to Mallarmé, and as a consequence of this constant risk of relapsing into incomprehension, the only truly effective way to participate in history would be by means of what he calls a book whose light (*éblouissements*), or truth, would not end in one, brief, and all-consuming flash. Such a written light, Mallarmé suggests, could only result from the highly mediated, and constantly renewed illumination, or textual explosion, of all the so-called facts of history, the journalistic *faits divers* that name and describe the disparate events of everyday life, though without subjecting them to genuine critical analysis. In Mallarmé's own words, which are themselves already so explosively mediated that they constantly require the readjustment and paraphrase of further exegesis: "I am delighted that there are some writers who remain off on the side to offend the *fait divers:* their very obliqueness thus calls into question, though otherwise than a bomb, those things that, beyond any doubt and at great expense, a capital is best able to furnish as a running commentary of its apotheoses" (652).[13] Whatever particular aims or issues Mallarmé sees as comprising the critical horizon of the writer, this much should be clear: authentically critical writing cannot, like a literal bomb, simply wipe out its object of analysis once and for all; nor can it, like the ordinary reporting, or *faits divers,* it must constantly call into question, merely announce and describe it.

What this task of critical vigilance, called for a century ago by Mallarmé, would ultimately consist in with respect to the actual *fait divers* of Paul de Man's wartime journalism for *Le Soir* is not itself easy to describe once and for all. Though it would most certainly *not* consist in a simple reduction of all of de Man's other writings, as well as the writings of other deconstructions, including the texts of Nietzsche referred to earlier, to the same dubious status as this one, certifiably true, historical fact. No, Mallarmé warns us that the truth of any given historical *fait divers,* as event and as mere description or report of events, must always be handled carefully, must in fact become the object of critical questioning in its own right, for such truth itself always has the potential to explode as a mere bomb of destruction, forever blotting out in definitive incomprehension precisely what it was meant to reveal and thus to preserve in a historical act of understanding.

Martin Heidegger, who, as the saying goes, may have had his reasons, said something remarkably similar to Mallarmé in a reflection on the truth of history that dates from 1935: "Every report or description [Bericht] about the past, in other words, about the steps leading up to the question . . . is concerned with what lies at rest; this kind of historical report [diese Art des historischen Berichts] is an explicit laying to rest of history [eine ausdrückliche Stillegung der Geschichte]—whereas history is on the contrary a happening [ein Geschehen]. We ask historically when we ask what is still happening, even when, to all appearances, something belongs to the past."[14] Heidegger tinkers here, as elsewhere, with the crucial distinction that is disclosed in German between the words *Historia* and *Geschichte*—history as a report or description of what has happened, and history as the actual event that must happen in its own right. The truth of history, then, is itself put into movement (*Bewegung*) when we interrogate such words, for history, Heidegger reminds us, can always be determined in at least two very different, and perhaps incompatible ways—as descriptive knowledge and as actual occurrence. Heidegger goes on to call this particular movement he is talking about, which is always waiting to take place between the two modes of history, "uncanny." In fact, Heidegger says that such a movement of history, arrested for the time being between the words and concepts of *Historia* and *Geschichte,* is "uncannier" (*unheimlicher*) than what we ordinarily call movement itself (34). Heidegger seems here, then, though in a very enigmatic way, to be asking about a kind of history that would consist in somehow moving the truth that is merely at rest in description toward a true occurrence.

Now before dismissing this uncanny idea of Heidegger's as a merely self-interested attempt to lay certain aspects of his own past to rest, let us also note that he does suggest here that simple reports about the past are not only inevitable, they are also indispensable insofar as they do provide the preliminaries (*Vorstufen*) for true historical questioning. There is, therefore, no question of hiding or laying to rest, much less condoning or excusing the simple fact of Heidegger's affiliation with the Nazi party of de Man's writing for a collaborationist newspaper. These are condemnable acts and one should have no difficulty in condemning them. But the risk, according to Heidegger as well as Mallarmé, is that a mere report or description—or condemnation or condonation for that matter—stops short because it can serve ultimately to remove us from another kind of necessary historical activity by remaining stuck in the affffirmations of mere commonplace. "If we do not want simply to parrot opinion," Heidegger warns us in his essay, "but would rather grasp what we ourselves are saying and usually mean, then we are immediately caught in a veritable maelstrom of questions" (36). Only by asking about the kind of truth that could *still* be happpening in every historical event, including all the texts now signed by Mallarmé, Heidegger, and de Man, would it be possible to avoid falsifying the truth of their historical occurrence in empty formulae. Each of these texts, of course, each of these signatures, has its own specificity, and only a detailed description and analysis of individual texts would be able to participate historically in the truth that may still be happening in any one of them. Some shorthand names for this participation in a historical truth that can only occur beyond the preliminaries or mere description—names as potentially misleading as they are economical, moreover—appear in Mallarmé's text as "writing," in Heidegger's as "questioning," or in de Man's as "reading." These names are not all the same for all three writers—and this could make an enormous difference in many different and important respects—nor are they the same in every one of each writer's texts. In ways specific to each writer and to any given text, though, they all begin to name that enigmatic relation between truth as description and truth as occurrence, between description and event, or between truth and history that is at issue for all of us.

At this point, of course, it becomes necessary to ask about how all that has just been said can be related to those names so prominently inscribed and displayed in Nietzsche's text on the actor: the "Jews" and "women" with which fragment 361 of *The Gay Science* seems to come to a grinding halt. But is it really still necessary to ask about what is resting, like a bomb, in the descriptions Nietzsche gives of those particular names? Do we not already know fully well, and with all the historical precision of its disastrous consequences, just how such descriptions must finally end up? But isn't it precisely because this knowledge and this history is still itself always in danger of disappearing in a mere catalogue of platitudes that can be thoughtlessly repeated and trotted out to justify the most aberrant intellectual and political behavior, that we remain obligated to ask once again, patiently, seriously, how much we actually know, once and for all, about the truth of our own history?

This question about repetition and history, about knowledge and thoughtlessness, about the necessity to continue asking questions even in the face of what we think we already know in order, finally, to produce a future for history itself, is treated by Nietzsche under the universally recognized and barely understood terms of the "eternal recurrence." The eternal return, according to Nietzsche, not only names the riddle of understanding how any truly historical moment must always confront the simultaneous challenge of overcoming an infinite past and opening up an infinite future, it names in addition the threat posed to true knowledge by the recurrent possibility of its relapse into empty chatter.[15] In the thought of the eternal return, Nietzsche writes in a fragment coming at the end of the fourth book of *The Gay Science,* lies the "greatest weight." But this greatest of weights, Nietzsche goes on to suggest, can be brought to bear on every single thing—every thought about truth and every historical action—only by putting it in the form of a question that also contains the potential to transform whatever it touches: "If this thought were to acquire power over you, it would transform you as you are and perhaps even crush you; the question, for each and every thing, 'do you want this again and again countless times,' would lie as the greatest weight on all your conduct!" (274). The weight of this thought, which Nietzsche also calls a "riddle," is itself liable to become an enormous burden for every understanding of history: for how could it be that by unremittingly returning to this question of the eternal return it would become possible to exert enough pressure on the usual patterns of our conduct to crush and transform the cycle of what otherwise always threatens to remain an even more vicious recurrence of the same beliefs and behavior?

We must return, then, to the bomb, or the stick of dynamite, lying in wait for us in Nietzsche's text, for it is only through tirelessly coming back to interrogate the complex nature of its actual explosive device that we could ever effectively register what may still be happening there historically, or may be waiting to happen there, and perhaps this time as a less familiar truth than the bomb of pure obliteration, or nihilism, that we so readily take for granted in all his texts. What is happening, for instance, not in the straightforward description of Jews and women easily readable at the end of the fragment, but rather what is happening in the relation Nietzsche's text articulates—and not just in this particular fragment—between the actor, or the artist, and the Jews and women? How, exactly, does the writing of the fragment prepare for and produce the naming of the Jews and women as actual historical examples of the more general epistemological problem raised by the dissimulation of truth? Asking the question in this way doesn't necessarily change anything at all, of course. In fact, the descriptions we have before us remain exactly the same, and they can still be read—descriptively and historically—to mean the same things we are mostly already familiar with. But then, on the other hand, this is not necessarily the way things have to turn out, either. It is true that historical things happen in ways we do not necessarily expect or control. And when it is a question of reading a text—like this one, for example—this means that we may not yet know all that is already truly happening in it.

If, for instance, we take Nietzsche at his word, we will perhaps not easily forget that the philosophical concept initially interrogated in this fragment is not simply a neutral or inert entity, but is itself inherently *dangerous:* "The problem of the actor has troubled me for the longest time; I felt uncertain (and sometimes still do) whether it was not only from this angle that one could get at the *dangerous* concept of the 'artist' " (316, emphasis added). The concept of the "artist," then, which first becomes accessible only by way of the art of acting, and which is later to be illustrated in a social context by the Jew—"What good actor is today *not* a Jew?" (317)—is "troubling," Nietzsche warns us. And this troubling aspect of the question is also associated with a subjective mood of "uncertainty" that is further aggravated by the presence of an unspecified "danger." Not the least unsettling thing about this dangerous concept, moreover, is the historical tendency of those who examine it not to take it and its uncertainties seriously enough. The unnamed danger in the concept is thus liable to become all the more serious and threatening since it is most often not even recognized *as* a danger: "I felt uncertain (and sometimes still do) whether it was not only in this way that one could get at the dangerous concept of the 'artist'—a concept that has so far been treated with unpardonable good-naturedness [mit unverzeihlicher Gutmütigkeit]." Just what is so dangerous about this concept of dissimulation that every relaxation of critical judgment toward it represents for Nietzsche an inexcusable lapse?

The answer, at least the one Nietzsche gives in this particular fragment, is that this concept involves a power so explosive that it is capable of wiping out the essence of a person's character: "the delight in dissimulation exploding as a power that pushes aside one's so-called 'character,' flooding it and at times *extinguishing* it . . ." (316, emphasis added).[16] Whenever we deal with the concept of the artist, then, we are always dealing with a *power* that threatens to break out (*als Macht herausbrechend*) of the limits assigned to it, and at the risk and peril of whoever seems originally to be the possessor of it. Because every subjective lapse of attention can therefore turn out to be fatal for the very one who undergoes it, none could ever be excused. The dissimulating power of the artist is dangerous, Nietzsche tells us, because it is in this way *excessively* "adaptable" or "flexible." As "an excess [ein Überschuss] of the capacity for all kinds of adaptations, [it] can no longer be satisfied in the service of the most immediate and narrowest utility," and thus it always threatens to eradicate the very "character" of the one it was supposed merely to manifest and preserve.

So far, of course, Nietzsche is merely describing, from the outside as it were, the essential traits of this excessive power to dissimulate that is the hallmark and the most dangerous risk of the actor. And to the extent that a clear distinction can still be made between the "dissimulator" being described and the philosophical "I" doing the describing, then no lapse of attention on the part of the text about dissimulation and its concomitant danger—loss of self or of its determinable needs and aims—need be considered or suspected. The claim to truth held out by the philosophical critique of the loss of essence or truth entailed in the aesthetic power to dissimulate is not therefore, at least at first, in question in this text by Nietzsche. But Nietzsche does not stop there, of course, for he goes on to add one more question to the inquiry, and this is decisive for any genuine reading and understanding of what will happen in the rest of the fragment: "perhaps all this describes not *only* the actor's essence? [alles das ist vielleicht nicht *nur* der Schauspieler an sich]?" (316). Is there a place, we must now ask in our turn as readers, where Nietzsche's own philosophical inquiry into the problem of the actor runs the risk of dissimulating itself, of a dissimulation so powerful and far-reaching, in fact, that it would threaten its own claim to truth with extinction by exploding beyond the reach of any properly philosophical understanding?

Such a question takes us back to the excess of "adaptability" Nietzsche associates with the artistic power of dissimulation. It is possible to dissimulate an essence only where we suppose there is first of all an essence that could eventually be disclosed, just as the concept of adaptability ordinarily presupposes a content or essence that can then be adapted *to* whatever lies around or beyond it. But Nietzsche's text also exceeds this traditional philosophical model of essence and accident, or interior and exterior, by introducing into his writing the possibility of an *original* power to dissimulate and adapt. What is most excessive in this regard is not simply that the power to adapt can eventually break free of its most immediate needs and desires, but rather that the power to dissimulate is itself conditioned only by a form of adaptability that has from the very beginning escaped the power of anything beyond itself. And this would still be the case even and especially when it managed to reintroduce the concept of a lost essence, whose very needs and desires it thus serves to dissimulate always and again. This particular excess is what Nietzsche refers to in this fragment as an *inner* craving for a role or mask, for an irreducible *Schein* or appearance that has itself no essence beyond it, "das *innere* Verlangen in eine Rolle und Maske, in einen *Schein* hinein" (316, emphasis added). Now this radically "inner" appearance, or *Schein,* so excessive that it can no longer be related back to an essence that would in any way be separable from it, either as its origin or its end, is also described in more detail by Nietzsche in an earlier fragment of the *Gay Science:*

> *The consciousness of appearance.*— . . . I suddenly woke up in the midst of this dream, but only to the consciousness that I am dreaming and that I *must* go on dreaming in order not to perish: as a sleepwalker must go on dreaming in order not to fall. What is 'appearance' for me now! Certainly not the opposite of some essence—what could I say about any essence except to name the attributes of its appearance! Certainly not a dead mask that one could place on an unknown x or remove from it! (116)

To wake up suddenly, then, but only to the consciousness that one is in fact dreaming, this is how Nietzsche describes the necessary outcome of the philosophical critique of appearance, or *Schein*. What could this mean with respect to the strange economy enacted within the fragment on the actor, which leads from the artistic power of dissimulation to the historical restriction of this attribute to Jews and women? First of all, it alerts us to the fact that the "adaptability" at issue in this fragment has very real, if problematic, limits. It may be possible, Nietzsche is warning us, to adapt ourselves to the state of epistemological sleepwalking into which we are plunged by our inability to know for sure anything about the essence of things. But that sudden recognition can it itself do nothing to change the fact that, at least philosophically speaking, we do indeed continue to fall asleep.

And the reason for this, Nietzsche points out, is that the radical falsity of appearance, or *Schein*—which, because it has been deprived of an essential and thus necessary origin and end, is as a consequence absolutely adaptable or flexible (*geschmeidig*) in its first position—tends also to become absolutely resistant or intractable once it assumes any given shape or form. The originary potential for infinite adaptability, Nietzsche's own writing describes and demonstrates, thus eventually hardens into an attribute that "becomes domineering, unreasonable, and intractable [herrisch, unvernünftig, unbändig]" in the long run (316–317). We are now prepared to note that two of the names Nietzsche's writing gives to this enigmatic structure of appearance, at least in this particular fragment, are "Jews" and "women." That is, the names "Jews" and "women" occupy the place in this fragment where the conceptual categories of radical flexibility and radical intractability come together in an impossible way and thus necessarily threaten the philosophical coherency of Nietzsche's own argument about dissimulation. For if, on the one hand, the words "Jews" and "women" can always be used in this fragment to name a generalized power of philosophical dissimulation that, as the fragment itself argues, could never legitimately be identified by reference to any give concrete empirical examples—since in that case it would no longer function *as* "dissimulation"—it is also true that, on the other hand, "Jews" and "women" are themselves proper names that ultimately cannot help but indicate as well as isolate and target actual groups of living human subjects. The philosophical argument, about the possibility of dissimulating the truth, cannot prevent itself from turning into the rhetorical example, and therefore potential error, of attempting to identify with historical and cognitive precision the locus of this truth of dissimulation.[17]

Why this should be so is also exemplified in an economical way within this fragment on philosophical and historical dissimulation. At the key moment in the demonstration, when the turn is being made from philosophical abstraction to historical actuality, Nietzsche makes use for the first time in the fragment of a very particular device, a rhetorical figure that in this case is a metaphor: "Such an instinct [of excessive adaptability] will have developed most easily in families of the lower class, who had to survive under changing pressures and coercions, in deep dependency, who had to cut their coat according to the cloth [welche sich geschmeidig nach ihrer Decke zu strecken hatten]" (316). "To cut one's coat according to the cloth," a mere rhetorical device, then, easy enough to read and understand as properly meaning, "to make the best of things" or "to adapt oneself to the situation at hand," cognitively or practically.

All such figures, of course, infinitely available to the writer of philosophical abstraction and argumentation, are themselves "adaptations" that have in essence no determinate value: for who would be so foolish as to believe, for instance, that Nietzsche is actually writing in this fragment about literal "coats"? The word *coat* here, like the dissimulation of *Schein* of which it is itself an example, is a mere covering, an envelope that in itself is absolutely empty and, therefore, absolutely adaptable to any circumstances whatsoever. But this mere appearance, this empty envelope of a purely adaptable rhetorical "coat," because it too, and by definition, is always capable of exceeding the "deep dependency" in which it originally seemed to function, can always come to lord it over all the other anthropological "instincts" it eventually finds itself surrounded by, whether they be speculative and philosophical, or normative and historical in nature. The rhetorical example, Nietzsche thus warns us—which, like the *Schein* of appearance it illustrates and necessarily dissimulates, is at first neither philosophically reliable nor historically precise—can always, though mistakenly, be taken to command the ultimate meaning of both history and philosophy.

What is excessive and intractable in this kind of adaptability, Nietzsche goes on to write in what is undoubtedly the fragment's most remarkable sentence, "gradually enables [those who possess it] to turn their coat to *every* wind and thus virtually to become a coat [befähigt allmählich, den

Mantel nach *jedem* Winde zu hängen und dadurch fast zum Mantel werdend]."[18] How is it possible to read and understand with any degree of philosophical or historical certainty the proper meaning of *this* "coat" (*Mantel*) that now serves to cover the meaning of Nietzsche's text? The sentence that uses the "coat" as a mere figure, or infinitely adaptable *Schein* with no intrinsic essence, value, or referent of its own, also asserts—simultaneously and thus abusively or impossibly—that this radically dissimulated "coat" is nonetheless in the process of becoming—a literal *coat*. But a coat that in essence is nothing but mere appearance and that, in spite of this, has as well to acquire the value of an actual coat is, in addition and equally necessarily, a cloak of pure deception for whoever would try to put it on or take it off, that is, for the mind that would understand it simply and definitively as either a literal or a figural coat. Nietzsche's own sentence therefore describes and enacts how an originally ungrounded tropic power in philosophical language has no reliable means to stop itself from coming to rest in the equally ungrounded literality of a referential name, or concept. The truth of dissimulation becomes absolutely false the minute it names itself with philosophical rigor, as it cannot fail to do if it is not to remain at the wholly preconscious level of utter confusion and chaos.

Now this particular logical inconsistency, so glaring in the case of the "rhetorical" coat of adaptability, is exactly parallel to the inconsistency that governs the gerneral economy of the entire fragment as it moves from the original philosophical category of dissimulation, or *Schein,* to the social and historical discrimination of actual "Jews" and "women."[19] For, although the logic of the fragment would require it, it is not simply possible for the names "Jews" and "women" in Nietzsche's text to function simultaneously as philosophical example for the radical dissimulation of a *Schein* devoid of essence *and* as straightforward descriptions of socially and historically identifiable human agents. And once we become aware in this way that the first part of the fragment not only describes the dangerous economy or disfigurative power—*die Verstellung als Macht*—of the "mask," or *Schein,* of artistic, that is, *rhetorical* adaptability, but also gives an example of this economy in the excessive figure and proper name of a "coat," it is no longer possible to understand the naming of the Jews and women at the end as a simple description. Or, rather, at this point in the analysis these names must themselves begin to exceed the strict limits of description and cognition that might otherwise be able to circumscribe and contain whatever activities and effects they come at any given moment to designate and stand for.

The excessive adaptability such names require of their eventual identification and meaning now produces a gap, a hole, or a far-reaching interruption, between the first part of the fragment—that describes what it knows to be true philosophically—and the last part—that truly names in spite of what it should already know about the deceptively unreasonable element in all such naming. The fragment is itself fragmented, or exploded, then, and in such a way that its own understanding is no longer easy to contain or control in a simple manner, good-humored or not. This explosion has itself a name, of course, and Nietzsche tells us what it is: "I am no man, I am dynamite."[20] Because it produces a textual, rather than a purely empirical, explosion, though, the dynamite in Nietzsche's text, like the bomb in Mallarmé or de Man moreover, requires the patience and the labor of reading its fragments prior to our deriving any values or actions from them. What would now be inexcusable (*unverzeihlich*), Nietzsche ultimately suggests, is no longer the written explosion that prevents description and naming, or truth as knowledge and truth as occurrence from coming together once and for all without a hitch, for such an explosion has in fact happened textually and therefore belongs irreversibly to history. We have no control whatsoever over the truth of that explosive occurrence, and for the same reason the question of excuses or accusations is no longer fully pertinent or adequate to it. What would be textually and historically inexcusable, though, would be to pretend we could go about our business, the strict business of naming, describing, understanding, evaluating and thus taking conscious action on things and others, as though nothing had taken place to upset—*beunruhigt,* Nietzsche says in the first line of his fragment, that is to say, to disturb and awaken—its day of rest, or sleep.

Notes

1. To a degree that is more or less explicitly pronounced, the belief that a present crisis in higher education can best be resolved by the determined return to traditional values and modes of thinking is shared by the following participants in this debate: Allan Bloom, *The Closing of the American Mind* (New York: Simon and Schuster, 1987); Dinesh D'Souza, *Illiberal Education: The Politics of Race and Sex on Campus* (New York: Free Press, 1991); Donald Kagan, "The Role of the West," *Yale Alumni Magazine,* November, 1990; Roger Kimball, *Tenured Radicals: How Politics Has Corrupted Higher Education* (New York: Harper & Row, 1990); and David Lehman, *Signs of the Times: Deconstruction and the Fall of Paul de Man* (New York: Poseidon Press, 1991). Further references appear in the text.

2. Friedrich Nietzsche, *On the Genealogy of Morals,* in *Basic Writings,* trans. Walter Kaufmann (New York: Random House, 1968), 456, emphasis added, translation modified. Nietzsche's own considerations on the value of higher education—which are neither simple nor straightforward—can be found in *On the Future of Our Educational Institutions,* trans. J. M. Kennedy, in

The Complete Works of Friedrich Nietzsche, vol. 3 (New York: Russell and Russell, 1964).

3. Friedrich Nietzsche, *Twilight of the Idols,* trans. R.J. Hollingdale (London: Penguin, 1968), 21, translation modified.

4. Paul de Man, "The Rhetoric of Persuasion," in *Allegories of Reading* (New Haven: Yale University Press, 1979), 119–131. Further references appear in the text.

5. Søren Kierkegaard, *Fear and Trembling,* trans. Howard V. and Edna H. Hong (Princeton: Princeton University Press, 1983), 27, emphasis added.

6. One of the necessary effects of such a definition would be the interrogation and testing of the ways words like "truth" and "history" have been thus far understood and to what extent these modes of understanding remain adequate to their own historical production and effects. For a concise description of some of the ways "history" is always and necessarily at stake for "deconstruction," see Jean-Luc Nancy's "Our History," *Diacritics* 20 (fall 1990): 96–115.

7. In itself, then, this book has little or nothing whatsoever to recommend it; its "importance" is therefore of extremely limited proportions and will undoubtedly not outlive the next few months. Unlike the texts of Nietzsche, which remain events in their own right, Lehman's book, and others like it, can be of interest to us only for what they might *occasion.* Such writings are aptly described by what Kierkegaard has said about all such "occasions": "The occasion, then, is nothing in and by itself and is something only in relation to that which it occasions, and in relation to that it is actually nothing" (*Either/Or* 1, trans. Howard V. Hong and Edna H. Hong [Princeton: Princeton University Press, 1987, 238]).

8. Friedrich Nietzsche, *The Gay Science,* trans. Walter Kaufmann (New York: Vintage, 1974), 316–317. Further references to this translation, sometimes modified, appear in the text. This fragment is referred to, described, and annotated in an exemplary way by Jacques Derrida in *Epérons: les styles de Nietzsche,* trans. Barbara Harlow (Chicago: The University of Chicago Press, 1978), 66–71. Other pertinent discussions of the fragment can be found in Pierre Klossowski, "Nietzsche, le polythéisme et la parodie," *Un si funeste désir* (Paris: Gallimard, 1963), 216–218; and in Gilles Deleuze, "Platon et le simulacre," in *Logique du sens* (Paris: Minuit, 1969), 292–307.

9. The fullest articulation of the relation of Nietzsche to the western metaphysical tradition, of course, is provided by Heidegger's study, *Nietzsche.*

10. De Man also wrote a number of articles for a Flemish newspaper, as well as for other publications, during the same period. The most complete documentation to date on this question is provided by *Wartime Journalism, 1939–1943,* ed. Werner Hamacher, Neil Hertz, and Thomas Keenan (Lincoln: University of Nebraska Press, 1988); and *Responses: On Paul de Man's Wartime Journalism,* ed. Werner Hamacher, Neil Hertz, and Thomas Keenan (Lincoln: University of Nebraska Press, 1989). To appreciate the misogynistic aspects of Nazi ideology, one need only consult the contemporary text by Alfred Rosenberg: *Der Mythus des 20.jahrhunderts* (Munich: Hoheneichen, 1934). For a concise

overview, see Rita Thalmann's chapter entitled "L'Ordre masculin," in *Etre femme sous le troisième Reich* (Paris: Robert Lafront, 1982).

11. Stéphane Mallarmé, *La musique et les lettres, Oeuvres complètes,* ed. Henri Mondor (Paris: Gallimard, 1945), 651–654. Further references appear in the text.

12. Max Nordau, *Degeneration,* trans. George L. Mosse (New York: Howard Fertig, 1968). A typical sentence: "It is precisely in France that the craziest fashions in art and literature would necessarily arise . . . precisely there that the morbid exhaustion of which we have spoken became for the first time sufficiently distinct to consciousness to allow a special name to be coined for it, namely, the designation of *fin-de-siècle*" (43). What is of interest from the critical perspective of a Mallarmé or a Nietzsche, as opposed to the polemical stance of a Nordau, is neither simply coining (*erfinden*) names nor encouraging and maintaining their unquestioned circulation; rather, it is the unremitting labor of verifying to what extent such "names" are adequate, in given situations, to the distinctions of "consciousness" they are supposed to reflect.

13. The French reads: "Qu'il y ait des écrivains à l'écart tenant . . . me captive . . . ils offensent le fait divers; que dérobent-ils, toujours jettent-ils ainsi du discrédit, moins qu'une bombe, sur ce que de mieux, indisputablement et à grands frais, fournit une capitale comme rédaction courante à ses apothéoses." Given other pronouncements by Mallarmé, it is possible that he actually wrote that writing is *more* effective than bombing: "*mieux* qu'une bombe." See, for example, the interview of 27 May, 1894, given to *Le Soir:* "And it is my opinion that there is no arm more effective than literature itself" (*Correspondance,* ed. Henri Mondor and Lloyd James Austin [Paris: Gallimard, 1981], 6:287); and the statement quoted by Sartre: "the only true bomb is a poem" (Jean-Paul Sartre, *Mallarmé, la lucidité et sa face d'ombre* [Paris: Gallimard, 1986], 157).

14. Martin Heidegger, *Die Frage nach dem Ding* (Tübingen: Max Niemeyer, 1987), 33. Further references appear in the text.

15. See *Thus Spoke Zarathustra,* trans. Walter Kaufmann (New York: Viking Penguin, 1966), Part 3, "On the Vision and the Riddle" and "The Convalescent." The difficulty of coming to terms with Nietzsche's thought of the eternal return—a thinking of history as the gateway under which past and future collide with and affront each other, *sie stossen sich gerade vor den Kopf*—without turning it into a mere platitude is aptly rendered by Martin Heidegger's commentary on Zarathustra's animals, the eagle and the serpent. It is much easier, according to Heidegger, to repeat the knowledge of the eternal return in mere prattle—by mindlessly deriding or celebrating it—than to think it: "Precisely this knowledge is the weightiest and most difficult; all too easily it flies off or slithers away in evasions and equivocations, in pure foolishness." See Heidegger's *Nietzsche* (Pfullingen: Neske, 1961), 1:301.

16. ". . . die Lust an der Verstellung als Macht herausbrechend, den sogenannten 'Charakter' beiseite schiebend, überflutend, mitunter auslöschend."

17. On the status of rhetorical figures within the philosophical argument of Nietzsche's text, see Andrzej Warminski, "Towards a Fabulous Reading," *Graduate Faculty Philosophy Journal* 15.2 (1991) 93–120.

18. The expression "to turn one's coat to the wind" is not, to my knowledge, an idiomatic equivalent in English for the concept of "adaptablity," and this makes the task of commentary and exegesis even more challenging in this instance. Translating the German into something like, "to trim one's sails to the wind," of course, would be more recognizable but for that very reason less demonstrative from a philosophical and rhetorical point of view. Translation, then, would be another name for the radical dissimulation of Nietzschean appearance and its infinite potential to become literalized in an aberrant way.

19. Nietzsche says, in fact, that the figure of the coat becomes *almost* a coat (*fast zum Mantel werdend*); the figural potential to dissimulate is thus never totally erased or neutralized by a final, definitive, and truly literal understanding here, although this critical insight is in turn put into question by the text's own straightforward naming of "Jews" and "women" at its conclusion. Therefore, the example of the coat—which, as pertaining specifically to language, is a genuinely rhetorical example—is not, in the end, exactly the same as the example of the "Jews" and "women," which are not strictly speaking, or exclusively, rhetorical figures. Between the rhetoric and the anthropology of the fragment, then, there is all the same the slightest gap—the gap of similarity, of which Nietzsche says elsewhere: "Precisely between what is most similar, illusion lies most beautifully; for the smallest gap is the most difficult to bridge" ("The Convalescent," *Thus Spoke Zarathustra*, 217).

20. "Why I Am a Destiny," *Ecce Homo*.

▼ Deborah Esch ▼

The Work to Come

> Something crisis-like was taking place at that moment, making practices and assumptions problematic that had been taken for granted.
> —Paul de Man, "Criticism and Crisis"

BY MOST ACCOUNTS, THE DISCLOSURE OF Paul de Man's wartime journalism precipitated something of a "crisis": the term recurs insistently in what is by now a host of reflections on the import, theoretical and political, of those early texts. In "Blindness and Hindsight," one of thirty-eight essays collected in *Reponses: On Paul de Man's Wartime Journalism,* Catherine Gallagher notes the way in which this crisis scenario dovetails with recent mainstream press reports of "the failure of the humanities in general and literary studies in particular"—an ongoing journalistic narrative, alarmist in tone, that casts "theory" as a kind of invading force on the cultural landscape. That story, of course, is traceable to academic sources, indebted to a rhetoric of crisis generated by some within the profession who take "theory"—by which they most often mean "deconstruction"—to be a threat to established habits of thought and what are called traditional values. Among the professors of literature who have gone on record as deploring theory's incursion into the humanistic disciplines, Walter Jackson Bate led the way with his manifesto "The Crisis in English Studies," published in *Harvard Magazine* in 1982. Bate's claim is that "The humanities are not merely entering, they are plunging into their worst state of crisis since the modern university was formed a century ago. . . . The humanities are not only in the weakest state they ever suffered but seem bent on a self-destructive course."[1] And he indicts "the strange stepchild of structuralism know as 'deconstructionism,' " a "nihilistic view of literature, of human communication, and of life itself," as chiefly responsible for the current crisis. As Gallagher rightly discerns, "The discovery that de Man had written for a collaborationist journal fit beautifully into this

From *Diacritics* 20.3 (Fall 1990). Copyright © 1990 by The Johns Hopkins University Press.

story because it provided a perfect symmetry between the beginning and the end. Deconstruction was no longer just the harbinger of outrages against humanity; it actually originated in such outrages. The outcome could no longer be in doubt because it was contained in the original."[2] In these terms, the disclosure of the wartime writings could elicit a collective "I told you so" from critics as well as journalisists who had judged deconstruction outrageous all along.

In one of the first substantive reviews of *Wartime Journalism, 1939–1943* and *Responses,* Lynne Higgins complicates this symmetrical narrative of origins and ends, even as she too adopts the rhetoric of crisis: "Reading the two volumes together," she writes, "gives one a sense of the current identity crisis within literary studies. The de Man 'affair' did not *create* that crisis, but it does magnify the complexities and raise the stakes."[3] For literary critics whose stake in the matter may amount in great part to self-interest, to fear for the possibility of their own contamination through the operative "logic of transmission," "Protection consists of mastering continuities and constructing distances. . . . It is the very indirect and mediated nature of the degrees of collaboration that makes it terrifying. The identity crisis takes the form of an urgent question: is the work I'm doing complicitous with something I would be horrified to be associated with?" In times of crisis—Higgins here invokes the current AIDS epidemic, not simply as an analogy—"we have to know who we are sleeping with. We want 'safe criticism' " (110).

The texts comprising the wartime journalism—a heterogeneous corpus including contributions to the Belgian dailies *Le Soir* and *Het Vlaamsche Land* and the monthly *Bibliographie Dechenne,* all issued under the control of the occupation authorities, as well as to *Jeudi* and the *Cahiers du Libre Examen,* the weekly newspaper and monthly journal of the socialist student circle at the Université Libre de Bruxelles, published prior to the occupation—were themselves written out of what the young Paul de Man repeatedly diagnosed as a "crisis," one whose dimensions were manifold. In "A la recherche d'un nouveau mode d'expression," a review of Charles Dekeukeleire's *L'Emotion sociale* published in *Le Soir* in March 1942 (a month in which, as the detailed chronology compiled by the editors of *Responses* notes, "German military authorities institute obligatory labor service for some categories of workers" [R, xvi], and in which *Le Soir,* with an average daily circulation of 255,000, is the most widely read periodical in the country [xvii]), he advises his readers that "the military events, as gigantic and full of consequence as they are, cannot make us forget that at the same time a crisis of spiritual order is proceeding whose historic import is incalculable."[4] And allusions like that to the "particularly delicate crisis that a man passes through around his twentieth year" ("Le problème de l'adolescence," *Le Soir* 6/30/42; *WJ*, 246) suggest that the "spiritual" crisis concomitant with the political upheaval had a biographical, an autobiographical aspect for the young journalist as well. This rhetoric of crisis, sustained in many of his contributions to *Le Soir* and *Het Vlaamsche Land,* is harnessed to a logic that argues collaboration to be a pragmatic, indeed a necessary, response to the current state of affairs, to the force of "facts," of "history": "There thus emerges the demonstration of the ineluctable truth of history," he writes in July 1942, in a review of the second volume of Fabre-Luce's *Journal de la France:* "the politics of collaboration results from the present situation not as an ideal desired by all of the people but as an irresistable necessity which none can escape, even if he thinks he ought to move in another direction" (*WJ*, 253; see also the review of Chardonne's *Voir la figure, Le Soir* 10/28/41; *WJ*, 158–159]. In "Qu'est-ce qu'un collaborateur?," Sartre identifies this logic (and ideologic) as that of "realism." Werner Hamacher elaborates the significance of Sartre's "insight":

> the ideology of realism, identified as a central element of collaboration, is itself a danger to democratically organized societies. The pragmatism, positivism and historicism which have long been a part of the ideological profile of democracies can hardly be regarded as anything other than variants of that realism which finds the final guarantee of reality of the power of so-called facts. This reality is actually first generated by all sorts of societal—and not only societal—institutions and all sorts of techniques—among them techniques of language. . . . It is in realism that Sartre marks the point of complicity between democratic and fascist systems. Putting this realism into question is an eminently political act, even if it is not articulated in explicitly political terms, but rather in linguistic and philological ones (as, for example, in de Man's later writings). No one with a critical mind will be startled that the institutions of this ideological realism try to denounce any such questioning as an attack on the basic foundations of "Western values." [*R,* 448]

Nor should it come as a surprise that the denunciations are couched in the rhetoric of crisis.

In the aftermath of the archival discovery that brought de Man's earliest publications once again to light, the "crisis" translates, especially for those indebted to his later work, as a need, an imperative to make sense of an event that has disrupted working premises and practices. Perhaps the event-character of the disclosure of the wartime journalism, which in the view of Samuel Weber as well as other commentators administered "a shock and an intensity in direct proportion to the influence of [de Man's] work and to the respect inspired by his person" (*R,* 410), might best be thought not so much as a contingent bibiographical find, but rather on the model of a missive, an open letter—or letter bomb— delivered after long delay. As Barbara Johnson speculates, "Whether or not these articles contributed in any way to the wartime history of Belgium, the arrival of this long-delayed letter strikes us *now* with the full disruptive force of an event. It is an event that is structured *like* what de Man describes as an 'occurrence'—an irreversible disruption of cognition." But in this case, she goes on to specify, "it is a disruption that is happening *to* his own acts of cognition. It is as though de Man had tried to theorize"—after the fact, in the mature work—"the disruption"—before the fact, in and by the pre-critical if not pre-theoretical journalism—"of his own acts of theorizing, had tried to include the theory's own outside within it. But that theory's outside was precisely, we now know, always already within. And he could not, of course, control the very loss of control he outlined as inevitable and defined as irony. . . . The arrival of this purloined letter, then, is an event not only for de Man but also for his readers, however uncannily his theory might have predicted its inevitability."[5] Johnson's account credits de Man's late essays—she quotes the 1983 lecture "Kant and Schiller," but could as well have cited "Hypogram and Inscription," "Anthropomorphism and Trope in the Lyric," "Aesthetic Formalization in Kleist" or "Phenomenality and Materiality in Kant"— with a reflection on the nature of historical occurrence, and specifically on its accessibility to cognition, that makes a particular claim on our attempts to make sense of the explosive event at hand, the belated disclosure of the abandoned writings. More generally, she helps to focus the question of the continuing importance of de Man's mature work not only for "the epistemological analysis of what 'reality' is and how it de-constitutes itself in the tension of language" (Hamacher, in *R,* 454), but also and especially "for any analysis of the totalitarian impulse insofar as it transmits itself in texts," "for the historico-political analysis of textuality in general," as "an effective analysis of historical acts [and events, 'occurrences'—DE] which are dissociated from cognition by language" (Kamuf, in *R,* 225).

Other formulations in *Responses* explore the pertinence of de Man's analysis of the dissociation of cognition from performance on the one hand, and from what he termed "the materiality of actual history" on the other. A number of these employ blindness as a figure for the disruption, the failure of cognition in the face of the event. As against Gallagher's summary assessment that "hindsight has revised nothing and confirmed everything" (*R,* 207), Cynthia Chase writes that "after the emergence of de Man's 1940-42 articles, one necessarily writes about his writing differently than before—insofar as one writes about a subject they do not as such address, about an occurrence they do not see. The reappearance of those abandoned texts is something that happens to de Man's writing from the outside"—an "outside" that, Johnson observes, was *always already* within, which is to say it is not so much an outside as a *before*—"which thus strikes it with blindness with regard to what is nevertheless its own situation, or rather ours, that of his students, readers. Here for the first time indubitably is an occurrence pertinent to his writing which it cannot see and about which it has nothing to say. But at the same time it says a great deal about just that predicament—the blindness of writing; and also—but why is it only now that one learns to read this?—about the implication of thought and writing in the violence of history, and particularly that European 20th-century violence, Nazism." Chase's argument, grounded in a meticulous reading and rereading of the journalism as well as the theoretical work, is not only that de Man's late essays on the aesthetic ideology (in particular "Aesthetic Formalization in Kleist") are crucial for thinking "the complicities of modes of education and models of history with the fascist totalitarian state," but also that "these writings' not knowing, not seeing their circumstances—which is not a matter of repressing or concealing—is a key dimension of what they give us to read" (*R*, 44). Reading, our reading, must account for the blindness, for the critical failure of cognition to inscribe a certain history.

In "Edges of Understanding," Rodolphe Gasché has recourse to the same figuartion in characterizing the severe shortcomings of the early work: "The essays of *Het Vlaamsche Land* and *Le Soir* do not show de Man to have sensed the catastrophic danger that Nazi Germany represented not only with respect to the Jewish people, but the whole of Europe and the celebrated values of Western civilization as well. This is rather difficult to understand today, after the fact. But if de Man did not come to grips with the horror that was in the offing, it was *among other things* because his analytical apparatus did not provide the means to capture the viciousness and aberration of the Nazi endeavor *on all fronts*" (*R*, 215). (As Hamacher specifies, "Despite the control [the articles] exercise over it, the vocabulary of the time is virtually never scrutinized or redefined" [*R*, 438].) And Gasché concludes that, if the young de Man's "intellectual instruments (like those of most of his contemporaries, and of many present intellectuals as well)" kept him from a precise understanding of events, "it was left to the later de Man to systematically put into question all those blinding schemes, categories and concepts by means of which he had, in his journalistic writings, unsuccessfully tried to gain insight into the political situation in Belgium in the early forties" (*R*, 215).

Among the most suggestive accounts of what it is that the event of the disclosure summons us to read and to think is Geoffrey Hartman's, in "Looking Back on Paul de Man," his two-part contribution to *Reading de Man Reading* (the essay's first part was written before, and the second after, the wartime journalism came to light). "By an irony that deserves a name of its own," he writes, "the disclosure of the early articles imbeds a biographical fact in our consciousness that tends to devour all other considerations. It may not spare the later achievement, whose intellectual power we continue to feel." We continue to feel, for example, the force of de Man's theorization of the blindness of writing, the limits of criticism and self-criticism. "One could argue," Hartman pursues, "that there is no relation between the young journalist, age twenty-one, and the distinguished theorist who published his first book at age fifty-one. Or that what relation obtains is one of reaction formation, as when he accuses Husserl of blindly privileging 'European supremacy' at the very time (1935) that Europe 'was about to destroy itself as center in the name of an unwarranted claim to be the center.' For de Man too was a European who 'escaped from the necessary self-criticism that is prior to all philosophical truth about the self.'" But, Hartman is careful to add, "what we are seeing here"—always allowing for our own blindness—"is a special case of what happens all the time. A new fact, often a new text, makes a difference in the way we read. Although history has moved more quickly in this case, we are always in the situation of having to revise our judgment of a work, however monumental it once appeared to be."[6]

It is no accident that the recurrent topoi of these responses—criticism and crisis, blindness and insight, irony and history among them—should be drawn from de Man's theoretical legacy. In particular, these formulations redirect us to *Blindness and Insight,* and to its opening essay "Criticism and Crisis," first published in 1967, where de Man interrogates the "recurrent epistemological structure that characterizes all statements made in the mood and the rhetoric of crisis."[7] As Hartman recalls, that analysis enlists ("[f]or reasons of economy") "an example from philosophy," the 1935 lectures that would later become Husserl's *The Crisis of The European Sciences and Transcendental Phenomenology,* and their "description of philosophy as a process by means of which naive assumptions are made accessible to consciousness by an act of critical self-understanding. Husserl conceived of philosophy primarily as a self-interpretation by means of which we eliminate what he calls *Selbstverhülltheit,* the tendency of the self to hide from the light it can cast on itself. The universality of philosophical knowledge stems from a persistently reflective attitude that can take philosophy itself for its theme" (15). But when Husserl's reader, "[a]lerted by this convincing appeal to self-critical vigilance," is led to apply the philosopher's standard to the very text in which it is established, that text is found wanting in its own terms, above all when it claims philosophy as "the historical privilege of European man."

> Husserl speaks repeatedly of non-European cultures as primitive, prescientific and pre-philosophical, myth-dominated and congenitally incapable of the disinterested distance without which there can be no philosophical meditation. This, although by his own definition philosophy, as unrestricted reflection upon the self, necessarily tends toward a universality that finds its concrete, geographical correlative in the formation of supratribal, supranational communities such as, for instance, Europe. Why this geographical expansion should have chosen to stop, once and forever, at the Caucasus, Husserl does not say. . . . The privileged viewpoint of the post-Hellenic, European consciousness is never for a moment put into question; the crucial, determining examination on which depends Husserl's right to call himself, by his own terms, a philosopher, is in fact never undertaken. As a European, it seems that Husserl escapes from the necessary self-criticism that is prior to all philosophical truth about the self. . . . Husserl's claim to European supremacy hardly stands in need of criticism today. Since we are speaking of a man of superior good will, it suffices to point to the pathos of such a claim at a moment when Europe was about to destroy itself as center in the name of its unwarranted claim to be the center. (15–16)

Writing "in what was in fact a state of urgent personal and political crisis about a more general form of crisis," Husserl unwittingly exemplifies what de Man takes to be "the structure of all crisis-determined statements. . . . The rhetoric of crisis states its own truth in the mode of error. It is itself radically blind to the light it emits, to the insight it makes possible. Husserl thus joins the ranks of thinkers in whose critical practice de Man discerns a cognitive mechanism figured as blindness and insight. As Wlad Godzich ably summarizes and situates de Man's analysis, its theoretical and potentially its ideological and institutional consequences:

> The blindness, for from being disabling, was constitutive of the insight, yet nonethess remained a blindness to the person affected with it. It was this predicament of critical activity that led de Man to formulate a more properly theoretical stance in which the mechanism of blindness and insight would be understood without being disabled, or at least not in such a way as to render further insights impossible. De Man's solicitude in the preservation of the mechanism has something profoundly disquieting, if

not downright scandalous, about it. Our impulse, bred in the bone by several centuries of education, is to correct an error when we come across it. De Man's willingness to let it be marked a profound break with a major component of the Western cognitive tradition, one that is the motor of the disciplines, especially the scientific ones.[8]

In the instance of Husserl's text, then, de Man is led to ask: "How does this pattern of self-mystification that accompanies the experience of crisis apply to literary criticism? Husserl was demonstrating the urgent philosophical necessity of putting the privileged European standpoint into question, but remained himself entirely blind to this necessity, behaving in the most unphilosophical way possible at the very moment when he rightly understood the primacy of philosophical over empirical knowledge. He was, in fact, stating the privileged status of philosophy as an authentic language, but withdrawing at once from the demands of this authenticity as it applied to himself" (16–17). In "Disfiguring the Monument," Weber glosses de Man's account: "De Man's 'point' . . . is that the notion of self-criticism, with reference to which Husserl seeks to define the specificity of Western philosophy, itself depends upon a highly contradictory set of assumptions which themselves may well comprise the enabling limit of 'criticism' itself (and which hence would have to remain uncriticized and uncriticizable). These assumptions have to do with Husserl's use of the term 'European' to define and determine the philosophical attitude of self-criticism he is engaged in defending against the crisis that has befallen it." In Weber's assessment, then, "the question raised by de Man with respect to Husserl (in both senses of that phrase)[9] involves the status of *criticism* itself, and concomitantly, the problem of judgment, that is, of proceeding from the particular (European man) to the general (the universal validity of the self-critical attitude of philosophical thought)"—this inscription of the particular in the general being for de Man "the purpose of any cognition."[10] "What is at stake in this problem," as Weber makes plain, "is the relation of thinking to alterity, to the others: here, the non-European. The question de Man is raising is that of self-limitation, of *demarcation*. . . . The point . . . is that the 'spiritual' generalization of European humanity in order to define a norm of thought valid beyond the limits of the European continent, requires necessarily the exclusion and subordination of other cultures" (*R*, 408).[11]

How then—if at all—are we to bring to bear on de Man's own history, on the grave pattern of self-mystification inscribed in the wartime writings, the lesson for which Husserl serves (the later de Man) as example? Do the terms and distinctions afforded in the theoretical work indeed make a particular claim on our efforts to render intelligible its relation to the early journalism—a claim that we ignore or reject at the expense of a better understanding? If we attend to the passage in which de Man locates the operation of blindness and insight in Husserl's text ("Husserl was demonstrating the urgent philosophical necessity of putting the privileged European standpoint into question, but remained himself entirely blind to this necessity, behaving in the most unphilosophical way possible at the very moment when he rightly understood the primacy of philosophical over empirical knowledge"), we find that much of the burden of the argument falls on the sense or senses of "demonstrating," among them "proving beyond the possibility of doubt by a process of argument or logical deduction" (*Oxford English Dictionary,* s. v. "demonstration"), by way of a line of reasoning that can close with *quid est demonstrandum.* Analysis of Husserl's demonstration thus yields a logic of blindness and insight, based on the principle of non-contradiction, that seems sufficient to his case, since the "blindness"—unphilosophical behavior—and the "insight"—right understanding—occur *"at the very [same] moment,"* since "[h]e was, in fact, stating the privileged status of philosophy as an authentic langauge but withdrawing *at once* from the demands of this authenticity as it applied to himself." The simultaneity that marks the operation of the logic, the law of blindness and insight in Husserl's text might seem to promise the possibility of a dialectical mediation of the two terms, but it is nonetheless "against any dialectical reappropriation or synthesis of blindness and insight that de Man is waging his most explicit, powerful attacks. In trying to define the relation of blindness and insight, he insists: 'The contradictions, however, can never cancel each other out, nor do they enter into the synthesizing dynamics of a dialectic' (*BI,* 102)."[12]

The impossibility of a dialectical resolution is all the more emphatic in de Man's own case. If we "apply de Man's statement about Husserl's claim to European supremacy to the writer of 'Inhoud der Europeesche gedachte' " (de Graef, in *R,* 119), we find that the de Manian corpus resists the imposition of the categories of blindness and insight conceived according to a logic that dictates their mutual cancellation or dialectical synthesis. For the two textual conditions do not occur simultaneously, are not co-present in this body of work, but are separated by more than a quarter-century. In these terms, a decisive difference between Husserl's case and de Man's—a difference that de Man's late writings helps us to read—is that in the latter the temporal dimension is not contingent but constitutive.[13]

The stakes—and the eventual outcome—of the crisis to which the disclosure of the wartime journalism has given rise thus depend upon the possible articulation of the early texts with the later ones, as a reading of *Responses* makes clear.[14] Gasché writes that "undoubtedly, it is the relation, the absence of a relation, or something other than a relation . . . between the early journalism and de Man's mature work that represents the most interesting problem . . . no analysis of what is to be related, of the *sort of relation that is possible, in the first place, between the relata*, seems to have been undertaken" (R, 215–216). "De Man's early writings . . . are a far cry from what he was later to become involved in, and thus it is no small task to demonstrate any *significant* relation between the two corpuses" (R, 217). In Derrida's formulation, that sizeable task is specifically "to articulate [the wartime writings] with the work to come while avoiding, if possible, two more or less symmetrical errors": that of declaring "no relation, sealed frontier between the two, absolute heterogeneity," and that of "amalgam, continuism, analogism, teleologism, hasty totalization, reduction and derivation" (R, 151), of "asserting complete identity, as though discontinuity and *history* were a mere ruse or epiphenomenon (Weber, in R, 410, emphasis added). An articulation that would do justice to such a history—and to history as such—must first pass by way of a thinking of temporality, a reading of the relation of past to present that presumes neither a straightforward economy of exchange, nor a homogenizing, totalizing narrative of origins and ends.

If we begin by rereading the conceptual metaphors of blindness and insight in light of the intervention of time that renders the terms radically asymmetrical, we find that the sense of "demonstrating" ("Husserl was demonstrating . . .") as the working out of an argument or a logical deduction yields to a more properly rhetorical (and practical) sense: that of the demonstration *effect* of the *example*. In these terms, Husserl was blindly offering himself as an example of blindness (the figure, again, for his "unphilosophical behavior") "at the very moment" when he was stating his insight into the superiority of philosophical over empirical knowledge.[15] And in de Man's case, the wartime writings could be understood in part to serve as examples—in advance—of the (pre-critical, ideological) blindness that the later (critical, theoretical) insight will expose, so unsparingly, as such.[16] This economy of the example would not be subsumable under any logic or dialectic: neither before nor after the fact can one control or fully account for one's own (or another's) status as example, with its unpredictable effects of meaning and force.[17]

Reflection on the demonstration effect of the example also prompts active consideration of the question of how occupied Belgium remains an example *for us*—a question that may be overlooked if our response to the disclosure takes the tempting form of simple condemnation. As Hartman writes in "History and Judgment," "Denunciation, at this point, is not enough; it tends to foster a paranoid style of localizing evil that removes the issues too far from our time."[18] "Mere reactions," concurs Hamacher, "are powerless, especially when dealing with the discourse of totalitarianism. . . . Elements of totalitarian ideologies live on—and most stubbornly in those who proclaim their own immunity" (R, 466–467). The question of how the then and there chronicled by the young journalist may implicate us, here and now, poses the challenge of thinking history not as a symmetrical, totalizing narrative of origins and ends, but in the precise terms of the material specificity of the event. " 'History,' this vague abstraction, seems then and now to function as a powerful means of homogenizing and making a taboo out of history—namely *that* history which exists only concretely, singularly, idiosyncratically, painfully. To judge history on the basis of its empty generality is to deny the past its particularities, and to run the risk of repeating it in its worst traits" (Hamacher, in R, 463). This is a risk we can hardly afford to run unawares—which is to say, blindly.

▼ ▲ ▼

>   Doch lies nur, lies!
>   —*Goethe*, Die Wahlverwandtschaften

>   . . . the gift of an ordeal, the summons to a work of reading, of historical interpretaion, of ethical-political reflection—an interminable analysis well beyond the sequence 1940–42. In the future and for the future. . . .
>   Derrida, *"Like the Sound of the Sea Deep Within a Shell: Paul de Man's War"*

Rather than resorting to empty generalities, summarizing the heterogeneous arguments of the wartime journalism as well as those of the responses to them, we may do better (not only "for reasons of economy") to explore these questions on the basis of an example—one of the few—of a text de Man engaged in his early as well as his later work, in order to posit a possible articulation of the two, and to substantiate what we have alluded to as his blindness and insight. The example is Goethe's *Die Wahlverwandtschaften* (*The Elective Affinities*), whose French translation de Man reviewed in *Le Soir* in May 1942. He undertook to analyze the novel again more than forty years later, in a lecture for "Reading and Rhetorical Structures," a course he taught in the Literature Major at Yale University in the spring of 1983; the late lecture is thus contemporaneous with his readings of Kant, Schiller, and Kleist, and their elaboration of his critique of the aesthetic ideology.[19] In it, de Man radically revises his former judgment of Goethe's text.

Before engaging the terms of de Man's commentaries on the novel, early and late, we might recollect a passage in which Goethe's text itself speaks to circumstances akin to those of the disclosure of the wartime journalism. In the novel's ninth chapter, the laying of the foundation stone for the new summer-house is marked with an elaborate ceremony, featuring an address by the mason on the importance for the architectural project of his own craft, which, "if it be not done in concealment, yet must pass into concealment."[20]

> But as the man who commits some evil deed has to fear, that, notwithstanding all precautions, it will one day come to light—so too must he expect who has done some good thing in secret, that it also, in spite of himself, will appear in the day; and therefore we make this foundation stone at the same time a stone of memorial [*Deswegen machen wir diesen Grundstein zugleich zum Denkstein*]. Here, in these various hollows which have been hewn into it, many things are now to be buried, as a witness to some far-off world [*Zeugnis für eine entfernte Nachwelt*]—these metal cases hermetically sealed contain documents in writing [*schriftliche Nachrichten*]; matters of various note are engraved on these plates; in these fair glass bottles we bury the best old wine, with a note of the year of its vintage. We have coins too of many kinds, from the mint of the current year. . . . There is space yet remaining, if guest or spectator desires to offer anything to the afterworld. . . . But in that we bury this treasure together with [the foundation stone], we do it in the remembrance—in this most enduring of works—of the perishableness of human things. We remember [*wir denken uns eine Möglichkeit*] that a time may come when this cover so fast sealed shall again be lifted. . . . [English 65–66; German 66–67].[21]

The written documents (*Nachrichten,* news reports, literally after-accounts) sealed in this time capsule—which is always potentially a time bomb—share an affinity with de Man's wartime writings: both are emphatically of their time in their referential function, but both reemerge at a future date, like the long-delayed letter (arriving, now, from before and beyond the grave), coming to light for what Hamacher terms "their second phase of use" (438).

In the concluding entry in his "Journals, Politics," one of the most consequential essays in *Responses* for thinking history as of the order of events and their possible articulation, Hamacher cites de Man's *Le Soir* review: "On May 26, 1942 de Man writes—under the title 'Universalisme de Goethe,' a discussion of Goethe's *Wahlverwandtschaften*—several sentences which are not written by an ideologue, a tactician in a politico-literary battle, or an accomplice of the collaborationist press, but by a *reader*. The other sentences must not be forgotten; these should be remembered as well. They concern the 'strange interlude' in the middle of the novel, in the early chapters of the second section, during which 'absolutely nothing happens which would advance the development of the drama.' " He goes on to translate de Man's text:

> There has been a great deal of discussion about the appropriateness of these pages, which seem unbearably long to some. And yet, they constitute one of the most alluring and original parts of the whole work.(. . .) It seems, though, that their principal *raison d'être* is the introduction into the novel of the factor of time, of the *duration* [de Man's emphasis] of events. Reality never presents itself as an uninterrupted movement towards a dénouement: it marks the stopping times [*temps d'arrêt*] during which, under the empire of inertia or human automatism, entirely eventless periods unroll their monotonous uniformity. A narrative which aims to produce the real rhythm of existence must insert such epochs. . . . [T]he interlude in the *Wahlverwandtschaften* is certainly one of the most successful attempts of this kind. (*R*, 467; *WJ*, 238)[22]

In attending to the economy of memory and forgetting crucial to our responses to these texts, Hamacher is right to mark, with emphasis, the distinction between de Man as an ideologue and as a reader: both play a role in the not altogether homogeneous corpus of the wartime journalism. Specifically, the youthful ideologue and tactician serves what the later theorist and reader would target under the rubric of the aesthetic ideology. The pursuit of the latter critique necessarily passes by way of what he termed "critical-linguistic analysis,"[23] including, importantly, a sustained investigation of the values associated, at least since the late eighteenth century, with symbolic and allegorical conceptions of language. With reference to Goethe, Schiller, and Schelling as well as to Coleridge, de Man argues in "The Rhetoric of Temporality" that the symbol, predicated on the assumed continuity and simultaneity of "the sensory image and the supersensory totality that the image suggests," in turn grounds an understanding of the subject-object relation "in which the experience of the object takes on the form of a perception or a sensation. The ultimate intent of the image is synthesis," and "the mode of this synthesis is defined as symbolic by the priority conferred on the initial moment of sensory perception"—i.e., on the *aesthetic* moment (*BI*, 189, 193). The symbol, then, proves to be the linguistic condition of possibility of "a certain claim for the autonomy and the power of the aesthetic which is being asserted in the wake of Schiller, but not necessarily in the wake of Kant"—that is, the aesthetic ideology.[24] Allegory, in de Man's reading, disrupts the possibility of the symbolic synthesis by opening up a constitutive temporal dimension, the difference that divides the allegorical sign from the previous sign to which it refers. Allegory confesses the failure of coincidence forgotten or repressed in the model of the symbol, in which the relationship of image and substance is taken to be "one of simultaneity, which, in truth, is spatial in kind, and in which the intervention of time is merely a matter of contingency" (207). In its detail and its scope, this analysis effects a radical revision of the conventional literary-historical and aesthetic categories through which we read romanticism (and idealism)—the same categories that are in full force in de Man's early review of *The Elective Affinities*.

In the review's first paragraph, the spirit of Goethe is said to be "independent of the conditions of space and time," and the novel, "one of Goethe's most perfect works," to be "the living image of the universalism of its author" (*WJ*, 238). De Man's assertion that there is nothing in or about the novel "that doesn't seem to us essentially modern" stands as an awkward precedent to the claim in his late essay on "Aesthetic Formalization in Kleist" that, "for all the attention it has received," the text on the marionette theater (published in 1810, and thus virtually contemporaneous with *Die Wahlverwandtschaften,* which appeared in 1809) has nonetheless "remained curiously unread and enigmatic," and "belongs among the texts of the period which our own modernity has not yet been able to confront, perhaps because the Schillerian aesthetic categories, whether we know it or not, are still the taken-for-granted premises of our own pedagogical, historical, and political ideologies" (*RR,* 266).

The review takes for granted the rhetoric and the ideology of the symbol, with its values of continuity, organicity, homogeneity, symmetry, and totality, and in a gesture akin to Husserl's use of the term "European" in his defensive demarcation of the properly philosophical, maps them onto European culture, based on a rigid logic of national stereotyping. As Hamacher comments, "It can appear as a logic, as a consistent mode of thought, because it makes the claim that the nation, the national community, is itself a homogeneous and substantial form not only of that which has been thought, but of thought itself. Therefore nationalism is a substantialism—a substantialism of community conceived of as nature" (439). Gasché and Chase, among others, point out that the ideo-logic of nationalism in the wartime writings does not simply serve the interests of the occupying power: "The issue which is a decisive thread running through most of the articles—the concern with national personality and difference, patriotic feeling, the protection . . . of national patrimony, the persistence of the independence of nationalities—is incongruous with the dominant Nazi ideology" [Gasché, in *R,* 211]. "The presence in the articles of such stereotyping by no means amounts to celebration of German nationality or the German nation; the characteristic qualities of at least three nations, France, Belgium, and Germany, are being identified and valued, in terms exerting some check or pressure upon the design of German domination. But while the stereotyping thus lacks a direct and pro-Nazi political significance, its deeper ideological significance persists" (Chase, in *R,* 50). Symptomatic of that ideological significance, as Chase remarks, is the fact that "the reviewer's strongest interest or enthusiasm is elicited by the co-presence of these [national] qualities or the circumvention of their opposition" [50], which he finds, for example, in Goethe's novel: "a latin as well as a germanic sensibility will be touched by its content in every sense. . . . [O]ne could take pains to situate the *Elective Affinities* in the norm of the literary traditions of all the great European creative centres. We will limit ourselves to examining the work with respect to the French and German artistic qualities: the synthesis of these two national termperaments, a rare and uneasy realization, being already amply sufficient to justify its particular attraction" (*WJ,* 238). The balance of the review is given over to this examination, culminating in the final paragraph: "In conclusion, this conjunction, in the same work, of so many different qualities, a conjunction obtained without the unity of the narrative and of the thought suffering for an instant, confers on it an unequaled merit. . . . At certain moments, the totality of riches dispersed among the nations forming western civilizations are concentrated in an elect, who thus becomes the universal genius. With this work, we witness one of these unique moments in the history of letters" (*WJ,* 239).

Such claims help to specify the blindness that crippled de Man's understanding in much of the wartime journalism. In a review of A.E. Brinckmann's *Geist der Nationen* (which he also co-translated), he writes that "What is proper to our time is the consideration of the national personality as a valuable condition, as a precious possession, which has to be maintained at the cost of all sacrifices. This conception is miles apart from sentimental patriotism. Rather, it concerns a sober faith, a practical means to defend Western culture against a decomposition from the inside or an overwhelming onrush by neighboring cultural norms" (*Het Vlaamsche Land* 29–30 March 1942; *WJ,* 303). Weber discerns the "pattern of self-mystification that accompanies the experience of crisis" here:

> What is "proper to our time," then, is not simply the valorization of the national or of nationalism, but rather the sense of these values being threatened: by internal "decomposition" or by "sur-

prise attack." What is "proper to our time," in short, is the sense of danger from without and from within. . . . It is not enough to define the identity of Europe internally, as it were, in terms of the "mutual exchanges" of the different national groups that inhabit the European continent. That identity must also be *set off* and *apart from* what it is not, from the non-European, the foreign. That is, from the Other. . . . Totality is never whole. . . . The other of the European . . . is, first and foremost: the Jew. It is the Jews who intrude, deranging the "continuity" and immanence of Western History: in this case, that of German Literature, thus causing it to deviate from its proper, predestined course. [R, 416]

The rhetoric of crisis is here yoked to the logic of nationalism as agonism that may be understood to yield (or, minimally, not to prevent) arguments like those in "The Jews in Contemporary Literature."[25] Thus the ideologue's "stereotypes, along with the models of thought they propagate, become among the most appalling products of the century" [Hamacher, in R, 438].

As tactically deployed and manoeuvred in de Man's review of the translation of *Die Wahlverwandtschaften,* the national stereotypes operate for the most part along predictable ideological lines. The traits that align the novel with "the great French classical tradition" also account for its strikingly "modern accent," chief among them "the eternal leitmotif of French prose: the primacy of the psychological motive." "In no recent work, even in an age in which the knowledge of the human soul has made considerable progress and the psychological *tournure d'esprit* has become more commonplace, can one indicate a clearer, more coherent analysis. The perfect harmony between the introspective and active parts of the content, the fact that each gesture finds its equivalent in the profound conformation of the one who performs it, these are the fundamental virtues that we find here" (238). The " 'French' virtues" of the novel, then, are those of "the equilibrium and mutual rapport of the component parts," the "perfection of the proportions among the different elements," "the rigor of the logical arrangement"—or, as he enumerates in "Le problème français. *Dieu est-il français?* de F. Sieburg," "the virtues of clarity, logic, harmony" that comprise "the constants of the latin spirit" [*Le Soir* 28 April 1942; *WJ,* 226–227].

Other aspects of Goethe's text, however, serve to remind the reader that it is "contemporaneous with that flowering of the germanic genius that is German Romanticism." De Man's review maintains that key elements in the novel exceed the psychological and the rational ("not everything is clarified by simple reason"), indicating a "supernatural power that eludes all analysis." "The death of the two lovers," for example "which is not explained by any illness or any physiological fact, symbolizes a supraterrestrial union, and thus no longer belongs to the realm of tangible verisimilitude." He remarks "the violence of certain passions that are raised above all contingency to enter into eternity," assimilating it to "the metaphysical sentiment of the infinite proper to German thought," through which "the novel reflects the nationality of its author." (Given that he is writing about a French translation of Goethe's prose, it is worth noting the absence here of anything presaging the mature reflection on translation, on the constitutive distance dividing the translated text from the original, that de Man provides in his late lecture on Walter Benjamin's "The Task of the Translator.")

Finally, he aligns *The Elective Affinities* with the German literary tradition by way of its subordination of aesthetic to ethical interests: if in the French canon, "from Racine to Gide," moral dilemmas are posed only for the sake of their aesthetic potential, "it is completely otherwise in the present case": Goethe's "profound germanism" enlists the aesthetic in the service of the ethical, "drawing practical conclusions with respect to education and to conduct." The same set of priorities is associated with the German tradition throughout the wartime journalism: for example in *Le Soir* 15 July 1941 (a review of Paul Willems's "Tout est réel ici") and 28 April 1942 ("Le problème français," cited earlier), and in *Het Vlaamsche Land* 20 August 1942, where, in "People and Books. A View on Contemporary German Fiction," de Man observes that "in present-day Germany there lives and flourishes a literature which is directly connected with that of the great precursors," with "the profound essence of [Germany's] artistic genius," "the spiritual property of the nation." The leitmotif (the red thread, as Goethe famously figures it) accounting for this continuity is "the profound moral disposition . . . the ambitious treatment of ethical problems," "the proper traditions of German art which had always and before everything else clung to a deep spiritual sincerity." That tradition, he argues here, was challenged in post-war German culture by the expressionist movement, in the work of "non-Germans, and specifically Jews," who pursued "an art with a strongly cerebral disposition, founded upon some abstract principles and very remote from all naturalness," resulting in "skillful artifices aimed at easy effects," and "a forced, caricatured representation of reality" (*WJ*, 325).

Gasché's rigorous, nuanced analysis of this blinded "View" points out among other things that "the cerebral quality of expressionism, that sets it over and against the other type of German literature, is an attribute associated throughout all the articles not only with Jewish thinking"—as in the reference to the Jews' "strongly cerebral disposition" in "The Jews in

Contemporary Literature"—"but with French culture in particular" (*R*, 210; cf. the "cérébralité qui a triomphé dans les lettres françaises de l'époque actuelle," *WJ*, 139). This cerebrality, abstraction and artifice are among the traits he will ascribe, in "The Rhetoric of Temporality," to allegory. Indeed, de Man's late work itself "exhibits all the negative characteristics cited by the young Paul: cerebrality, abstraction, a tendency to 'différencier à outrance' " (Johnson, xvi). But in the wartime journalism, the values associated with the symbol prevail virtually unchallenged.

Those values give the impetus to articles like "Le destin de la Flandre" (*Le Soir* 1 September 1941; *WJ*, 139–140), a programmatic text in which de Man seeks to define and demarcate the "nation"—in this instance the Flemish nation—to establish its origin and its essence according to aesthetic criteria. The particular "genius" of Flemish art, with its "elective virtues" of pictorialism and realism, accords Flanders the status of an art-nation whose cultural and political autonomy must be preserved in the face of the current imperialist threat ("one can pose the question of its political destiny only as a function of its cultural qualities"). Hamacher assesses the ideological import of this national aestheticism:

> as a theory of the originality, autonomy and essence of a nation, [it] demonstrates unmistakable affinities with the national-aesthetic myths of origin propogated in fascist Germany at the same time. There can be no doubt about the proto-fascist substance of this theory. But—with it de Man makes himself the defender of the art-nation Flanders against the cultural and political imperialisms of the neighboring nations and above all against the pan-Germanic annexation policy of the National Socialist regime. De Man turns the national-aesthetic ideologeme—which not only suited the occupation powers and their organized Belgian supporters, but was even borrowed from their own ideological resources—against the Nazi's integration plans . . . and uses it as an argument not only for the cultural autonomy but also for the political independence of Belgium. (443)[26]

A few months later, in the review of Willems's "Tout est réel ici," de Man argues the participation of Belgian fantastic realism, the outgrowth of Flemish pictorial realism, in both the German romantic and the French surrealist traditions, at no cost to its (relative) autonomy. In this sense, contemporary Belgian art is the privileged locus of the synthesis of the great cultural blocs of Europe, France and Germany, now at war. "But what in the antagonistic art-nations ought to join together to create this Belgian unity must itself already have the character of the European synthesis": it is in this context that "de Man praises Goethe's combination of a *sensibilité latine* and a *sensibilité germanique, la sythèse de ces deux tempéraments nationaux;* and he lauds Ernst Jünger, the only other German author for whom he shows unrestrained admiration, for his combination of myth and reality" (Hamacher, 454).

Given the virtually uninterrupted, rapid-fire deployment of national stereotypes in these articles, those few junctures at which the reviewer hestiates, however briefly, warrant further consideration. In the course of enumerating the " 'French' virtues" of Goethe's novel ("the rare perfection of the proportions . . . the rigor of the logical arrangements," etc.), he writes that "one point in this admirable architecture"—one of the novel's own figures for proportion, balance, and symmetry—"merits that one pause over it longer." This is followed by the sentences, singled out by Hamacher as written by a reader rather than an ideologue, on the "strange interlude" early in the novel's second part, which suspends the narrative development, but functions crucially to introduce "the factor of time, of the *duration* of events." De Man pauses, takes time (a quantity in short supply in journalism, particularly of the daily variety) to single out for attention the place where the novel itself pauses, interrupts itself to introduce the time factor. He takes the time, that is—if only a moment—to read. The review then resumes its ideological course, and its brisk pace, as de Man goes on to align the introduction of the time factor, of duration, with "the 'French' virtues of the 'Affinities,' " ascribing it to the "rigor of the logical arrangement," specifically that of the mimetic logic of realism: "a narrative which aims to produce the real rhythm of existence must insert such epochs." He then proceeds directly to catalogue the novel's "German" features.

To read such a passage now, after the fact (the fact of its first and its second appearance, the fact of the late work), is in part to ask whether the factor of time can indeed be understood as contingent (upon national origin, for example), whether it can be subsumed under one or another "logical arrangement." The de Man of "The Rhetoric of Temporality" and the essays that followed would answer that, where texts are concerned, it cannot. When the factor of time is understood not as contingent but as constitutive, it resists assimilation to such a logic (of nationalism, of realism, of blindness and insight). In the review of *The Elective Affinities,* it might serve to skew the opposition and the synthesis of the art-nations, as allegory skews the symbol, as the fact that the foundation-stone of the summer-house is also and at the same time (*zugleich*) a memorial stone—at once a time capsule and a grave marker—may skew the spatial symmetry of the "admirable architecture" both of the building and of the novel itself.

The "introduction of the time factor," then, may be understood to disrupt the rhetoric and the ideology of the symbol that, when mapped onto European culture and politics in 1940–43, yielded the national aestheticism (the phrase is Lacoue-Labarthe's in his *La fiction du politique*) that determines much of the wartime journalism. The argument of de Man's late work, its theoretical reflection on rhetoric and ideology, is that, in Hartman's words, "Any mode of analysis that sees the text as an organicist unity or uses it for a totalizing purpose is blind, and the text itself will 'deconstruct' such disclosures" ("Looking Back," 19). This would include the argument of his 1983 lecture on the *Wahlverwandtschaften*.

The lecture begins by invoking the novel's "sombre," "upsetting" and "haunting" quality, suggesting that the reader "can be unaware of [the] sombreness until it catches hold," with a "belated shock effect" (like that of a time bomb). De Man goes on to assert that the novel's "dreamlike" overdeterminations are "not symbolic, not transposable into a single symbolic register," that the "different registers [are] not necessarily compatible." The claims that he makes for the unity of the novel's symbolic system in the *Le Soir* review are in the late lecture subsumed under the first of "three levels of reading." The initial level or moment is that of "trope," of the text's "literal [and] figural diction."[27] "This novel is, more than any other text you can read, about language," and de Man's reading first takes into account its system of symmetrical "exchanges" and "substitutions." He offers a "summary in terms of geometrical figures" of the relations among the principal characters: they are "structured like a circle or rather a sphere," and also as a "cross"; the tropology thus draws on the "highly formalized, symbolic language" of Rosicrucianism and freemasonry that "hangs over eighteenth and nineteenth century literature" (he mentions *Wilhelm Meister* and *Die Zauberflöte*, and adds, ironically, "once you're aware of this you'll go crazy. The less you know about it the better." That irony takes a sharp turn in light of the wartime journalism, for example the "Introduction to Contemporary German Literature" (*Le Soir* 3/2/42; *WJ*, 200–201], an account of the 1942 German Book Exposition that Alice Kaplan calls the "rhetorical apogee of de Man's collaborative writing" [*R*, 276]).[28] The cross within the circle figures the "principle of totalization" conveyed most notably through the "analogy of the chemical reactions" elaborated in the novel's fourth chapter. In the "equation between elements" ($CaCO_3 + H_2SO_4 = CaSO_4 + CO_2 + H_2O$), the "original formulation is symmetrical," reflecting the "balance," the "specular relation between [the] two sides of [the] equal sign" and "allowing for crossing over." The "affinities [that] develop" between Eduard and Ottilie, the Captain and Charlotte do so according to this "rigorously symmetrical" model: hence the "double adultery," the "double resemblance" in the child, the "baptism [of the child]" and the "death [of the priest]." That "symmetry is the principle of totalization" that organizes the narrative.

It is fitting that the chemical formula provided is that for limestone and gypsum, for the "principle of building" that is a "constant" in the novel "is itself a principle of symmetry." Its thematic function is multiple, since building (e.g. the construction of the summer house) is also "the figure of marriage," "tied to the institution of marriage" as a "balance between *Blutverwandtschaft* (filiation) and *Seelenverwandtschaft* (affinity)," between the genetic and the erotic (he here alludes to Benjamin's essay on the novel, and its citation of Kant's *Metaphysics of Morals,* which defines marriage as "the union of two people of different sexes in lifelong reciprocal possession of one another's sexual properties"). Thus the "equation sets [the] pattern of the book. [The] polarities, by crossing over, result in totalizations," "all under [the] aegis of [the] fundamental metaphor of building," of "*Stiftung* as the grounding of an institution," the "property on which the stability of [the] balance [between] genetic [and] erotic rests." And the story itself, "based on [the] principle of symmetry [is] as such like a building, an architectonic."

De Man reads the text's symmetries in terms of the tropological function of language, the operation of figures like chiasmus and prosopopoeia: the "elaborate system of symmetries," of "specular relations," is "one of [the] most powerful forces of trope—it is the system of trope, [with] its overdeterminations," that establishes the "integrated unity in [the] presentation of the novel" ("everything relates to everything else") that the young journalist praised in the *Le Soir* review. But in the lecture, de Man goes on to discern a "disturbance of [the] symmetry on the level of tropes." And it is here that the later encounter with *Die Wahlverwandtschaften* locates the intervention of the time factor, for this disturbance occurs "temporally": "what seems to work in space doesn't work on [the] temporal level." As evidence, he cites the insistent role in the narrative of "impatience" and haste (*Eile*), associated especially with the impetuous Eduard, who "plays the flute too hurriedly" in his duets with Charlotte, such that the "tempos don't coincide." He recalls as well the symptomatic scene of reading in which "Charlotte runs ahead in reading over [his] shoulder as Euard reads aloud," resulting in a "distortion that disrupts [the] spontaneous illusion of representation, of voice, in reading"; Eduard likens the effect to being "torn in two," a figure that anticipates the subsequent fate of Nanni, Ottilie's companion, who is "literally" dismembered (then re-membered) near the novel's end. Such "confusion of literal and figurative" accounts for the always possible "fundamental error of reading, of interpretation" that consists in "taking one for the other"—as in taking death for life in the *tableau vivant,* which depends on effects "achieved by trope" for its "complex balance of life and death." "To represent dead painting as alive is [a] mistake. The *tableau* is not *vivant*"—with consequences for Goethe's text, whose "narration in [the] present [tense] affords a "succession of tableaux vivants." The sense that "reading is dangerous in the novel" is confirmed when, in the "movement from adultery to infanticide" in the narrative's "succession of crimes," the drowning of the child is presented "as a result of Ottilie's reading" (in a scene in which she is represented allegorically, as the "emblematic figure of the patron saint of Alsace, book in hand," fatally forgetful of death). The "system of symmetrical tropes is undone in this play with life and death." More precisely, the symmetry established "at the level of trope [is] undone by temporality," "disturbed by a temporal lack of convergence," by the introduction of the factor of time. "The epistemological asymmetry of knowing" is a *temporal* asymmetry: "things don't come together in time." Yet this "undoing" can be "recuperated on [the] level of representation," to the extent that this story of negative knowledge can still be told.

The lecture goes on to elaborate what disrupts or resists totalization in terms of other moments of reading, other functions of language. De Man invokes the "level" or "system of the letter," the "asemantic" function associated with the terms *Buchstabe* ("mistranslated as symbol") and *Zeichensprache,* and embodied in the figure of Ottilie as "allegorically overdetermined element" (the several characters "thematize" one or another "linguistic function": "there are no persons in this book"). In scenes like that in which Ottilie copies Eduard's contract ("by means of which property is acquired, [the] house set up") in handwriting that comes to resemble his own—or in which, at any rate, he can only see his own—the "crossing takes place on the literal level of *Handschrift,*" of the "materiality of writing, of inscription." The "level of the letter" "undoes [the] level of representation, of trope"; it is "no longer [a] thematics, no longer [the] realm of trope and substitution," "no longer of [the] order of representation," but rather of the order of "allegory." The fate of the characters is "inscribed in the nature of language": "Ottilie becomes mute, [the] letter loses its voice." And the "hopelessness of this is intolerable. Hard to take. No escape. Intolerable. That's the way it is."

Finally, de Man suggests the possibility of a further "recuperation" at the "level of narrative control" (of "Goethe's '*wir*' "), a possibility he terms "dialogism."[29] But again, the intervention of time prevents this recovery from being complete. For in the novel itself, "wrong stories [are] constantly being told at [the] wrong time," in the manner of "gaffes" that are "fine, coherent as stories, but told in untimely fashion," with results that are "deeply and fundamentally embarassing," indeed "catastrophic" (he recalls the effects of Mittler's remarks on Ottilie, and especially those of the interpolated tale of the "strange young neighbors" on Charlotte). For readers of the novel, the lecture concludes, the dialogic "asymmetry" raises the questions: "is [Goethe's] story timely for us? Can we attain

Goethe's serenity?" The answer afforded in the lecture—a far cry from the reassuring assertion of the "universalism of Goethe" in the early review—is that the story "never comes at the right time," is "always untimely," that it is "always a catastrophe to understand it." "This is dialogism—[the] fundamental asymmetry of [the] dialogical situation": the asymmetry between the text and its reading that troubles our own efforts to read the past in the present, to read (for example) the wartime journalism in this, its second phase of use.

If we reread the *Le Soir* review in the retrospective light of the late lecture, we find that the apparent unity, symmetry, and harmony it prizes in Goethe's novel are made possible by a highly formalized system of tropes, a system on which knowledge and cognition depend. The moment in which the review pauses to consider the time factor—and so, potentially, its disfiguring, asymmetricalizing effect, its exposure of the precarious status of the text's totalizations—is immediately reinscribed in the symbolic system, according to the mechanism analyzed in the late work whereby the threat posed to cognition is, inevitably but erroneously, reinscribed in a tropological system, whereby the historical event is recuperated for, implemented in, one or another aesthetic and political program. It would be left to essays like "Aesthetic Formalization in Kleist" to analyze "the complicity between the aesthetic valorization of form"—specifically the model of trope, the "transformational turns and substitutive exchanges of which are necessarily informed by a telos of infinite totalization"—and "totalitarian claims to hegemony" (Weber, in *R*, 413, 415). The late essays seek to elaborate, to make explicit the articulation of "textual models and the historical and political systems that are their correlate" (de Man, *RR*, 289). As Chase suggests, "the correlation . . . between a totalitarian state and a model of the text as a 'formal system of tropes' [*RR*, 285] is more than an impression and other than an analogy" (*R*, 55). The burden imposed by the correlation of the textual and the political, like that imposed by the attempt to articulate early with late de Man, is that of reading: the relations (whether of continuity and complicity, or discontinuity and distance) cannot be presumed, but must be read, again and again, in each here and now. "The suspension of the necessity of reading needs to be resisted because it closes down the possibility of a future. In doing so, it is inevitably totalitarian, whereas reading, in suspending, is not *inevitably* totalitarian, which does not mean that it is inevitably democratic either—reading is not inevitably anything, that's why it holds out the promise of a future" (Warminski, in *R*, 387–388).

This is also the burden (and the promise) of the effort to correlate text and history, the order of language and the order of the event. It is the burden assumed, in no uncertain terms, in de Man's late work. As Weber argues, the conception of history in the essays from "Shelley Disfigured" to "Kant and Schiller" is a far cry from that advanced in *Le Soir* and *Het Vlaamsche Land,* for example in "Criticism and Literary History," where history appears as a "continuity" in which "one generation ensues logically from the preceding one" (*Het Vlaamsche Land* 6/7–8/42, *WJ,* 313–314); the two understandings "are separated by a practice of reading which is both informed by a theory of language and which transforms it in turn" (*R,* 413–414). The order of events, as theorized in de Man's mature writings, is assimilable neither to a logic (or dialectics), nor to the tropology of cognition, nor, finally, to temporality. History, as "Kant and Schiller" demonstrates, is not a movement of mediation, not a temporal process, but a radical transformation "from cognition, from acts of knowledge . . . to something which is no longer a cognition but which is to some extent an *occurrence,* which has the materiality of something that actually happens, that actually occurs . . . that leaves a trace on the world" (*AI*). In this sense, history is *"what is happening,"* as Derrida writes, and "happening to *us.*" For Derrida, as for de Man, as for Goethe's eloquent mason, history "belongs to the order of the absolutely unforeseeable, which is always the condition of any event"—for example, the disclosure of the wartime journalism. "Even when it seems to go back to a buried past, what comes about always comes from the future" (*R,* 128). From the work to come.

Notes

1. Walter Jackson Bate, "The Crisis in English Studies," *Harvard Magazine* 85.1 (Sept.–Oct. 1982): 46.

2. In Werner Hamacher, Neil Hertz, and Thomas Keenan, eds., *Responses: On Paul de Man's Wartime Journalism* (Lincoln: U of Nebraska P, 1988) 204. Cited hereafter as *R.*

3. Lynne A. Higgins, rev. of Paul de Man, *Wartime Journalism, 1939–1943* and Hamacher, Hertz, and Keenan, *Responses, South Central Review* 6:2 (Summer 1989): 105–106.

4. Paul de Man, *Wartime Journalism, 1939–1943,* ed. Werner Hamacher, Neil Hertz, and Thomas Keenan (Lincoln: U of Nebraska P, 1988) 208. Cited hereafter as *WJ.*

5. Barbara Johnson, "Preface to the Paperback Edition: A Note on the Wartime Writings of Paul de Man," *A World of Difference,* 2nd ed. (Baltimore: Johns Hopkins UP, 1988) xii.

6. Geoffrey Hartman, "Looking Back on Paul de Man," *Reading de Man Reading,* ed. Lindsay Waters and Wlad Godzich (Minneapolis: U of Minnesota P, 1989) 18.

7. Paul de Man, *Blindness and Insight: Essays in the Rhetoric of Contemporary Criticism,* 2nd ed., rev. (Minneapolis: U of Minnesota P, 1983) 14. Cited hereafter as *BI.*

8. Wlad Godzich, "Religion, The State, and Post(al) Modernism," afterword to Samuel Weber, *Institution and Interpretation* (Minneapolis: U of Minnesota P) 155. See also Graff, in *R*, 249.

9. "De Man treats Husserl with a 'respect' that is more than mere politeness; it acknowledges his own indebtedness, since if he questions Husserl, it is only by extending Husserl's conception of critical self-reflection to the philosopher's determination of self-criticism as 'the historical privilege of European man' (de Man), in order to argue that the very project of attributing universal validity to a localized phenomenon reveals that the notion of self-criticism itself reposes upon an uncriticized, and perhaps uncriticizable, presumption of 'self' " (Weber, in *R*, 423, n. 11). We do well to keep in mind such indebtedness when we make use of the critical tools with which de Man has provided us in seeking to dismantle the ideologemes operative in his own early writings.

10. Paul de Man, *The Rhetoric of Romanticism* (New York: Columbia UP, 1984) 276. Cited hereafter as *RR*.

11. "Derrida, in his recent study of Heidegger, *De l'esprit,* is drawn to cite the same passage. . . . And to the question 'Why recall such a passage and cite it today?' Derrida replies, in part: 'Using the example [*sur l'exemple*] of a discourse that in general is not suspected of [harboring] the worst, it is good to recall that referring to the *spirit,* to *freedom* of the spirit and to the spirit as *European,* could and still can be allied with a politics to which one would like to oppose it.' [Jacques Derrida, *De l'esprit. Heidegger et la question*. Paris: Galilée, 1987, 95 n.2]" (Weber, in *R*, 409).

12. Richard Klein, "The Blindness of Hyperboles; the Ellipses of Insight," *diacritics* 3.2 (1973): 36.

13. In his reading of Rousseau's *Second Discourse,* de Man allows for such a temporal intervention in what initially appears as a logical contradiction: "Are we forced to conclude that Rousseau's paradoxes are genuine contradictions, that he did not know, in the *Discourse,* what he stated in the *Essay,* and vice versa? Perhaps we should heed his admonition: 'in order not to find me in contradiction with myself, I should be allowed enough time to explain myself' " (Paul de Man, *Allegories of Reading: Figural Language in Rousseau, Nietzsche, Rilke and Proust* [New Haven: Yale UP, 1979] 149. Cited hereafter as *AR*).

14. Higgins examines the "recurrent motif of continuity and rupture" in the efforts of *Responses* to articulate early with late de Man. She also interrogates possible continuities and discontinuities between de Man and deconstruction, collaboration and resistance, journalism and scholarship (108–109).

15. On the constitutive blindness of philosophical reflection, see also Zizek: "There is the theatre in which your truth was performed before you took cognizance of it. The confrontation with this place is unbearable because philosophy as such *is defined* by its blindness to this place" (*The Sublime Object of Ideology* [London: Verso, 1989] 19–20].

16. The operation of blindness and insight, as de Man understood it, could be summoned as a partial explanation—if one were required—for the disinclination to meet in advance the demand made by John Brenkman and

others that he set the record straight with a public confession or apology ("De Man eschewed any acknowledged reflection on his writing and activity during the war. He participated in fascism publicly, but did not abandon it publicly [R, 21]—although, as several essays in *Responses* attest, de Man made his writings for the collaborationist press known to a number of people at critical junctures in his career). Once again, Godzich provides an economical summary: "A blindness constitutive of an insight was far more interesting than the result of its correction would be: at best, the latter would smooth out the argumentative path through which the insight was obtained; at worst, it would erase the traces of the functioning of a cognitive mechanism that forced anyone examining it into wondering about the provenance of insight, and thus of the workings of cognition in general. Correcting errors sets the record straight, eliminates impediments to thought; reflecting on blindness, on the other hand, forces thought into a reflective judgment about its own tortuous and discontinuous path, the very blindness of which consists in the fact that it has no guide to warn against its vagaries" (155).

17. With reference to de Man's praise of Charles Peguy as a Dreyfusard in the "Chronique littéraire" for 5/6/41 (*WJ*, 85–86), Ian Balfour takes note of the effect that the example of Peguy may have exercised on de Man: "By holding up Peguy's life as exemplary, [de Man] offers an implicit contrast to his own position" (*R*, 8).

18. Geoffrey Hartman, "History and Judgment: The Case of Paul de Man," *History and Memory* (1989): 69.

19. The version of the lecture cited here was compiled from three sets of notes recorded by colleagues and students in attendance, including my own. Taken together, the notes make for a full and detailed, if not verbatim, transcription.

20. Johann Wolfgang von Goethe, *Die Wahlverwandtschaften* (Frankfurt am Main: Insel, 1976) 66. *Elective Affinities*, trans. James A. Froude and R. Dillon Boylan (New York: Frederick Ungar, 1962) 64.

21. In his *Life and Works of Goethe*, George Henry Lewes cites the author's reflection on the novel: "In it, as in a burial urn, I have deposited many a sad experience. The 3rd of October 1809 (when the publication was completed) set me free from the work: but the feelings it embodies can never depart from me' " ([London: J. M. Dent, 1908] 520).

22. Lewes provides an example of the "discussion about the appropriateness" of the interlude, commenting, "A dear friend of mine, whose criticism is always worthy of attention, thinks that the long episodes which interrupt the progress of the story during the interval of Eduard's absence and return, are artistic devices for impressing the reader with a sense of the slow movement of life; and, in truth, it is only in fiction that the denouement usually lies close to the exposition. I give this opinion, for the reader's consideration; but it seems to me more ingenious than just. I must confess that the stress Goethe lays on the improvements of the park, the erection of the moss hut, the restoration of the chapel, the making of new roads, &c., is out of all proportion, and somewhat

tedious" (525). I am grateful to Lesley Turner for calling this passage to my attention, and for noting that the view of Lewes's friend (possibly George Eliot) corresponds to that of de Man in the *Le Soir* review.

23. Paul de Man, *The Resistance to Theory*. (Minneapolis: U of Minnesota P, 1986) 121. Cited hereafter as *RT*.

24. Paul de Man, *Aesthetic Ideology*, ed. Andrzej Warminski (Minneapolis: U of Minnesota P, forthcoming.). Cited hereafter as *AI*.

25. "Nationalism is an agonism. It draws its life not from the natural community of a nation, but from the will to destroy the other, in whose image it is at the same time supposed to be created. The logic of nationalism is the logic of homicidal, suicidal identification" (Hamacher, in *R*, 439). Hamacher deliberately poses the question as "what was it that *did not prevent* such articles?" For "Only when it is asked in this way is the question not really a question about a hidden determinism to which the intellectuals of that time would have fallen victim; and only when asked in this way does the question give the answer a chance to isolate factors in the situation of intellectuals that would still, *even today,* not prevent a comparable commitment to a no less disastrous politics" (440). He also reminds us that we should not forget the articles in *Jeudi* that call for a practical critique of the nationalist spirit (439).

26. A "decisive ideological-political point" in such an instance is, in Hamacher's formulation, "to be able, in a given hisorical moment, to estimate precisely how far the resistance and how far the exploitability of a particular ideologeme reaches" (*R*, 444).

27. The model of language as trope was addressed in detail in the lecture preceding this one in the course, given by J. Hillis Miller. See his "A Buchstäbliches Reading of *The Elective Affinities*": "The basic paradigm of *The Elective Affinities* is the following: Human relations are like the substitutions in metaphorical expressions, or, to put it the other way, since these metaphorical analogies are reversible, the laws of language may be dramatized in human relations" (*Glyph* 6 [1979]: 7).

28. De Man cites the Reichsleiter Baldur von Schirach, who "situates the problem with complete clairvoyance": " 'He who calls Goethe a freemason or the "Magic Flute" a freemason opera is not taken seriously by our people. . . . Each great work . . . is always the expression of an isolated personality and, at the same time, of the entire nation. But the nation is not only the current and the immediate, but the eternal community of language and of blood. . . .' " And de Man comments in conclusion: "It is because German literature has conformed to these sage precepts that it has been able to realize its goals and to prepare the way for future greatness" (*WJ*, 201).

29. De Man interrogates the concept of dialogism as developed in the work of Bakhtin in "Dialogue and Dialogism" (*RT*).

Rethinking Responsibility: Politics and Ethics

▼ JUDITH BUTLER ▼

Contingent Foundations
Feminism and the Question of "Postmodernism"

THE QUESTION OF POSTMODERNISM is surely a question, for is there, after all, something called postmodernism? Is it a historical characterization, a certain kind of theoretical position, and what does it mean for a term that has described a certain aesthetic practice now to apply to social theory and to feminist social and political theory in particular? Who are these postmodernists? Is this a name that one takes on for oneself, or is it more often a name that one is called if and when one offers a critique of the subject, a discursive analysis, or questions the integrity or coherence of totalizing social descriptions?

I know the term from the way it is used, and it usually appears on my horizon embedded in the following critical formulations: "if discourse is all there is . . . ," or "if everything is a text . . . ," or "if the subject is dead . . . ," or "if real bodies do not exist . . . " The sentence begins as a warning against an impending nihilism, for if the conjured content of these series of conditional clauses proves to be true, then, and there is always a then, some set of dangerous consequences will surely follow. So "postmodernism" appears to be articulated in the form of a fearful conditional or sometimes in the form of paternalistic disdain toward that which is youthful and irrational. Against this postmodernism, there is an effort to shore up the primary premises, to establish in advance that any theory of politics requires a subject, needs from the start to presume its subject, the referentiality of language, the integrity of the institutional descriptions

From *Feminists Theorize the Political,* ed. Judith Butler and Joan W. Scott (New York: Routledge, 1992).

it provides. For politics is unthinkable without a foundation, without those premises. But do these claims seek to secure a contingent formation of politics that requires that these notions remain unproblematized features of its own definition? Is it the case that all politics, and feminist politics in particular, is unthinkable without these prized premises? Or is it rather that a specific version of politics is shown in its contingency once those premises are problematically thematized?

To claim that politics requires a stable subject is to claim that there can be no *political* opposition to that claim. Indeed, that claim implies that a critique of the subject cannot be a politically informed critique but, rather, an act which puts into jeopardy politics as such. To require the subject means to foreclose the domain of the political, and that foreclosure, installed analytically as an essential feature of the political, enforces the boundaries of the domain of the political in such a way that that enforcement is protected from political scrutiny. The act which unilaterally establishes the domain of the political functions, then, as an authoritarian ruse by which political contest over the status of the subject is summarily silenced.[1]

To refuse to assume, that is, to require a notion of the subject from the start is not the same as negating or dispensing with such a notion altogether; on the contrary, it is to ask after the process of its construction and the political meaning and consequentiality of taking the subject as a requirement or presupposition of theory. But have we arrived yet at a notion of postmodernism?

A number of positions are ascribed to postmodernism, as if it were the kind of thing that could be the bearer of a set of positions: discourse is all there is, as if discourse were some kind of monistic stuff out of which all things are composed; the subject is dead, I can never say "I" again; there is no reality, only representations. These characterizations are variously imputed to postmodernism or poststructuralism, which are conflated with each other and sometimes conflated with deconstruction, and sometimes understood as an indiscriminate assemblage of French feminism, deconstruction, Lacanian psychoanalysis, Foucauldian analysis, Rorty's conversationalism and cultural studies. On this side of the Atlantic and in recent discourse, the terms "postmodernism" or "poststructuralism" settle the differences among those positions in a single stroke, providing a substantive, a noun, that includes those positions as so many of its modalities or permutations. It may come as a surprise to some purveyors of the Continental scene to learn that Lacanian psychoanalysis in France positions itself officially against poststructuralism, that Kristeva denounces postmodernism,[2] that Foucauldians rarely relate to Derrideans, that Cixous and Irigaray are fundamentally opposed, and that the only tenuous connection between

French feminism and deconstruction exists between Cixous and Derrida, although a certain affinity in textual practices is to be found between Derrida and Irigaray. Biddy Martin is also right to point out that almost all of French feminism adheres to a notion of high modernism and the avant-garde, which throws some question on whether these theories or writings can be grouped simply under the category of postmodernism.

I propose that the question of postmodernism be read not merely as the question that postmodernism poses for feminism, but as the question, What is postmodernism? What kind of existence does it have? Jean-François Lyotard champions the term, but he cannot be made into the example of what all the rest of the purported postmodernists are doing.[3] Lyotard's work is, for instance, seriously at odds with that of Derrida, who does not affirm the notion of "the postmodern," and with others for whom Lyotard is made to stand. Is he paradigmatic? Do all these theories have the same structure (a comforting notion to the critic who would dispense with them all)? Is the effort to colonize and domesticate these theories under the sign of the same, to group them synthetically and masterfully under a single rubric, a simple refusal to grant the specificity of these positions, an excuse not to read, and not to read closely? For if Lyotard uses the term, and if he can be conveniently grouped with a set of writers, and if some problematic quotation can be found in his work, then can that quotation serve as an "example" of postmodernism, symptomatic of the whole?

But if I understand part of the project of postmodernism, it is to call into question the ways in which such "examples" and "paradigms" serve to subordinate and erase that which they seek to explain. For the "whole," the field of postmodernism in its supposed breadth, is effectively "produced" by the example which is made to stand as a symptom and exemplar of the whole; in effect, if in the example of Lyotard we think we have a representation of postmodernism, we have then forced a substitution of the example for the entire field, to effect a violent reduction of the field to the one piece of text the critic is willing to read, a piece which, conveniently, uses the term "postmodern."

In a sense, this gesture of conceptual mastery that groups together a set of positions under the postmodern, that makes the postmodern into an epoch or a synthetic whole, and that claims that the part can stand for this artificially constructed whole, enacts a certain self-congratulatory ruse of power. It is paradoxical, at best, that the act of conceptual mastery that effects this dismissive grouping of positions under the postmodern wants to ward off the peril of political authoritarianism. For the assumption is that some piece of the text is representational, that it stands for the phenomenon, and that the structure of "these" positions can be properly and economically discerned in the structure of the one. What authorizes such an assumption from the start? From the start we must believe that theories offer themselves in bundles or in organized totalities, and that historically a set of theories which are structurally similar emerge as the articulation of an historically specific condition of human reflection. This Hegelian trope, which continues through Adorno, assumes from the start that these theories can be substituted for one another because they variously symptomatize a common structural preoccupation. And yet, that presumption can no longer be made, for the Hegelian presumption that a synthesis is available from the start is precisely what has come under contest in various ways by some of the positions happily unified under the sign of postmodernism. One might argue that if, and to the extent that, the postmodern functions as such a unifying sign, then it is a decidedly "modern" sign, which is why there is some question whether one can debate for or against this postmodernism. To install the term as that which can be only affirmed or negated is to force it to occupy one position within a binary, and so to affirm a logic of noncontradiction over and against some more generative scheme.

Perhaps the reason for this unification of positions is occasioned by the very unruliness of the field, by the way in which the differences among these positions cannot be rendered symptomatic, exemplary, or representative of each other and of some common structure called postmodernism. If postmodernism as a term has some force or meaning within social theory, or feminist social theory in particular, perhaps it can be found in the critical exercise that seeks to show how theory, how philosophy, is always implicated in power, and perhaps that is precisely what is symptomatically at work in the effort to domesticate and refuse a set of powerful criticisms under the rubric of postmodernism. That the philosophical apparatus in its various conceptual refinements is always engaged in exercising power is not a new insight, but then again the postmodern ought not to be confused with the new; after all, the pursuit of the "new" is the preoccupation of high modernism; if anything, the postmodern casts doubt upon the possibility of a "new" that is not in some way already implicated in the "old."

But the point articulated forcefully by some recent critics of normative political philosophy is that the recourse to a position—hypothetical, counterfactual, or imaginary—that places itself beyond the play of power, and which seeks to establish the metapolitical basis for a negotiation of power relations, is perhaps the most insidious ruse of power. That this position beyond power lays claim to its legitimacy through recourse to a prior and implicitly universal agreement does not in any way circumvent the charge, for what rationalist project will designate in advance what counts as agreement? What form of insidious cultural imperialism here legislates itself under the sign of the universal?[4]

I don't know about the term "postmodern," but if there is a point, and a fine point, to what I perhaps better understand as poststructuralism, it is that power pervades the very conceptual apparatus that seeks to negotiate its terms, including the subject-position of the critic; and further, that this implication of the terms of criticism in the field of power is *not* the advent of a nihilistic relativism incapable of furnishing norms, but, rather, the very precondition of a politically engaged critique. To establish a set of norms that are beyond power or force is itself a powerful and forceful conceptual practice that sublimates, disguises and extends its own powerplay through recourse to tropes of normative universality. And the point is not to do away with foundations, or even to champion a position that goes under the name of antifoundationalism. Both of those positions belong together as different versions of foundationalism and the skeptical problematic it engenders. Rather, the task is to interrogate what the theoretical move that establishes foundations *authorizes,* and what precisely it excludes or forecloses.

It seems that theory posits foundations incessantly, and forms implicit metaphysical commitments as a matter of course, even when it seeks to guard against it; foundations function as the unquestioned and the unquestionable within any theory. And yet are not these "foundations," that is, those premises that function as authorizing grounds, are they themselves not constituted through exclusions which, taken into account, expose the foundational premise as a contingent and contestable presumption? Even when we claim that there is some implied universal basis for a given foundation, that implication and that universality simply constitute a new dimension of unquestionability.

How is it that we might ground a theory or politics in a speech situation or subject position which is "universal," when the very category of the universal has only begun to be exposed for its own highly ethnocentric biases? How many "universalities" are there?[5] And to what extent is cultural conflict understandable as the clashing of a set of presumed and intransigent "universalities," a conflict which cannot be negotiated through recourse to a culturally imperialist notion of the "universal" or, rather, that will only be solved through such recourse at the cost of violence? We have, I think, witnessed the conceptual and material violence of this practice in the United States' war against Iraq, in which the Arab "other" is understood to be radically "outside" the universal structures of reason and democracy and, hence, calls to be brought forcibly within. Significantly, the U.S. had to abrogate the democratic principles of political sovereignty and free speech, among others, to effect this forcible return of Iraq to the "democratic" fold, and this violent move reveals, among other things, that such notions of universality are installed through the abrogation of the very universal principles to be implemented. Within the political context of contemporary postcoloniality more generally, it is perhaps especially urgent to underscore the very category of the "universal" as a site of insistent contest and resignification.[6] Given the contested character of the term, to assume from the start a procedural or substantive notion of the universal is of necessity to impose a culturally hegemonic notion on the social field. To herald that notion then as the philosophical instrument that will negotiate between conflicts of power is precisely to safeguard and reproduce a position of hegemonic power by installing it in the metapolitical site of ultimate normativity.

It may at first seem that I am simply calling for a more concrete and internally diverse "universality," a more synthetic and inclusive notion of the universal, and in that way committed to the very foundational notion that I seek to undermine. But my task is, I think, significantly different from that which would articulate a comprehensive universality. In the first place, such a totalizing notion could only be achieved at the cost of producing new and further exclusions. The term "universality" would have to be left permanently open, permanently contested, permanently contingent, in order not to foreclose in advance future claims for inclusion. Indeed, from my position and from any historically constrained perspective, any totalizing concept of the universal will shut down rather than authorize the unanticipated and unanticipatable claims that will be made under the sign of "the universal." In this sense, I am not doing away with the category, but trying to relieve the category of its foundationalist weight in order to render it as a site of permanent political contest.

A social theory committed to democratic contestation within a postcolonial horizon needs to find a way to bring into question the foundations it is compelled to lay down. It is this movement of interrogating that ruse of authority that seeks to close itself off from contest that is, in my view, at the heart of any radical political project. Inasmuch as poststructuralism offers a mode of critique that effects this contestation of the foundationalist move, it can be used as a part of such a radical agenda. Note that I have said, "it can be used": I think there are no necessary political consequences for such a theory, but only a possible political deployment.

If one of the points associated with postmodernism is that the epistemological point of departure in philosophy is inadequate, then it ought not to be a question of subjects who claim to know and theorize under the sign of the postmodern pitted against other subjects who claim to know and theorize under the sign of the modern. Indeed, it is that very way of framing debate that is being contested by the suggestion that the position articulated by the subject is always in some way constituted by what must be displaced for that position to take hold, and that the subject who theorizes is constituted as a "theorizing subject" by a set of exclusionary and selective procedures. For, indeed, who is it that gets constituted as the feminist theorist whose framing of the debate will get publicity? Is it not always the case that power operates in advance, in the very procedures that establish who will be the subject that speaks in the name of feminism, and to whom? And is it not also clear that a process of subjection is presupposed in the subjectivating process that produces before you one speaking subject of feminist debate? What speaks when "I" speak to you? What are the institutional histories of subjection and subjectivation that "position" me here now? If there is something called "Butler's position," is this one that I devise, publish and defend, that belongs to me as a kind of academic property? Or is there a grammar of the subject that merely encourages us to position me as the proprietor of those theories?

Indeed, how is it that a position becomes a position, for clearly not every utterance qualifies as such. It is clearly a matter of a certain authorizing power, and that clearly does not emanate from the position itself. My position is mine to the extent that "I"—and I do not shirk from the pronoun—replay and resignify the theoretical positions that have constituted me, working the possibilities of their convergence, and trying to take account of the possibilities that they systematically exclude. But it is clearly not the case that "I" preside over the positions that have constituted me, shuffling through them instrumentally, casting some aside, incorporating others, although some of my activity may take that form. The "I" who would select between them is always already constituted by them. The "I" is the transfer point of that replay, but it is simply not a strong enough claim to say that the "I" is situated; the "I," this "I," is *constituted* by these positions, and these "positions" are not merely theoretical products, but fully embedded organizing principles of material practices and institutional arrangements, that matrix of power and discourse that produces me as a viable "subject." Indeed, this "I" would not be a thinking, speaking "I" if it were not for the very positions that I oppose, for those positions, the ones that claim that the subject must be given in advance, that discourse is an instrument or reflection of that subject, are already part of what constitutes me.

No subject is its own point of departure; and the fantasy that it is one can only disavow its constitutive relations by recasting them as the domain of a countervailing externality. Indeed, one might consider Luce Irigaray's claim that the subject, understood as a fantasy of autogenesis, is always already masculine. Psychoanalytically, that version of the subject is constituted through a kind of disavowal or through the primary repression of its dependency on the maternal. And to become a *subject* on this model is surely not a feminist goal.

The critique of the subject is not a negation or repudiation of the subject, but, rather, a way of interrogating its construction as a pregiven or foundationalist premise. At the outset of war against Iraq, we almost all saw strategists who placed before us maps of the Middle East, objects of analysis and targets of instrumental military action. Retired and active generals were called up by the networks to stand in for the generals on the field whose intentions would be invariably realized in the destruction of various Iraqi military bases. The various affirmations of the early success of these operations were delivered with great enthusiasm, and it seemed that this hitting of the goal, this apparently seamless realization of intention through an instrumental action without much resistance or hindrance was the occasion, not merely to destroy Iraqi military installations, but also to champion a masculinized subject whose will immediately translates into a deed, whose utterance or order materializes in an action which would destroy the very possibility of a reverse strike, and whose obliterating power at once confirms the impenetrable contours of its own subjecthood.

It is perhaps interesting to remember at this juncture that Foucault linked the displacement of the intentional subject with modern power relations that he himself associated with war.[7] What he meant, I think, is that subjects who institute actions are themselves instituted effects of prior actions, and that the horizon in which we act is there as a constitutive possibility of our very capacity to act, not merely or exclusively as an exterior field or theater of operations. But perhaps more significantly, the actions instituted via that subject are part of a chain of actions that can no longer be understood as unilinear in direction or predictable in their outcomes. And yet, the instrumental military subject appears at first to utter words that materialize directly into destructive deeds. And throughout the war, it was as if the masculine Western subject preempted the divine power to translate words into deeds; the newscasters were almost all full of giddy happiness as they demonstrated, watched, vicariously enacted, the exactitude of destructiveness. As the war began, the words one would hear on television were "euphoria," and one newscaster remarked that U.S. weapons were instruments of "terrible beauty" (CBS) and celebrated prematurely and phantasmatically its own capacity to act instrumentally in the world to obliterate its opposition and to control the consequences of that obliteration. But the consequentiality of this act cannot be foreseen by the instrumental actor who currently celebrates the effectivity of its own intentions. What Foucault suggested was that this subject is itself the effect of a genealogy which is erased at the moment that the subject takes itself as the single origin of its action, and that the effects of an action always supersede the stated intention or purpose of the act. Indeed, the effects of the instrumental action always have the power to proliferate beyond the subject's control, indeed to challenge the rational transparency of that subject's intentionality, and so to subvert the very definition of the subject itself. I suggest that we are in the midst of a celebration on the part of the United States government and some of its allies of the phantasmatic subject, the one who determines its world unilaterally, and which is in some measure typified by the looming heads of retired generals framed against the map of the Middle East, where the speaking head of this subject is shown to be the same size, or larger, than the area it seeks to dominate. This is, in a sense, the graphics of the imperialist subject, a visual allegory of the action itself.

But here you think that I have made a distinction between the action itself and something like a representation, but I want to make a stronger point. You will perhaps have noticed that General Colin Powell, the chair of the Joint Chiefs of Staff, invoked what is, I think, a new military convention of calling the sending of missiles "the delivery of ordinance." The phrase is significant, I think; it figures an act of violence as an act of law, and so wraps the destruction in the appearance of orderliness; but in addition, it figures the missile as a kind of command, an order to obey, and is thus itself figured as a certain act of speech which not only delivers a message—get out of Kuwait—but effectively enforces that message through the threat of death and through death itself. Of course, this is a message that can never be received, for it kills its addressee, and so it is not an ordinance at all, but the failure of all ordinances, the refusal of a communication. And for those who remain to read the message, they will not read what is sometimes quite literally written on the missile.

Throughout the war, we witnessed and participated in the conflation of the television screen and the lens of the bomber pilot. In this sense, the visual record of this war is not a *reflection* on the war, but the enactment of its phantasmatic structure, indeed, part of the very means by which it is socially constituted and maintained as a war. The so-called "smart bomb" records its target as it moves in to destroy it—a bomb with a camera attached in front, a kind of optical phallus; it relays that film back to a command control and that film is refilmed on television, effectively constituting the television screen and its viewer as the extended apparatus of the bomb itself. In this sense, by viewing we are bombing, identified with both bomber and bomb, flying through space, transported from the North American continent to Iraq, and yet securely wedged in the couch in one's own living room. The smart bomb screen is, of course, destroyed in the moment that it enacts its destruction, which is to say that this is a recording of a throughly destructive act which can never record that destructiveness, indeed, which effects the phantasmatic distinction between the hit and its consquences. Thus as viewers, we veritably enact the allegory of military triumph: we retain our visual distance and our bodily safety through the disembodied enactment of the kill that produces no blood and in which we retain our radical impermeability. In this sense, we are in relation to this site of destruction absolutely proximate, absolutely essential, and absolutely distant, a figure for imperial power which takes the aerial, global view, the disembodied killer who can never be killed, the sniper as a figure for imperialist military power. The televsion screen thus redoubles the aerial view, securing a fantasy of transcendence, of a disembodied instrument of destruction which is infinitely protected from a reverse-strike through the guarantee of electronic distance.

This aerial view never comes close to seeing the *effects* of its destruction, and as a close-up to the site becomes increasingly possible, the screen conveniently destroys itself. And so although it was made to seem that this was a humane bombing, one which took buildings and military installations as its targets, this was, on the contrary, a frame which excludes from view the systematic destruction of a population, what Foucault calls the modern dream of states.[8] Or perhaps we ought to state it otherwise: precisely through excluding its targets from view under the rubric of proving the capacity to target precisely, this is a frame that effectively performs the annihilation that it systematically derealizes.

The demigod of a U.S. military subject which euphorically enacted the fantasy that it can achieve its aims with ease fails to understand that its actions have produced effects that will far exceed its phantasmatic purview; it thinks that its goals were achieved in a matter of weeks, and that its action was completed. But the action continues to act after the intentional subject has announced it completion. The effects of its actions have alread inaugurated violence in places and in ways that it not only could not foresee but will be unable ultimately to contain, effects which will produce a massive and violent contestation of its phantasmatic self-construction.

If I can, then, I'll try to return to the subject at hand. In a sense, the subject is constituted through an exclusion and differentiation, perhaps a repression, that is subsequently concealed, covered over, by the effect of autonomy. In this sense, autonomy is the logical consequence of a disavowed dependency, which is to say that the autonomous subject can maintain the illusion of its autonomy insofar as it covers over the break out of which it is constituted. This dependency and this break are already social relations, ones which precede and condition the formation of the subject. As a result, this is not a relation in which the subject finds itself, as one of the relations that forms its situation. The subject is constructed through acts of differentiation that distinguish the subject from its constitutive outside, a domain of abjected alterity conventionally associated with the feminine, but clearly not exclusively. Precisely in this recent war we saw "the Arab" figured as the abjected Other as well as a site of homophobic fantasy made clear in the abundance of bad jokes grounded in the linguistic sliding from Saddam to Sodom.

There is no ontologically intact reflexivity to the subject which is then placed within a cultural context; that cultural context, as it were, is already there as the disarticulated process of that subject's production, one that is concealed by the frame that would situate a ready-made subject in an external web of cultural relations.

We may be tempted to think that to assume the subject in advance is necessary in order to safeguard the *agency* of the subject. But to claim that the subject is constituted is not to claim that it is determined; on the contrary, the constituted character of the subject is the very precondition of its agency. For what is it that enables a purposive and significant reconfiguration of cultural and political relations, if not a relation that can be turned against itself, reworked, resisted? Do we need to assume theoretically from the start a subject with agency *before* we can articulate the terms of a significant social and political task of transformation, resistance, radical democratization? If we do not offer in advance the theoretical guarantee of that agent, are we doomed to give up transformation and meaningful political practice? My suggestion is that agency belongs to a way of thinking about persons as instrumental actors who confront an external political field. But if we agree that politics and power exist already at the level at which the subject and its agency are articulated and made possible, then agency can be *presumed* only at the cost of refusing to inquire into its construction. Consider that "agency" has no formal existence or, if it does, it has no bearing on the question at hand. In a sense, the epistemological model that offers us a pregiven subject or agent is one that refuses to acknowledge that *agency is always and only a political prerogative*. As such, it seems crucial to question the conditions of its possibility, not to take it for granted as an a priori guarantee. We need instead to ask, what possibilities of mobilization are produced on the basis of existing configurations of discourse and power? Where are the possibilities of reworking that very matrix of power by which we are constituted, or reconstituting the legacy of that constitution, and of working against each other those processes of regulation that can destabilize existing power regimes? For if the subject is constituted by power, that power does not cease at the moment the subject is constituted, for that subject is never fully constituted, but is subjected and produced time and again. That subject is neither a ground nor a product, but the permanent possibility of a certain resignifying process, one which gets detoured and stalled through other mechanisms of power, but which is power's own possibility of being reworked. It is not enough to say that the subject is invariably engaged in a political field; that phenomenological phrasing misses the point that the subject is an accomplishment regulated and produced in advance. And is as such fully political; indeed, perhaps *most* political at the point in which it is claimed to be prior to politics itself. To perform this kind of Foucauldian critique of the subject is not to do away with the subject or pronounce its death, but merely to claim that certain versions of the subject are politically insidious.

For the subject to be a pregiven point of departure for politics is to defer the question of the political construction and regulation of the subject itself; for it is important to remember that subjects are constituted through exclusion, that is, through the creation of a domain of deauthorized subjects, presubjects, figures of abjection, populations erased from view. This becomes clear, for instance, within the law when certain qualifications must first be met in order to be, quite literally, a claimant in sex discrimination or rape cases. Here it becomes quite urgent to ask, who qualifies as a "who," what systematic structures of disempowerment make it impossible for certain injured parties to invoke the "I" effectively within a court of law? Or less overtly, in a social theory like Albert Memmi's *The Colonizer and the Colonized,* an otherwise compelling call for radical enfranchisement, the category of women falls into neither category, the oppressor or the oppressed.[9] How do we theorize the exclusion of women from the category of the oppressed? Here the construction of subject-positions works to exclude women from the description of oppression, and this constitutes a different kind of oppression, one that is effected by the very *erasure* that grounds the articulation of the emancipatory subject. As Joan Scott makes clear in *Gender and the Politics of History,* once it is understood that subjects are formed through exclusionary operations, it becomes politically necessary to trace the operations of that construction and erasure.[10]

The above sketches in part a Foucauldian reinscription of the subject, an effort to resignify the subject as a site of resignification. As a result, it is not a "bidding farewell" to the subject per se, but, rather, a call to rework that notion outside the terms of an epistemological given. But perhaps Foucault is not really postmodern; after all, his is an analytics of *modern* power. There is, of course, talk about the death of the subject, but *which* subject is that? And what is the status of the utterance that announces its passing? What speaks now that the subject is dead? That there is a speaking seems clear, for how else could the utterance be heard? So clearly, the death of that subject is not the end of agency, of speech, or of political debate. There is the refrain that just now, when women are beginning to assume the place of subjects, postmodern positions come along to announce that the subject is dead (there is a difference between positions of postructuralism which claim that the subject *never* existed, and postmodern positions which claim that the subject *once* had integrity, but no longer does). Some see this as a conspiracy against women and other disenfranchised groups who are now only beginning to speak on their own behalf. But what precisely is meant by this, and how do we account for the very strong criticisms of the subject as an instrument of Western imperialist hegemony theorized by Gloria Anzaldúa,[11] Gayatri Spivak,[12] and various theorists of postcoloniality? Surely there is a caution offered here, that in the very struggle toward enfranchisement and democratization, we might adopt the very models of domination by which we were oppressed, not realizing that one way domination works is through the regulation and production of subjects. Through what exclusions has the feminist subject been constructed, and how do those excluded domains return to haunt the "integrity" and "unity" of the feminist "we"? And how is it that the very category, the subject, the "we," that is supposed to be presumed for the purpose of solidarity, produces the very factionalization it is supposed to quell? Do women want to become subjects on the model which requires and produces an anterior region of abjection, or must feminism become a process which is self-critical about the processes that produce and destabilize identity categories? To take the construction of the subject as a political problematic is not the same as doing away with the subject; to deconstruct the subject is not to negate or throw away the concept; on the contrary, deconstruction implies only that we suspend all commitments to that to which the term, "the subject," refers, and that we consider the linguistic functions it serves in the consolidation and concealment of authority. To deconstruct is not to negate or to dismiss, but to call into question and, perhaps most importantly, to open up a term, like the subject, to a reusage or redeployment that previously has not been authorized.

Within feminism, it seems as if there is some political necessity to speak as and for *women,* and I would not contest that necessity. Surely, that is the way in which representational politics operates, and in this country, lobbying efforts are virtually impossible without recourse to identity politics. So we agree that demonstrations and legislative efforts and radical movements need to make claims in the name of women.

But this necessity needs to be reconciled with another. The minute that the category of women is invoked as *describing* the constituency for which feminism speaks, an internal debate invariably begins over what the descriptive content of that term will be. There are those who would claim that there is an ontological specificity to women as childbearers that forms the basis of a specific legal and political interest in representation, and then there are others who understand maternity to be a social relation that is, under current social circumstances, the specific and cross-cultural situation of women. And there are those who seek recourse to Gilligan and others to establish a feminine specificity that makes itself clear in women's communities or ways of knowing. But every time that specificity is articulated, there is resistance and factionalization within the very constituency that is supposed to be *unified* by the articulation of its common element. In the early 1980s, the feminist "we" rightly came under attack by women of color who claimed that the "we" was invariably white, and that the "we" that was meant to solidify the movement was the very source of a painful factionalization. The effort to characterize a feminine specificity through recourse to maternity, whether biological or social, produced a similar factionalization and even a disavowal of feminism altogether. For surely all women are not mothers; some cannot be, some are too young or too old to be, some choose not to be, and for some who are mothers, that is not necessarily the rallying point of their politicization in feminism.

I would argue that any effort to give universal or specific content to the category of women, presuming that that guarantee of solidarity is required *in advance,* will necessarily produce factionalization, and that "identity" as a point of departure can never hold as the solidifying ground of a feminist political movement. Identity categories are never merely descriptive, but always normative, and as such, exclusionary. This is not to say that the term "women" ought not to be used, or that we ought to announce the death of the category. On the contrary, if feminism presupposes that "women" designates an undesignatable field of differences, one that cannot be totalized or summarized by a descriptive identity category, then the very term becomes a site of permanent openness and re-signifiability. I would argue that the rifts between and among women over the content of the term ought to be safeguarded and prized, indeed, that this constant rifting ought to be affirmed as the ungrounded ground of feminist theory. To deconstruct the subject of feminism is not, then, to censure its usage, but, on the contrary, to release the term into a future of multiple significations, to emancipate it from the maternal or racialist ontologies to which it has been restricted, and to give it play as a site where unanticipated meanings might come to bear.

Paradoxically, it may be that only through releasing the category of women from a fixed referent that something like "agency" becomes possible. For if the term permits of a resignification, if its referent is not fixed, then new configurations of the term become possible. In a sense, what women signify has been taken for granted for too long, and what has been fixed as the "referent" of the term has been "fixed," normalized, immobilized, paralyzed in positions of subordination. In effect, the signified has been conflated with the referent, whereby a set of meanings have been taken to inhere in the real nature of women themselves. To recast the referent as the signified, and to authorize or safeguard the category of women as a site of possible resignifications, is to expand the possibilities of what it means to be a woman and in this sense to condition and enable an enhanced sense of agency.

One might well ask: but doesn't there have to be a set of norms that discriminate between those descriptions that ought to adhere to the category of women and those that do not? The only answer to that question is a counter-question: who would set those norms, and what contestations would they produce? To establish a normative foundation for settling the question of what ought properly to be included in the description of women would be only and always to produce a new site of political contest. That foundation would settle nothing, but would of its own necessity founder on its authoritarian ruse. This is not to say that there is no foundation, but rather, that wherever there is one, there will also be a foundering, a contestation. That such foundations exist only to be put into question is, as it were, the permanent risk of the process of democratization. To refuse that contest is to sacrifice the radical democratic impetus of feminist politics. That the category is unconstrained, even that it comes to serve antifeminist purposes, will be part of the risk of this procedure. But this is a risk that is produced by the very foundationalism that seeks to safeguard feminism against it. In a sense, this risk is the foundation, and hence is not, of any feminist practice.

In the final part of this paper, I would like to turn to a related question, one that emerges from the concern that a feminist theory cannot proceed without presuming the materiality of women's bodies, the materiality of sex. The chant of antipostmodernism runs, if everything is discourse, then is there no reality to bodies? How do we understand the material violence that women suffer? In responding to this criticism, I would like to suggest that the very formulation misconstrues the critical point.

I don't know what postmodernism is, but I do have some sense of what it might mean to subject notions of the body and materiality to a deconstructive critique. To deconstruct the concept of matter or that of bodies is not to negate or refuse either term. To deconstruct these terms means, rather, to continue to use them, to repeat them, to repeat them subversively, and to displace them from the contexts in which they have been deployed as instruments of oppressive power. Here it is of course necessary to state quite plainly that the options for theory are not exhausted by *presuming* materiality, on the one hand, and *negating* materiality, on the other. It is my purpose to do precisely neither of these. To call a presupposition into question is not the same as doing away with it; rather, it is to free it up from its metaphysical lodgings in order to occupy and to serve very different political aims. To problematize the matter of bodies entails in the first instance a loss of epistemological certainty, but this loss of certainty does not necessarily entail political nihilism as its result.[13]

If a deconstruction of the materiality of bodies suspends and problematizes the traditional ontological referent of the term, it does not freeze, banish, render useless, or deplete of meaning the usage of the term; on the contrary, it provides the conditions to *mobilize* the signifier in the service of an alternative production.

Consider that most material of concepts, "sex," which Monique Wittig calls a thoroughly political category, and Michel Foucault calls a regulatory and "fictitious unity." For both theorists, sex does not *describe* a prior materiality, but produces and regulates the *intelligibility* of *materiality* of bodies. For both, and in different ways, the category of sex imposes a duality and a uniformity on bodies in order to maintain reproductive sexuality as a compulsory order. I've argued elsewhere more precisely how this works, but for our purposes, I would like to suggest that this kind of categorization can be called a violent one, a forceful one, and that this discursive ordering and production of bodies in accord with the category of sex is itself a material violence.

The violence of the letter, the violence of the mark which establishes what will and will not signify, what will and will not be included within the intelligible, takes on a political significance when the letter is the law or the authoritative legislation of what will be the materiality of sex.

So what can this kind of poststructural analysis tell us about violence and suffering? Is it perhaps that forms of violence are to be understood as more pervasive, more constitutive, and more insidious than prior models have allowed us to see? That is part of the point of the previous discussion of war, but let me now make it differently in yet another context.

Consider the legal restrictions that regulate what does and does not count as rape: here the politics of violence operate through regulating what will and will not be able to appear as an effect of violence.[14] There is, then, already in this foreclosure a violence at work, a marking off in advance of what will and will not qualify under the signs of "rape" or "government violence," or in the case of states in which twelve separate pieces of empirical evidence are required to establish "rape," what then can be called a governmentally facilitated rape.

A similar line of reasoning is at work in discourses on rape when the "sex" of the woman is claimed as that which establishes the responsibility for her own violation. The defense attorny in the New Bedford gang rape case asked the plaintiff, "If you're living with a man, what are you doing running around the streets getting raped?"[15] The "running around" in this sentence collides grammatically with "getting raped": "getting" is procuring, acquiring, having, as if this were a treasure she was running around after, but "getting raped" suggests the passive voice. Literally, of course, it would be difficult to be "running around" and be "getting raped" at the same time, which suggests that there must be an elided passage here, perhaps a directional that leads from the former to the latter? If the sense of the sense is "running around [looking to get] raped", which seems to be the only logical way of bridging the two parts of the sentence, then rape as a passive acquisition is precisely the object of her active search. The first clause suggests that she "belongs" at home, with her man, that the home is a site in which she is the domestic property of that man, and the "streets" establish her as open season. If she is looking to get raped, she is looking to be the property of some other, and this objective is installed in her desire, conceived here as quite frantic in its pursuit. She is "running around," suggesting that she is running around looking under every rock for a rapist to satisfy her. Significantly, the phrase installs as the structuring principle of her desire "getting raped," where "rape" is figured as an act of willful self-expropriation. Since becoming the property of a man is the objective of her "sex," articulated in and through her sexual desire, and rape is the way in which that appropriation occurs "on the street" (a logic that implies that rape is to marriage as the streets are to the home, that is, that "rape" is street marriage, a marriage without a home, a marriage for homeless girls, and that marriage is domesticated rape), then "rape" is the logical consequence of the enactment of her sex and sexuality outside domesticity. Never mind that this rape took place in a bar, for the "bar" is, within this imaginary, but an extension of the "street," or perhaps its exemplary moment, for there is no enclosure, that is, no protection, other than the *home* as domestic marital space. In any case, the single cause of her violation is here figured as her "sex" which, given its natural propensity to seek expropriation, once dislocated from domestic propriety, naturally pursues its rape and is thus responsible for it.

The category of sex here functions as a principle of production and regulation at once, the cause of the violation installed as the formative principle of the body is sexuality. Here sex is a category, but not merely a representation; it is a principle of production, intelligibility, and regulation which enforces a violence and rationalizes it after the fact. The very terms by which the violation is explained *enact* the violation, and concede that the violation was under way before it takes the empirical form of a criminal act. That rhetorical enactment *shows*—that "violence" is produced through the foreclosure effected by this analysis, through the erasure and negation that determines the field of appearances and intelligibility of crimes of culpability. As a category that effectively produces the political meaning of what it describes, "sex" here works its silent "violence" in regulating what is and is not designatable.

I place the terms "violence" and "sex" under quotation marks: is this the sign of a certain deconstruction, the end to politics? Or am I underscoring the iterable structure of these terms, the ways in which they yield to a repetition, occur ambiguously, and am I doing that precisely to further a political analysis? I place them in quotation marks to show that they are under contest, up for grabs, to initiate the contest, to question their traditional deployment, and call for some other. The quotation marks do not place into question the urgency or credibility of sex or violence as political issues, but, rather, show that the way their very materiality is circumscribed is fully political. The effect of the quotation marks is to denaturalize the terms, to designate these signs as sites of political debate.

If there is a fear that, by no longer being able to take for granted the subject, its gender, its sex, or its materiality, feminism will founder, it might be wise to consider the political consequences of keeping in their place the very premises that have tried to secure our subordination from the start.

Notes

This paper was first presented in a different version as "Feminsim and the Question of Postmodernism" at the Greater Philadelphia Philosophy Consortium in September 1990. This essay is reprinted from *Feminists Theorize the Political,* ed. Judith Butler and Joan Scott (New York: Routledge, 1994).

1. Here it is worth noting that in some recent political theory, notably in the writings of Ernesto Laclau and Chantal Mouffe, *Hegemony and Socialist Strategy,* (London: Verso, 1986); William Connolly, *Political Theory and Modernity* (Madison: University of Wisconsin Press, 1988); as well as Jean-Luc Nancy and Philippe Lacoue-Labarthe, "Le Retrait du politique," in *Le Retrait du politique* (Paris: Editions Galilée, 1983), there is an insistence that the political field is of necessity constructed through the production of a determining exterior. In other words, the very domain of politics constitutes itself through the production and naturalization of the "pre-" or "non-" political. In Derridean terms, this is the production of a "constitutive outside." Here I would like to suggest a distinction between the constitutive outside and a political field that produces *and naturalizes* that constitutive outside and a political field that produces and *renders contingent* the specific parameters of that constitutive outside. Although I do not think that the differential relations through which the political field itself is constituted can ever be fully elaborate as well *ad infinitum,* I do find useful William Connolly's notion of constitutive

antagonisms, a notion that finds a parallel expression in Laclau and Mouffe, which suggest a form of political struggle which puts the parameters of the political itself into question. This is especially important for feminist concerns insofar as the grounds of politics ("universality," "equality," "the subject of rights") have been constructed through unmarked racial and gender exclusions and by a conflation of politics with public life that renders the private (reproduction, domains of "femininity") prepolitical.

2. Julia Kristeva, *Black Sun: Depression and Melancholy* (New York: Columbia University Press, 1989).

3. The conflation of Lyotard with the array of thinkers summarily positioned under the rubric of "postmodernism" is performed by both the title and the text of an essay by Seyla Benhabib: "Epistemologies of Postmodernism: A Rejoinder to Jean-François Lyotard," in *Feminism/Postmodernism,* ed. Linda Nicholson (New York: Routledge, 1989).

4. This is abundantly clear in feminist criticisms of Jürgen Harbermas as well as Catharine MacKinnon. See Iris Young, "Impartiality and the Civic Public: Some Implications of Feminist Criticisms of Modern Political Theory," in *Feminism as Critique: Essays on the Politics of Gender in Late-Capitalism,* ed. Seyla Benhabib and Drucilla Cornell, (Oxford: Basil Blackwell, 1987); Nancy Fraser, *Unruly Practices: Power and Gender in Contemporary Social Theory* (Minneapolis: University of Minnesota Press, 1989), especially "What's Critical about Critical Theory: The Case of Habermas and Gender"; Wendy Brown, "Razing Consciousness," *The Nation* 250:2, January 8/15, 1990.

5. See Ashis Nandy on the notion of alternative universalities in the preface to *The Intimate Enemy: Loss and Recovery of Self Under Colonialism* (New Delhi: Oxford University Press, 1983).

6. Homi Bhabha's notion of "hybridity" is important to consider in this context.

7. Michel Foucault, *The History of Sexuality, Vol. I: An Introduction,* trans. Robert Harley (New York: Random House, 1980), p. 102.

8. "Wars are no longer waged in the name of a sovereign who must be defended; they are waged on behalf of the existence of everyone; entire populations are mobilized for the purpose of wholesale slaughter in the name of life necessity: massacres," he writes, "have become vital." He later adds, "the principle underlying the tactics of battle—that one has to be capable of killing in order to go on living—has become the principle that defines the strategy of states. But the existence in question is no longer the juridical existence of sovereignty; at stake is the biological existence of a population" (Foucault, *History of Sexuality,* p. 137).

9. "At the height of revolt," Memmi writes, "the colonized still bears the traces and lessons of prolonged cohabitation (just as the smile or movements of a wife, even during divorce proceedings, remind one strangely of those of her husband)." Here Memmie sets up an analogy which presumes that colonizer and colonized exist in a parallel and separate relation to the divorcing husband and wife. The analogy simultaneously and paradoxically

suggests the feminization of the colonized, where the colonized is presumed to be the subject of men, *and* the exclusion of the women from the category of the colonized subject. Albert Memmi, *The Colonizer and the Colonized* (Boston: Beacon Press, 1965), p. 129.

10. See the introduction to Joan W. Scott, *Gender and the Politics of History* (New York: Columbia University Press, 1988).

11. Gloria Anzaldúa, *La Frontera / Borderlands* (San Francisco: spinsers Ink, 1988).

12. Gayatri Spivak, "Can the Subaltern Speak?" in *Marxism and the Interpretation of Culture,* ed. Cary Nelson and Lawrence Grossberg (Chicago: University of Illinois Press, 1988).

13. The body posited as prior to the sign is always *posited* or signified as prior. This signification works through producing an *effect* of its own procedure, the body that it nevertheless and simultaneously claims to discover as that which *precedes* signification. If the body signified as prior to signification is only known as an effect of signification, then the mimetic or representational status of language, which claims that signs follow bodies as their necessary mirrors, in not mimetic at all; on the contrary, it is productive, constitutive, one might even argue *performative,* inasmuch as this signifying act appears to produce the body that it then claims to find prior to any and all signification. This is not to claim that language causes or composes the body which it signifies. It is only to claim that there is no reference to the body outside of the apparent circularity of this metalepsis.

14. For an extended analysis of the relationship of language as rape, see Sharon Marcus, "Fighting Bodies, Fighting Words," in *Feminists Theorize the Political,* ed. Butler and Scott.

15. Quoted in Catharine MacKinnon, *Toward a Feminist Theory of the State* (Boston: Harvard University Press, 1989), p. 171.

▼ DIANA FUSS ▼

Inside/Out

THE PHILOSOPHICAL OPPOSITION BETWEEN "heterosexual" and "homosexual," like so many other conventional binaries, has always been constructed on the foundations of another related opposition: the couple "inside" and "outside." The metaphysics of identity that has governed discussions of sexual behavior and libidinal object choice has, until now, depended on the structural symmetry of these seemingly fundamental distinctions and the inevitability of a symbolic order based on a logic of limits, margins, borders, and boundaries. Many of the current efforts in lesbian and gay theory have begun the difficult but urgent textual work necessary to call into question the stability and ineradicability of the hetero/homo hierarchy, suggesting that new (and old) sexual possibilities are no longer thinkable in terms of a simple inside/outside dialectic. But how, exactly, do we bring the hetero/homo opposition to the point of collapse? How can we work it to the point of critical exhaustion, and what effects—material, political, social—can such a sustained effort to erode and to reorganize the conceptual grounds of identity be expected to have on our sexual practices and politics?

The figure inside/outside cannot be easily or ever finally dispensed with; it can only be worked on and worked over—itself turned inside out to expose its critical operations and interior machinery. To the extent that the denotation of any term is always dependent on what is exterior to it (heterosexuality, for example, typically defines itself in critical opposition to that which it is not: homosexuality), the inside/outside polarity is an indispensable model for helping us to understand the complicated workings of semiosis. Inside/outside functions as the very figure for signification

> This piece was originally written as the introduction to an edited collection of essays entitled *Inside/Out: Lesbian Theories, Gay Theories,* ed. Diana Fuss (New York: Routledge, 1991). It is reprinted here, in slightly altered form, by permission of Routledge.

and the mechanisms of meaning production. It has everything to do with the structures of alienation, splitting, and identification which together produce a self and an other, a subject and an object, an unconscious and a conscious, an interiority and an exteriority. Indeed, one of the fundamental insights of Lacanian psychoanalysis, influenced by a whole tradition of semiotic thought, is the notion that any identity is founded relationally, constituted in reference to an exterior or outside that defines the subject's own interior boundaries and corporeal surfaces.[1]

But the figure inside/outside, which encapsulates the structure of language, repression, and subjectivity, also designates the structure of exclusion, oppression, and repudiation. This latter model may well be more insistent to those subjects routinely relegated to the right of the virgule—to the outside of systems of power, authority, and cultural legitmacy. Interrogating the position of "outsiderness" is where much recent lesbian and gay theory begins, implicitly if not always directly raising the questions of the complicated processes by which sexual borders are constructed, sexual identities assigned, and sexual politics formulated.[2] How do outsides and insides come about? What philosophical and critical operations or modes produce the specious distinction between a pure and natural heterosexual inside and an impure and unnatural homosexual outside? Where exactly, in this borderline sexual economy, does the one identity leave off and the other begin? And what gets left out of the inside/outside, heterosexual/homosexual opposition, an opposition which could at least plausibly be said to secure its seemingly inviolable dialectical structure only by assimilating and internalizing other sexualities (bisexuality, transvestism, transsexualism . . .) to its own rigid polar logic?

For heterosexuality to achieve the status of the "compulsory," it must present itself as a practice governed by some internal necessity. The language and law that regulates the establishment of heterosexuality as both an identity and an institution, both a practice and a system, is the language and law of defense and protection: heterosexuality secures its self-identity and shores up its ontological boundaries by protecting itself from what it sees as the continual predatory encroachments of its contaminated other, homosexuality. Of course, any sexual identity, based on the complicated dynamics of object choice, works through a similar defensive procedure. Read through the language of psychoanalysis, sexual desire is produced, variously and in tandem, through acts and experiences of defense, ambivalence, repression, denial, threat, trauma, injury, identification, internalization, and renunciation. Indeed, sexual object choice is not even so "simple" a matter of psychical identifications and defenses; it is also a result of the complex interaction of social conflicts, historical pressures, and cultural prohibitions.

The difference between the hetero and the homo, however, is that the homo becomes identified with the very mechanism necessary to define and to defend any sexual border. Homosexuality, in a word, becomes the excluded; it stands in for, paradoxically, that which stands without. But the binary structure of sexual orientation, fundamentally a structure of exclusion and exteriorization, nonetheless constructs that exclusion by prominently including the contaminated other in its oppositional logic. The homo in relation to the hetero, much like the feminine in relation to the masculine, operates as an indispensable interior exclusion—an outside which is inside interiority making the articulation of the latter possible, a transgression of the border which is necessary to constitute the border as such.

The homo, then, is always something less and something more than a supplement—something less in that it signifies lack rather than addition, and something more in that it signifies an addition to a lack, a lack which, importantly, may not be its own. Recent work on sexual subjectivities has begun to challenge the usual association, prevalent even in some poststructuralist thinking, of the outside (of sexual, racial, and economic others) with absence and lack. This work has begun to recognize that any outside is formulated as a consequence of a lack *internal* to the system it supplements. The greater the lack on the inside, the greater the need for an outside to contain and to defuse it, for without that outside, the lack on the inside would become all too visible.[3]

To protect against the recognition of the lack within the self, the self erects and defends its borders against an other which is made to represent or to become that self-same lack. But borders are notoriously unstable, and sexual identities rarely secure. Heterosexuality can never fully ignore the close psychical proximity of its terrifying (homo)sexual other, any more than homosexuality can entirely escape the equally insistent social pressures of (hetero)sexual conformity. Each is haunted by the other, but here again it is the other who comes to stand in metonymically for the very occurrence of haunting and ghostly visitations. A striking feature of much current lesbian and gay theory is a fascination with the specter of abjection, a certain preoccupation with the figure of the homosexual as specter and phantom, as spirit and revenant, as abject and undead. Those inhabiting the inside can only comprehend the outside through the incorporation of a negative image. This process of negative interiorization involves turning homosexuality inside out, exposing not the homosexual's abjected insides but the homosexual as the abject, as the contaminated and expurgated insides of the heterosexual subject. Homosexual production emerges under these inhospitable conditions as a kind of ghost-writing, a writing which is at once a recognition and a refusal of the cultural representation of "the homosexual" as phantom Other.

Paradoxically, the "ghosting" of homosexuality coincides with its "birth," for the historical moment of the first appearance of the homosexual as a "species" rather than a "temporary aberration"[4] also marks the moment of the homosexual's disappearance—into the closet. That the first coming out was also simultaneously a closeting; that the homosexual's debut onto the stage of historical identities was as much an egress as an entry; and that the priority or "firstness" of homosexuality, which preceded heterosexuality in Western usage by a startling eleven years,[5] nonetheless could not preempt its relegation to secondary status: all these factors highlight, in their very contradictoriness, the ambigous operations of ins and outs. "Out" cannot help but to carry a double valence for gay and lesbian subjects. On the one hand, it conjures up the exteriority of the negative—the devalued or outlawed term in the hetero/homo binary. On the other hand, it suggests the process of coming out—a movement into a metaphysics of presence, speech, and cultural visibility. The preposition "out" always supports this double sense of invisibility (to put out) and visibility (to bring out), often exceeding even this simple tension in the confused entanglement generated by a host of other active associations.[6]

To be out, in common gay parlance, is precisely to be no longer out; to be out is to be finally outside of exteriority and all the exclusions and deprivations such outsiderhood imposes. Or, put another way, to be out is really to be in—inside the realm of the visible, the speakable, the culturally intelligible. But things are still not so clear, for to come out can also work not to situate one on the inside but to jettison one from it. The recent practice of "outing," of exposing well-known public figures as closet homosexuals, is (among other things) an attempt to demonstrate that there have been outsiders on the inside all along. To "out" an insider, if it has any effect at all, can as easily precipitate that figure's fall from power and privilege as it can facilitate the rise of other gays and lesbians to positions of influence and authority. Because of the infinitely permeable and shifting boundaries between insides and outsides, the political risks or effects of outing are always incalculable.

Recently, in the academy, some would say it is "in" to be "out." An avant-garde affinity for the liminal space of the marginal energizes many of those disciplines and programs (Women's Studies, African-American Studies, Multicultural Studies) still routinely denied sufficent funding and support from their home institutions adequate to meet the excess in student demand. Supporters of "Gay Studies," a recently emergent interdisciplinary yet autonomous field of inquiry, must grapple with many of the same issues its predecessors confronted, including the vexed question of institutionalization and the relation of gay and lesbian communities to the academy. The issue is the old standoff between confrontation and assimilation: does one compromise oneself by working on the inside, or does one shortchange oneself by holding tenaciously to the outside? Why is institutionalization overwritten as "bad" and anti-institutionalization coded as "good"? Does inhabiting the inside always imply cooptation? (Can incorporation be so easily elided with recuperation?) And does inhabiting the outside always and everywhere guarantee radicality?

The problem, of course, with the inside/outside rhetoric, if it remains undeconstructed, is that such polemics disguise the fact that most of us are both inside and outside at the same time.[7] Any misplaced nostalgia for or romanticization of the outside as a privileged site of radicality immediately gives us away, for in order to idealize the outside we must already be, to some degree, comfortably entrenched on the inside. We really only have the leisure to idealize the subversive potential of the power of the marginal when our place of enunciation is quite central. To endorse a position of perpetual or even strategic outsiderhood (a position of powerlessness, speechlessness, homelessness . . .) hardly seems like a viable political program, especially when, for so many gay and lesbian subjects, it is less a question of political tactics than everyday lived experience. Perhaps what we need most urgently in gay and lesbian theory right now is a theory *of* marginality, subversion, dissidence, and othering. What we need is a theory of sexual borders that will help us to come to terms with, and to organize around, the new cultural and sexual arrangements occasioned by the movements and transmutations of pleasure in the social field.[8]

Recent and past work on the question of sexual difference has yet to meet this pressing need, largely because, as Stephen Heath accurately targets the problem, our notion of sexual difference all too often subsumes sexual differences, upholding "a defining difference of man/woman at the expense of gay, lesbian, bisexual, and indeed *hetero* heterosexual reality."[9] Homosexuality is produced inside the dominant discourse of sexual difference as its necessary outside, but this is not to say that the homo exerts no pressure on the hetero nor that this outside stands in any simple relation of exteriority to the inside. Every outside is also an alongside; the distance between distance and proximity is sometimes no distance at all. It may be more accurate to say that the homo, occupying the frontier position of inside out, is neither completely outside the bounds of sexual difference nor wholly inside it either. The fear of the homo, which continually *rubs up against* the hetero (tribadic-style), concentrates and codifies the very real possibility and ever-present threat of a collapse of boundaries, an effacing of limits, and a radical confusion of identities.

In its own precarious position at/as the border, homosexuality seems capable of both subtending the dominance of the hetero and structurally subverting it. Much has been made, in discussions of deconstruction's textual and political efficacy, of the tendency of hierarchical relations to reestablish themselves. Such retrenchments often happen at the very moment of the supposed transgression, since every transgression, to establish itself as such, must simultaneously resecure that which it sought to eclipse. Homosexuality, read as a transgression against heterosexuality, succeeds not in undermining the authoritative position of heterosexuality so much as reconfirming heterosexuality's centrality precisely as that which must be resisted. As inescapable as such a logic might be, it does not diminish the importance of deconstruction in addressing the admittedly stubborn and entrenched hetero/homo hierarchy. That hierarchical oppositions always *tend toward* reestablishing themselves does not mean that they can never be invaded, interfered with, and critically impaired. What it does mean is that we must be vigilant in working against such a tendency: what is called for is nothing less than an insistent and intrepid disorganization of the very structures which produce this inescapable logic. Perhaps what we cannot escape at *this* moment in history is an "analysis interminable," a responsibility to exert sustained pressure from/on the margins to reshape and to reorient the field of sexual difference to include sexual differences.

But how do we know when the homo is contributing to the confirmation of the hetero and when it is disturbing it? How can we tell the difference—if we hold to the by no means certain assumption that there is a difference? Questions of epistemology ("how do we know?") enjoy a privileged status in theorizations of gay and lesbian identity. How does one know when one is on the inside and when one is not? How does one know when and if one is out of the closet?[10] How, indeed, does one know if one is gay? The very insistence of the epistemological frame of reference in theories of homosexuality may suggest that we *cannot* know—surely or definitively. Sexual identity may be less a function of knowledge than performance, or, in Foucauldian terms, less a matter of final discovery than perpetual reinvention.[11] This is why, while not entirely abandoning the demands of the epistemological, we need to shift away from the interrogative mode and toward the performative mode—toward the imaginative enactment of sexual redefinitions, reborderizations, and rearticulations.

"What we need," Foucault writes in "the Gay Science," is "a radical break, a change in orientation, objectives and vocabulary."[12] While this writer remains suspicious of the faith Foucault places in epistemological "breaks," since such breaks inevitably seem to reassert what they sought to supersede, the call for new orientations, new objectives, and especially new vocabularies is still admittedly a seductive one. It would be difficult, not to say delusionary, to forget the words "inside" and "outside," "heterosexual" and "homosexual," without also losing in this act of willed amnesia the crucial sense of alterity necessary for constituting any sexed subject, any subject as sexed. The dream of either a common language or no language at all is just that—a dream, a fantasy that ultimately can do little to acknowledge and to legitimate the hitherto repressed differences between and within sexual identities. But one can, by using these contested words, use them up, exhaust them, transform them into the historical concepts they are and have always been. Change may well happen by working on the insides of our inherited sexual vocabularies and turning them inside out.

Notes

1. For the importance of inside/outside in theorizing the psychical constitution of the sexed subject, see Jacques Lacan's "The Mirror Stage" in *Ecrits*, trans. Alan Sheridan (New York: Norton, 1977), 1–7, especially his remarks on the *Innenwelt* and the *Umwelt*.

2. The essays in the *South Atlantic Quarterly* special issue on "Displacing Homophobia," to take one recent example, are linked with a shared concern with the tenuous border (generic, thematic, ideological, immunological, historial, linguistic) distinguishing insides from outsides. Lee Edelman's "The Plague of Discourse: Politics, Literary Theory, and AIDS" and Robert Caserio's "Supreme Court Discourse vs. Homosexual Fiction" are the pieces perhaps most directly invested in deconstructing the inside/outside binary. See *South Atlantic Quarterly* 88, no. 1 (1989).

3. On the question of lack and supplementarity, see Jacques Derrida's *The Truth in Painting*, trans. Geoff Bennington and Ian McLeod (Chicago: University of Chicago Press, 1987), 57–59. For an interesting reading of the "spectacle of male lack," and an important revision of Lacan's theorization of castration and subject formation, see Kaja Silverman's "Historical Trauma and Male Subjectivity," in *Psychoanalysis and Cinema*, ed. E. Ann Kaplan (New York: Routledge, 1990), 110–127, and her *Male Subjectivity at the Margins* (New York and London: Routledge, 1992).

4. This by-now-famous distinction, of course, belongs to Michel Foucault; see *The History of Sexuality, Vol. I: An Introduction* (New York: Vintage Books, 1980), 43.

5. According to historian Jonathan Ned Katz, *homosexuality* and *heterosexuality* were privately coined in 1868 by the nineteenth-century German sodomy law reformer, Karl Maria Kertbeny. *Homosexuality* made its first public appearance in an 1869 appeal for reforming the German sodomy laws, and *heterosexuality* followed eleven years later in an 1880 published defense of homosexuality. See Katz's "The Invention of Heterosexuality," *Socialist Review* 21, no. 1 (1990): 7–34. On this subject of the delayed or secondary emergence of heterosexuality into the public sphere, David Halperin wittily

observes that "it came into being, in fact, like Eve from Adam's rib." See Halperin's *One Hundred Years of Homosexuality and Other Essays on Greek Love* (New York: Routledge, 1990), 17.

6. "Out" can also signify an end or resolution (outcome; school's out); an excuse, alibi, or means of escape (an easy out); a beyond or surpassing (outdoing); an expiration or exhaustion (outmoded, outdated); a fullness or excessiveness (to deck out or rig out); or an utterance or cry (to call out). The term cannot escape certain contradictory class connotations as well. The phrase "coming out" can refer to a debutant's ceremonious and ostentatious introduction to high society, while the phrase "ins and outs" was coined in the nineteenth century to label the nomadic poor who regularly sought readmission to the workhouse.

7. Very few of Jacques Derrida's works, a corpus to which the present essay is obviously indebted, fail to take up and to work over this classical figure of inside/outside; readers might wish, in particular, to consult the following: "Writing Before the Letter," in *Of Grammatology,* trans. Gayatri Chakravorty Spivak (Baltimore and London: The Johns Hopkins University Press, 1974); "Violence and Metaphysics: An Essay on the Thought of Emmanuel Levinas," in *Writing and Difference,* trans. Alan Bass (Chicago: University of Chicago Press, 1987); "Living On: Border Lines," in *Deconstruction and Criticism, trans.* James Hulbert (New York: Seabury Press, 1979); "Plato's Pharmacy" and "The Double Session," in *Dissemination,* trans. Barbara Johnson (Chicago: University of Chicago Press, 1981); *Positions,* trans. Alan Bass (Chicago: University of Chicago Press, 1981); and *The Truth in Painting,* trans. Geoff Bennington and Ian McLeod (Chicago: University of Chicago Press, 1987).

8. For example, any changes in sexual practices prompted by AIDS necessarily creates the conditions and the means for the continuing resocialization of gay, lesbian, bisexual, as well as heterosexual identities and pleasures.

9. Stephen Heath, "The Ethics of Sexual Difference," *Discourse* 12, no. 2 (1990): 132

10. Michelangelo Signorile, one of the editors of the lesbian and gay magazine *Outweek* and the journalist most frequently associated with the practice of outing, deftly poses the question this way: "how many people must one confide in to be 'out of the closet'?" Signorile adamantly disclaims any responsibility for coining the term "outing," attributing the neologism not to *Outweek* but to *Time*—another example of the way in which the outside can be produced as an effect of the inside. See *Outweek* 46 (May 16, 1990): 40.

11. For a persuasive and powerful reading of identity as performance, see Judith Butler's *Gender Trouble: Feminism and the Subversion of Identity* (New York: Routledge, 1990). On the centrality of epistemology in theories of gay identity, see Eve Sedgwick's aptly titled and evocative study, *Epistemology of the Closet* (Berkeley: University of California Press, 1990).

12. I am grateful to D. A. Miller and Michael West for bringing this interview to my attention and for Michael West's excellent unpublished translation from which I quote here.

▼ HARRIET DAVIDSON ▼

"I Say I Am There"

Siting/Citing the Subject of Feminism and Deconstruction

IN HER 1980 POEM "Frame" Adrienne Rich narrates the story of a young black college student who is harassed, arrested, and assaulted by the police for being in the wrong place at the wrong time. At first reading this seems to be one of Rich's "simple" political poems that hostile critics like to hold against her. But poetically her strategy is, as I think it always is, complicated and provocative. In italicized passages Rich comments on her own marginality as narrator of the scene: "*I am / standing though somewhere just outside the frame / of all this, trying to see.*"[1] But the epistemological difficulties which she often writes about in her poetry give way by the end of the poem to a more interesting presentation of herself as subject: "*What I am telling you / is told by a white woman who they will say / was never there. I say I am there*" (305). The defiance and bearing witness of the final sentence is not an assertion of empirical fact, as the curious disjunction of "I am there" rather than "I am here" indicates. The poem makes it clear that she could not have experienced everything she narrates, not only because she projects the narrative into the future, but also because as a white privileged outsider, she is not there in the same way as the young black woman. The poem considers how being there is a discursive as well as material condition: the young black woman must doubt if the policeman can "see her at all", while the narrator, who "is not supposed to be / there," occupies that invisible spot of an unreliable narrator, a spot which uncomfortably shifts to the invisible place of the woman who is not supposed to see, hear, or especially to speak.

Copyright © 1994 by Harriet Davidson

The final sentence in its doubled "I" of enunciation and enounced—"I say I"—and in its assertion of being there but not here presents a subject who is contradictorily both situated and cited. The self-assertion, which is characteristic enough of Rich's writing that it forms a signature for her work, is here deliberately split and diffused: which "I" is being asserted? She situates herself "there" only because she can cite herself as "I," thus entering a discourse which has excluded her. But she can cite herself as "I" only because she is a material (as she will say, located) being who is not the signifier "I" but is different from it and exceeds it. The oscillation of the "I" between saying and being diffuses the sense of a coherent, autonomous subject into discursive systems and into material indeterminacy: "what I says I say I?" can be extended in an endless *mise en abime* (recalling Lacan's "I think where I am not"). But the performative effect of bearing witness, the sense of the subject's agency, does not seem denied by this splitting and doubling. Rather, the indeterminate effect seems to give her space to operate in, opening the prison of discursive determinism as well as the prison of material essentialism. As Judith Butler puts it in the context of an similar *mise en abime* of gender identity: "This perpetual displacement constitutes a fluidity of identities that suggests an openness to resignification and recontextualization, and it deprives hegemonic culture and its critics of the claim to essentialist accounts of gender identity." And in his analysis of the performative speech act in his "Signature, Event, Context" Derrida asks: "Would a performative statement be possible if a citational doubling did not eventually split, dissociate itself from the pure singularity of event?"[2] Derrida insists that while the doubling of citation will always undermine the control of consciousness or intention on the performative, citation is also what makes the performative possible, thus, I will argue, basing the possibility of agency upon the split subject.[3]

If Adrienne Rich is widely regarded by fans and detractors alike as an essentialist feminist (or culturalist feminist) it is because of the constant performance of self-assertion in her work. But I would claim that her self-assertion is based on a rigorous deconstruction of the subject within a material and discursive matrix which disallows essentialism, idealism, or transcendence—everything but the saying, the telling, the self-assertion which is the basis for her poetry. This deconstruction of the subject can be traced back to her poems of the sixties, but it is especially evident in her work in the eighties. Rich's position as representative of essentialist or empirical feminism in opposition to poststructuralist feminism can only be maintained by not carefully reading her recent work. Her influential essay "Notes Toward a Politics of Location" (1984), which I will discuss at length below, disperses her own subjecthood into discursive systems as well as into the dense unyielding material of her own body, while the "subject" of feminism is completely undone; "Who is we?" she asks at the end of the essay. But importantly, this question is not spoken in despair. Instead, the last sentence of the essay asserts, "This is the end of these notes, but it is not an ending." As in so many of her poems, she avoids the abyss of fragmentation, uncertainty, and silence to which her critique of the subject might lead and turns instead to an assertion of her writing self.[4]

I would like to use Rich as the representative of feminist thought often cited in opposition to deconstruction and show that she shares a critique of the subject with deconstruction and more particularly with that figure most often critiqued by political thinkers—Jacques Derrida. In turn I would like to examine the subject in Derrida—a subject many claim to be missing or at least lacking in any viable agency—and show how he constructs a performative subject, one no less noticeable than in Rich (in fact, the arrogance of his self-assertion irritates many detractors), but less valued in his work. As in Rich's poem, Derrida splits the subject between citational dispersion and situational density and opens up a place for a subject with agency. This performative subject asserts its ability to act even while any stable ground for subjectivity is questioned. In Derrida's work agency is asserted with surprising frequency, even in the midst of his greatest attacks on the humanistic subject, as in the 1968 essay "The Ends of Man," which ends with a question about the subject echoing Rich: "But who, we?"[5]

This essay begins, not so uncharacteristically for Derrida, with a reference to the time and place in which he is writing and speaking the lecture (originally delivered in New York) and to his own presence within this context: "Let me be permitted to speak in my own name here," he asks. "When I was invited to this meeting, my hesitation could only end when I was assured I could bear witness here, now, to my agreement, and to a certain point my solidarity with those in this country who were fighting what was then their country's official policy in certain parts of the world, notably Vietnam" (113).

This statement unequivocally invokes the ability of individuals and groups to bear witness, a resolutely humanist gesture to begin this antihumanist meditation. He makes the statement in part to emphasize a point about the democratic form which allows statements of dissent; and he does not think that the freedom to bear witness is a sign that "evil complicities [are] undone." Nevertheless the act stands, unjustified by any moral or ethical imperatives, buttressed only by a historical placement of himself:

> Such in its most general and schematic principle, is the question which put itself to me during the prepartions for this encounter,

> from the invitation and the deliberations that followed, up to the acceptance, and then to the writing of this text, which I date quite precisely from the month of April 1968: it will be recalled that these were the weeks of the opening of the Vietnam peace talks and of the assassination of Martin Luther King. A bit later, when I was typing this text, the universities of Paris were invaded by the forces of order—and for the first time at the demand of a rector—and then reoccupied by students in the upheaval you are familiar with. This historical and political horizon would call for a long analysis. I have simply found it necessary to mark, date, and make known to you the historical circumstances in which I prepared this communication. (114)

A quite determinate and empirical situating of himself, as well as his audience ("which you are familiar with"), this passage calls forth the authority of history, the urgency of political agency, and the curious intertwining (or as he says, chiasmus) of chance and necessity that attends historical event. In this light, the ending "But who, we?" both notes and splits the fragile solidarity he has established at the beginning, replacing his firm stance with one balanced precariously on the "eve" of change, as he says at the end.

The question at the conclusion of the essay dislocates the "we," making it into a citation; the question "But who, we?" asks both whether the who is we and also who is we. For Derrida, the ability to cite any utterance, an ability based on the material articulation of language, is profoundly disruptive to intention, context, and presence (as we will see that for Rich the material articulation of particular subjects in the world disrupts and disperses the "we"). But this citing is always connected to a siting; it is the material locatedness of words, as of bodies, that makes it possible for them to be somewhere else, to exceed their context. His question, like Rich's, indicates the undecidable, not to remove us from the world, but to point to difference, change, the unknown future—all the things necessary for a politics of liberation.

Derrida has come in for strong criticism from critics oriented toward more political or more historical paradigms. His indeterminant subject, his typical move from history to rhetoric, his often coy evasion of recognizable political statement are justifiably irritating to feminists, marxists, and historians. Feminists have a particularly hard time with this figure of intellectual authority; yet deconstruction has become more and more prominent in feminist work as we move into the nineties. The deconstructive pressure on feminism now comes not only through theoretical debates of the French school, but increasingly from political praxis. Every attempt to define a politically viable female subject has come under scrutiny on the front lines, so to speak, where the women marginalized by those definitions—the non-white, non-Western, non-middle-class, non-heterosexual women—press for a subject that can accommodate differences among and within women, instead of only the binary female/male. The search for such a subject animates much postmodernist theory as well as the debates of identity politics.[6]

By recovering the deconstructive strain in Rich's work and the irrepressible agency in Derrida's, we may find that deconstruction and feminism yet can learn from each other. Rich and Derrida are trying to think a fully material subject, one that is defined not only by the empirical, determinate conditions analyzed by materialism, but also the radical alterity of matter that as excessive, indeterminate, and unavailable, complicates any empirical analysis. These two forms of material are always mediated to us and each other by the materiality of language, the constant doubleness and oscillation of language I would like to capture in the homonym *cite/site*. The signified/signifier structure of language as meaningful reference and non-meaningful material inscription is complicated by an understanding that the structure of reference undermines determinate reference by the possibility of citation (in order to refer a word must be universal, able to be repeated, not a determined reference at all), while curiously, the material inscription of the letters provides an "example" of a particular fact, but an example that is odd, tenuous and different from referential fact. In other words language doubly denies reference and determinate meaning in both the signified and signifier, but language use doubly affirms determinate reference in conventional meaning and in what I would call the performative aspect of language as materiality. In both Rich's and Derrida's writing of the self we see a play over all these possibilities in various passages of empirical description, desconstructive dispersion, and a performance of these possibilities of language in passages which call attention to the writing self, as in "I say I am there."[7] The materiality of language introduces the forces of difference and chance into the necessities of history. If these forces necessarily disrupt the clarity of political ideas, they also may be seen as an opening to a nontranscendent freedom which makes political agency possible. Rich's influential notion of location may be compared with the crucial idea of spacing in Derrida, while each presents a subject that asserts its agency in a writing that courts both necessity and chance.

Save the Spacing: Derrida and Writing at the Wheel

Derrida has made it his central task over the years to present and in part theorize a subject of difference, especially in recent years as his interest has focused on psychoanalysis and literature. But quite early on, Derrida said in response to a question, "I don't destroy the subject, I situate it. . . . It is a question of knowing where it comes from and how it functions."[8] Derrida presents a subject both sited and cited, situated in a radical empiricism of materiality, locality, contingency, and finitude that leads finally to the singularity of event, but an event that is always already a citation, caught up in discourses. The crossing of siting and citing becomes a more problematized chiasmus through the understanding that the site can only be defined as a place of discourses, mapped in discursive ways, while the citation reveals the disruptive operation of space and time. Thus site and citation are not opposed to each other in a dialectical arrangement. They are, rather, implied in each other.

This situated subject has radical implications in Derrida's work. For the situatedness involves both the situation within discourses, as a historical being, that is, the construction of the subject, but also the situatedness in space and time as a material being which spaces these discourses in unexpected, though always already discursive, ways. In this, the operation of chance as part of material finitude is crucial for Derrida, entwining as it does with the necessity of discourse. In tying materiality to chance, Derrida goes back beyond Plato's hierarchy of form over matter to the atomism of the pre-Socratics, for whom the principle of indeterminate deviation or *clinamen* necessarily disrupts the clarity of form. Difference, freedom, and pleasure all finally ride on the entwining of chance and freedom in the material subject. While feminists are likely to set necessity off against conscious agency, slighting chance, Derrida is likely to set necessity off against chance, slighting conscious agency. Yet all three elements—necessity, chance, agency—have a place here, implicitly if not explicitly. Recovering the implicit agency in Derrida's project is one task; recovering chance in feminist/political discourse is another.

The crucial Derridean term for understanding siting/citing is "spacing." Spacing is in some senses quite simple in that it calls attention to the material space and time in which we exist. In "Différance," for example, Derrida argues against the self-presence of consciousness, a consciousness, "before distributing its signs in space and in the world" (*Margins,* 16). For Derrida consciousness is an *effect* as much as a cause of signs articulated into the world, thus consciousness is always already material, relational, mutating, different—in no sense full and present. Derrida moves away from an idealist definition of consciousness by emphasizing its historical construction, which decenters consciousness from a transcendent position, but does not disperse it. For consciousness as discourses, as citations, is in a body, a determinate site. That being in the body is what makes it historical, thus spacing in this case refers both to the material body and to historical discourses.

Similarly, language for Derrida is never the full, intuitive presence of idea, but is always already articulated into space and the world, into Saussure's signifiers. The conventional spacing between words is one sign of this distribution and articulation into space.[9] Many have become familiar with Saussure's observation that because the physical form of words varies so much throughout history—not to mention among languages—the word cannot refer to the thing in a one-to-one manner. This materiality of language has two consequences. First, it insists that language can only work as a diacritical, relational system which casts nets of meaning. But second, much to Saussure's distress, the mutability of the material thing makes language highly unstable, finite, contingent, and local.[10] Contemporary hermeneutics focuses on the first consequence and undertakes the difficult task of understanding these complex webs of meaning, which are not dependent on a speaker or situation, but signify broadly, giving us not just a situation, but a world. As Paul Ricoeur writes: "Here again the spirituality of discourse manifests itself through writing, which frees us from the visibility and limitation of situations by opening up a world for us, that is, new dimensions of our being-in-the-world."[11]

Some theorists object to this hermeneutic vision because it slights the contextual determinants of meaning in favor of the world of codes. Derrida, too, understands that context will always disrupt, change, and mutate the codes at work; even as he agrees with hermeneutics that codes lift meaning out of contexts.[12] But Derrida is more interested in the second consequence of the materiality of language, which does not have to do with meaning at all. Situation for Derrida implies more than semiotic context; it also implies chance, which risks rending the net of meaning altogether. Derrida says in "My Chances/*Mes Chances*":

> Language, however, is only one among those systems of *marks* that claim this curious tendency as their property: they *simultaneously* include toward increasing the reserves of random indetermination *as well as* the capacity for coding and overcoding or, in other words, for control and self-regulation. Such competition between randomness and code disrupts the very systematicity of the system while it also, however, regulates the restless, unstable interplay of the system.[13]

Because of the spacing of language into space and time, meaning arises through systems (codes) as well as through semiotic contexts, but this very spacing leads to randomness, indeterminacy. In "Signature, Event, Context" Derrida meditates on the fragility and inadequacy of both code and context for meaning; the mark of spacing can be enclosed by neither, though we are always in a context, always ruled by conflicting codes. We have not only polysemia, the many meanings of hermeneutics, but dissemination, the mutation of language not governed by systems of meaning, but caused by an accident of spacing (*Margins,* 316). The homonym is a clear example of dissemination, as a material accident of language which disrupts the clarity of idea. Aristotle condemns the homonym as a scandal; Derrida uses undecidable homonyms frequently as a means of disrupting the clear boundaries between ideas, but also to show how material accidents of language may shape our thought.

The spacing which Derrida equates with *différance* and "the play of the trace" is not, he says in "Signature, Event, Context," "the simple negativity of a lack, but the emergence of the mark" in some sense apart from any meaning or relation (*Margins,* 317). It is crucial to understand how tangible this central term of spacing or *différance* is in Derrida as a mark, not a negativity, how nonmetaphysical it is, though conceptually we can only approach the completely nonmetaphysical, the completely material, through the route of metaphysics. In speaking of the trace Derrida says it is "situated as the change of site" (*Margins,* 24). The spacing, *différance,* or trace is the *change* and properly has no site; it is the necessary movement of space and time that all material things are subject to. Yet it is the change of *site,* never an idealized movement, a change that happens only because of the site.

The subject, too, is spaced. It is made up of discourses; therefore, it is not essential, organic, or a thing-in-itself. But as spaced, it is also not a representation of those discourses, a pointing to a model preceding it. The subject as constructed by discourses can never be as mechanically produced as the word "constructed" suggests. The notion of construction opposes the notion of the organic or natural self, but the word "construction" carries its own unfortunate burden of implying an orderly process. The intervention of space-time introduces difference; the notion of a copy of a model, a representation, cannot be maintained. This double movement undermines the determinacy of essentialism and of discourses; as Gregory Ulmer says, it is a double writing, "one that refers only to itself, and one that refers indefinitely to other texts," making it both highly idiomatic and also highly impersonal.[14] Neither model, nor copy, neither sufficient unto itself, nor referring elsewhere, the extreme subject of difference would be, Derrida suggests, "when nothing takes place but the place."[15] Characteristically, Derrida stresses the nothing in this statement, and indeed absence and dislocating play are emphasized by him as well as by most commentators. But the place remains, and is necessary to keep Derrida from what he calls "the romantic pathos of negativity"—the concern with trying to find an outside to occupy (for which he criticizes the avant-garde).[16] I would like to emphasize this placing, perhaps more than Derrida would wish, as a way to focus on the subject being presented and theorized in Derrida's work. This placing yields a subject that is material, historical, and always balanced on the edge of the unknown where chance, invention, and bearing witness make a difference and mark a difference—that we are unfinished.

Derrida's work not only theorizes but also *presents* a complex portrait of the subject, one that is by no means passive, dispersed, or unaccountable. Some of the most complacent critique directed at Derrida has been occasioned by his insistence that he can bear witness and that he be read in context, with attention to his rhetoric and the status of his utterance. This complacency is especially evident in responses to Derrida's heated retort to the critics of his essay on apartheid, "Racism's Last Word." These critics accuse him of being ahistorical, of severing word from history, of finally not effectively "bearing witness" to the evil of apartheid.[17] Derrida angrily responds in "But, Beyond . . . ," not that he has been misread, but that he hasn't been read at all: "historians must be attentive to rhetoric, to the type and status of utterances, at the very least to their grammar."[18] He insists that his method in general is deeply historical, indeed "deconstructive readings are . . . political and institutional interventions that transform contexts" (367). Critics delight in what they see as the spectacle of Derrida being hoist on his own petard, as the philosopher of indeterminacy, who has deconstructed any stable referential context or history, must in order to be understood now insist upon that context, history, and determinate meaning.[19] But rather than deconstruct the historical reality of apartheid, he wants to deconstruct the language which tries to erase the material subject—not only the legal language of apartheid but the scientific discourse of his critics. His insists upon the writing subject whose material context and history is always intertwined with a received history. Thus in the essay, Derrida's extraordinarily novelistic presentation of himself can be seen as a way to present a material subject, both to counter the claims that he detaches words from history, and also to show how much the subject of ordinary academic discourse is detached from the materiality that he would like to see complicating even materialist discourse. In this essay he addresses his critics by the personal "you" rather than the more standard last names, in order, he says, to "save the space" needed for more formal address (354). There is surely a buried pun here in Derrida's attempt to save the "spacing" of the material subject. But his tactic situates his critics in the dialogue and the material context of the discussion. It also allows him to launch a personal attack on them, revealing an anger beyond the normal etiquette of academic disagreement. The highly personal quality of his voice in this response, a quality highlighted by the letter form he preserves, indicates a type of bearing witness here, whether selfishly or not. Calling attention to himself is a way to space the discourse which his critics had tried to unspace; ignoring both Derrida's context and their own, they produced a "scientific" account of history. Derrida would drag them into a dirtier fray and hold them accountable to their own context and for the unknown future being shaped by discourse.

Derrida's stance of consciousness, accountability, and agency reveals the "positive" side of the subject, the siting whose "negative" side is citation. Situating is one of Derrida's most common moves. In fact, reading a great deal of Derrida at once, one is struck by the forceful presence of the situated "I" throughout his writings. This impression is partly a result of happenstance, that chance so embraced by Derrida. So many of the essays in his books are written for a particular context, either as a lecture to a particular audience or for a particular event, that the explanatory headnotes throughout his books begin to form a little narrative on their own, a litany of Derrida's travels to international academic conferences, colloquia, and lectures. Derrida confirms this impression by the frequency with which he refers to his context, especially at the beginnings of his essays.

Derrida also draws attention to this ongoing narrative by way of parody in the "Envois" section of *The Post Card*. One of the recurring motifs in these fragmented, but carefully dated, letters is the narrator's academic travels which indeed provide the conventional narrative excuse for the letters themselves, the dislocation of the I from the you. Yet the incessant movement of the narrator and the constant placing of himself at specific airports, train stations, universities, as well as on specific dates, form a dizzying counterpoint to the movement of the letters throughout the postal system.[20] This travelling I, this parody of Ulysses, an academic Leopold Bloom, is both firmly located in space and time and dislocated by the self-reflexivity of the letters and the postal system. As Derrida writes in a final letter, printed as an advertisement on the back of *The Post Card*: "At the very instant when from its address it [the post card] interpellates, you, uniquely you, instead of reaching you it divides you or sets you aside, occasionally overlooks you."[21]

The "you, uniquely you" is not, I think, meant derisively here, though it has some ironic overtones. Interpellation is a word associated with Althusser's ideological hailing by which the individual is always already constituted as subject (and in the West, as a subject who believes herself to be unique). The "uniquely you" is set between this interpellation and the possibility of a mis-hailing, we might say, by which the hailing, the address, the post card functions imperfectly, goes off course, disseminates in unexpected ways, gets misdelivered. The address is thus both a means of locating and dislocating the subject. The ideological locating of the address is a place of citation, making you not you, no longer a concrete individual that, Althusser points out, would be too particular to be known at all, but an ideological subject we can know.[22] But the spatial locating of the address splits the citational dislocating through the chance disruptions of space and time, restoring some concreteness. In an early letter (6 June 1977) the narrator writes, "I write you letters of a travelling salesman hoping that you hear the laughter and the song—the only ones (the only what?) that cannot be sent, nor the tears. At bottom I am only interested in what cannot be sent off, cannot be dispatched in any case" (*Post Card*, 14–15). The parenthetical question here indicates the problem—there is no-thing that cannot be sent off, cited, dislocated, but in that crossing of siting and citing is that moving target that can't be sent off.

Derrida presents this moving subject again in "Ulysses Gramophone" as he chronicles his "experiences" in preparing for the lecture to Joyce scholars he is "now" giving. As he thinks of this lecture, he is again on the academic circuit traveling in Tokyo and Ohio and constantly finding himself echoing experiences in *Ulysses*. Every siting of himself also becomes a citation. This quite recent essay moves closer and closer to a Shandean mode as he ends the lecture by writing: "I decided to stop here because I almost had an accident just as I was jotting down this last sentence, when, on leaving the airport, I was driving home after the trip to Tokyo."[23] Everyone has seen drivers who like to *read* at the wheel, but this convoluted evoking of writing at the wheel is a frightening image for the extension of writing (speech, consciousness) in space and time, as we are always both located and dislocated, always on the go.

Thus, the situated I is also the intensely self-reflexive I which erases itself, as in the opening to "Qual Quelle" when Derrida writes, "I mark(s) the division" where the I of agency, a signified I, gets entwined and for many readers swallowed up in the "I" of the signifier (*Margins*, 275). This sentence shifts from a use of "I" to a mention of "I"—between a siting and a citation—and they both mark the division, the difference, of the historical body always referred to by "I" and the systemic function of the shifting pronoun itself. Derrida's emphasis on the dislocation of writing and on the location of situation may be seen in a recent neologism he has coined: programmatology. Programmatology is

> the intersection of a pragmatics and a grammatology. Open to a different sense of the dispatch (envoi) and of dispatches (envois), programmatology should always take the situation of the marks into account; in particular that of utterances, the place of senders and addressees, of framing and of the sociohistorical circumscription, and so forth. It should therefore take account of the prob-

lematics of randomness in all fields where it evolves: physics, biology, game theory, and the like. ("My Chances," 27–28)

The "therefore" in the last sentence provides the equation of situation and chance.

Derrida does not consign the subject to the ethereal nominalism of indeterminacy; rather he sees a subject with a future, and not just a past. If feminism is to continue to rely on an experience not yet fully mapped and represented by an ideology (as well as continued analysis of clearly measurable conditions), experience must be turned toward the unknown, the future. For scientific analysis would take what we know or can imagine as a tool to shape the unknown future; the unknown is faced with what is known. But the material subject must reverse that direction and let the known be faced by the unknown, letting that unknown affect what we know. As Derrida says in his essay on Bataille, "From Restricted to General Economy":

> [Scientific discourse] has as its meaning (as its discursive content and direction) the relation oriented from the unknown to the known or knowable, to the always already known or to anticipated knowledge. Although general writing [a deconstructive writing] also has a meaning, since it is only a relation to nonmeaning, this order is reversed within it. And the relation of absolute possibility of knowledge is suspended within it. The known is related to the unknown, meaning to nonmeaning.[24]

This difficult movement is central to Derrida's thought and opens him to the charges of frivolity; as he writes in the same essay, "this writing must assure us of nothing, must give us no certitude, no result, no profit. It is absolutely adventurous, is a chance, and not a technique" (273).

What is the profit for feminism in such a profitless enterprise? I would like to claim three: It is a way to think freedom while maintaining a materialist stance (without science); it is a way to define experience as both mapped by discourses and disruptive of them; it is a way to turn toward a future we cannot imagine, even while we try to imagine it. This opening to chance, to the unknown, is essential for a movement of liberation: Derrida says in "My Chances/*Mes Chances*" that while chance "does not imply a conscious freedom or will," nevertheless he claims that it "is what makes the conscious freedom of man fathomable" (8). What, indeed, for the materialist, are choice, agency, action, without chance? Without the sense that we are not in the grip of immutable forces and that power is never total? Feminism as a movement of liberation and one moreover that must be based on what is not fully known, not yet fully represented—

women's experience—must be a politics crossed by its own contradictions, armed by both the known and the disruptions of the unknown.

Begin with the Material: Rich and the Kudzu Principle of Writing

When one reads Adrienne Rich in tandem with Derrida two things become evident: first, that her idea of location is a way to combine chance and determinism into a definition of experience; second, that she also tries to allow her writing performance to foreground her particular situation and the material chances it offers. The happenstance of where she is, as well as the material mutations of language so dear to her poetic ear, are often at odds with her emphasis on her own cultural determinants and the force of her own political desires.

"Notes Toward a Politics of Location," originally a lecture, begins with a repudiation of the universality of women and an erasure of the words she once "would have spoken." What is left after abstract woman disappears from her discourse is only "notes" which "are the marks of a struggle to keep moving, a struggle for accountability."[25] Her writing as "marks" is reciprocally related to the movement; both are in contrast to the stasis of the abstract concept. And both are related to accountability, which seems distinctly harder to come by in a world of marks and movement than in a world of clear concepts. The sense of movement is what she continually tries to foreground in her writing and thinking about location, so that the relatively static and empirical word "location" gradually comes to mean a moving, spatial articulation which extends the subject into both citational and situational possibilities.

The essay itself keeps moving by shifting rhetorically among different subject positions, as well as shifting among meditations, facts, personal reminiscences, reporting, and quotations. Each move tends to complicate and question the other parts of the essay. For instance, in the third paragraph, the "speaking" voice established at the beginning rhetorically shifts as she self-reflexively writes, "Beginning to write, then getting up. Stopped by the movement of a huge early bumblebee which has somehow gotten inside this house" (*BBP*, 211). By calling attention to herself (citing herself) as a situational, material subject, who is yet constructed by her language (what is the force of "this"?), she reenforces her opening rejection of the universal woman and emphasizes that it is not from a transcendent point of view that she makes that rejection. In another section, the logic of her reference to Marx is partially undermined by her earlier remark that *The German Ideology* "happens" to be lying on her table. In other sections she overtly problematizes her pronouns, questions her feelings with facts, and questions her reporting of facts with poetry.

In one particularly striking passage these movements and shifts are combined into one sentence. In this passage, Rich speaks of the first woman astronaut with aggravation at the young woman's blithe advocacy of the military and industrial uses of the space program and ignorance of the human costs: "Women, too, may leave the earth behind," she comments (*BBP*, 222). Then Rich's writing shifts gears:

> On a split screen in my brain I see two versions of her story: the backward gaze through streaming weightlessness to the familiar globe, pale blue and green and white, the strict and sober presence of it, the true intuition of relativity battering the heart;
> and the swiftly calculated move to a farther suburb, the male technocrats and the women they have picked and tested, leaving the familiar globe behind: the toxic rivers, the cancerous wells, the strangled valleys, the closed-down urban hospitals, the shattered schools, the atomic desert blooming, the lilac suckers run wild, the blue grape hyacinths spreading, the ailanthus and kudzu doing their final desperate part—the beauty that won't travel, that can't be stolen away. (*BBP*, 223)

This remarkable passage of jeremiad and poetic vision, fury and love, doubles its vision more than once as it veers away from the logical political discourse which precedes it. The beauty of transcendence is imaged literally in the movement out to space, contrasting with the bleak cultural landscape left behind. But within the second vision, the common association of the atomic cloud with a bloom provides a point of material mutation from destruction to creation—from a familiar globe of stagnant disaster to a familiar globe of movement and recovered beauty. The flowers and notorious kudzu take over the sentence, as they will take over any landscape. These spreading plants, some of which are colloquially known as "travellers," paradoxically create the beauty that won't travel—movement is its location and it moves because it is located. The parasitical kudzu also images the running wild of language which escapes discursive restraints in its material articulation, as Rich's political discourse is complicated and obscured by a poetic play of language. She reverses her direction in this sentence, moving from what Derrida might call a restricted to a general writing as she first gives us the unknown future as seen from what we now know—the toxic wasteland—and then gives us a mysterious, mutating future, letting the unknown impinge upon what she knows. Rich's insistence that we see the sad facts of the world's exploitation makes that world no less the familiar globe where the story is not yet over, the speaking and writing not done, the ending not yet here. What can't be stolen away is the materiality, change, and particularity which, even though always connected to patterns of culture and forms of power, yet do, in turn, mutate and change those forms, too, in ways we cannot always predict. Her shifting writing, like the spreading kudzu, plays havoc with her own too-determined vision of the future.

Throughout the essay, Rich tries to remain true to the feminist first principle that one must appeal to female experience, while she defines that experience away from transparency and toward two different opacities: the materiality of the body and the proliferation of discourses. Her battle is "against lofty and privileged abstraction" (*BBP*, 213) even in the service of feminism. Thus she finds she must reject "a form of feminism so focused on male evil and female victimization that it, too, allows for no differences among women, men, places, times, cultures, conditions, classes, movements" (*BBP*, 221). In repudiating the simple dualism of male/female her awareness is decidedly deconstructive: "Living in the climate of an enormous either/or, we absorb some of it unless we actively take heed" (221). Rich's metaphor, suggesting that she understands the difficulty of protecting herself from something so pervasive as the climate, points to her complicity in an ideology she thought she was opposing. She suggests that we can, however, begin to take heed of difference through the seemingly simple task of "recognizing our location, having to name the ground we're coming from, the conditions we have taken for granted" (*BBP*, 219).

The word "location" seems oddly neutral and empirical for this visionary poet, but as she complicates the term more and more, its ordinariness may provide one more moment of a writing undermining itself. Rich's understanding of location is similar in purpose to the feminist theorists who speak in terms of *positionality* as a way to define a fluid but determinate subject, but location is distinctly less metaphorical than positionality.[26] Even though Rich uses location to refer beyond her physical location to her location within discourses—she locates herself as female, white, Jewish, American, Southern—she also insists on a bodily, material location, as well. Rich can't ignore the drag of materiality, of the body, of suffering, of the unconscious, of the invisibility of ideology. "Position" is a word easily and frequently idealized; a position may for good or ill become the way we transcend the material constraints of location to find clear meaning. Position is also a word that adheres closely to the subject. Someone's position can be described with no reference beyond herself (she's standing up, she's a democrat, etc.). But location is less easily idealized and less tied to meaning.

Location entails being some place, not only at the locus of different discourses, but spatially and temporally there. It emphasizes that one is in a body—a position may be in one's mind, but a location must be in a body which spaces positions in often unexpected ways, but which also gets spaced by those positions. In the body, material forces, driven by chance, desire, and repetition, work in excess of meaning and position. Obviously, this emphasis on location over position makes it more difficult actively to construct meaning in politically useful ways. But becoming aware of differences is a political act, too, and one that avoids some of the self-righteousness of constructing meaning: " 'To see the light' too often has meant rejecting the treasures found in darkness," Rich reminds us (*BBP,* 143).

Rich begins her project of location with a map on which she must find herself, no longer content to say in Virginia Woolf's words, "as a woman I have no country" (*BBP,* 210). While she agrees with what she sees as Woolf's rejection of nationalistic rhetoric, she can no longer so blithely detach herself from it. In the past she would have spoken as a feminist "who 'happened' to be a white United States citizen" (*BBP,* 211). But now that particular happenstance, that chance, seems more and more primary. She knows she does have a country and she writes, "I need to understand how a place on the map is also a place in history within which as a woman, a Jew, a lesbian, a feminist I am created and trying to create" (*BBP,* 212). But this place on the map, a semiotic place, a place created by discourse, is occupied by something not quite defined by those coordinates: "Begin, though, not with a continent or a country or a house, but with the geography closest in—the body. Here at least I know I exist, that living human individual whom the young Marx called 'the first premise of all human history.' " But, she continues, "it was not as a Marxist that I turned to this place . . . It was as a radical feminist" (*BBP,* 212). In turning away from Marxism Rich rejects not only any lingering scientific transcendence in Marxist thought, but also the way the body is mapped in the discourse of materialism. Rich wants to understand this mapping but also to retreat another step: "Begin with the material," she insists: "To reconnect our thinking and speaking with the body of this particular living human individual, a woman. Begin, we said, with the material, with matter, mma, madre, mutter, moeder, modder, etc., etc." (*BBP,* 213). Rich has revised her beginning from the coordinates of the map, to the body, still a geography, to material, the mute matter of philosophy. Yet she refuses this endgame. She knows that matter, too, exists in a discourse in which women have come to represent matter as opposed to masculine mind. The suspicious return to essentialism as Rich embraces the matter/mother is countered by a curious moment of writing, as the poetic play of alliteration on "m" coincides with the cultural discourse connecting women and matter. But the play is suddenly stopped even before she gets to her own English "mother" by the force of the harsh sounding and odd-looking abbreviations "etc., etc."

There are many things going on here. First, Rich is undoubtably referring to the inconclusive research that purports to show that one of the first sounds made by suckling babies in every culture is "mma." But her chain of associations begins with abstract matter and ends with "etc." enclosing the "natural" connection in a chain of conventional associations both cultural and linguistic. The iteration of "etc." is of course redundant, though a common colloquial redundancy. "Etc." is already an abbreviation of an abbreviation, standing for a continuation of the chain. It suggests one could go on, but doesn't need to, in a kind of logic of the supplement which indicates that there is more to be said and also suggests that everything that needs to be said has been. In Rich's sentence the repeated "etc."'s indicate both a continuing wealth of examples, but also an exhaustion with this connection, as the "etc." points to shared cultural discourse we all know and can pursue on our own. This unending process indicated by "etc., etc." undermines essentialism in favor of the graphic connection; both the continuing play of alliteration and the repeated "etc." point to conventions of writing, thus threatening the naturalism of the connection of matter and mother. The sudden poetic play on "mma" undermines the possibility of stable reference even while it insists on cultural determination.

The material at which Rich wants to begin thus oscillates between an excessive writing of materiality, something more particular and fluid than experience, and a cultural ideology of materialism, something more encompassing than experience, that cultural "etc." indicating an ideology. Rich's attempt to move away from essentialism leads her into a materialism thoroughly charged with the effects of materiality, where each particular location is mapped by discourses, but also tends toward an atomistic dispersal: "You cannot speak for me. I cannot speak for us" (*BBP*, 224). Materiality, that being in space and time, introduces temporal disjunction, particularity, and chance into the largely conceptual analyses of materialism. With this focus on the material, Rich moves toward difference rather than the politically more useful category of similarity. Her essay states a problem rather than a resolution: "Two thoughts: there is no liberation that only knows how to say 'I'; there is no collective movement that speaks for each of us all the way through" (*BBP*, 224). Nevertheless, she says, "I need to move outward from the base and center of my feelings, but with a corrective sense that my feelings are not *the* center of feminism" (*BBP*, 231).

Rich defines a self that is always a material, situated body, simultaneously subjected to determination by forces of history, culture, and language, and yet grounded in a materiality that opens itself to chance and escapes determination. But she also wants a self that can "actively take heed"; human agency must be found in the midst of the forces of materialism and materiality. Rich is trying to work out a political and poetic stance that will remain responsible to history, to chance, and to agency, in "a struggle for accountability." This struggle once again comes down to "marks" as she backtracks one final time from the material body to something less abstract:

> Perhaps we need a moratorium on saying "the body." For it's also possible to abstract "the" body. When I write "the body," I see nothing in particular. To write "my body" plunges me into lived experience, particularity: I see scars, disfigurements, discolorations, damages, losses, as well as what pleases me. Bones well nourished from the placenta; the teeth of a middle-class person seen by a dentist twice a year since childhood. White skin, marked and scarred by three pregnancies, an elected sterilization, progressive arthritis, four joint operations, calcium deposits, no rapes, no abortions, long hours at a typewriter—my own, not in a typing pool—and so forth. (*BBP,* 215)

Again she moves, from map, to body, to material, to her scars. The particularity Rich seeks resides in the marks of experience on her body and in her body as a mark determining experience. The marking of her body is a sign of discourses passing through a particular material point, but the mark itself changes, deflects, and determines the discourse, as well. In other words, the discourses about subjectivity are always spatialized in particular subjects and this spatialization mutates the discourse. This does not mean that power does not continue to insist upon its own conclusions, but only that materiality provides experience with a certain fluidity and particularity that may be marshalled to oppose the forces of institutionalized injustice.

As Derrida says in regard to spacing, the conscious subject is an effect of the mark, not its cause. But the doubling of citing and siting in the mark undermines the determinism attributed to the notion that existence precedes consciousness. For the citational quality of the mark not only refers to discourses but also opens possibilities for change and surprise, for doubling, splitting, and changing context. And the siting of the mark not only mires it in material destiny, but also lets it move, change, and mutate in the unfinished world of finitude. Rich's writing subject, like Derrida's, asserts this dual movement, though Rich critically engages the practical politics that Derrida only critiques. The possibility that "you cannot speak for me" and "I cannot speak for us" is a condition of the possibility that "I say I am there." For Rich, the feminist subject must risk the perils of deconstruction—the uncertainty of "Who is we?"—and stay attuned to the entwining of chance and necessity which leads to freedom and an unknown future.

Notes

1. Adrienne Rich, *The Fact of a Doorframe: Poems Selected and New 1950–1984* (New York: Norton, 1984), 303.

2. Judith Butler, "Gender Trouble, Feminist Theory, and Psychoanalytic Discourse," in Linda Nicolson, ed., *Feminism/Postmodernism* (New York: Routledge, 1990), 338. Jacques Derrida, *Margins of Philosophy,* trans. Alan Bass (Chicago: University of Chicago Press, 1982), 326. Cited hereafter as *Margins.*

3. Derrida's writings on speech-act theory have been collected in *Limited Inc.,* trans. Samuel Weber and Alan Bass (Evanston: Northwestern University Press, 1988).

4. Adrienne Rich, *Blood, Bread, and Poetry: Selected Prose 1979–85* (New York: Norton, 1986), 231. Linda Alcoff terms Rich a representative of "cultural feminism" in her admirable essay "Cultural Feminism versus Poststructuralism: The Identity Crisis in Feminist Theory," *Signs: Journal of Women in Culture and Society* 13 (Spring 1988): 413.

5. Jacques Derrida, "The Ends of Man," in *Margins,* p. 136; also see his "Violence and Metaphysics: An Essay on the Thought of Emmanuel Levinas," in *Writing and Difference,* trans. Alan Bass (Chicago: University of Chicago Press, 1978), 79–153.

6. The relation of feminism and deconstruction has a complicated history consisting of three parts: Derrida's "feminine" metaphors; the *écriture féminine* of predominantly French women writers such as Hélène Cixous and Luce Irigaray; and the analysis of deconstruction by Anglo-American feminists. Derrida's best known work on Woman is his essay on Nietzsche, *Spurs: Nietzsche's Styles,* trans. Barbara Harlow (Chicago: University of Chicago Press, 1979). In this work Derrida seems more interested in examining the use of gendered metaphors in philosophical writing than in endorsing Nietzsche's scandalous equation of truth and woman as absence. While Derrida does use gendered metaphors himself (hymen and invagination), I will argue below that Derrida turns away from negativity and, by implication, from Woman as lack. Explorations of feminism and deconstruction may be found in Mary Poovey, "Feminism and Deconstruction," *Feminist Studies* 14 (Spring 1988): 51–65; Gayatri Chakravorty Spivak, "French Feminism in an International Frame," *Yale French Studies* 62 (1981): 154–184; Alice A. Jardine, *Gynesis: Configurations of Women and Modernity* (Ithaca: Cornell University Press, 1985); Linda Nicolson, ed. *Feminism/Postmodernism* (New York: Routledge, 1990); and Elizabeth Meese, *(Ex)Tensions: Refiguring Feminist Criticism* (Urbana: University of Illinois Press, 1990).

7. Paul de Man describes this pointing to the writing as a parabasis, which Cynthia Chase describes as "a gesture of address that suddenly confronts the

audience of a representation with the framework of its performance. . . . This parabasis suddenly gives a face to the agent who has been producing the text" ("Translating Romanticism," *Textual Practice* 4, no. 3 [1990]: 363). DeMan's term comes in a discussion of Hegel in "Hypogram and Inscription" in *The Resistance to Theory* (Minneapolis: University of Minnesota Press, 1986), 27–53. My thanks to Cathy Caruth for calling my attention to these texts.

8. This quotation appears in the question-and-answer session included in the version of "Structure, Sign, and Play in the Discourses of the Human Sciences" published in *The Structuralist Controversy: The Languages of Criticism and the Sciences of Man*, ed. Richard Macksey and Eugenio Donato (Baltimore: Johns Hopkins University Press, 1970), 247–272, esp. 271.

9. Jacques Derrida, *Of Grammatology*, trans. Gayatri Chakravorty Spivak (Baltimore: John Hopkins University Press, 1976), 21.

10. Ferdinand de Saussure, *Course in General Linguistics*, trans. Wade Baskin (New York: McGraw-Hill, 1966), 65–78.

11. Paul Ricoeur, "The Model of the Text: Meaningful Action Considered as Text," *Social Research* 38 (Winter 1971): 529–562, esp. 536.

12. The contextualist argument is made against both hermeneutics and deconstruction by Walter Benn Michaels and Stephen Knapp in "Against Theory 2," *Critical Inquiry* 14 (Autumn 1987), 49–68.

13. Jacques Derrida, "My Chances/*Mes Chances*: A Rendezvous with some Epicurean Stereophonies," in *Taking Chances: Derrida, Psychoanalysis, and Literature*, ed. Joseph H. Smith and William Kerrigan (Baltimore: Johns Hopkins University Press, 1984), 1–32, esp. 2. Cited hereafter as "My Chances."

14. Gregory L. Ulmer, *Applied Grammatology: Post(e)-Pedagogy from Jacques Derrida to Joseph Beuys* (Baltimore: Johns Hopkins University Press, 1985), 178.

15. Jacques Derrida, *Dissemination*, trans. Barbara Johnson (Chicago: University of Chicago Press, 1981), 285.

16. Jacques Derrida, *Positions*, trans. Alan Bass (Chicago: University of Chicago Press, 1981), 86.

17. See Anne McClintock and Rob Nixon, "No Names Apart: The Separation of Word and History in Derrida's 'Le Dernier Mot du Racisme,' " in *"Race," Writing, and Difference*, ed. Henry Louis Gates, Jr. (Chicago: University of Chicago Press, 1986), 339–353, esp. 353.

18. Jacques Derrida, "But, Beyond . . . (Open Letter to Anne McClintock and Rob Nixon)," in Gates' *"Race," Writing and Difference*, 354–369, esp. 359.

19. This argument is made by Mark Edmunson, "The Ethics of Deconstruction," *Michigan Quarterly Review* 27 (Fall 1988): 622–643, esp. 635. Edmundson is, nevertheless, sympathetic to Derrida.

20. The narrator in "Envois" is highly unreliable and Derrida's preface warns us not to trust "him." Nevertheless, many particulars of the narrator's travels coincide with historical events in Derrida's life.

21. Jacques Derrida, *The Post Card: From Socrates to Freud and Beyond,* trans. Alan Bass (Chicago: University of Chicago Press, 1987). Cited hereafter as *Post Card.*

22. See Louis Althusser, "Ideology and Ideological State Apparatuses," in *Lenin and Philosophy and Other Essays,* trans. Ben Brewster (London: New Left Books, 1971), 121–173. Compare Lacan's: "I think where I am not, therefore I am where I do not think," in *Ecrits: A Selection,* trans. Alan Sheridan (New York: Norton, 1977), 166.

23. Jacques Derrida, "Ulysses Gramophone: Hear say yes in Joyce," in *James Joyce: The Augmented Ninth,* ed. Bernard Benstock (Syracuse: Syracuse University Press, 1988), 27–75, esp. 71.

24. Jacques Derrida, "From Restricted to General Economy: A Hegelianism without Reserve," in *Writing and Difference,* 251–277, esp. 270–271.

25. Adrienne Rich, *Blood, Bread and Poetry: Selected Prose 1979–85* (New York: Norton, 1986), 210–211. Cited hereafter as *BBP.*

26. Linda Alcoff's essay (cited earlier) consolidates many of the arguments about positionality, relying especially on work by Denise Riley and Teresa de Lauretis. I would argue that de Lauretis's terms "space-off" and "the elsewhere of the here and now" are closer to Rich's location than Alcoff's positionality. See Teresa de Lauretis, *Technologies of Gender: Essays on Theory, Film, and Fiction* (Bloomington: Indiana University Press, 1987), 26. At the end of *Positions,* Derrida states his discomfort with and interest in the notion of position. (93–96).

▼ THOMAS KEENAN ▼

Deconstruction and the Impossibility of Justice

"Justice," she said. "I've heard that word. It's a cold word. I tried it out," she said, still speaking in a low voice. "I wrote it down. I wrote it down several times and always it looked like a damn cold lie to me. There is no justice."
—Jean Rhys[1]

DID SOMEONE SAY justice was possible?[2]

We should not proceed too hastily from the fact that there was a conference, and later a volume, called "Deconstruction and the Possibility of Justice," that the phrase "possibility of justice" has been tried out, written down, even several times, to the conclusion that this possibility has been established. That a claim has been made goes, as they say, without saying, but the status of this claim must remain an open question, if we are to give justice its due.

But would thinkers or activists, even radical or critical ones, seriously consider putting the *possibility* of justice into question? Certainly some questions about its existence, its realization, have been raised—especially in the United States where every day and every night more and more women, people of color, gays and lesbians, prisoners, people without housing, and poor people are singled out for discrimination and death, in an ongoing wave of violent economic, psychic, social, political, medical, and juridical assaults. But the critical questions about this violence have generally operated well within the horizon of justice's possibility. Indeed, it is on the basis of the presumed possibility of justice that the critiques would seem to have their meaning and pertinence: because justice is possible, but not actual, action is called for to bring it out of the taunting ideality of the potential and into reality. And yet—the phrase ". . . and the possibility of justice," without abandoning any of the critical force associated recently with the more daring wings of literary and political and legal studies, hints at a more unsettling thought: the possibility that justice might not be simply possible. What might deconstruction (not that it's any more possible than justice) have to contribute to the question of the impossibility of justice?³

That deconstruction could contribute something to the question of justice, possible or impossible, is taken as either self-evident or met with outrage these days (and hence in both cases remains unthought). More than a quarter century after *De la grammatologie* and a decade after *Allegories of Reading,* academic and journalistic commonplaces remain unaccountably but desperately impoverished in their encounters with this question. Deconstruction's ethico-political pertinence is either (1) taken for granted (often but by no means always presumed to be "progressive") with an appeal to its thematic or referential considerations of issues (democracy, torture, "race," feminism, the university and teaching, apartheid) or to its formal homologies with political interventions (the deconstruction of authority as emancipatory or as ideology-critique), or (2) condemned (as nefariously antipolitical or paralyzing) because it appears to ruin the categories on which political discourse has tried to found itself for as long as anyone can remember: subjectivity and agency, and the reliable knowledge (meaning, whether positively, theologically, or hermeneutically determined) that "allows" it to act.

This choice (either familiar or foreign) needs to be obliterated. It guarantees that whatever ethico-political force anything called deconstruction might have will be evaded or casually recognized by reference to the reassuring certainties of well-known themes and categories. The opposed poles unite themselves symetrically around the axiom that ethics and politics are, in the first or last instance, matters of choice: determinations and acts of a subject with an identity (man, agent, consciousness, state or nation, or people) held to be—in some sense, whether strong or weak—free. To be free means to be capable of understanding and of integrating that knowledge with a response to the demand to act. "Subject" names the time and place, always some sort of present, within which knowledge can be articulated with and provide the basis for action. The subject *is* the right to, and the responsibility for, this passage from knowing to doing.

Much of the discussion concerning this articulation (the condition of the possibility of justice, it seems) has turned around those most vexed of deconstructive topoi, undecidability (Derrida) or unreadability (de Man). Even with those for whom deconstruction provides recognizably useful ethico-political benefits, the politics in question is that of decision or of reading, determined as that of the subject who reads. Christopher Norris provides an exemplary summary of the position:

> De Man's texts quite explicitly *ask* to be read in this "political"
> mode. They insist that the field of rhetorical tensions is always
> ("contrary to what one might think") a space where the politics
> of reading is inevitably brought into play. . . . [T]he "burden" of
> politics, as de Man conceives it, is a negative labor (like that of
> deconstruction) relentlessly trained upon its own liability to error
> and delusion. . . . If the political unconscious is structured like a
> language, then the politics of reading is both more error-prone
> *and* more radically unsettling than criticism (Marxist and otherwise) can easily allow.[4]

Reading is also *the* political paradigm for those who fear, on the other hand, that questioning its possibility means plunging ethics and politics, justice, into an abyss of uncertainty—incapacity and paralysis. The back-cover text—its institutional anonymity gives it another sort of exemplary status—of one such effort expresses the predictable worry economically: the author, it promises, criticizes those

> many theorists of the "subject" [who] routinely deny the possibility of human agency and the "subject"'s resistance to the pressures of the ideological, . . . and calls instead for a view of the "subject" which will allow for genuine social and political action.[5]

The blurb allows us to formalize the troubled theory with some precision. Its idealism or theoreticism, which grants to "theorists" the privilege of "deny[ing]" permission to act and to their "view" the authority to "allow" such action, turns crucially around the determination of the subject as a locus of possibility. Idealism of idealism, in fact, insofar as theory does not simply found or ground action but the theory that does it is one of the subject (theorist) whose capacity to articulate cognition with "genuine" action, to rely on what it knows (ideas) to base its active resistance to other ideas (the ideological), is explicitly exempted from interrogation. No doing without (first) knowing, it seems. Theory is required to ground practice, to permit it (routinely), and the theory that will do it is that of a subject whose knowledge allows (makes possible, but in the strong sense of "guarantees reliably") action. "The possibility of human agency"—the certainty of a knowledge or a meaning which grants a reason to action, and to which action can appeal for guidance—is the possibility of reading as determined interpretation or decision.[6] But surely justice, like reading, involves some exposure to language and its alterities, and hence can only exceed the horizon of the human subject, its understandings and guarantees.

▼ ▲ ▼

Deconstruction and Justice ▼ 265

Drucilla Cornell has raised this spectre of justice's impossibility, at the end of what I can only imagine must have marked the stunning intrusion into critical legal studies of a rigorously political deconstruction.7 If her essay hesitates in its concluding call for ethico-political vigilance and responsibility, withdrawing just that sharp differential edge (the repeated insistence on the "remaining of the other") which had earlier allowed its most politically provocative operations (we will return to them), it is the doubly-bound structure of the hesitation that is of most interest.

Cornell quotes Emmanuel Levinas on this question of the possible conditions for rendering justice:

> Justice is impossible without the one that renders it finding himself in proximity. His function is not limited to . . . the subsuming of particular cases under a general rule. The judge is not outside the conflict, but is in the midst of proximity. . . . This means that nothing is outside of the control of the responsibility of one for the other. (quoted 1627–1628; ellipses mine)

The emphasis is of course on the "without," and the constant and irrevocable impact of the other on the one who judges or responds, the interference or the disappearance of exteriority (not being "outside the conflict" is here called "proximity"), provides the paradoxical condition of the possibility of justice. Because we (who judge, as we do all the time) are implicated, are in the midst of conflict, justice is possible. Because we are all implicated, because the absence of any exterior has plunged us all into the proximity of one another ("nothing is outside"), there can be justice and responsibility. Justice cannot simply be the application of general rules to particular cases, because any exteriority from which the general might govern its particulars is lacking. We are involved, which is why we have to judge. This requires that the decisions or judgments made not be of the order of the constative or cognitive, of the actually present and interpretable ("we can no longer read off what the ideal is as if it were *there,* present in the actual" [1628]). To this new responsibility belongs the future-oriented temporality of the performative or positing (an active, ungrounded, initiatory call to some ideal not yet available), of what Cornell's redemptive Benjaminian strategy allows her to call "hope," as a promise and a call from within the confusion and the blurred boundaries of conflict:

> When we interpret, we posit the very ideal we purportedly find "there" in the legal text, and as we posit the ideal or the ethical we promise to remain true to it. Our promise of fidelity to the ethical or to the ideal is precisely what breathes life into the dead letter of the law and provides a barrier against the violence of the

word. . . . To heed the call to responsibility within the law is both to remind our students of the disjuncture between law and the ideal and to affirm our responsibility to make the promise to the ideal, to aspire to counter the violence of our world in the name of universal justice. (1628)

This promise would not be thinkable outside our contaminated implication in the conflict, which disqualifies the definition of justice as the impartial application of universal laws to particular cases (justice as fairness) just as it erodes any pretense to interpret something with the status of an object for a subject, some fact outside of our investments. There's no there there, because all theres are too unavoidably here, others fracturing our present, proximately interfering with the self-sameness and self-certainty of our interpretations. Of course, objectivity has not been replaced with the whimsical arbitrariness of subjectivity, because the thought of our implication in the other has to imply the other's intervention into our "present," that effect of a "here and now" constructed only thanks to the trace of the other's having already traversed and disrupted it. The "positing" is not that of a subject but a response to the call of something else radically immune to any intention or cognitive mastery. Who are we to know what we do when we respond? As Cornell suggests, "better to do it even if one thinks one cannot say what one does" (1621), even or particularly if that doing is saying.[8]

If Cornell describes as "a double gesture" (1628) this blind and self-blinding "aspiration" to nothing short of universal justice, this in-spiriting of the dead letter with the breath of life, its doubleness nevertheless does appear to lack the asymmetrical negativity, the respect for impossibility, often associated with such gestures in Derrida's work. To breathe life into the dead letter, to mark the disjunction between actual and possible (as ideal), and hence to offer against particular violences the protection of the universally just, all suggest a certain resurfacing of the phono- or logo-centrism that has dominated (and largely crippled) critical political discourse and to which deconstruction has formulated the most startling challenges. Cornell "remains true" in this to the dialectical negativity of Levinas' claim (which she cites) that "justice can be established only if I . . . always in non-reciprocatable relationship with the other, always for the other, can become an other *like* others" (quoted 1625; my emphasis). Because we all are, or can be(come), others for the others, we have something in common—this is the transcendental condition of possibility for what is called justice here. This "establishment" of justice, and of some universal justice at that, has to be predicated on the aberrant and utterly unreliable tropological substitution of myself for the other, the dialectical identification of the two of "us" as equally or at least comparably (and a little comparision goes a long way) nonreciprocally related to "each" other. The possibility of justice is the possibility that "I . . . can become an other like others." This is likewise the temporal structure of the "promise" directed toward the "ideal," which depends on the interpretation of the futurity of that future as simply an accidentally not-yet-present present. The possibility of (the establishment of) justice means that the "disjuncture" between now and then, me and the other, the actual state of injustice and the ideal future of universal justice, can in principle, however negatively, be reduced. These promises are also promises to the ideal, to an ideal of comprehension or understandability, of universality, an ideal universality that the very performative structure of the promise has to disregard and indeed to disfigure.⁹

Doesn't the appeal to a universal justice of the future, with which to counter the evident violence of today and tonight, risk precisely this erasure of the alterity of the future (which is to say its futurity) that the thought and practice of the promise first opens? If elsewhere Cornell's deconstructive gestures push at the very limits of, and threaten to shake, our most oppressively familiar and powerful political theories, these last pages of her essay seem to begin, in their hope- or wishfulness, a retreat from its otherwise militant and activist demand that "we mark the ethical relationship as the limit of the possible, and therefore, as the Saying, rather than as the said. The possibility of the ethical lies in its impossibility; otherwise, the ethical would be reduced to the actual, to the totality of what is" (1616). Cornell associates this reductive maneuver with a certain politics, denouncing "a right-wing Hegelian's complacency that reduces the ethical to the actual and therefore . . . to the perpetuation of order" (1616). Refusing to take the possibility of ethics or justice for granted, marking instead "the limits of the possible" breached in the ethical relation (to the other in its utter and incomprehensible difference, the futurity of a saying without predetermined or predictable content), resists this totalizing affirmation of the permanence of the present (order) and its unlimited extension into (and thus erasure of) the future. If this resistance is not as optimistic or wishful as Cornell's final phrases, they should not be understood as pessimistic either. "By the impossible we should not understand an absolute barrier, for to erect such a barrier would be again to mistakenly attempt closure. Nor should the impossible simply be understood as the not-possible, a formulation that would also reduce the ethical to the mere Other of the same. As Derrida reminds us, the impossible occurs at every moment" (1616).

Nor should the fact of this occurence be taken to mean that the impossible is simply possible, at every moment, or even actual, especially when we're speaking of justice or responsibility. Impossibility means that ethics, and justice, can find no privileged ground for their articulation, no unquestionable epistemological standpoint somehow removed from the strife, investments, and contamination regularly associated with them. Justice and responsibilty are only possible, if they have a chance of happening at all, starting from their exposure to their strict and unpredictably recurring impossiblity. Because that privilege is impossible, we have what we call ethics and politics, and responsibility is an ineluctable necessity. The "we" here can be a community only in the strangest sense, a community without ground in any common "like"-ness and without a universal law, without the present in which any subject might articulate itself, but only a terrifying proximity.

> A community of decision, of initiative, of absolute initiality, but also a threatened community, in which the question has not yet found the language it has decided to seek, is not yet sure of its own possibility within the community. A community of the question about the possibility of the question. This is very little—almost nothing—but within it, today, is sheltered and encapsulated an unbreachable dignity and a duty of decision. An unbreachable responsibility. Why unbreachable? Because the impossible has *already* occured.[10]

If the impossible calls for a response that exceeds its own possibility, what gives it that right?

▼ ▲ ▼

If there is a certain persistence to the rhetoric of rights and responsibilities, beyond and thanks to their deconstruction, this survival enacts something irreducible and unforgiving about politics: that it is a game with the highest of stakes and without the security of predictability or of uncontaminated instruments, without even the comfort of reliable standpoints or positions, without guarantees—that it is just this "experience" of the failure of guarantees. And far from being a contingent or neutral piece in this game, a discourse that might just as easily be replaced with another one, "rights" and "responsibilities" have a certain unavoidability to them, an inevitability continuous with that of the political itself.

Elsewhere I have pursued this question in the work of Michel Foucault, who has often been understood to advocate the simple abandonment of this discourse because it has been surpassed by political techniques ("discipline") irreducible to it.[11] In the last pages of *La volonté de savoir*, though, Foucault underlines the odd way the vocabulary of right has of outliving itself, of living beyond its uselessness, and of extending itself into a realm where it does not belong: "It is life much more than right which has come to be at stake in [recent] political struggles, even if these [struggles] are formulated on the basis of affirmations of rights. . . . This right, so incomprehensible for the classical juridical system, has been the political reply to all these new procedures of power which did not derive, either, from the traditional right of sovereignty."[12] How are we to understand this "even if"? Perhaps the theory is in error, and the break between life and right, between the power of the disciplinary apparatus to say "yes" to bodies and the power of the king to say "no" to his subjects, isn't so radical after all? Or perhaps the practice is simply outdated, and the struggles woefully undertheorized? Or perhaps these are new rights, new kinds of rights, long hidden within the discourse of "human rights," rights to different kinds of events and experiences which never could have been reduced to rights of sovereignty but which have now become available to us? Or perhaps right in general, the claim to rights, is another name for the complex stategic situation in which political demands are made *because* epistemologically justified grounds are not available, not in the nature or the essence of humanity, not in the experience of a subject or a group, not even in this very reality of the body, not anywhere. If claims to rights persist as the rhetorical structure of our political responses, whatever their content, then we need to raise the possibility that rights and politics are coextensive.

What does it mean to claim a right, or what is it to do such a thing, since to assume in advance that it is meaningful is to presume too much. Who claims, and on what (if any) basis? The most obvious answer is simply: *I* claim, I claim something that belongs to me as my property, as what is proper and essential to me in virtue of what I am or what I have or what I do (and I am, for starters, human, but I am all sorts of other things too, various identities, understood here as given or better as taken, taken for granted). Right is my (own) right, not even right of or on behalf of others (no representation is possible here), what is owed to me as me and no one else—the claim to a right is justified here precisely on the grounds that the site of the claim and of the right are identical. In short, *I am right,* and claiming rights is really nothing other than reclaiming or rescuing them, since they are essentially mine and their loss can only be accidental or contingent.

But what of this claim? Why claim what is one's own? Why even open up the relation to the other that the linguistic act of claiming implies, when my relation to my rights is essentially a relation to myself without mediation through, or openness to, an other? This claim could only be a statement, the constative declaration of a fact that had fallen into temporary oblivion. Is this act of claiming necessary? For if rights must be claimed, then (1) the relation to the other, and the supposed "loss" of rights in the other, cannot be merely contingent, and (2) the rights claimed cannot simply preexist the claim that is made for them. In other words, if there is an irreducibility to the act of claiming rights, then they cannot simply be given, and the I that claims them for itself cannot be given either but must occur only in relation with an other, an other that always implies the possibility of the dispropriation of oneself and one's "rights" and "property," an other whose inevitability is this experience of dispropriation, i.e. of language as something other than a system of signs or representations.

Claude Lefort has argued something like this in an important essay on "Droits de l'homme et politique."[13] Unfortunately, Lefort's text does insufficient justice to the "paradox" which it exactingly articulates: without a king or any transcendental authority, rights have no foundation, and so they come to depend on the very declaration which would seem to refer them to that missing elsewhere:

> [T]he rights of man are declared [*énoncés*]; they are declared as rights that belong to man; but, simultaneously, man appears through his representatives as the being whose essence it is to declare his rights. Impossible to detach the statement [*l'énoncé*] from the utterance [*l'énonciation*] as soon as no one is able to occupy the place, at a distance from all others, from which he would have the authority to grant or ratify rights. Thus rights are not simply the object of a declaration, it is their essence to be declared. (67; Eng. trans. 256–257)

As Derrida has argued, in the case of an ungrounded declaration not of rights but of independence, this declaration must be one that aims at producing the condition it requires as its condition (freedom).[14] Here, who has the right to claim a right? Without exteriority, the declaration cannot appeal to any elsewhere for its authority. The word "human" at best marks or holds the place of an aporia: who could decide whether something like humanity exists before it claims its rights? The declaration is the declaration of the right to declare.

This difficult situation parallels the one Paul de Man analyzes in his reading of the so-called "blessed babe" passage in Book 2 of Wordsworth's *Prelude*.[15] This babe's "soul claims manifest kindred with an earthly soul," namely that of his mother. De Man argues that this event of claiming is nothing like the stereotyped scenarios we have come to expect of the *droits de l'homme:* "this encounter is not a recognition, a shared awareness of a common humanity. It occurs as an active verbal deed, a *claim* of 'manifest kindred' which is not given in the nature of things" (91). De Man here exploits the difference that opens up between the verb "claim" and its object "manifest kindred." If the relationship, the shared identity or the commonality, the community to be exact, is manifest—not latent, not hidden, but as evident as the hand that reaches out to touch—then why the necessity to claim it? What is strange here, as in Lefort's paradox, is that the claim ought to be a constative utterance, a statement of the facts, the fact of a relation or a state of things. Why is the noise, the clamor, of the speech act required to make what's already so manifest manifest? It seems as though this right, the right to the mother and to the natural intimacy of the relation of the mother, is not so much being taken for granted here as it is being thrown into some doubt. Why is this baby screaming? Because, manifestly, the attachment to the mother is somewhat questionable, because the apparently natural legitimacy of the relation is not guaranteed by anything other than the most fragile of conventions. The baby has to claim what is so obvious because it threatens to disappear, because the legitimacy or the foundation of the relation is lacking: when the guarantee is missing, when there is no certainty, then we claim. In this sense, the baby's claim is a performative speech act in the strongest Austinian sense (an active verbal deed, like a promise), one that does what it says and makes something happen: a claim claims, and in its wake—and only then—can we say that something has been claimed. But this is no ordinary performative, because in fact it does *claim* a fact, the fact of a relation, of a state of things: I am related to you. It superimposes a performative and constative in a way that renders the difference very difficult to make out. It claims in a way that is in principle discontinuous with (and irreducible to) any declaration of the facts of the case and with the performance of any already constituted subject: it is thanks to the absence of this cognitive foundation, in the default of any grounded guarantee, that the baby claims— and claims precisely this foundation.

"We" are that child. We should not hesitate to call our predicament a literary one (a fable). Not in order to aestheticize it, nor to appropriate the ethico-political for the discipline of literary criticism, but to insist on the linguistic character of this difficult conflation and disarticulation of constative and performative, cognition and position, without which no politics would be necessary or possible.

Without cognition, without recognition, and without any sharing, least of all of a common humanity.[16] Not because we are monadic and singular subjects, but because language—as it opens (breaches) us to others—removes the foundations to which we might refer together. If we claim a right, a right to justice, we try it out, write it down, several times, and it nevertheless continues to taunt or haunt us, to deny itself: "there is no justice"—then its difficulty and its persistence stem from its terrifying, challenging, removal of guarantees. We can take nothing for granted, least of all the we of any right—or of any justice. But without that unreadably cold word, without its irreducible conflation and disarticulation of constative and performative, cognition and position, present and future, no politics would be necessary or possible. This impossible claim is what politics is like for us, we who are not alike and are only barely human; what we call justice is the undergoing of this impossibility. Without a we, we have politics, the politics of claiming our right to it, still speaking in a low voice.

Notes

1. Jean Rhys, *Wide Sargasso Sea,* in *The Complete Novels* (New York: Norton, 1985), 548.

2. An earlier version of this article first appeared in *Deconstruction and the Possibility of Justice,* which corresponds to *Cardozo Law Review* 11, nos. 5–6 (July–August 1990): 1675–1686 (the title reproduces that of a symposium, including some participants from the Critical Legal Studies movement, that took place at the Cardozo Law School in New York City in October 1989).

3. The formula "deconstruction and the possibility of X" stems, I believe, from Robert Bernasconi's "Deconstruction and the Possibility of Ethics," in *Deconstruction and Philosophy,* ed. John Sallis (Chicago: University of Chicago Press, 1987), 122–139. Bernasconi argues that when the demand for an ethics is submitted to a deconstruction, as it must be, "the *possibility* of ethics is referred, not to its actuality, but to its *impossibility*" (135). He concludes that "we find the ethical enactment above all in the way deconstruction ultimately refuses to adopt the standpoint of critique, renouncing the passing of judgments on its own behalf in its own voice" (136).

4. Christopher Norris, *The Contest of Faculties* (New York: Methuen, 1985), 44–45. It is, of course, also to "reading" that Hillis Miller has turned in his effort to pose the question of ethics: see J. Hillis Miller, *The Ethics of Reading* (New York: Columbia University Press, 1987).

5. Paul Smith, *Discerning the Subject* (Minneapolis: University of Minnesota Press, 1988), back cover.

6. Drucilla Cornell comes close to this position as well when she insists on differentiating between the deconstructions of foundations and of intelligibility: "[R]ecent debates on legal interpretation which have predominantly turned around linguistic intelligibility have focused on the wrong question. The issue is not whether there is intelligibility, but rather what figure the Good can take on after the deconstruction of foundationalist phi-

losophy" ("From the Lighthouse," *Cardozo Law Review* 11, nos. 5–6 [July/August 1990]: 1690).

7. Drucilla Cornell, "Post-Structuralism, the Ethical Relation, and the Law," *Cardozo Law Review* 9, no. 6 (August 1988): 1587–1628.

8. This remark comes in a discussion of Derrida's "hesitancy to name the ethical desire that pushes deconstruction forward," but it has a certain exemplary value.

9. As Werner Hamacher has pointed out, the tropes are capricious here: "the performative act of promising a possible understanding must be structured as an epistemologically illegitimate rhetorical figure, as metalepsis, in order to be carried out. For what is announced by the promise only for the future—a possible understanding—is asserted to be already effective in the present. The rhetorical figure of confounding a future with a present . . . is unavoidably a figure of deceit, insofar as that which it implicitly states to be present can be opened up only by the illocutionary act as futurial" ("LECTIO: De Man's Imperative," trans. Susan Bernstein, in *Reading de Man Reading*, ed. Wlad Godzich and Lindsay Waters [Minneapolis: University of Minnesota Press, 1989], 197).

10. Jacques Derrida, "Violence et métaphysique," in *L'Écriture et la différence* (Paris: Seuil, 1967), 118; "Violence and Metaphysics," in *Writing and Difference*, trans. Alan Bass (Chicago: University of Chicago Press, 1978), 80.

11. Thomas Keenan, "The 'Paradox' of Knowledge and Power: Reading Foucault on a Bias," *Political Theory* 15, no. 1 (February 1987): 5–37.

12. Michel Foucault, *La Volonté de savoir* (Paris: Gallimard, 1976), 190–91; *The History of Sexuality*, vol. 1, trans. Robert Hurley (New York: Random House, 1978), 145.

13. Claude Lefort, "Droits de l'homme et politique," in *L'Invention démocratique: les limites de la domination totalitaire* (Paris: Fayard, 1981), 45–86; "Politics and Human Rights," in *The Political Forms of Modern Society*, trans. Alan Sheridan, ed. John B. Thompson (Cambridge: MIT Press, 1986), 239–272. On human rights, see also Jean-Fraçois Lyotard and Jacob Rogozinski, "La Police de la pensée," *L'Autre Journal* 10 (December 1985): 27–34, and Emmanuel Levinas, "Les Droits de l'homme et les droits de l'autrui," in *Hors sujet* (Montpellier: Fata Morgana, 1987), 173–187.

14. Jacques Derrida, "Déclarations d'Indépendance," in *Otobiographies* (Paris: Galilée, 1984), 22; "Declarations of Independence," trans. Thomas Keenan and Thomas Pepper, *New Political Science* 15 (Summer 1986): 7–15. Derrida argues that this impossible event is structured like a "fable": "This happens every day, but it is fabulous." He has continued this argument in "Psyché" and "Admiration de Nelson Mandela, ou Les Lois de la réflexion," in *Psyché: Inventions de l'autre* (Paris: Galilée, 1987), 11–61 and 453–475, and, since this article was first written, in "Force de Loi/Force of Law," trans. Mary Quaintance, *Cardozo Law Review* 11, nos. 5–6 (July/August 1990): 919–1045.

15. Paul de Man, "Wordsworth and the Victorians," in *The Rhetoric of Romanticism* (New York: Columbia University Press, 1984), 83–92.

16. On the question of this commonality, see Jean-Luc Nancy, *La Communauté désœuvrée* (Paris: Christian Bourgeois, 1986); *The Inoperative Community*, trans. Peter Connor et al. (Minneapolis: University of Minnesota Press, 1991), and Nancy's special issue of *Cahiers Confrontation* 20: Après le sujet qui vient (Winter 1989); Eduardo Cadava et al, ed., *Who Comes After the Subject?* (New York: Routledge, 1991).

▼ JILL ROBBINS ▼

Visage, Figure
Speech and Murder in Levinas's *Totality and Infinity*

The Figure of the Face

WHAT WOULD IT MEAN TO FACE what Derrida has called "the ethics of ethics"? That is to say, to confront the very opening of the question of ethics—the grounds of both its possibility and impossibility—prior to the production and elaboration of all moral rules or precepts? According to Emmanuel Levinas, the face of the other *(le visage d'Autrui)* is the very site and privileged figure for such an opening. In the face-to-face encounter, responsibility in its most original form of response, or language-response, arises. The pages that follow will consider the specificity of this language-response as Levinas describes it, the originary speech or "conversation" with the other. It will follow Levinas's description up to the point where all conversation ceases, namely in the paradigmatic situation of murder that Levinas analyzes in his 1961 *Totality and Infinity*, the 1953 essay "Freedom and Command," and in other early texts. In the course of this discussion, the Levinasian account of violence, as well as the relationship of violence to "face" and "speech," will be closely examined.

This essay will also take up the question of the textual status of the face. Can there be a figure for the ethical? a figure for the face? The very question is problematic in that rhetoric, as a (derivative) science of figures, may be incommensurable with the more originary level of Levinas's

This essay takes as its point of departure an essay of mine that originally appeared in *Yale French Studies* 79 (1991), under the title, *"Visage, Figure:* Reading *Totality and Infinity."* It has been significantly revised and expanded. Permission to reprint the original essay is gratefully acknowledged.

description. Could the opening of the question of the ethical be marked with a certain figurality? And supposing that one can speak about an alterity that is rhetorical or textual, can the alterity of the other and textual alterity be even addressed in one breath? Here too, the question of ethics and the question of language come into their closest possible proximity.

Just Speaking

"The alterity of the other," asserts Levinas in *Totality and Infinity*, "is not 'other' like the bread I eat, the land in which I dwell, like, sometimes, myself for myself" (*TI*, 33). A relation to this latter, finite alterity characterizes the "I" in its primordial work of identification, that is, its tendency to absorb otherness into its identity as thinker or possessor (*TI*, 33). Levinas also calls it the economy of the Same, and it refers to the *habitual* exchanges—for example, dwelling, being at home (*chez soi*)—that make up the self's concrete relationship with the world. However, the alterity of the other is *infinite*. Encountered neither as a phenomenon nor as a being (something to be mastered or possessed), the other is encountered as a *face*.

The first reference to the face in *Totality and Infinity* reads as follows:

> For the presence before the face, my orientation toward the Other can lose the avidity of the gaze only by turning into generosity [*l'avidité du regard se muant en générosité*], incapable of approaching the other with empty hands. This relationship, established over the things henceforth possibly common, that is, susceptible of being said, is the relationship of discourse [*discours*]. The way in which the other presents himself, exceeding the idea of the other in me, we here name face [*nous l'appelons, en effet, visage*]. (*TI*, 50)

Levinas describes a radical change in orientation that the encounter with the face of the other may produce. The avaricious gaze *turns into* generosity and discourse. This transformation is necessary because, for Levinas, vision is inherently violent: it "immobilizes its object as a theme." As a form of adequation (*TI*, 34), it is unable to respect what is infinitely other. In this way, vision is just one instance—albeit an emblematic instance—of the self's *habitual* economy, an economy that always fails to do justice to the other. Other instances within this habitual economy include knowledge, representation, understanding, recognition, or any form of the theoretical relation. Each of these possibilities would reduce and deny alterity, would draw the other into the play of the Same. Note that even the apparent attempts to respect the other, by way of recognition or comprehension, end up doing violence to him or her, precisely because recognition and comprehension are adequating and phenomenalizing forms.

Hence vision, a relation of adequation, turns into generosity and discourse, relationships of nonadequation. The face is preeminently *inadequation*. Levinas describes it in accordance with the formal structure of infinity, "an *ideatum* that surpasses its idea" (*TI,* 49), a thought that thinks more than it can contain.[1] He defines the face as a surplus, or, in the passage above, as "the way in which the other presents himself, *exceeding* the idea of the other in me." When vision becomes generosity and discourse, then, everything that belongs to the habitual economy— its tendency to see and to know, to grasp with an appropriative gaze—is suspended and transformed. The transformation is no less than paradigmatic of what Levinas calls ethics: "we name this calling into question of my spontaneity by the presence of the other ethics" (*TI,* 43). (And one will note the distance between this sense of ethics and its ordinary understandings as right conduct or any particular morality. This calling into question of the self, occurring on a primordial level, *opens* ethics, is its upsurge.) Moreover, and this is a point to which I will return, the ethical transformation or transfer is a figural transfer as well. The turn from vision to generosity (*l'avidité du regard se muant en générosité*) and to discourse (*discours*), from seeing the face to giving to the face (not an "empty-handed approach") and to speaking to the face, resembles a synesthesia, a crossing of sensory attributes. The verb which marks the transformation, *se muer,* "to turn, to moult, to metamorphose," implies a break, within the figural turn, in phenomenality.

For Levinas, then, ethics is a calling into question of the self's spontaneity, an interruption *of* self that is produced in the presence of the other. The "spontaneity" to which Levinas refers has nothing psychological about it; it does not happen *in* the world, but is the very possibility of world, is the world *as* possibility,, as a space where I can (*je peux*). In Levinas's descriptions, *pouvoir*—in the sense of possibility and also power—characterizes the self's very being in the world.[2] But over the other, Levinas says, *je ne peux pouvoir;* that is, I have no power (and this will be significant for Levinas's murder analysis); I am no longer my possibilities (or if you will, I am no longer I). Possibility itself is interrupted by the other's face.

But to characterize ethics as an interruption (that is, in somewhat negative and formal terms) should not obscure its positive significance, indeed, the ethical positivity that Levinas assigns to the concrete instances of generosity and discourse. The only nontotalizing ways of relating to the other which are proposed in *Totality and Infinity,* generosity and discourse are exceptional modes which affirm and welcome alterity. Levinas says, in a grammatical figure, "the other does not appear in the nominative," but "in the dative" or "in the vocative." (*DF,* 7).³ The dative is the case of the gift, the vocative the case in which to call upon the other. The generosity which goes out *unto* the other without return and the aneconomical gift that demands, consequently, a radical ingratitude, preserve an asymmetrical and nonreversible relation to the other, as I have elaborated elsewhere.⁴ "Discourse," in the particular sense in which Levinas understands it, namely, as a unique form of interpellation, also preserves asymmetry and nonreversibility.⁵ It reaches the other without touching him. Discourse maintains a relation of infinite distance, "without this distance destroying this relation and without this relation destroying this distance" (*TI,* 41). It is as if the discourse had the very moment of infinity in it.

In the *fact* of this speaking relationship to the face of the other can be found the entire significance of the ethical relation. The other who is called upon is "maintained in his heterogeneity," whatever the content of the discourse. Before all comprehension, discourse—as interpellation, interlocution, and address—respects the other's alterity. The whole possibility of a *just* relation to the face is there. Discourse is a direct and immediate relation to the other. The term Levinas uses to characterize this language relation is *droiture,* which means "straightforwardness," "uprightness," "rectitude,"and "justice." Not only is the language relation *to* the face characterized by a singular straightforwardness, but the language *of* the face is also said to possess an exceptional "sincerity"and "frankness": "the eyes break through the mask—the language of the eyes, impossible to dissemble (*indissimulable*)" (*TI,* 66). Levinas opposes the *droiture,* the direct and straightforward rapport with the face, to the indirection and obliqueness he associates with rhetoric. Unlike the ethical language which faces, "rhetoric," asserts Levinas, "approaches the other not to face him but obliquely" (*TI,* 70). Rhetoric approaches the neighbor from an angle, with an angle, with ruse: it is, for Levinas, manipulation, violence, injustice. Levinas's entire discourse on ethical language (and its distinction from nonethical language or rhetoric) is dominated by an opposition between the geometrical figures of facing and the angle.

Levinas's denigration of rhetoric, which he invariably conceives as persuasion, is essentially classical and Platonic. But even if Levinas assimilates *all* rhetoric to persuasion (to action between subjects, to an *inter*subjective level) and ignores the level of rhetoric that Paul de Man calls trope (a level which is cognitive and *intra*linguistic), it is not easy to assign a place to this fact, or to evaluate the consequences of Levinas's denigration of rhetoric and his privileging of ethical language. The "straightforwardness," the "sincerity" that is at issue occurs not on the positivistic level of a denotative phrase universe, but on the level of an originary language response to the other that *opens* ethics. With ethical language and rhetoric opposed as direct/indirect, facing/angle, justice/violence, we have to do not with an opposition *within* meaning (a semantic opposition) but an opposition between nonmeaning and meaning, between something that *precedes* meaning, and meaning.⁶ There is an asymmetry between what Levinas calls ethical language and rhetoric, just as there is an incommensurability between the originary discourse and the derivative science of figures. Even if this incommensurability turns out to be only apparent (if, say, a Levinasian view of ethical language and a de Manian view of rhetoric can be brought together), there may still be good reasons why figure is hostile to what Levinas calls "face."

Speaking Face

To figure a face is to de-face it. Perhaps it is the legacy of *figura,* and the "plastic form" that is, for Erich Auerbach, its earliest meaning (even if, in the later, rhetorical usage, the sense of "figure" is nonplastic). Figure invariably implies a certain plasticity, but the face, in every description Levinas gives of it, is precisely that which is *not* reducible to a plastic image, to any phenomenal or visible figure. Levinas says in an interview: "I can certainly look at a face while defacing it [*je peux certes regarder le visage en le dévisageant*], like any plastic form."⁷ But there is violence in reducing a face to an object or thing seen, "transforming faces into objective and plastic forms, into visible—but defaced—figures" [*transformation des visages . . . en figures visibles, mais dévisagées.*]⁸ One can try to dominate the face with a look, but to encounter the face *as* face is, as in the paradigmatically ethical transfer when my gaze turns into discourse, to face the other as interlocutor. Alphonso Lingis comments: "To face someone is both to perceive him and to answer to him."⁹ The facing *happens* in language.

But we cannot take for granted that we know what we mean here by language. Levinas describes the discourse with the face as "a conversation [*entre-tien*] which *proposes* the world. This proposition is held between [*se tient entre*] two points which do not constitute a system, a cosmos, a totality" (*TI,* 96). The speech that ensues in response to the face of the other cannot be understood according to hermeneutic models of "conversation" or "dialogue." It is a conversation *before* conversation, a relationship, as said in the above-cited passage, "established over the things henceforth possibly common, that is, susceptible of being said" (*TI,* 50). A conversation rigorously without communality, it makes *lieux communs* possible. Rather than being a searching together for consensus, it is what makes possible the difference between consensus and disagreement.

Nor is this to be mistaken for any form of communication. It is "prior" to language understood as an exchange of signs. The face signifies in a distinctive manner which Levinas calls expression *kath 'auto* ("according to itself"), or that which signifies only relative to itself. Usually when we encounter things we do so within a system of relations, across a generality, or as categorized by disclosure (FC, 20). The signification of a being is relative to a context or in its relation to another thing (EI, 86). But a *direct* encounter with a being "is that which puts us in contact with a being that is not simply uncovered, but divested of its form, of its categories, a being becoming naked, an unqualified substance breaking through its form and presenting a face" (FC, 20).

In Levinas's descriptions, expression is always about the way in which the face presents itself as a phenomenon and also exceeds the phenomenon, lodges itself within form and also breaks through the form:

> The way for a being to break through its form, which is its apparition, is concretely, its look, its aim [*sa visée*]. There is not first a breakthrough, and then a look; to break through one's form is precisely to look; the eyes are absolutely naked. A face has a meaning not by virtue of the relationships in which it is found, but *out of itself;* that is what expression is. (FC, 20)

> The life of expression consists of undoing the form in which the existent, exposing itself as a theme, in this way dissimulates itself. The face speaks. The manifestation of the face is already discourse. [*Le visage parle. La manifestation du visage est déjà discours*]. (TI, 66)

The *concrete* way in which the face accomplishes this breaking through the sensible form is with its look and its speech: expression is a combination of glance and speech. With the expression the face comes from behind its appearance (T, 352), or, as Levinas states above, each time with an active verb, it "undoes the form," "breaks through the form," "divests itself of the form." Face is an active surplus over the form that would enclose it. Never reducible to plastic image, surface, or mask, it is by definition always on the move. Expression is a mobile interpellation. Note also that in these descriptions of expression, there is a reversal: the face that I would grasp with the look, looks back. This reversal was already implied in the word *visage*. Despite its Latin root, *visum*, "a thing seen," the *visage* is not just a thing seen or intended. It is also that which intends me, as Levinas etiologizes it: "Regarder un regard, c'est regarder ce qui ne s'abandonne pas, ne se livre pas, mais qui vous vise: c'est regarder le *visage*" (DF, 8). Hence, it is not simply that my look becomes discourse and I face the face in language. The face, which breaks through its form, looks back, and speaks, also faces in language.¹⁰ To encounter a face is always (already) to encounter a speaking face: *Le visage parle.*

Derrida has remarked in "Violence and Metaphysics" that it may be "tempting" to consider this discourse on the face a prosopopeia (VM, 101). Surely this is because in the most general sense, the giving of face or prosopopeia is the governing figure of Levinas's discourse. More specifically, when Levinas gives the face *as* voice, as he repeatedly does, he in a sense de-faces it, gives it as *figure*. At times it is as if figuration performs the desired (ethical) break in phenomenality, the turn away from the optical. Yet while this, like the earlier transformation or ethico-figural transfer ("l'avidité du regard se muant en générosité") seems tropological, prosopopeia or any other rhetorical term may be, once again, inapplicable here. There is a tension between the ethico-figural transfers operative in Levinas's description (*from* vision *to* voice), which seem to imply a sequential narrative, and the anteriority of the experience that is described. The facing face does not become discourse; "the manifestation of the face is *already* discourse" (*TI*, 66). While the sequential narrative proceeds forward, the (quasi-transcendental) description proceeds backwards. The "already" here belongs to an immemorial past that is accessible to no present.

Let us look more closely at the conceptual figure of facial expression, in particular Levinas's description of the distinctive way in which expression signifies. The face, as we have said, does not signify in relation to a context or within any system of relations, but *kath 'auto,* according to itself. While Levinas's discussion of the *kath 'auto* has a technical sense, takes in an entire philosophical heritage, and includes a polemic against Heidegger which contrasts the face's signification with the disclosure and dissimulation that is proper to forms, there is a simple meaning as well. Unlike other signs, facial expressions signify only themselves. They do not refer to something else, to states of mind or feeling. Their auto-signification is presemiotic and has no cognitive content:

> Expression does not consist in presenting to a contemplative consciousness a sign which that consciousness interprets by going back to what is signified. What is expressed is not just a thought which animates the other; it is also the other present in that thought. Expression renders present what is communicated and the one who is communicating [*le communiqué et le communiquant*]; they are both in the expression. But that does not mean that expression gives us knowledge about the other. The expression does not speak about someone, is not information about a coexistence, does not invoke an attitude in addition to knowledge;

expression invites one to speak to someone. The most direct attitude before a being *kath 'auto* is not the knowledge one can have about him, but is precisely social commerce with him. (FC, 20–21)

Expression speaks not with any kind of denotative speech; it is more like that mode of speech that Roman Jakobson calls conative, oriented toward the addressee. Its force is performative rather than constative.[11] Expression is this interlocutionary address; it is an invitation to speak, a greeting. It doesn't say anything except itself. There is thus a type of self-coincidence within facial expression, between (to use a terminology that is inadequate) addressor and message. Levinas would distinguish this self-coincidence from a Romantic (or proto-Romantic) view of facial expression as the exteriorization of an inward state. For example, Augustine formulates the self-coincidence of facial expression semiotically: in the face of a friend he finds "the signs which proceed from the heart . . . and are revealed in the face, the voice, the eyes." In describing a coincidence between the movement of the heart and facial expression, he proposes that the face's signs have a necessary rather than arbitrary relation to their meaning.[12]

Of course, Levinas would distinguish his view of facial expression from all semiotic accounts; he opposes expression *kath 'auto* to sign. If the face signified in the manner of other signs, it would be reducible to a play of immanence, which is how Levinas describes the referrals inherent in sign systems. It would be an apparent contour, a surface, like "the face of a building." It would be a mask, which is for Levinas derivative upon face. In the 1963 essay "The Trace of the Other," Levinas distinguishes the face's signification from the order of disclosure, the symbolic, and the semiotic order: "A face . . . is not a form concealing, but thereby indicating, a ground, a phenomenon that hides, but thereby betrays a thing itself. Otherwise a face would be one with a mask—but a mask presupposes a face" (T, 355). Face signifies in a manner which, unlike revelation, disclosure, or indication, is a specific form of signification *in retreat* that Levinas calls "trace." The opposition between expression *kath 'auto* and the sign will later become an opposition between "trace" and sign.

The face signifies not solely with reference to a context, horizon, or world. It is a disturbance, a shaking up of the mundane; it occurs as a collision between world and that which exceeds world. To the extent that the face is out of world, it appears *in* the world as naked and destitute. Naked—that is, without clothing, covering, or mask—it signifies without attributes, outside any categories, not across its generality, but by itself, and this is the technical sense of Levinas's term expression *kath 'auto*.

He says: "There is first the very uprightness of the face, its upright exposure, without defense (*la droiture même du visage, son exposition droite, sans défense*). The skin of the face is that which stays the most naked . . . the most destitute (*la plus nue . . .la plus dénuée*): there is an essential poverty in the face" (*EI,* 86). The face's destitution is an essential destitution. Its nakedness, its wretchedness, indeed, its strangeness are a mark of its absence and exile from world. In the nakedness of expression, the face signifies—before all semiosis—with an exceptional *droiture,* presenting itself in person, present to itself as a "coincidence of the expressed with him who expresses" (*TI,* 66).

The question arises: can facial expressions be kept altogether apart from sign relations? Let us come back to the semiotic version of the self-coincidence of facial expression suggested by Augustine: the face's signs reveal the movement of the heart and thus, in facial expression, the relationship between sign and meaning, usually conventional and arbitrary, is necessary. Such a view that sign and meaning coincide in the face is not untypical.[13] However, it can be argued that a facial expression can always *become* a conventional sign, that is, one in which there is discrepancy between sign and meaning. Paul de Man uses the example of "a smile that hides rage or hatred" in an examination of the double consequences of the arbitrary nature of the sign: "It is the distinctive privilege of language to be able to hide meaning behind a misleading sign . . . but it is the distinctive curse of all language, as soon as any kind of interpersonal relation is involved, that it is forced to act this way."[14] The discrepancy between sign and meaning liberates the subject, who is "privileged" to exploit and manipulate signs in a playful manner, to hide rage behind a smile (to privilege sign over meaning). But it also puts into question the subject, "who," in the case of an authentic smile (that is, in a case where he would wish meaning to predominate over sign), is "forced" to use the same sign. For de Man, the impossibility of making sign and meaning coincide results in a world of "potentially inauthentic" social relationships.[15] But for Levinas and his philosophy of face, is this not to acknowledge that facial expressions necessarily employ semiotic conventions?

Of course, this is precisely what Levinas does *not* mean by face. The face in Levinas's descriptions cannot dissimulate; it is *prior* to rhetoric, mask, semiosis—to meaning itself. "The alternative between truth and lies, between sincerity and dissimulation, is the privilege of him who abides in the relation of absolute frankness" (*TI,* 66). For Levinas, to decode a face in the manner of other signs would be to reduce it violently, to turn it—horribly—into a mask, that is, not just a surface, but something petrified and immobile.[16] To *figure* a face would have to be accounted a similar violence (and there is surprising agreement on this point between de Man and Levinas). If the face is presemiotic, it is certainly prior to figure as well.

All of the oppositions which organize Levinas's discourse—face and mask, mobility and immobility, direct and indirect language, ethical language and rhetoric, expression and sign—are not oppositions within meaning, but again, between that which precedes meaning and meaning. This asymmetry makes a difference, for it is not as if Levinas were simply championing a direct, denotative, or constative language on a positivistic level. But one may still reflect on the necessity by which Levinas nonetheless seeks to privilege meaning over sign, on *this* side of meaning, on a level that precedes meaning, or the necessity by which Levinas reconstitutes metaphysical oppositions such as direct/indirect, expression/sign, *p*resemiotically, asymmetrically, situating the first term of the oppostion on a quasi-transcendental level.

There is a certain phonocentrism in Levinas's description of the self-coincidence of expression, which renders it complicit with what Derrida has called the metaphysics of presence. Such turns of phrase as "expression renders present what is communicated and the one who is communicating" (FC, 21) or, elsewhere in his work, the assertions that expression means "being behind the sign," or that "he who manifests himself comes, according to Plato's expression, to his own assistance" (*TI*, 66), all seem part of a privileging of oral discourse as "plenitude" (*TI*, 96), as presence to oneself.[17] As Blanchot remarks, it is at just these moments that what Levinas describes as discourse or *entretien* "becomes a tranquil humanistic speaking again" (*IC*, 56). This is largely a result of the privileging of oral discourse in Levinas. (For Levinas rarely uses the word "man." Recall that the *visage* is defined as the way in which the other presents himself, exceeding the idea of the other in me. The *visage* is man in his infinite alterity, man *insofar as* he is infinitely other. *Visage* is not a description added on to the conception of "man"; it is prior to it.) But that the Levinasian *entretien* would revert to a humanistic conversation is also due to a fault of the language ("our" language), which is weighted towards the hermeneutical and the dialectical. (Recall again that the face's speaking, which belongs to the "already," does not take place in the present and is accessible to no present.)

Thus the radicality of the Levinasian *entretien*, of the language relation with the other, should be insisted upon. As Blanchot elaborates it in *L'Entretien infini*, in this encounter, which maintains distance and separation, the asymmetry between discussants is absolute. The other is described alternately by Levinas as the Most-High and the weak one. At times he seems the overlord, and at times the utterly helpless and destitute. He is, as we shall see, the one who commands me and the one to whom I am infinitely obligated. Thus, despite the seeming symmetry of the exchange of glances and speech, despite the formal symmetry of the phrase "face-to-face," and despite, in Blanchot's phrase, "l'affrontement de deux figures" that it invariably suggests, the confrontation, the encounter face-to-face, has nothing symmetrical about it. Blanchot comments: "I never face the one who faces me. My manner of facing the one who faces me is not an equal confrontation of presences. The inequality is irreducible" (*IC*, 62). And this is why at the close of *Totality and Infinity*, Levinas formulates the relation to the other as "the curvature of intersubjective space which inflects distance into elevation," or simply, "the curvature of space" (*TI*, 291). This "curvature," the only "ethical" variation on the geometrical figure of the straight line of ethical discourse, denotes nonreciprocity.[18]

The speaking relation to the other in the face-to-face does not bring the two parties close, does not familiarize; it is, as Blanchot comments further, "the access to man in his strangeness by speech" (*IC*, 62). How can such a speaking maintain "the strangeness of this strangeness" and not "repatriate it?" (*IC*, 68) Again, this will be a kind of speaking that is not a speaking about the other, but rather a speaking *to* him, an invocation. Not a referential or denotative speech, but conative, not a speech which merely constates the ethical relation, but one which accomplishes and performs it. And a question that arises concerning such a claim, and that has been posed by both Lyotard and Derrida, is, how to speak about this invocation of the other without neutralizing the relation, transforming it into a form of knowledge? How to speak about Levinas's discourse without rendering its performative dimension constative, assimilating it to the denotative language of the same? How, for that matter, to speak *to* the other without comprehension (a form of "repatriation")? Would this not occasion the grossest misunderstanding?[19]

If this speaking to the other is "to maintain the strangeness of this strangeness," it must be characterized by nonreciprocity and noncomprehension. "Parole sans entente et à laquelle je dois cependant répondre" (*IC*, 65), writes Blanchot. Such a speech, is thus, in an important sense, impossible. *Parler sans pouvoir* is what Blanchot calls it, that is, to speak without power, to speak without being able (to speak), to speak without ability.[20] This is a speech which affirms impossibility, takes it up as the space where—within the economy of the Same—the alterity of the other becomes legible.

It is a strange speech, this speech that is "the access to man in his strangeness." It is not a speech between two already constituted entities, but speech that "founds" the rapport, and that *is* the rapport (without rapport). In this *entretien*, Blanchot writes, the *entre* designates an interval held up over a void, an abyss. This speech with the *visage* is a speech with the outside (although Levinas generally uses the term "exteriority"), for *Autrui* is "always coming from the outside" (*IC,* 56). A speech with the outside, it is speech with the "stranger, the destitute, the proletarian" (*TI,* 75), or, in the biblical locution that Levinas frequently invokes, "the stranger, the widow, the orphan." The other is "always, in relation to me, without country, stranger to all possession, dispossessed and without dwelling, he who is as if 'by definition' the proletarian" (*IC,* 56).

Speaking Murder

> The being that expresses itself, that faces me, says *no* to me by his very expression. (FC, 21)

> [The Other] opposes to me not a greater force . . . but precisely the infinity of his transcendence. This infinity, stronger than murder, already resists us in his face, is his face, is the primordial expression, is the first word: "thou shalt not kill." (*TI,* 199)

> The face, it is inviolable; these eyes absolutely without protection, the most naked part of the human body, offer, nevertheless, an absolute resistance to possession, an absolute resistance in which the temptation of murder is inscribed: the temptation of an absolute negation. The Other is the sole being that one can be tempted to kill. This temptation of murder and this impossibility of murder constitute the very vision of the face. To see a face is already to hear: "Thou shalt not kill." (*DF,* 8)

Levinas had described expression as an autosignification and as an invitation to speak, within the originary language encounter with the face of the other. It is only in Levinas's analysis of murder that the face's speaking is given a particular content, albeit negative. In the passages above Levinas asserts that the expression "says no," that the "primordial expression," "the first word" is an order, "thou shalt not kill," that "to see a face is already to hear: 'thou shalt not kill.' " How to understand this primordial expression? As an utterance it is imperative and interlocutionary. To call it a prohibition may be to take too much for granted. (What is a prohibition, if it can occur on such a primordial level?) Jean-François Lyotard likens the Levinasian description of the primordial utterance to the biblical diction in which God commands, "Listen!" or "Hear O Israel." This is a prescription which in effect tells its addressee, "Get yourself into a situation where you are ready to hear a prescription." This prescription arises from the very fact of the other's speaking to me. That is why as paradigm, "thou shalt not kill" has something misleading about it. Most of the time in Levinas's descriptions the other's command is not a categorical prescription but a more general "prescription that there be prescriptions."[21] In other words, most of the time there is something deliberately empty and general about the other's speaking command. There is, however, a more general (noncategorical) sense of the primordial "you shall not kill" in Levinas's work: it brings about a cessation of power and possibility in the I who is thus addressed. As Lyotard reads it, the prescription "you shall not kill" turns the I into a *you,* into the recipient of a command.[22]

"Thou shalt not kill," or its shortened form, "no," is the only utterance that Levinas, in his earlier work, proposes for the primordial lexicon. This choice suggests the enigmatic relation between murder and primordial speech. It suggests the way in which the (im)possibility of murder inhabits the language relation to the other at its origin. Blanchot writes:

> Such would be the speech that measures the relation of man face-to-face with man, when there is no choice but to speak or to kill. A speech as grave, perhaps, as the death of which it is the detour. The speech/murder alternative is not the tranquil exclusion of one by the other, as if it were a matter of choosing once and for all between good speech and bad death . . . in this situation, either to speak or to kill, speech does not consist in speaking, but first of all in maintaining the movement of the *either/or;* it is what founds the alternative. (IC, 62)

The speech with the face occurs on the level at which killing is avoided. With this primordial speech, an alternative presents itself: either to welcome infinity or to reject it, to speak or to kill. The sense of killing must be enlarged here beyond its literal meaning to a more general sense. The warrant for this will be found in the very continuity between Levinas's account and his account of all instances of transcendental violence. The speech/murder alternative, however, does not belong to a subject who could choose or initiate an action. In this alternative, there is *in*ability. The (ethical) speaking without *pouvoir* is a speech which takes its life from a certain experience of impossibility. With the other, then, it is a matter of not a humanistic speech that keeps the peace, but a "grave" speech—in both senses of the term—a speech in which there circulates the violence that belongs to the very nature of possibility.

Just as the speech with the other is precisely not part of a dialogue in the usual sense—for the ordinary concept has been reread and reinscribed—so too the other's primordial expression is not an utterance in any usual sense where the sender and the receiver are already constituted entities. This is because the speaking occurs on the level of face, that is, on the level of distress, nudity, and exposure to violence. In Levinas's descriptions, the face wears a double aspect. It is at once absolutely defenseless—"naked," that is, "without covering, clothing, or mask" (FC, 21), naked because of its eyes, its look which breaks through form, and causes it to be "divested of its form" (FC, 20)—and also that which "opposes my power over it, my violence, and opposes it in an absolute way" (FC, 21). The face is delivered up to my powers and, at the same time, refuses them. It challenges them, saying "no," offering resistance. This double aspect of the face was already evident in the descriptions of the other at once as the destitute one and as overlord. The interruptive force of the face was evident as well when the encounter with the other was said to call into question and transform the self's habitual economy, its possibilities and its powers (*pouvoir*).

These powers are, at the limit, murderous. Vision is a violence; it would possess the other; it is even "by essence murderous." The habitual economy is shot through with violence and the drive for possession. According to the account Levinas gives in "Freedom and Command" and *Difficult Freedom,* there is violence within the habitual economy "whenever one acts as though one were alone" (FC, 18; cf. DF, 6). This extends to satisfaction of a need, knowledge of an object. "Knowledge seizes an object; it possesses it" (DF, 8). What departs from the order of violence is the fact of facing and the discourse that ensues. "What characterizes a violent act is the fact that one does *not* face" (FC, 19).

But in the violence specific to vision there is a temptation of murder ("this temptation of murder . . . constitutes the very vision of the face" [DF, 8]). The temptation would seem to arise in the face's phenomenalization, in the sensuous moment of expression (*ex-primere,* to press out), that is, to the precise extent that the face can be seized by an adequating vision. But ultimately, the manner in which the temptation arises is more complicated. It is due to an ambiguity within expression itself, namely, the fact that the face lodges itself in form and also goes beyond the form. Not just its presenting itself in sensible form, but also its divesting itself of its form, its nakedness, exposes it to murder. The temptation is inscribed then, not just in the face's phenomenality but in its beyond-phenomenality. Hence the face's expression invites murder. Yet, Levinas stresses, it also prohibits it. In its very defenselessness, it absolutely resists the murderous intent: "This temptation of murder *and this impossibility of murder* constitute the very vision of the face" (DF, 8).

There are several registers of this impossibility that we will let resonate in the following discussion of Levinas's analysis of murder. The first and the plainest sense is that murder is, morally, abhorrent: "The authority of the prohibition is maintained in the bad conscience of the accomplished evil—malignancy of evil" (EI, 87). But the central emphasis that

Levinas gives this impossibility is this: murder is doomed in advance to a certain failure. He writes: "Murder exercises a power over what escapes power. It is still a power, for the face expresses itself in the sensible, but already impotency, because the face rends the sensible" (*TI*, 198). Murder wants to kill the other, who is (by definition) beyond the sensible. Yet in murdering the other, it arrives only at the sensible. In this way, murder always misses its mark. No doubt it effects an annihilation of the other in his being. But it thereby misses the genuine alterity of the other, namely that which in him goes beyond the sensible (and that which in him is beyond being).

It is here that we might begin to think the relation of murder and speech in yet another way. Does not murder aim at speech itself, at that language possibility (or language-trace) of the other that is his alterity? Does it not necessarily aim at the discourse by which the other comes from behind his appearance, namely, at a speaking face? There is not space here to pursue these complex questions. Suffice it to remark that in the other's language-trace, in the infinity that the other speaks, lies the impossibility of murder and the indestructibility of the other.[23]

One of the difficulties of Levinas's analysis of murder comes from his assertion that it is in the face's absolute resistance to possession that the temptation of murder is inscribed. How is it that the resistance itself is the temptation? What is the nature of this resistance? As Levinas explains it, the face is "total resistance without being a force" (FC, 19). In murder, however, "one identifies the absolute character of the other with his force" (FC, 19). In other words, one mistakes the other's resistance *for* a force. The mistake comes from not facing, from indirection, from the angle: "Violence consists in ignoring this opposition, ignoring the face of a being, avoiding the gaze, and catching sight of an angle whereby the *no* inscribed on a face by the very fact that it is a face becomes a hostile or submissive force. Violence is a way of acting on every being and every freedom by approaching it from an indirect angle" (FC, 19). Blanchot explains this colossal "mistake" as a violent misreading—as it were—of infinity: murder takes the infinity by which *Autrui* presents himself as if it were a property of *Autrui* and wishes to reject it absolutely. Thereby it misses *Autrui*; "it changes him into absence, but does not touch him" (*IC*, 61). Thus the one who murders is caught in a substitutive structure; he is like a man who must aim at his target (infinity) over and over again, and always miss it. (That is why he cannot kill his victim enough times.) The infinite alterity of the speaking face is "incommensurate with a power exercised"; there is a "disproportion between infinity and my powers" (*TI*, 198). And it is in this sense that while murder is a *real* possibility, it is what Levinas calls an *"ethical* impossibility."

"The face defies not just the weakness of my powers but my power of power (*mon pouvoir de pouvoir*)" (*TI*, 198). The other opposes to me "not a greater force" (*TI*, 199), but "the resistance of that which has no resistance—ethical resistance" (*TI*, 199) or "intelligible resistance," as Levinas calls it in "Freedom and Command."²⁴ Derrida terms this a "strange, unthinkable notion of unreal resistance" (VM, 104). The face's opposition is one that "no finite power can restrict" (VM, 104). The ethical impossibility of murder means precisely, and here is, again, its enlarged sense: the face's expression, "which prohibits me with the original language of its defenseless eyes" (TH, 90), brings about a cessation of my murderous *pouvoir* at the level on which any particular power could originate. Levinas has described it as an intentionality in reverse.²⁵ But here is also the positive significance of the impossibility of murder. In "Freedom and Command," Levinas explains that the "no" that the face opposes to me is "not the *no* of a hostile force or threat . . . it is the possibility of encountering a being through an interdiction." (FC, 21). Again, not a force in the world, interdiction is unlike repression. It has an ethical positivity; it signals an ethical relationship. The interruption of the "imperialism of the same" (*TI*, 39), is also welcome, gift and the originary response of responsibility.

As in earlier textual instances in Levinas's work, this interruption is marked by an ethico-figural turn of speech, a quasi-synesthetic turn from my vision to the other's voice, or from the sense of seeing to that of hearing: "to see a face is already *to hear* 'Thou shalt not kill.' " But is this a matter of hearing, with its connotation of self-coincidence, at all? The face's primordial expression is a *citation,* that is, it is characterized not by phenomenality, but by the structure of the mark, with the constitutive absence that implies. Moreover, the "voice" delivers a commandment from an immemorial past, accessible to no present: "To see a face is *already* to hear: 'thou shalt not kill' " (*DF,* 8). This "already" ruptures self-coincidence. Thus when Levinas gives the face as voice here, again he gives the face *as* (nonphenomenal, nonplastic, ethical) *figure.* He gives the face as a figure for, one might add, the (biblical version of the) originary donation of the law, in all the literality of its imposition. But that the face (*visage*) could be a figure (*figure*) was always possible within the semantic destination of the word.

Similarly, within the semantic field and also before the semantic field, face and mask can converge. Even an ethical reading of face yields this possibility. The murderer who takes violent aim at the face of the other does not truly *face* the other. He thus loses not only the face of the other but also his own face—that is, he is ashamed, and, as it were, forfeits his own alterity. "When Cain saw that the Lord did not accept his sacrifice, he became inflamed and his face fell" (Gen. 4:5). There is something overdetermined about the biblical diction here, beyond any physiognomy. Cain's face falls, denoting displeasure, anger, a feeling of rejection. He loses face proleptically, for he is about to try to make himself master of that which exceeds him absolutely, the other, Abel. (In Blanchot's reading, "the incomprehensible inequality of the divine favor" is, precisely, the other's transcendence [*IC*, 61]). Cain loses face, or is out of face, in part because that face was never anything but a showing, a mask, a violent angle on the other, like the ruse of a rhetoric. A great deal is at stake in Levinas's work in being able to keep separate face, the locus of the revelation of alterity, and mask, the covering or cloak for face. But if one *can* lose face (within a rigorously ethical understanding and in accordance with an ethical diction), cannot face be given? Is there not a dimension of face that is rhetorical in yet another sense (in the sense not of persuasion but of trope)? If one *can* lose face, then it is always possible that the face can be a mask. Always possible and hence a necessary possibility: mask is structured as a necessary possibility of face.[26] Despite the asymmetry between face and mask, like that between facing/angle, ethical language/rhetoric, justice/violence, expression/sign, trace/sign, the consequences of this necessary possibility would be a certain intercontamination of the governing oppositions of Levinas's discourse. Then there would be, again, a rhetorical dimension, a figurality, of face, of the very face that commands ethical response. This means that the face is to some extent a face-mask or a figure-face.[27] It also means that there can be "face" in figure. But is not "figuration" itself transformed by such a usage? What is figure, if there can be face in it?

It remains to consider the theological dimension of Levinas's description. After all, the primordial expression is a *biblical* citation, one of God's commandments, the Sixth Commandment, even if it is revealed not by God but, in Levinas's rewriting, in the face of the other man. Does its presence imply that Levinas's ethics are dependent on the revealed morality of positive religion? In brief, it does not, for Levinas's definition of religion is as removed from the ordinary sense of the term as is his definition of ethics: "We propose to call religion the bond that is established between the same and the other without constituting a totality" (*TI*, 40). Yet Levinas does, nonetheless, cite one of one of the Ten Commandments, which are at the center of the revealed morality of the Judeo-Christian tradition. Here it is necessary to observe that Levinas is concerned not with a unitary Judeo-Christian tradition but rather with the Judaic, and particularly the rabbinic, tradition as a "source" or a resource for his ethics. Moreover, Levinas distances the Judaic from the interpretation it has received within the unitary Judeo-Christian tradition, an interpretation that is often negative and privative. He reinscribes it to bring out its positive force, even the alternative intelligibility it offers. For example, the law in Judaism—the 613 laws—is not a yoke, a servitude, a legalism; in the minutiae of ritual observance is hidden the primacy of obligation to the other, even a certain break in the logic of possibility. The Judaic, as Levinas recovers it, gives access to the ethical structures that he himself describes: it is an originary responsibility.[28] This means, however, that we cannot take for granted that we know what we mean by "Judaism" in Levinas's work. The Judaism in question is a reinscribed "Judaism," a post-Heideggerian Judaism that is equivalent neither to the determinations it has received within the dominant "Greco-Christian" conceptuality nor to Judaism as a historical or positive religion, although it necessarily takes off from there.[29]

One may still wish to ask, what is the specific religious meaning of the commandment "Thou shalt not kill"? Is it not significant that within historical Judaism, the concept of murder is enlarged, according to one commentator, to include even *"the omission* of any act by which a fellow-man could be saved in peril, distress or despair"?[30] Such a reference may help to illuminate the spirit of Levinas's analysis of murder and the way in which interdiction produces the very positivity of obligation, generosity, gift and discourse. But Levinas's phenomenological descriptions of the relation to the other already make the "religious" (in his sense) meaning of the commandment quite explicit. Its "religious" meaning is the imperative of response or responsibility that arises in the encounter with the other who faces in language.

And Cain Said to Abel

What did Cain say to Abel immediately before he murdered him? In Gen. 4:8, there is a lacuna in the text (preserved in the Masoretic tradition), where the verse is incomplete: "And Cain said to Abel his brother . . ." "The Hebrew *vayommer* means not 'told' or 'spoke to' but 'said unto,' and the words said ought to follow"[31] The text of Gen. 4:3–8, in Everett Fox's translation, reads:

> It was, after the passing of days that Kayin brought, from the fruit of the soil, a gift to YHWH, and as for Hevel, he too brought—from the firstborn of his flock, from their fat parts. YHWH had regard for Hevel and his gift, for Kayin and his gift he had no regard. Kayin became exceedingly enraged and his face fell. YHWH said to Kayin: Why are you so enraged? Why has your face fallen? Is it not thus: If you intend good, bear-it-aloft, but if you do not intend good, at the entrance is sin, a crouching-demon, toward you his lust—but you can rule over him. Kayin

said to Hevel his brother . . . But then it was, when they were out in the field, that Kayin rose up against Hevel his brother and he killed him.[32]

In numerous versions of the Bible (such as the Samaritan, Greek, Syriac, Old Latin, and Vulgate), and consequently, in most translations, the missing phrase is supplied: "let us go outside." This metonymic response seeks to provide a bridge to the place of the action that follows. The midrashic response to this lacuna in *Bereshith Rabbah* 22:16 is freely embellishing. It interpolates an extended discussion between Cain and Abel. This response, like that of Philo, assumes that the brothers had a *quarrel*. Philo even writes: "The plain is a figure of contentiousness."[33] And although the midrash explains alternately that the two quarreled about material possessions, religious ideology, and sexual jealousy, the fact of the quarrel seems more important than its content.[34]

Within contemporary interpretations of the episode as a whole, André Neher remarks Cain's silence in response to God's question, "Why has your face fallen?"[35] This silence is not entirely unreasonable, given the notorious obscurity, indeed, the near-unintelligibility of the admonitory verse that follows, "If you intend good, bear-it-aloft . . ."[36] But, writes Neher, "in place of God, he chose his brother as the recipient of his answer: And 'Cain said unto Abel his brother . . .' "[37] And thus, as Elie Wiesel remarks, he turned his quarrel against God against his brother instead.[38] What did Cain say to Abel here? For Neher, the initial "rupture in communication" between Cain and God underscores the failure of dialogue that is central to the episode as a whole: "Abel does not speak, whereas Cain speaks all the time" ("incessantly," Wiesel notes). Thus "dialogue was swallowed up in silence and death." Neher concludes: "It is as if the obliteration of the dialogue were the cause of murder."[39] The "dialogue" of which Neher speaks, based on an ideal of symmetry and an understanding of language as communication, is derivative of the Blanchotian "speech or death," the asymmetrical *parole* that founds the possibility of "dialogue" in such a sense. Yet Neher's comment gives pause: it is as if the textual gap or lacuna in its very materiality were the cause of the murder the episode recounts.

What did Cain say to Abel? Perhaps, as Neher suggests, he simply repeated God's words to him "in all their fearful ambiguity." These words were not only obscure, but as Elie Wiesel comments, "cruel": "Repudiated by God, Cain sank into a black depression. Whereupon God, with a cruelty as startling as it was unprovoked asked why he looked so crestfallen, why he was so depressed. As though He did not know, as though He was not the cause!"[40] Perhaps, Wiesel continues, Cain wanted to unburden himself to Abel, who did not listen.

And Cain said to Abel, "Let us go outside." Why did he direct him toward the outside?" "Outside, where there were no witnesses," says one commentator.[41] Blanchot writes, "as if he knew that the outside is the place of Abel, but also as if he wished to lead him back to that poverty, to that weakness of the outside where every defense falls away" (IC, 61).[42]

Notes

The following abbreviations are used in the text for frequently cited works:

DF Emmanuel Levinas, *Difficult Freedom*. Translated by Sean Hand. Baltimore: Johns Hopkins University Press, 1990. Originally published as *Difficile liberté*, 2d ed. (Paris: Albin Michel, 1976).

EI Emmanuel Levinas, *Ethics and Infinity*. Translated by Richard A. Cohen. Pittsburgh: Duquesne University Press, 1985. Originally published as *Éthique et infini* (Paris: Fayard, 1982).

FC Emmanuel Levinas, "Freedom and Command." In *Collected Philosophical Papers*. Translated by Alphonso Lingis. Dordrecht: Martinus Nijhoff, 1987. Originally published as "Liberté et commandement," *Revue de métaphysique et de morale* 58 (1953).

IC Maurice Blanchot, *The Infinite Conversation*. Translated by Susan Hanson. Minneapolis: University of Minnesota Press, 1993. Originally published as *L'Entretien infini* (Paris: Gallimard, 1969).

T Emmanuel Levinas, "The Trace of the Other." Translated by Alphonso Lingis. In *Deconstruction in Context*, ed. Mark C. Taylor. Chicago: University of Chicago Press, 1986. Originally published as "La trace de l'autre," in *En découvrant l'existence avec Husserl et Heidegger*, 2d ed. (Paris: Vrin, 1974).

TH Emmanuel Levinas, "Transcendance et hauteur." *Bulletin de la Société Française de Philosophie* 56 (1962): 89–113.

TI Emmanuel Levinas, *Totality and Infinity*. Translated by Alphonso Lingis. Pittsburgh: Duquesne University Press, 1969. Originally published as *Totalité et infini* (The Hague: Martinus Nijhoff, 1961).

VM Jacques Derrida, "Violence and Metaphysics." In *Writing and Difference*, trans. Alan Bass. Chicago: University of Chicago Press, 1978. Originally published as "Violence et métaphysique," in *L'Écriture et la différence* (Paris: Seuil, 1967).

1. The Cartesian idea of infinity is a guiding notion of Levinas's work and one of the privileged moments in his history of philosophy. The first reference to the face in *Totality and Infinity*, cited above, introduces it as a "deformalization or concretization of the idea of infinity" (TI, 50).

2. Compare Heidegger's description, in which *Dasein* doesn't *have* its possibilities; it *is* its possibilities. Levinas's polemical reading of Heidegger is problematic insofar as it seems deliberately to confuse possibility, an *existentiale,* with power, a relation between already constituted entities. See the reading of Levinas and Heidegger by Jacques Derrida in VM, 134ff.

3. These grammatical terms are only provisional and will later be abandoned. Ultimately, the relationship to the other cannot be conceived in terms of a grammar.

4. "On Call from the Other," a chapter of a forthcoming work on Levinas and literature.

5. The interpellative sense Levinas gives "discourse" is at a distance from ordinary definitions. Compare Paul Ricoeur who, summarizing a tradition which goes back to Aristotle, defines discourse as "the intertwining of noun and verb," the conjunction of which "brings forth a predicative link." *Discourse and the Surplus of Meaning* (Fort Worth: Texas Christian University Press, 1976), 1–2.

6. I am indebted to Cathy Caruth for helping me to arrive at this formulation.

7. Francois Poirié, *Emmanuel Levinas: Qui êtes-vous* (Lyon: La Manufacture, 1987), 94.

8. *Répondre d'Autrui: Emmanuel Levinas,* ed. Jean-Christophe Aeschlimann (Neuchâtel: Editions de la Baconnière, 1989), 10–11.

9. Alphonso Lingis, Translator's Introduction to Emmanuel Levinas, *Collected Philosophical Papers,* xxx.

10. See ibid.

11. This is the guiding thread of the readings of Levinas by Jean-François Lyotard and Jacques Derrida, which I discuss in "On Call from the Other." See Lyotard, "Levinas's Logic," in *Face to Face with Levinas,* ed. Richard A. Cohen (Albany: State University of New York Press, 1986), 117–158, and Jacques Derrida, "At This Very Moment in This Work Here I Am," trans. Ruben Berezdivin, in *Re-Reading Levinas,* ed. Robert Bernasconi and Simon Critchley (Bloomington: Indiana University Press, 1991); originally published as "En ce moment même dans cet ouvrage me voici," in *Textes pour Emmanuel Levinas,* ed. François Laruelle (Paris: Éditions Jean-Michel Place, 1980), 21–60.

12. *Confessions* 4.8. In *On Christian Doctrine* 2.1–2, Augustine will describe facial expression as an example of a borderline case between the two types of signs, natural and conventional.

13. It is at the basis of physiognomy, the idea that the signs of facial expression reveal character. Edouard Dhorme summarizes the biblical view that "the affections of the soul . . . are painted on the face." He writes: "It is thus that the state of the soul of an individual appears on the face; it is by his face that one can know his passions, his emotions, his feelings and even his wishes. His entire being is imprinted on his face and is expressed by it. If the soul or the heart characterizes his being in itself, the face characterizes it for

others." *L'emploi métaphorique des noms de parties du corps en hébreu et en akkadien* (Paris: Librairie orientaliste Paul Geuthner, 1963), 51, 59.

14. Paul de Man, "Criticism and Crisis," in *Blindness and Insight: Essays in the Rhetoric of Contemporary Criticism,* 2d ed, rev. (Minneapolis: University of Minnesota Press, 1983), 11. The essay was first published in 1967.

15. De Man's assertion that "there is no a priori privileged position of sign over meaning or meaning over sign" and his emphasis on "inauthenticity" as a consequence may be compared to Umberto Eco's discussion of the close relationship between signification and lying. Eco writes: "Semiotics is concerned with everything that can be taken as a sign . . . Thus semiotics is in principle the discipline studying everything which can be used in order to lie." *A Theory of Semiotics* (Bloomington: Indiana University Press, 1976), 7.

16. For this reason, Erving Goffman's analyses and decoding of "facework," however suggestive for a (social) idiom of face, would be derivative upon the Levinasian conception.

17. See Derrida, VM, 101–102.

18. On the image of the line and its relation to writing, figurative language, and narrative, see J. Hillis Miller, *Ariadne's Thread: Story Lines* (New Haven: Yale University Press, 1992), especially chapter 1, entitled "Line."

19. See Lyotard, "Levinas' Logic," and Derrida, "At This Very Moment."

20. For a discussion of the *in*ability in responsibility, see Ann Smock, "Disastrous Responsibility," *L'Esprit Créateur* 24 (1984): 5–20.

21. Jean-François Lyotard and Jean-Loup Thébaud, *Just Gaming,* trans. Wlad Godzich (Minneapolis: University of Minnesota Press, 1985), 22, 63; originally published as *Au juste* (Paris, Christian Bourgois, 1979). Lyotard writes: "First there is this prescription to place myself in a prescriptive situation" (22).

22. Jean-François Lyotard, *The Differend: Phrases in Dispute,* trans. Georges Van Den Abbeele (Minneapolis: University of Minnesota Press, 1988), 111; originally published as *Le Différend* (Paris: Minuit, 1983).

23. Blanchot's reflections on the indestructible, in a section of *The Infinite Conversation* devoted to Robert Antelme's *L'espèce humaine,* are indispensable for such a direction of thought. IC, 130–135.

24. "If the impossibility of killing were a real impossibility, if the alterity of the other were only the resistance of a force, his alterity would be no more exterior to me than that of nature which resists my energies, but which I come to account for by reason; it would be no more exterior than the world of perception which, in the final analysis, is constituted by me. The ethical impossibility of killing is a resistance made to me, but a resistance which is not violent, an intelligible resistance" (FC, 21–22).

25. Emmanuel Levinas, interview with Richard Kearney in *Face to Face with Levinas,* ed. Richard A. Cohen (Albany: State University of New York Press, 1986), 25, cited and discussed by Robert Bernasconi in "Levinas and Derrida: The Question of the Closure of Metaphysics," in the same volume. See also Bernasconi's "Deconstruction and the Possibility of Ethics," in *Decon-*

struction and Philosophy: The Texts of Jacques Derrida, ed. John Sallis (Chicago: University of Chicago Press, 1987), 122–139.

26. Cf. Jacques Derrida, "Signature Event Context," trans. Samuel Weber and Jeffrey Mehlman, *Glyph* 1 (1977).

27. For a careful and rigorous discussion of what is at stake in the production of the rhetorical figure that gives face, especially in the writings of de Man, see Cynthia Chase, *Decomposing Figures: Rhetorical Readings in the Romantic Tradition* (Baltimore: Johns Hopkins University Press, 1986), 82–112.

28. See Levinas's *Difficult Freedom* and *Nine Talmudic Lectures,* trans. Annette Aronowicz (Bloomington: Indiana University Press, 1990). See also my discussion in "An Inscribed Responsibility: Levinas's *Difficult Freedom,*" *Modern Language Notes* 106 (1991): 1052–1062.

29. I develop this in my *Prodigal Son/Elder Brother: Interpretation and Alterity in Augustine, Petrarch, Kafka, Levinas* (Chicago: University of Chicago Press, 1991).

30. *Pentateuch and Haftorahs,* ed. J. H. Hertz (London: Soncino Press, 1978), 299.

31. Harry M. Orlinsky, ed. *Notes on the New Translation of the Torah* (Philadelphia: The Jewish Publication Society, 1969), 68.

32. *In the Beginning: A New English Rendition of the Book of Genesis,* trans. with commentary and notes by Everett Fox (New York: Schocken, 1983).

33. *Philo,* vol. 2, with an English translation by F. H. Colson (Cambridge, Mass.: Harvard University Press, 1929), 205.

34. See the discussion by Nehama Leibowitz in *Studies in Bereshit Genesis,* trans. Aryeh Newman (Jerusalem: World Zionist Organization, 1972), 38–45.

35. As Claus Westermann notes, "J" understands Cain's reaction to the rejection of his gift as "psychosomatic." "He became inflamed . . . his face fell." *Genesis 1–11: A Commentary,* trans. John J. Scullion (Minneapolis: Augsburg Publishing House, 1984), 297. Everett Fox reminds us that "the text is punctuated . . . by changing connotations of the word 'face.' " *In the Beginning,* 19.

36. Commentators agree that the Hebrew of this verse is obscure, and its textual difficulties irresolvable. U. Cassuto reports that "in ancient times the Rabbis counted it among the indeterminate verses because of the doubt in regard to the syntactic relationship of the word $\acute{s}^{e}$'*ēth* ['to lift, carry']." One interpretive suggestion (based on the passage "then you will lift up your face without blemish" [Job 11:15]) "would imply an antithesis here to *the falling of the countenance* mentioned in the previous verses; but just the vital word *face* is wanting!" *A Commentary on the Book of Genesis* I, trans. Israel Abrahams (Jerusalem: The Magnes Press, 1961), 208–209.

37. André Neher, *The Exile of the Word: From the Silence of the Bible to the Silence of Auschwitz,* trans. David Maisel (Philadelphia: The Jewish Publication Society, 1981), 97–98. See also the related discussion by Neher in *L'existence juive: solitude et affrontements* (Paris: Seuil, 1962), 34–46.

38. Elie Wiesel, *Messengers of God: Biblical Portraits and Legends,* trans. Marion Wiesel (New York: Pocket Books, 1977), 54.

39. Neher, *Exile of the Word,* 95.

40. Wiesel, *Messengers,* 58.

41. Westermann, *Genesis 1–11,* 302.

42. Although the reading of Gen. 4 that I have proposed (via Blanchot, Neher, Wiesel, and others) is more or less "Levinasian," this is not to say that Levinas would necessarily endorse this particular reading of the biblical chapter. Indeed, at one of the annual Colloques des Intellectuels Juifs de Langue Française, at which André Neher presented a version of his Cain and Abel reading, Levinas registered his disagreement. Neher's reading emphasizes both the impossibility of dialogue that leads to violence and also the "arbitrariness" and the "inadvertency" of God's dealings with man. The arbitrariness is in accepting Abel's sacrifice and not accepting Cain's for although one can argue (as many midrashim do) that Cain's sacrifice was less well intentioned than Abel's (fruits of *the ground* versus *first* of the flock), Neher says, "the last nuance of the text asks us to admit that the sacrifices were equivalent." Moreover, Neher continues: "God only intervenes when it is too late. . . . God intervenes like someone who will have seen nothing at the moment when the [murder] comes to pass." This "heedlessness" and "inadvertency" on the part of God invites us to think God's distance from man. But Cain senses that God is also close, facing him and speaking to him, hence, Neher proposes, "the poignant need for Cain to speak and at the same time to say: I do not understand; If I could lay my complaint before you I would be able to understand, but I am not able to, you grip me, as it were, by the throat, you are suffocating me."

Tellingly, Levinas took the other side of the debate and objected to what he termed "these Kierkegaardian paradoxes" concerning the distance and nearness of God. Levinas reasserted God's preference for Abel's sacrifice over Cain's, following the midrashim which "insist on the quality of the Gift." See André Neher, "Caïn et Abel," and the "Débats" that follow in *La Conscience juive: données et débats* (Paris: P.U.F., 1963), 34–53.

I would like to thank Rebecca Comay for her comments on the earliest version of this essay.

▼ Notes on Contributors ▼

DEREK ATTRIDGE teaches in the English Department of Rutgers University, New Brunswick. His books include *Peculiar Language: Literature as Difference from the Renaissance to James Joyce* (Cornell, 1988) and—as editor or co-editor—*Post-Structuralist Joyce: Essays from the French* (Cambridge, 1984), *Post-structuralism and the Question of History* (Cambridge, 1986), and *Acts of Literature,* by Jacques Derrida (Routledge, 1992).

E. S. BURT, who has published articles on autobiography and nineteenth-century poetics, has a book on Rousseau forthcoming from the Johns Hopkins University Press.

JUDITH BUTLER is the author of *Gender Trouble: Feminism and the Subversion of Identity* (Routledge, 1990) and *Bodies that Matter* (Routledge, 1993) and coeditor with Joan W. Scott of *Feminists Theorize the Political.* She is Professor of Rhetoric at the University of California at Berkeley.

CATHY CARUTH is Associate Professor of English at Yale University. She is the author of *Empirical Truths and Critical Fictions: Locke, Wordworth, Kant, Freud* (Johns Hopkins, 1990), and of *Unclaimed Experience: Trauma, Narrative, and History* (Johns Hopkins, forthcoming). She has also edited *Trauma: Explorations in Memory* (Johns Hopkins, 1995).

CYNTHIA CHASE is Professor of English at Cornell University. She is the author of *Decomposing Figures: Rhetorical Readings in the Romantic Tradition* (Johns Hopkins, 1988) and editor of *Romanticism* (Longman Critical Readers, 1993). She has also coedited *Wordsworth and the Production of Poetry, Diacritics* 17 (Winter 1987). She is currently working on a book on romanticism and literary theory.

HARRIET DAVIDSON is Associate Professor of English and Comparative Literature at Rutgers University. She is the author of *T. S. Eliot and Hermeneutics: Absence and Interpretation in "The Waste Land"* (Louisiana State University Press, 1985) and is now editing a collection of essays on

Eliot and contemporary theory and working on a book on contemporary poetry and theories of location.

DEBORAH ESCH is Associate Professor of English at the University of Toronto. She is the author of *The Senses of the Past,* on Henry James and Alice James, and a coeditor of Jacques Derrida's *Negotiations* and *Institutions of Philosophy.* Most recently, she collaborated with artist Stephen Andrews on a bookwork entitled *Safe.*

DIANA FUSS is Associate Professor of English at Princeton University. She is the author of *Essentially Speaking: Feminism, Nature and Difference* (Routledge, 1989) and editor of *Inside / Out: Lesbian Theories, Gay Theories* (Routledge, 1991).

THOMAS KEENAN teaches in the English Department at Princeton University. He is the author of *Fables of Responsibility* (forthcoming from Stanford) and coeditor of *Paul de Man's Wartime Journalism 1939–43* (Nebraska, 1988) and *Responses* (Nebraska, 1989).

KEVIN NEWMARK teaches at Boston College and is the author of *Beyond Symbolism: Textual History and the Future of Reading* (Cornell, 1991).

JILL ROBBINS is Associate Professor of English and Comparative Literature at the State University of New York at Buffalo. She is the author of *Prodigal Son / Elder Brother: Interpretation and Alterity in Augustine, Petrarch, Kafka, Levinas* (Chicago, 1991) and *Ethics and the Literary Instance: Reading Levinas,* forthcoming.

ANDRZEJ WARMINSKI is Professor of Comparative Literature at the University of California, Irvine, and the author of *Readings in Interpretation: Holderlin, Hegel, and Heidegger* (Minnesota, 1987). His book of essays in allegorical reading and critique of ideology is forthcoming.

Index

abjection, 225
accountability, 253
action, and cognition, 157, 163, 165, 166, 222, 252, 264
actor, problem of the, 168, 169, 174, 178
Adorno, Theodor, 22, 216
aesthetics, 42–44, 54, 55, 59, 72, 78; aesthetic ideology, 16, 56; national aestheticism, 203
agency, 223–225, 242, 244, 246, 250, 252
aletheia, 167
allegory, 197
alterity, 276
Althusser, Louis, 28, 250, 251
antifoundationalism, 217
Anzaldúa, Gloria, 225
apartheid, 249
Aristophanes, 106
Aristotle, 107, 248
Artaud, Antonin, 107
"Athenaeum, The," 47–49, 52, 76
Attridge, Derek, 4
Auerbach, Erich, 279
Augustine, 281, 283
Austin, J. L., 72, 107, 271
autobiography, 98–101
autrui, 289

Barthes, Roland, 21, 24, 33, 59, 114
Bataille, Georges, 114, 252
Bate, Walter Jackson, 184
Baudelaire, Charles, 107, 136, 163
Beckett, Samuel, 114

Benjamin, Walter, 22, 42, 61, 77, 200, 204, 265
Blanchot, Maurice, 7, 8n5, 46–49, 51, 52, 54, 62, 65–69, 114, 117, 119, 285, 287, 294
body, the, 94–96, 102, 103, 227, 244, 246, 256, 258, 284
Boileau, Nicolas, 62
Brinkman, A. E., 198
Burt, E. S., 3
Butler, Judith, 242

Caruth, Cathy, 56, 76
catachresis, 137
chance, 246, 247, 252, 253
Chase, Cynthia, 3, 8n2, 96n8, 187, 188, 197, 198, 206
chiasmus, 72, 244
choice, 252
citability, 118
Cixous, Hélène, 214, 215
claim, 271
clinamen, 246
Coleridge, Samuel, 196
communication, 279
community, 268
consciousness, 77, 142, 246, 250; natural consciousness, 80; self-consciousness, 34; speaking consciousness, 64
constative, 270, 271. *See also* performative
context, 110
contingency, 214
Cornell, Drucilla, 265, 267

Cratylis, 128, 129, 139, 142
critique of subject, 127
Culler, Jonathan, 108, 112
cultural studies, 214

Dante, 106
Davidson, Harriet, 7
decision, 254, 265
deconstruction, 1, 2, 8, 108, 120, 157, 158–161, 165–167, 170, 185, 214, 215, 225, 242, 244, 262, 263, 268
deferral, 113
Dekeukleire, Charles, 185
de Man, Paul, 2, 11, 29, 30, 34, 42–43, 45, 48–51, 55, 56, 58, 59, 61, 62, 69, 98, 99, 142, 158, 159, 163, 165, 166, 167, 169, 170, 171, 173, 184, 185, 188, 191, 193, 194, 195, 196, 197, 198, 200, 203–205, 263, 264, 271, 279, 284; "Aesthetic Formalization in Kleist," 94–101, 187, 188, 206; "Anthropomorphism and Trope in the Lyric"; "Autobiography as Defacement," 72; "Criticism and Crisis," 189, 283; "Hypogram and Inscription," 26, 43, 64–67; 68, 72–80, 83, 139, 187; "The Image of Rousseau in the Poetry of Hölderlin," 80; "An Interview with Paul de Man," 27–29; "Kant and Schiller," 207; "Nietzsche and the Rhetoric of Persuasion," 157; "Phenomenality and Materiality in Kant," 81, 82, 94, 95, 96, 102, 103, 187; "Reading and History," 68; "The Rhetoric of Temporality," 201, 202; "The Resistance to Theory," 21, 26, 61, 66, 81, 92, 93, 94; "The Return to Philology," 44, 68; "Semiology and Rhetoric," 12–20, 22–25, 33; "Shelley Disfigured," 207; "Sign and Symbol in Hegel's Aesthetics," 66, 75; "Wordsworth and Hölderlin," 58
democracy, 218, 223, 225, 243, 263
Derrida, Jacques, 2, 11, 50, 61, 62, 67, 106–117, 118–121, 158, 159, 163, 165, 166, 197, 207, 214, 215, 245–249, 254, 258, 263, 266, 267, 284, 285, 290
Descartes, René, 68, 106, 131, 250, 251, 252, 253
description, 161, 163, 172, 176
dialogue, 293
difference, 246; sexual, 237
différance, 113, 248
dissemination, 248
distance, 278

economy, 277
essentialism, 242, 257
ethics, 113, 119, 263, 264, 275, 277, 278; ethical language, 279, 289, 290, 291
event, 118
example, 77, 83, 84, 102, 103, 193, 215, 245
experience, 1, 252, 253, 268, 269
expression, 280, 282, 284, 285
exteriority, 285

face, the, 275, 276, 278, 280, 281, 282, 283, 285, 287, 288, 289, 290, 291
feminism, 213, 214, 225, 226, 242, 243, 244, 246, 258
fiction, 22–23.
figure, 134, 137, 179, 276, 279, 281, 283, 290, 291
Fineman, Joel, 128, 129, 142, 147
force, 95
forgetting, 78–80, 83
form, 280
Foucault, Michel, 128, 214, 220, 224, 228, 238, 268, 269
freedom, 246, 252, 259, 290
Freud, Sigmund, 62
Fuss, Diana, 5, 6

Gallagher, Catherine, 184, 187
Gasché, Rodolphe, 67, 109, 112, 120, 187, 192, 197, 198, 200
gay/lesbian studies, 233, 234, 235, 236
gaze, 276, 277, 289

generosity, 276, 277, 278
Genette, Gérard, 60
Gide, André, 200
gift, 7, 13
Godzich, Wlad, 190
Goethe, Johann Wolfgang, 194, 195, 196, 197, 198, 200, 201, 202, 203, 204, 205, 206, 207
grammar, 12, 93, 98, 102, 249

Hamacher, Werner, 186, 187, 188, 193, 194, 195, 196, 197, 198, 201, 202
Hardy, Thomas, 80
Hartman, Geoffrey, 188, 190, 193
Heath, Stephen, 237
Hegel, Georg Wilhelm Friedrich, 28–31, 47–48, 52, 64, 67, 68, 69, 73, 75, 76, 77, 78, 79, 80, 83, 107, 130, 143, 163, 216, 267
Heidegger, Martin, 67, 107, 117, 172, 173, 281
Henri IV, 133
Hertz, Neil, 55, 68, 83
Higgins, Lynne, 185
history, 1, 2, 4, 110, 163, 165, 170, 171, 172, 173, 187, 193, 194, 243, 246, 251, 257; historical particularity, 13, 14, 29, 52, 92, 113; new historicism, 128, 161; and truth, 163, 167, 186, 244, 249
Hölderlin, Friedrich, 8n5, 58, 67, 68, 80, 117
Hugo, Victor, 47, 66, 67, 68, 69, 73, 75, 76, 78, 79, 130, 131, 132, 133, 134, 135, 136, 137, 139, 143, 145, 146, 147
Husserl, Edmund, 107, 188, 190, 191, 192, 193, 197

identity politics, 225, 226, 234
ideology, 28, 48, 252; of progress, 146; of realism, 186, 263
imperialism (cultural), 217
infinity, 275, 276, 277
inside/outside, 233, 234
intention, 244
interpellation, 250

Irigaray, Luce, 214
iterability, 118, 257

Jakobsen, Roman, 23, 60
Jameson, Fredric, 13; *The Ideology of Theory*, 14, 15
Jauss, Hans Robert, 45
Johnson, Barbara, 187, 188
Johnson, Samuel, 68
Joyce, James, 107, 251
judgment, 265
Jünger, Ernst, 202
justice (possibility/impossibility of), 262, 263, 265, 266, 267, 268, 272, 278

Kafka, Franz, 99, 101, 107
Kakutani, Michiko, 8n3
Kant, Immanuel, 44, 81, 82, 94, 95, 96, 97, 99, 100, 101, 102, 107, 130, 143, 194, 204
Kaplan, Alice, 203
Keats, John, 47, 62
Keenan, Tom, 5, 6
Kierkegaard, Søren, 16, 21, 27–28, 99, 101, 160
Kleist, Heinrich von, 94, 95, 96, 97, 98, 100, 101, 102, 103, 194
knowledge, 6; self-understanding, 82
Kristeva, Julia, 214

labor, 160
Lacan, Jacques, 214, 242
Lacoue-Labarthe, Phillipe, 203
language: and consciousness, 31; materiality of, 33, 54; phenomenality of, 45, 61
Laplanche, Jean, 140
literary science, 23–25
Leavis, F. R., 14
Lefort, Claude, 270, 271
Lehman, David, 163, 164, 165, 166, 167
Leibniz, Gottfried Wilhelm, 107
Levinas, Emmanuel, 6, 8n4, 265, 266, 275, 277, 279, 280, 282, 283, 284, 286, 287, 288, 289, 290, 291, 292

Lingis, Alphonso, 279
listening, 6
literary (versus philosophical), 107–121
logocentrism, 111, 115
Louis XVI, 130, 134
Lukács, Georg, 14
Lyotard, Jean-François, 215, 285, 286, 287

Mallarmé, Stéphane, 68, 107, 117, 119, 135, 170, 171, 172, 173, 180
Martin, Biddy, 215
Marx, Karl, 21–22, 26–27, 28–32, 81, 159, 163, 253, 256
materiality, 2, 33, 77, 82, 227, 246, 257; of language, 245, 247; of writing, 147
mathematics, 94; and nonreferentiality, 97
Memmie, Albert, 224
Milton, John, 68
mimesis, 110
Montaigne, Michel de, 102, 131
murder, 288, 290

nationalism, 78, 197, 198, 199, 200, 201
natural law, 92
necessity, 246
negation, 30
Neher, André, 293
Newmark, Kevin, 3
Newton, Isaac, 93, 94, 95
Nietzsche, Friedrich, 44, 64, 67, 75, 156, 159, 167, 168, 169, 170, 173, 174, 175, 176, 177, 178, 179, 180
nominalism, 252
Norris, Christopher, 109, 112, 263

O'Brien, Michael, 164

performative, 72, 92, 94, 271. See also constative
Petrarch, Francesco Petrarca, 129
phallocentrism, 111
phonocentrism, 111, 113
Pilon, Germaine, 135

Plato, 107, 121, 246, 284
pleasure, 246
political science, 161
polysemia, 248
Pontalis (Lefévre-) J. P., 140
positionality, 255, 219
possibility, 277, 278. See also power
postal system, 250
postcolonialism, 218, 225
postmodernism, 213, 214, 215, 216, 217
poststructuralism, 217, 218
power, 216, 223, 224, 252, 277, 287, 288, 290. See also possibility
pragrammatology, 251
presence, 244
pre-Socratics, 246
promise (the), 51, 100, 265, 266, 267
property, 269
prosopopeia, 51, 75, 76, 82, 131, 132, 136, 139, 281
Proust, Marcel, 12, 60, 163
psychoanalysis, 219, 246

Racine, Jean, 200
racism, 249
reading, 13–14, 34, 114, 173
reference, 1, 2, 4, 96, 100, 110, 113, 227; denominative system, 134; referential context, 249; self-referentiality, 11, 24, 93, 127, 129, 130
responsibility, 5, 118, 258, 264, 265, 266, 268, 290
Revolution (French), 130, 131, 132, 134, 135, 137, 138, 140, 143, 144, 146
rhetoric, 12, 44–45, 50, 93, 249, 268, 278, 279, 291
Rhys, Jean, 262
rhythm, 142
Ricoeur, Paul, 247
Rich, Adrienne, 241, 243, 245, 253, 254, 255, 256, 257
Riffaterre, Michel, 45, 48, 56, 60, 68, 72, 73, 80, 130, 131
right, 264, 268, 269, 270, 272
Rilke, Rainer Maria, 117

Robbins, Jill, 3, 6, 8n4
Robespierre, Maximilien, 132
Romanticism, 44–46, 48, 49, 51, 55, 58, 59, 66, 68, 69, 80, 84, 85, 282; German, 199
Rorty, Richard, 214
Rousseau, Jean-Jacques, 28, 44, 47, 51, 61, 131, 139

same (economy of), 276
Saussure, Ferdinand, 62, 74–76, 164, 247
Schelling, Fredrich Wilhelm Joseph von, 196
Schiller, Johann Christoph Friedrich, 194
Schlegel, Fredrich, 46
Scott, Joan, 224
semiology, 21–22; semiotic system, 134
Shakespeare, William (*Romeo and Juliet*), 116, 128, 142
Shelley, Percy, 47
Sieberg, F., 199
signature, 118
singularity, 6, 7
situation, 247
spontaneity, 277
subject, 214, 217, 219, 220, 222, 224, 225, 243, 246, 248, 249, 251, 263, 264, 266; self-reflexivity of, 250
supplement, 257

Terror (the), 46–47, 49, 51, 143, 144, 146

theology, 161
theoreticism, 264
totality, 279
trace, 248
transcendance, 242
translation, 85
trauma, 7n11

Ulmer, Gregory, 248
undecidability, 263
unheimlich, 172
unreadability, 263

Valéry, Paul
value, 155, 156, 159
violence, 170, 275, 277, 279, 289
vision, 277
voice, 66, 135

Warminski, Andrzej, 34, 67, 68, 84, 206
Warren, Robert Penn, 68, 83
Weber, Samuel, 186, 191, 198, 206
Weisel, Elie, 293
Willem, Paul, 200, 201
Winckelmann, Johann Joachim, 102, 103
witnessing, 249
Wittig, Monique, 228
Woolf, Virginia, 256
Wordsworth, William, 44, 47, 48, 54, 55, 58, 68, 82, 84, 270
writing, 170

GENERAL THEOLOGICAL SEMINARY.
NEW YORK.